Thomas Conzelmann / Randall Smith (eds.)

Multi-level Governance in the European Union: Taking Stock and Looking Ahead

Nomos

Die Deutsche Nationalbibliothek verzeichnet diese Publikation in der Deutschen Nationalbibliografie; detaillierte bibliografische Daten sind im Internet über http://www.d-nb.de abrufbar.

Die Deutsche Nationalbibliothek lists this publication in the Deutsche Nationalbibliografie; detailed bibliographic data is available in the Internet at http://www.d-nb.de.

ISBN 978-3-8329-3838-3

1. Auflage 2008

Table of Contents

Contributors

Ian Bache is Reader in Politics at the University of Sheffield, the United Kingdom. E-mail: i.bache@sheffield.ac.uk

Kathrin Birkel is Researcher in the Department of Political Sciences of the Environment at Radboud University Nijmegen, the Netherlands. E-mail: k.birkel@fm.ru.nl

Thomas Conzelmann is Associate Professor of International Relations and EU External Relations at Maastricht University, the Netherlands. E-mail: t.conzelmann@politics.unimaas.nl

Leeda Demetropoulou is a Researcher at the Institute of Urban Environment and Human Resources of Panteion University, Athens, Greece. E-mail: leedem@uehr.panteion.gr

Jenny Fairbrass is Lecturer in Strategy at the University of Bradford, the United Kingdom. E-mail: j.fairbrass@bradford.ac.uk

Panagiotis Getimis is Professor of Urban and Regional Policy at Panteion University of Political and Social Sciences, Athens, Greece. E-mail: pget@panteion.gr

Hubert Heinelt is Professor for Public Policy, Public Administration and Urban Research at Darmstadt University of Technology, Germany. E-mail: heinelt@pg.tu-darmstadt.de

Christoph Knill is Professor of Political and Administrative Science at the University of Konstanz, Germany. E-mail: christoph.knill@uni-konstanz.de

Charalampos Koutalakis is Senior Lecturer at the Department of Political Science and Public Administration at the University of Athens, Greece. E-mail: ckoutalakis@pspa.uoa.gr

Brigid Laffan is Professor of European Politics at University College Dublin (UCD), Ireland. E-mail: brigid.laffan@ucd.ie

Andrea Lenschow is Professor of European Integration and Politics and Jean Monnet Chair at the University of Osnabrück, Germany. E-mail: andrea.lenschow@uos.de

Duncan Liefferink is Senior Researcher in the Department of Political Sciences of the Environment at Radboud University Nijmegen, the Netherlands. E-mail: d.liefferink@fm.ru.nl

Klaudijus Maniokas is Chairman of the Board of the consultancy Europos, Socialiniai, Teisiniai ir Ekonominiai Projektai (ESTEP), Vilnius, Lithuania. E-mail: k.maniokas@estep.lt

Yannis Papadopoulos is Professor of Political Science at the University of Lausanne, Switzerland. E-mail: ionnais.papadopoulos@unil.ch

Christos J. Paraskevopoulos is Assistant Professor of European Public Policy at the University of Macedonia, Thessaloniki, Greece, and Visiting Research Fellow at the London School of Economics (LSE), the United Kingdom. E-mail: c.paraskevopoulos@lse.ac.uk

Simona Piattoni is Associate Professor of Comparative Politics and European Union Politics at the University of Trento, Italy. E-mail:simona.piattoni@unitn.it

Katja Rottmann is liaison officer to European institutions for the parliamentary group 'Bundnis 90/Die Grünen' in the Brussels office of the German Bundestag. E-mail: katja.rottmann@gruene-bundestag.de

Jale Tosun is a Ph.D. candidate of Political and Administrative Science at the University of Konstanz, Germany. E-mail: jale.tosun@uni-konstanz.de

I. Efficient and Legitimate? Reflections on Multi-level Governance

A New Mode of Governing? Multi-level Governance between Co-operation and Conflict

Thomas Conzelmann

The emergence of a new mode of governing

In recent years, the debate on the future institutional shape of the European Union has centred on the Constitutional Treaty and the Lisbon Treaty as its less ambitious (but possibly equally abortive) successor. This debate has two distinct features. On the one hand, the nation state still seems to serve as the foremost frame of reference. Ideas such as the establishment of a second 'national' chamber in addition to the European Parliament, the direct election of the Commission president, or the introduction of an EU foreign minister dominated the constitutional debate. Only a few observers have asked whether such proposals merely "rehearse institutional myths" (Kohler-Koch, 1999: 8), i.e. put forward institutional concepts derived from nation state practice that may however be of limited viability in the context of a non-state polity like the European Union. On the other hand, the debate looks almost exclusively at the Union's formal institutions, e.g. the decision-making procedures in the Council, the powers and composition of the Commission, or the distribution of competences between member states and the Union. The discussion has thus painted a relatively one-sided picture of the institutional development of the Union. What is missing from this picture is the fact that policy-making in the EU is increasingly characterised by the delegation and diffusion of authority to sub-national and private actors, the use of 'soft' (i.e. non-binding) forms of regulation, and the emergence of networked forms of governing that span several territorial levels or policy arenas. Koutalakis, in this volume, mentions "a wide range of different policy processes such as the open method of co-ordination, voluntary accords, standard setting, delegation to regulatory networks and agencies, regulation 'through information', benchmarking, peer review, [and] informal agreements" as examples of these new instruments (see also Héritier, 2002; Sabel and Zeitlin, 2007). Koutalakis also suggests that the new style of governing linked with these instruments is characterised by the principles of voluntarism (i.e. the use of non-binding targets), subsidiarity (i.e. delegation to lower levels or to private actors) and the inclusion of actors not on the basis of formal competence, but on the basis of the resources these actors can bring into play.

While it may, of course, be argued that the constitutional process was never intended to shape and reorient the finer details of institutional development at EU level, the predominant focus of the debate on the constitutional issues distracts from these less visible, but nevertheless sweeping, institutional transformations. The current volume seeks to address that bias in the topical debate on the future institutional shape of the Union. It focuses on newly emerging forms of governing at the EU level, in particular the convoluted and multi-level nature of decision-making in the EU, the increasing role of private actors and the greater use made of 'soft' non-regulatory techniques. In particular, the volume seeks to move on from earlier scholarship that discussed these modes of governance as novel and interesting ways to overcome the legitimacy and efficiency deficits of EU policy-making in areas where traditional hard law did not seem to produce the desired results. It rather seeks to contribute to 'second generation'[1] research on governance in the Union by asking questions about the conditions under which these instruments are applied, to what extent they can be considered successful, and how traditional political science concerns about power, conflict, and interests are playing out in governance in the EU.

In asking such questions, the volume builds on the assumption that – no matter what the outcome of the current treaty debate might be – these forms of multi-level and soft or non-coercive governance witnessed at the European level are here to stay at least in the medium run and therefore form an important subject of study in the context of the institutional development of the Union. This assumption has to do less with certain intrinsic normative qualities of these forms of governance, such as an enhanced efficiency and effectiveness of policy making (Héritier, 2003) or opportunities for more and better democratic participation (Gbikpi, 2002). Rather, it is that 'soft' and 'multi-level' forms of governance are seen by policy-makers as offering possibilities to address a number of structural problems of policy-making in the European Union. As explained by Schmitter (2004: 49-51), the different forms of "multi-level and polycentric governance" are a product of gradual and incremental institutional formation at EU level and an attempt to inject a dose of flexibility into an otherwise cumbersome policy process; which is to grow even more unwieldy following the accession of twelve new member states since 2004. A further plausible interpretation of the increasing use of 'soft' forms of governance is the protection of member state autonomy in the highly legalized environment of the EU (Schäfer, 2006). In addition, for the Commission, 'new' and 'multi-level' modes of governance offer a welcome opportunity for building up relations with societal actors and to sideline member states in the development and implementation of policies.[2] All this implies that these forms of governance may not be the sort of efficiency and legitimacy panacea that they are often portrayed as. Quite on the contrary, these forms of governance may very well give rise to elitist and non-participatory or otherwise undemocratic forms of governance (Hooghe and Marks, 2001: 120-122; see also Papadopoulos, this volume), and may end up in merely symbolic or declaratory (and thus inefficient) policies.

---

1 I borrow this expression and the underlying distinction from Pollack (2008).

2 See, for example, the debate about the gate-keeping role of EU member states in the implementation of structural funds (Bache, 1999).

Against this background, the present volume sets out to take stock of what we know about the functioning of new and multi-level forms of governance. In particular, it challenges the implicitly positive and harmonist conceptions that often surround research on multi-level governance in structural policy. Furthermore, it extends the analytical scope of multi-level governance by looking at the policy area of environmental policy and the various forms of public-private and internationalized networks that have developed in that area. In that connection, the book also seeks to build bridges between the debates on 'multi-level' and 'new' forms of governance, that take influential roles in the structural funds and environmental policy areas, respectively. Finally, normative aspects are highlighted in chapters on the effectiveness and legitimacy of multi-level governing, and on the power relations that exist in the seemingly harmonious and consensual world of multi-level governing. In that sense, the volume will also discuss the extent to which these forms are actually 'new' in the sense of departing from the Laswellian world of 'who gets what, when and how' in favour of a more consensual and problem-solving mode of discharging government functions.

A definition of key terms

The recent 'governance turn' in EU studies (Kohler-Koch and Rittberger, 2006; see also Bache and Flinders, 2004; Jachtenfuchs and Kohler-Koch, 2004; Börzel, 2005) has discussed the phenomena sketched above both under the labels of both 'multi-level governance' (MLG) and 'new modes of governance' (NMG). Common features highlighted by both these concepts are the use of non-hierarchical forms of governing, the emergence of multi-level structures of policy implementation, and the enhanced role of non-state actors within them. Still, the two debates are neither congruent nor is there a great deal of commonality in how these somewhat vague concepts are defined. It is therefore useful at the outset to delineate 'multi-level' and 'new' modes of governance more precisely and also to identify aspects in respect to which the two debates depart from one another.

The multi-level governance discourse originally focused strongly on questions of regional mobilisation and constitutional transformation of the nation state. The main point of reference was efforts by the Union to tap the potential of local and regional authorities as well as non-state and private actors in contributing to the goals of the Union in the structural funds area. Gary Marks initially described this process as one of "decentralization of decision-making to subnational levels of government as well as centralization of new powers at the supranational level". Together, these created a "centrifugal process in which decision-making is spun away from member states in two directions", namely to the subnational as well as the supranational levels (Marks, 1993: 401-402). In its more recent versions, the MLG discourse has begun to address more generally the diffusion of political authority into a less hierarchical and more network-like structure of EU policy-making. In conjunction with this broadening of scope, actor strategies in multi-level systems and the risks associated with *Politikverflechtung* in multi-level systems moved more into the focus (Grande, 2000; Benz, 2004). 'New' modes of governance (NMG) in the EU bear some important resemblance to these processes, although the debate puts greater emphasis on the use of non-binding regulatory instruments and the potential of such instruments to overcome decisional deadlock. Furthermore, the NMG debate often takes a more normative approach, e.g. by focusing on the effectiveness of these modes of governing, on questions of democratic legitimacy, and on the rule of law (Best, 2003; Borrás and Greve, 2004; Borrás and Conzelmann, 2007).

An interesting recent attempt to account for the broadening use of the MLG concept is done by Marks and Hooghe (2004), who, as two of the most important writers on the concept, have begun to distinguish between two sorts of multi-level governance. The more traditional 'Type 1' form of MLG is associated with a state-centric concept of politics and sharing of power among governmental actors at different levels. Consequently, federalism is described as the "intellectual foundation" for Type 1 MLG (op.cit.: 17). Taking this view, MLG emerges as a reaction to the simultaneous processes of European integration and regionalisation, both of which lead to a diffusion of powers away from the nation state. One institutional blueprint that takes up this vision of MLG is the 'Europe of the Regions' idea that received much attention during the 1980s and 1990s (Conzelmann, 1996). 'Type 2' multi-level governance as identified by Hooghe and Marks is characterised by task-specific (instead of territorial) boundaries, intersecting memberships and a flexible design that is responsive to temporary need (Marks and Hooghe, 2004: 20-22). As explained by the authors (op. cit.: 29), "Type 2 multi-level governance (…) consists of special-purpose jurisdictions that tailor membership, rules of operation, and functions to a particular policy problem". If one uses such a broadly conceived concept, the notion of 'levels' becomes unfastened from territorially defined entities (such as regions). Rather, 'levels' can be any sort of task-specific policy network that stands in interaction with other networks. As observed by Knill and Tosun (this volume), the effectiveness problems of detailed European legislation and an emerging 'implementation gap' necessitated the development of a 'new' approach to governance, which gave implementing actors "more flexibility in adapting national arrangements to European requirements. Furthermore, it aims to create positive incentives for voluntary participation and co-operation by various societal actors at different institutional levels during policy formulation and implementation" (p.154). Pretty much as in the structural funds area, we thus see a situation where relatively flexible policy rules emanating from the European level are taken up by functionally defined implementation networks at lower levels that consist of a variety of actors. The governance arrangements in environmental policy can therefore also be described as 'multi-level', even though they may not include regional or local actors.

While the authors in the present volume were not confined to making exclusive reference to the Marks/Hooghe definition of multi-level governance, the broader notion sketched above is able to cover experiences from a wide variety of policy fields, including those discussed in the present volume. Most importantly, it blurs the increasingly unsustainable delineation of discussions on 'multi-level' and 'new' modes of governance (see also Eberlein and Kerwer, 2004). New modes of governance may be 'new' in that they "depart from the Community Method of legislating through the use of regulations and directives" (ibid.: 123), i.e. use distinct policy instruments.[3] They do not differ, however from the general picture of multi-level governing in that they also rely on the interaction of policy networks at different levels that are organized along shared functions (and not territory).

The unsustainability of conceiving of 'multi-level' governance as *necessarily* including regional and local actors can also be shown by taking a closer look at the role of these actors in structural policy. In retrospect, it seems that the original excitement about the empowerment of subnational actors and the possible emergence of a 'Europe of the Regions'[4] was to a large degree due to the state-centric analytical lenses that observers used when analysing these phenomena. These did not allow for a conception of the emergence of the new implementation structures of the structural funds as part of a larger phenomenon of governance in the Union. In fact, federalism was never something the Commission had in mind when pushing for the inclusion of regional actors in the implementation of the structural funds. Rather, regional (and other sub-national) actors were seen by the Commission as crucial partners in producing more meaningful regional development plans than those drawn up by remote member state bureaucracies. But regional actors never managed to play a role beyond that task-specific and basically temporary function and in principle acted on a par with the other "social partners" that were mentioned in the implementation regulations for the structural funds from 1993 onwards. In that sense, the multi-level governing structures set up in the context of the implementation of the structural funds more closely resemble 'Type 2' multi-level governance. The geographical and functional delimitation of networks set up for structural funds purposes clearly vary over time and usually do not coincide with the borders of territorially defined regional entities. Furthermore, although elected regional governments or decentralised executives often play an important role in the various networks, these networks do not pretend to represent a certain 'region' (rather, they represent an intervention area of the structural funds), and are also not intended to contribute to the emergence of more formalised regional structures.[5] This viewpoint is further underlined by the

3 See Knill and Tosun (this volume) for a discussion of the extent to which the 'new' instruments in the environmental policy area are actually new.

4 Some early experiments in the context of the 'Integrated Mediterranean Programmes' during the early 1980s and a crucial reform in 1988 paved the way for greater emphasis on the regional level in EU structural policy (see Piattoni, this volume). As part of the implementation of the structural funds, processes of regional empowerment and mobilisation as well as a large amount of direct interaction and alliance-building between the Commission and the regional level have been observed (Marks, 1993; Conzelmann 1995; Heinelt and Smith, 1996; Hooghe, 1996). This was one important trigger for applying the much older (cf. Conzelmann, 1996: 63-65) 'Europe of the Regions' concept to the structural funds area.

5 Even in the UK, where the implementation of the reformed structural funds coincided with (and sometimes seems to have triggered) the emergence of a certain degree of regional

context in which regional participation is discussed in the often-quoted 2001 White Book on 'Governance in the European Union' (European Commission 2001). It is argued there that "a stronger interaction with regional and local governments and civil society" is needed (p. 4) and that "target-based, tripartite contracts (...) between Member States, regions and localities designated by them for that purpose, and the Commission" (i.e. the structural funds model) should be exported to other policy areas, such as environmental policy in order to bring forward a "greater flexibility" of EU policy-making (ibid.: p. 13).

What becomes clear from all of this is that the original multi-level governance debate and the more recent discussion on flexible and 'soft' instruments in EU policy-making (often discussed in the area of environmental policy; cf. Knill and Tosun, this volume) have important common traits. Multi-level and 'new' modes of governance are just two facets of a larger phenomenon of changing forms of governance in the EU. In that sense, it seems worthwhile not only to look for exports of the structural funds model to other policy areas (such as the environment), but also to systematically compare different governance phenomena across regional and environmental policy and to discuss questions of effectiveness, legitimacy, power and interest related to governance in the Union. It is this task that the present volume focuses on.

The contributions in this book

The present volume[6] is divided into three parts, the first of which (including this introductory chapter) offers reflections on the notion of network governance, MLG and the difficult issue of democratic accountability. The second part looks at the structural funds area, while the third part seeks to widen the debate by looking at a number of cases from environmental policy broadly conceived.

The chapter by *Papadopoulos* starts from the idea developed above that the emergence of cooperative forms of governance is not primarily triggered by its potential for democratisation of policy making, but is meant as "a solution to functional problems, like the management of interdependence" (p.34). In that sense, we cannot expect multi-level and new modes of governance to enjoy democratic legitimacy *per se*. Rather, there are four problems in holding the participants within networks accountable, namely their poor transparency and the lack of credible democratic control by parliaments and voters, the overrepresentation of weakly accountable func-

identification, and – after the advent of the Blair Government – the creation of regional development agencies, both the importance of the EU's structural funds and the long term institutional implications of that development should not be overstated (Bache and Conzelmann, this volume).

6 The book is the outcome of a 'thematic stocktaking conference' on the topic of multi-level governance in the EU that was organised under the auspices of the EU Network of Excellence CONNEX. It includes both revised papers given at the conference and subsequently commissioned articles. For more information on Connex, see www.connex-network.org

tional representatives (such as bureaucrats, experts, and interest group representatives) at the cost of representatives of the general public (such as parliamentarians), the multi-level character of networks, and finally the prevalence of 'peer' forms of accountability. With respect to the multi-level character of policy processes, Papadopoulos points out that they lead not only to a dilution of responsibility between levels or between functional networks (the problem of 'many hands'), but also create problems of lengthy chains of delegation and of 'two-level' accountability. Concerning the former, the actors in all forms of networks may in principle be accountable to the public, but only remotely so: The public can only hold elected politicians to account, which themselves then need to hold functional delegates to account – without, however, having sufficient insight into network dynamics: The policy process is visible and understandable only to those principals who are relatively close to network members. The problem of two-level accountability relates to those actors who are directly accountable to the public and still take part in networks: Because they are also accountable to their negotiation partners in the sense of having to build trust and cooperative relationships, they cannot simply follow the demands of their democratic principals. In the words of Papadopoulos, "peer accountability can hardly be achieved without some loss of accountability at home" (p.44). In sum, Papadopoulos argues that the democratic problems intrinsic to network governance are exacerbated by the emerging multi-level character of many governance processes. MLG thus seems to produce or at least to accentuate accountability problems that are linked to lengthy chains of delegation and a heavy overweight of specialized viewpoints and interest to the disadvantage of representatives of general interests. In that sense, the potential for democratic participation often seen in networks seems to be much more accentuated than is usually assumed. On the other hand, Papadopoulos makes clear that democratic control mechanism appropriate to multi-level forms of decision-making could well be developed. Furthermore, he clearly states that one needs to empirically research the extent to which the dangers for democratic accountability outlined in his contribution actually materialize.

The call for empirical research is taken up in the subsequent chapter by *Heinelt* who discusses conditions of achieving 'governability' in multi-level systems. This ability to purposefully direct and shape societal interactions and policy-making, and thus the social environment is faced with a number of challenges in multi-level systems. By looking at the experiences in structural and in environmental policy, Heinelt describes the fragmentation and different logics of action between decision-making and implementation networks and between sectoral policy networks concerned with different aspects of structural or environmental policy as a key element of multi-level governing (see also Knill and Tosun, this volume; Getimis, Demetropolou and Paraskevopoulos, this volume). While this multitude of networks and actors involved in them may offer important opportunities for policy learning and policy experimentation (Sabel and Zeitlin, 2007), Heinelt also highlights challenges for effective governance. These are not only rooted in the complexity of modern societies, but also in the divergent outlooks between players at different levels on "what is desired, known and perceived as possible". How, then, is governance –

understood as a "continuous political process of setting explicit goals for society, of providing incentives and sanctions for their achievement [and] of monitoring and controlling compliance" (Kohler-Koch, 2005: 6) – possible, given the multitude of actors and interests involved in multi-level and new governance arrangements? The answer, according to Heinelt, is that actors and organisations at different levels and of different types are linked through mechanisms of "loose coupling" (see also Heinelt et al., 2005). Such coupling mechanisms could be policy paradigms that suggest generalized conceptions of 'sound' policy while leaving policy details open; or formal institutions that establish a obligation to meet, to interact and, if necessary, to explain and justify specific courses of action. Heinelt points out that concepts such as sustainability in the environmental policy domain and partnership in the structural funds domain have the potential to act as such paradigms that can gently coordinate the actions and interactions of players at various levels. At the same time, the monitoring committees in the structural funds domain and instruments such as environmental impact assessments and eco-audits can provide institutional arenas for the exchange of experiences and the erection of 'soft' pressures for compliance. Still, Heinelt concludes that "there is no inevitability of the development and the effectiveness of these mechanisms" (p.63), and that in order to be successful, coherence mechanisms must rely on the willingness of actors to align and adapt their policy orientations and routines. Therefore, an important question in the context of the present volume is to what extent we can empirically confirm the evolution of such loose coordination mechanisms and a corresponding willingness on the side of actors in implementation networks to adapt their routines and rationales of action. Heinelt also highlights the importance of a shadow of hierarchy for the effectiveness of such mechanisms, i.e. the capacity of the Commission or the Council to resort to a hierarchical mode of decision-making in the case of failure of these softer forms of coordination. In a similar vein, the 'light of the public' (i.e. the danger of being exposed in public for misperformance or deviation from collective norms) is considered by Heinelt to be helpful, thus reflecting on the earlier discussion of public and peer accountability in the Papadopoulos chapter. Again, it is important to know in what ways the 'shadow of hierarchy' and the 'light of the public' are actually used and are effective in keeping fragmented and dispersed actor networks on track, thus contributing to successful governance.

The following two sections of the book discuss these principal themes for the area of the structural funds and for environmental policy. Each section is opened by a more general chapter highlighting the development of policy paradigms and steering mechanisms over time, while the following more empirically oriented contributions then look at the viability and successes of these paradigms in different real world environments. The empirical chapters usually single out 'hard' cases, i.e. situations where there is a high degree of policy conflict and where a general weakness of administrations can be observed. While political tensions e.g. between centre and periphery will likely impair the willingness of actors to reorient and approximate conceptions of sound policies, the case of weak administrations is interesting because one can expect that they are unable to creatively use the latitude given to them by horizontal and non-regulatory instruments of implementation.

The opening chapter of the structural funds section by *Piattoni* poses the question whether the structural funds can be considered a success, both as regards their potential to overcome the problems highlighted in the Heinelt chapter, but also with respect to wider objectives of the policy (such as contributing to the development and system integration of the EU as a whole). She demonstrates that beginning with the Integrated Mediterranean Programs in the 1980s, the structural funds were far more than a simple tool for distributing funds, but instead aspired to transform the governance structures of the Union in a more fundamental way. This is true both in the sense of establishing regional and local authorities as interlocutors of the Commission under the slogan of 'subsidiarity', and with respect to the introduction of the partnership principle in regional policy. The notion of "all parties acting as partners in pursuit of a common goal",[7] and the erection of implementation structures that to some extent sidelined member state administrations are witness to this system-transforming effect. At the same time, Piattoni shows how, in official parlour, the regional level was enhanced as the level where citizen participation could best be organized and where concerns for social and environmental sustainability of the integration process could best be channelled into the EU's decision-making processes. This is for example expressed in the Commission's White Paper on European Governance (European Commission, 2001: 12-13), where the regional level is presented as an "elected and representative channel interacting with the public on EU policy" (top down aspect), and in terms of providing input bottom up: Thus, in the words of the White Paper, it should be ensured (by the Commission) "that regional and local knowledge and conditions are taken into account when developing policy proposals". Relating to such ideas, Piattoni argues that "multi-level governance has developed into a new mode of governance for all those policies where several territorial jurisdictions are fundamentally involved", although the picture remains mixed concerning the extent to which the regions took up the challenge: "Some regions did learn and imported EU standards and procedures into their overall programming. Others clearly dragged their feet, feigned ignorance or simply ignored the possibilities" (p.90). In addition to such actor-oriented explanations of a limited impact of EU

7 This is a quotation from the second (1993) framework regulation on the structural funds (Regulation 2081/93, OJ L 193, 31 July 1993). The full wording is: "Community operations shall be (...) established through close consultations between the Commission, the Member State concerned and the competent authorities and bodies - including, within the framework of each Member State's national rules and current practices, the economic and social partners, designated by the Member State at national, regional, local or other level, with all parties acting as partners in pursuit of a common goal". It includes, for the first time, reference to "economic and social partners". A similar wording can be found in Article 8 (1) of the successor regulation for the 2000-2006 funding period (Regulation 1260/99, OJ L 161, 26 June 1999). The successor regulation for the 2007-2013 period contains a slightly more 'renationalised' version of the partnership principle (Article 11 (1), Regulation 1083/2006, OJ L 210, 31 July 2006).

policies on regional governance, one can certainly detect bottlenecks concerning administrative capabilities.

Reflecting on this latter dimension, the two following chapters look at the experiences with the adaptation of regional players in Greece, Ireland and Portugal as well as in Lithuania to European imperatives. The chapter by *Getimis, Demetropolou and Paraskevopoulos* on the cohesion countries analyses the extent to which the implementation of the structural funds has shaped intra-regional interactions and promoted local institutional capacity in accordance with the wider institutional goals of structural policy (as highlighted by Piattoni). The comparison between Greece, Ireland, and Portugal reveals both significant differences between these countries and a number of important commonalities. Among these are the relatively circumscribed role of regional and local authorities in the implementation of the structural funds in all three countries. Furthermore, we see the creation of specialized agencies and public-private partnerships at the national level that oversee the use of structural monies in their countries and act as a prime point of contact for the Commission. Interestingly, therefore, it is at the *national* and not at the regional or local level that the largest institutional transformations have occurred. There is some limited extent of institutional transformation also at the regional level and an increased role of societal actors in policy-making, most clearly in Ireland and Portugal, and much less pronounced in Greece. Even in the Irish and Portuguese cases, however, these transformations have been largely coordinated and mediated by the centre, and the authors find little evidence for the occurrence of organized feedback loops and societal learning in the implementation of the structural funds. In other words, the adaptations that can be observed mainly have to do with the strategic rationale to access European funds more easily. The authors hypothesise that these observations can be linked to pre-existing patterns of state-society relations as well as to softer variables such as a specific civic culture and identity that impede both the smooth adaptation to European imperatives in general and to the specific implementation model of the structural funds in particular.

The centralisation of policy-making highlighted by Getimis, Demetropolou and Paraskevopoulos in their chapter is underlined in the analysis of the Lithuanian case by *Maniokas*. In what can be read as a scathing critique of the 'Type 1' conception of multi-level governance as identified by Marks and Hooghe (2004), he highlights that neither subnational nor national governmental actors were the main beneficiaries of the implementation of the structural funds, but non-majoritarian institutions at the central level: "It is these quasi-independent agencies created and remodelled through the years of accession – and not regional actors – which can be seen as the (…) major players in the new multi-level governance networks. The implication is that Europeanization in the new member states resulted not so much in territorial, but in functional redistribution of power. It is no longer the 'Europe of Regions'. It is about the 'Europe of Agencies'" (p.115). This echoes some of the findings in the earlier chapter by Getimis and his colleagues, which pointed to the emergence of national managing authorities working outside the regular civil service for the implementation of structural funding programmes in Greece and Portugal and to some extent also in Ireland. These bodies then also play a pivotal role in interacting with local implementation structures (where they exist), thus to some extent detaching the whole implementation process from formal governmental structures. Another commonality is the relatively strong sectoral orientation of these agencies. Six of them operate in Lithuania in the management of the structural funds, and also for the Greek case a number of sectoral bodies can be observed. For Lithuania as well as other Central and East European Countries (CEECs), Maniokas explains the development of such structures with the lacking tradition of regional policy, the relatively small geographical size of many CEECs, the large sums channelled into these countries through the structural funds, and the concerns by the other member states to ensure efficient and sound management of the funds. While it remains unclear to what extent this structure will be modified in future rounds of implementation of the structural funds, it underlines that the structural funds implementation model does not always imply the use of strictly regionalized structures, but may in fact favour a more sectoral and privatized approach to governance. In addition, both chapters identify a relatively weak societal input into these implementation structures, making them, in the words of Maniokas, "distant from the applicants and consequently (...) less user friendly" (p.121).

The final contribution in this section by *Bache and Conzelmann* looks at the question of how the embeddedness of regional policy and politics into the European context played out in Britain. Given that the UK is a member state with a considerable history of regional policy ranging back well into the early post-war years, adaptation to the European model differs considerably from the countries discussed in the previous chapters. While the authors observe an enhancement of the regional tier, the emergence of more partnership-oriented, inter-agency work, and the incorporation into domestic governance and policies of practices first developed in EU programmes, it becomes clear that such changes were and still are firmly under governmental control. Thus, the prime factor in the convergence process of domestic and European policy was the change in government in 1997 and not any direct impact of Europe on the British polity. Furthermore, it is clear that the central government remains the 'financial gatekeeper' in terms of control over structural funds allocations. Another line of argument by the authors is that even though one can observe a strengthening of the regional and local levels in Britain, this does not add up to a strong decentralization of the British polity or the emergence of 'Type 1' multi-level governance. Rather, "governance arrangements are task-specific and, as such, may be disbanded once they have fulfilled their tasks" (p. 138). In this context, the authors also highlight the tendency to delegate the implementation of the structural funds to public-private governance networks operating outside the normal governmental structures and overseen only by the democratically unaccountable Regional Development Agencies created in the 1990s.[8]

8 This is true for the English case. In Scotland, and Wales, the Regional Development Agencies are under oversight by the democratically controlled Welsh Assembly Government and the Scottish Executive.

The third part of the book then seeks to extend the debate by looking at multi-level governance in the domain of environmental policy as well as on 'new' instruments and modes of governance, such as regulatory networks, public-private partnerships and voluntary self-regulation. The opening chapter by *Knill and Tosun* on 'emerging patterns of multi-level governance in EU environmental policy' gives an overview of the emergence of 'new' instruments in environmental policy such as economic, context-oriented and decentralized instruments. Two important explanations advanced by the authors for the emergence of these forms of political steering are the increasing prominence of the subsidiarity principle in the EU and the implementation gaps that occurred under the old regulatory paradigm in environmental policy. These developments led to a situation where "interventionist regulations which encroached on member states' room for manoeuvre were no longer as politically legitimate as in the past" (p. 153). The 'new' context-oriented instruments that were first introduced through the 5th Environmental Action Programme (1993) seemed to address both of these problems by shifting responsibility for policy formulation and implementation downwards and by creating incentives for the voluntary participation of societal actors. In an important sense, these developments reflect the development of steering instruments in the structural funds. The shift from substantial to procedural regulation and the increasing participation of societal actors in the implementation of European policies are common features of both policy domains, a fact that is also highlighted in the chapter by Heinelt (this volume).

Still, has EU environmental policy thus "re-entered the 'right' path", as Knill and Tosun formulate? The answer can be given on a variety of levels. Quantitatively, the significance of the new instruments when compared to classical regulatory measures still seems to be marginal (Jordan, Wurzel and Zito, 2003; but see also Rottmann and Lenschow, this volume). It can also be observed that in cases where the EU originally embarked on voluntary self-regulation (such as in the case of reduction of CO_2 emissions from passenger cars), it has in the meantime returned to a classical regulatory approach (Lenschow and Rottmann, this volume; see also Conzelmann, 2008). Qualitatively, the question arises whether the governance capacity of the EU has been improved by this shift from 'hierarchical' to 'context-oriented' instruments. Possible criteria in this respect could be the effectiveness of EU policies, as well as the democratic quality of EU governance. The present volume is seeking to give answers by looking at two cases of more traditional top down implementation of EU environmental policies (chapters by Fairbrass and Laffan) and at two cases of 'new' policy instruments (chapters by Koutalakis and by Rottmann and Lenschow). Furthermore, each of the chapters offers a distinct and novel view of the multi-level problematique in EU governance.

The chapter by *Laffan* focuses on the implementation of the Habitats Directive in Ireland, Greece and Finland, thus reflecting on two countries that were also discussed in the earlier chapter by Getimis et al. Reflecting on points made in the chapters by Heinelt and Knill and Tosun, Laffan argues that the process of implementation and compliance can usefully be seen as a multi-level process in which several political arenas are interconnected. Importantly, this process is characterised by severe political conflict between the Commission, the member states, and domestic NGOs in all three member states researched by Laffan. While this is largely due to the demanding and controversial nature of the Habitat directive, it also shows that 'multi-level' policy processes are not *per se* consensual. Two further points are noteworthy when comparing the findings of Laffan with those from the structural funds area: First, there is ample evidence of the emergence of subnational actors as aides in the implementation of environmental policy. In all three member states, environmental NGOs acted as watchdogs that alerted the Commission to implementation or compliance problems at the domestic level. On the other hand, there is also considerable opposition from domestic actors. In Ireland, the Commission faced an effective alliance of governmental and domestic actors (in particular the farmer's lobby). In Greece, a management authority put into place for the operation of a marine park met with formidable local opposition. In Finland, finally, a similar pattern of supporting and opposing coalitions of domestic actors emerged, with both sides becoming increasingly Europeanized as the dispute over site designation began to reach the courts. These examples show that even though there is increasing interaction between the Commission and subnational actors, it does not always lead to a harmonious 'partnership' among all the actors involved. Partly in relation to this, European policies open up new alliances and channels of influence for hitherto marginalized actors, even though domestic governments remain the key 'gatekeepers' in this respect. A second interesting parallel between the implementation of the Habitats directive and structural funding is that the Commission used the withdrawal or freezing of structural fund monies as a lever to pressurize unwilling domestic actors into compliance. Instances of this can be seen both in Ireland and in Greece.

The subsequent chapter by *Fairbrass* analyzes the evolution of environmental governance in the UK, and the impact that devolution in the UK has had on these processes. It is argued that devolution created a number of weak administrations at the regional level of Wales and England that are now 'jockeying for position' (i.e. seeking to extend their political influence) under the conditions of increasing European embeddedness of environmental policy. Fairbrass arrives at the conclusion that both devolution and the introduction of non-traditional approaches in environmental policy have led to the dispersion of decision-making powers, and have at the same time opened up new channels of influence for subnational actors. Interestingly, it is not regional public actors, but public-private partnerships and resource-rich business organisations that seem to profit most in this context. Fairbrass echoes a finding from the Bache and Conzelmann and Laffan chapters in again pointing out the key role of central government as a gate keeper in the structuring of this new dynamism. On the other hand, regional public bodies often find allies in other regions or at the EU level and can try to push their interests alongside the formal channels provided by the government. The supranational actors in particular see regional actors as "a source of political support and information" (p.203) and are therefore willing to coalesce with them. In summary, while the devolution agenda in the UK has given rise to some forms of 'Type I' multi-level governance, it is not devolution, but functional need that seems to give the strongest push to the emergence of multi-level structures in the context of EU governance. At the same time, it is clearly not the case that these 'Type 2' MLG structures work consensually and free from conflict. While it is true that hitherto marginalized actors are increasingly drawn into processes of policy making and policy implementation for functional reasons, this does not imply that all partners are actually working "in pursuit of a common goal", as the prose on partnership in the structural funds regulations would have it.

This point is further underlined in the chapter by *Koutalakis*, which looks at a particular instance of 'new' environmental governance, namely the functioning of participatory environmental networks in the context of the so-called Seville Process. These networks are made up of a host of different actors (such as Commission, the member states, business associations, individual firms, environmental organisations, research institutes, universities, plus national and EU regulatory agencies) and are coordinated by a European bureau in Seville. Their main task is to implement the Integrated Pollution Prevention and Control Directive which is innovative in that it does not prescribe harmonised emission limit values, but seeks to install co-regulatory processes through which best practices and techniques are identified and disseminated. The key concern of Koutalakis is whether the hopes for an increased effectiveness of policy-making through networks (due to their potential to bring together all actors concerned by a particular piece of environmental regulation, and the chance of policy learning and exchange of best practises that result from the repeated interaction within networks) do actually materialize: "In other words, can new forms of governance reduce the influence of conflicting national interests over the level of environmental regulatory standards?" (p.209). Through a thorough analysis of the composition of these networks, Koutalakis reveals that there is a strong overrepresentation of government and business representatives to the detriment of environmental NGOs and research institutes. He explains this outcome again by the lack of necessary resources on the side of many NGOs, in particular lacking knowledge about the often highly complex technical issues having to do with the determination of best available technologies (BATs). Concerning the issue of whether regulatory standards are raised by this 'new' form of environmental governance, Koutalakis remains undecided. Even though the outcomes may differ from that of classical command and control regulation, the issue of whether these outcomes represent a higher standard boils down to a determination of what the BAT in a given field actually is – an issue that is difficult to determine scientifically. In this context, Koutalakis concludes that the key to a higher environmental standard would actually be a more balanced participation structure within the networks. Unless the imbalances in participation are addressed, Koutalakis concludes, the outcomes of participatory networks will not differ significantly from classical forms of regulation.

The following chapter by *Rottmann and Lenschow* looks at yet another example of 'new' modes of governance, namely voluntary agreements between industry actors and the Commission in the areas of environmental protection. Voluntary agreements follow an idea similar to that of participatory networks and the structural funds, namely to incorporate concerned actors into processes of policy shaping and implementation. The analysis of the two voluntary agreements reveals that both agreements emerged from a situation in which the Commission openly threatened to regulate if the business associations would not adopt the targets set politically by the Commission and the Council. However, the success of the two agreements and especially the willingness of industry actors to join them differ considerably, a finding that seemingly has to do with the different membership and structures of the two industry associations as well as with the success that the Commission had in negotiating similar agreements with extra-EU competitors. The authors conclude that for voluntary agreements to work, the maintenance of a credible shadow of hierarchy by the Commission is crucial. Concerning the nature of participation in these agreements, there is naturally a limited role for non-governmental actors, even though both agreements seem to acknowledge the problem and have experimented with different forms of monitoring and inclusion of societal actors. Still, Rottmann and Lenschow conclude that participatory input into these steering arrangements is minimal and that "similar to regulatory policies of the EU, voluntary agreements gain public legitimacy not through the democratic and transparent organisation of 'input' but rather through policy output and problem solving capacity" (p. 251).

The chapter by *Birkel and Liefferink,* while staying within the environmental policy domain, opens up a completely new dimension of the debate by extending the idea of multi-level governing beyond the confines of the EU to the global level. At the same time, the authors give a useful summary of the MLG debate and point out some of its blind spots: Apart from the neglect of the global level, Birkel and Liefferink argue that many MLG authors somewhat precipitately use a positivist concept of power and authority: For example, the idea that competences are "spun away from member states" (Marks, 1993: 402) in the direction of supranational and subnational actors seems to carry a notion of power and authority as givens that can be distributed and redistributed over levels in a basically zero-sum fashion. However, one open question for Birkel and Liefferink is why such a spinning away is considered to be appropriate and legitimate in the first place, and how the newly 'empowered' actors then come to be viewed as rightful participants in multi-level governing. Part of the answer is likely the shared policy paradigms that Heinelt and others have highlighted in their chapters, and that seem to justify the increasing role of subnational and societal actors in EU policy-making. In a similar vein, Birkel and Liefferink argue that concerning the role of the EU at the global level there needs to be a recognition by the other negotiation partners that the participation of supranational actors is rightful, and a willingness on the side of the EU member states to collaborate with the supranational level in order to increase the political clout of the Union as a whole. The authors hypothesise that EU member states and EU institutions are increasingly aware of the fact that internal power struggles have negative effects on the overall ability of the EU to act effectively at the international level. Although actors within the EU will still strive to maintain or enhance their own authority, they will at the same time be constrained by the need for external coherence. This discussion mirrors the earlier point about conflict-driven explanations of multi-level governance versus more functional explanations, yet highlights the importance of the ideational context within which multi-level governance arrangements are embedded.

Conclusion

Taken together, a number of key arguments emerge from the present volume that seem to have the potential to add some fresh elements to the debate on multi-level governance. Even though not all of them are completely new, it seems that they do not receive that much attention in the respective debates as would be appropriate.

Type 1 and Type 2 multi-level governance: Both variants cover important aspects of the multi-level governance phenomenon. Still, if we want to extend the MLG concept into a more general notion of governing in the EU, the concept of 'levels' must be defined broader than just in territorial (regional or local) terms. A functional delineation of governing arenas seems to offer advantages here: Not only is it able to cover fields beyond the structural funds area, such as environmental policy. In addition, it also seems to be more appropriate to analyze the policy shaping and policy implementation structures in the field of regional and structural policies. As was argued above, even though many implementation networks are situated at the regional or local level, their boundaries often do not converge with administrative delineations. In addition, they are often of a more ephemeral nature than formal regional structures in decentralized or federal systems. In that sense, functional need and not regional empowerment or federalism is the key concept standing behind multi-level governance. Nevertheless, it is still useful to keep the notion of 'levels' – not only for want of a better term, but also because functionally delineated, but still '*subnational'* policy-making arenas become increasingly prominent in EU governance.

Second generation research on governance in the EU: It was claimed in the beginning of this chapter that the present volume is representative of what one may term 'second generation' research on governance in the EU. As argued by Pollack (2008), the first generation of research on multi-level and new forms of governance was characterized by a debate on the novelty of these forms of governance and the extent to which they could transform basic institutional features of the Union. In this discussion, those who saw a more regionalized or a more deliberative form of governing emerging in the EU were pitted against those who offered "corrective evaluations demonstrating the limited impact and implementation of new governance practices" (ibid.). This volume takes a different approach. It acknowledges the existence of a growing body of new and multi-level forms of governing while at the same time not sounding the death knell for more traditional forms of regulation. Both approaches exist in parallel, and the most interesting debates for political science probably are centred around the relationship between the two and their comparative strengths and weaknesses.

Starting from this, it becomes an empirical question whether and under which conditions these non-traditional forms of governance are applied and can increase the effectiveness and legitimacy of governance in the EU. The chapters in this volume give a range of different answers to this question: On the one hand, there are authors who think about this problem predominantly in terms of 'getting the instruments right', for example by making use of the mechanisms of loose coupling identified in the Heinelt chapter. For others, effectiveness is more an outcome of actor strategies that can favour or impede broad participation of actors and joint policy-making in the pursuit of a common goal. Yet, for most authors in the present volume there is no such clear juxtaposition between actor-centred and structural approaches. As expressed by Heinelt (p. 63), "there is no inevitability in the development and the effectiveness of these mechanisms [of loose coupling]". Rather, the extent to which actors are willing to adapt their routines is crucial for the form that governance in the EU takes. This problem is recognized for example in the chapters by Getimis et al. and by Laffan: They argue that established patterns of state-society interaction and the availability of institutionalized access channels for subnational actors determine the extent to which central governments are able to play a gatekeeping role, thus effectively undermining the participatory potential of multi-level governance (see also the chapters by Bache and Conzelmann and by Fairbrass). A similar finding emerges in the chapters by Koutalakis and by Rottmann and Lenschow who both observe a predominance of governmental and business actors in the networks they research. It is obvious that considerations of power and autonomy continue to play a role, and that, therefore, governance research cannot get rid of the old Lasswell questions of 'who gets what, when, and how'). In a similar vein, the role of the Commission becomes fairly important in multi-level and new governance arrangements. Heinelt and Rottmann and Lenschow in particular point to the importance of keeping up a shadow of hierarchy (i.e. a regulatory threat) in order for governance arrangements to remain effective. While the Commission is dependent upon the member states in this respect, the experiences reported in the Getimis et al. and the Laffan chapters show that the Commission can also gain influence unilaterally, for example through withholding structural funding. These experiences may caution against the portrayal of the Commission as a politically neutral moderator and enabler.

Normative qualities: The ultimate criteria against which to judge the significance of new and multi-level governance arrangements are normative ones. While effectiveness issues have already been dealt with above, a further key issue is the democratic legitimacy of these forms of governance. One important aspect of this discussion is against which conception of democracy the normative credentials of MLG and NMG should be gauged. As pointed out above, some of the most novel forms of governance in the European Union are centred round the idea of transparency of standards, steering by benchmarks and decentralised participation by citizens and civil society actors. Whether or not one wants to see an amelioration of the democratic quality of EU governance in this strongly depends on the conceptual starting point: Such arrangements may hollow out traditional parliamentary control rights, but may also imply new opportunities for deliberative democracy and post-parliamentarian accountability (Borrás and Conzelmann, 2007).

Starting from liberal and participatory conceptions of democracy, the authors in this volume draw a largely negative conclusion. Neither the uneven forms of representation in the several networks and governance arrangements researched here nor the limited role of the public and of parliaments speak in favour of these newly emerging forms of governance at EU level. In addition, the functional nature of the governance arrangements researched in this volume point to problems of uneven access and a bias towards resource-rich actors such as business organizations. The uneven distribution of resources that are necessary to become part of horizontal networks of governance is mentioned by almost all authors in this volume, as well as the strong positions of the Commission and member state governments. While one may argue that the latter actors are under democratic scrutiny at least in principle, the observations in the Papadopoulos chapter caution against such an optimistic assessment. The tendency of networks to develop 'groupthink' and to exclude opponents, the lengthy chains of delegation and democratic control, and the problems of 'many hands' and of 'two-level accountability' are very real problems. The instruments through which new and multi-level governance arrangements can be held democratically accountable in a robust manner are still to be devised.

References

Bache, I. (1999): The Extended Gatekeeper. Central Government and the Implementation of EU Regional Policy in the UK *Journal of European Public Policy*, *6* (1), pp. 28-45.

Bache, I. and Flinders, M. (2004). *Multi-level Governance*. Oxford: Oxford University Press.

Benz, A. (2004): Multilevel Governance - Governance in Mehrebenensystemen; in: A. Benz (eds.): *Governance - Regieren in komplexen Regelsystemen: Eine Einführung* (pp. 125-146). Wiesbaden: VS Verlag für Sozialwissenschaften.

Best, E. (2003): Alternative Regulations or Complementary Methods? Evolving Options in European Governance *Eipascope*, *2003* (1), pp. 2-11.

Borrás, S. and Conzelmann, T. (2007): Democracy, Legitimacy and Soft Modes of Governance in the EU: The Empirical Turn *Journal of European Integration*, *29* (5), pp. 531-548.

Borrás, S. and Greve, B. (2004): Concluding Remarks: New Method or Just Cheap Talk? *Journal of European Public Policy*, *11* (2), pp. 329-336.

Börzel, T. A. (2005): European Governance - Nicht neu, aber anders; in: G. F. Schuppert (eds.): *Governance-Forschung: Vergewisserung über Stand und Entwicklungslinien* (pp. 72-94). Baden-Baden: Nomos.

Conzelmann, T. (1995): Networking and the Politics of EU Regional Policy: Lessons from North Rhine-Westphalia, Nord-Pas de Calais and North West England *Regional and Federal Studies*, 5 (2), pp. 134-172.

Conzelmann, T. (1996): Europa der Regionen; in: B. Kohler-Koch and W. Woyke (eds.): *Europäische Union* (pp. 61-68). München: C.H.Beck.

Conzelmann, T. (2002). Große Räume, kleine Räume: Europäisierte Regionalpolitik in Deutschland und Großbritannien. Baden-Baden: Nomos.

Conzelmann, T. (2008): A New Public-Private Divide in the European Union?; in: B. Kohler-Koch and F. Larat (eds.): *Efficient and Democratic Governance in the European Union* (Connex Report Series No. 9). Mannheim: Mannheimer Zentrum für Europäische Sozialforschung (forthcoming).

Eberlein, B. and Kerwer, D. (2004): New Governance in the European Union: A Theoretical Perspective *Journal of Common Market Studies*, *42* (1), pp. 121-142.

European Commission (2001). *European Governance. A White Paper* (COM(2001) 428 final). Brüssel: Europäische Kommission.

Gbikpi, B. G. J. R. (2002): From Democratic Government to Participatory Governance; in: J. R. Grote and B. Gbikpi (eds.): *Participatory Governance: Political and Social Implications* (pp. 17-34). Opladen: Leske + Budrich.

Grande, E. (2000): Multi-Level Governance: Institutionelle Besonderheiten und Funktionsbedingungen des europäischen Mehrebenensystems; in: E. Grande and M. Jachtenfuchs (eds.): *Wie problemlösungsfähig ist die EU? Regieren im europäischen Mehrebenensystem* (pp. 11-30). Baden-Baden: Nomos.

Heinelt, H. et al. (2005). Die Entwicklung der EU-Strukturfonds als kumulativer Politikprozess. Baden-Baden: Nomos.

Heinelt, H. and Smith, R. (1996). *Policy Networks and European Structural Funds*. Aldershot: Avebury.

Hooghe, L. (1996). Cohesion Policy and European Integration. Building Multi-Level Governance. Oxford: Oxford University Press.

Hooghe, L. and Marks, G. (2001). *Multi-level Governance and European Integration*. Lanham etc.: Rowman & Littlefield.

Héritier, A. (2002). *New Modes of Governance in Europe: Policy Making without Legislating?* (Working Paper, Institute for Advanced Studies, Political Science Series No. 81). Wien: Institute for Advanced Studies.

Héritier, A. (2003): New Modes of Governance in Europe: Increasing political efficiency and policy effectiveness; in: T. Börzel and R. Cichowski (eds.): *The State of the European Union, 6 - Law, Politics, and Society* (pp. 199-243). Oxford: Oxford University Press.

Jachtenfuchs, M. and Kohler-Koch, B. (2004): Governance in der Europäischen Union; in: A. Benz (eds.): *Governance - Regieren in komplexen Regelsystemen: Eine Einführung* (pp. 77-101). Wiesbaden: VS Verlag für Sozialwissenschaften.

Jordan, A., Wurzel, R. and Zito, A. R. (2003). *New Instruments of Environmental Governance? National Experiences and Prospects*. London: Frank Cass.

Kohler-Koch, B. (1999). *A Constitution for Europe?* (MZES Working paper 8/1999). Mannheim: Mannheimer Zentrum für Europäische Sozialforschung.

Kohler-Koch, B. (2005). European Governance and System Integration (European Governance Papers No. C-05-01; Online: http://www.connex-network.org/eurogov/pdf/egp-connex-C-05-01.pdf).

Kohler-Koch, B. and Rittberger, B. (2006): Review Article: The Governance Turn in EU Studies *Journal of Common Market Studies*, *44* (Annual Review), pp. 27-49.

Marks, G. (1993): Structural Policy and Multilevel Governance in the EC; in: A. W. Cafruny and G. G. Rosenthal (eds.): *The State of the European Community. The Maastricht Debates and Beyond, Volume 2* (pp. 391-410). Boulder Col: Harlow Longman.

Marks, G. and Hooghe, L. (2004): Contrasting Visions of Multi-level Governance; in: I. Bache and Flinders Matthew (eds.): *Multi-level Governance* (pp. 15-30). Oxford: Oxford University Press.

Marks, G., Hooghe, L. and Blank, K. (1996): 'European Integration and the State'; in: K. Armingeon (ed.): *Der Nationalstaat am Ende des 20. Jahrhunderts: Beiträge im Rahmen der Berner Vortragsreihe: 'Die Schweiz im Prozess der Globalisierung'* (pp. 91-126). Bern, Stuttgart, Wien: Haupt.

Pollack, M. A. (2008): Discussion: The Community Method and New Modes of Governance; in: B. Kohler-Koch and F. Larat (eds.): *Efficient and Democratic Governance in the European Union;* Connex Report Series No. 9. Mannheim: Mannheim Centre for European Social Research (forthcoming).

Sabel, C. and Zeitlin, J. (2007). Learning from Difference: The New Architecture of Experimentalist Governance in the European Union (European Governance Papers (EUROGOV) No. C-07-02).

Schmitter, P. C. (2004): Neo-neo-functionalism; in: T. Diez and A. Wiener (eds.): *European Integration Theory* (pp. 45-74). Oxford: Oxford University Press.

Schäfer, A. (2006): Resolving Deadlock: Why International Organisations Introduce Soft Law *European Law Journal*, *12* (2), pp. 194-208.

Problems of Democratic Accountability in Network and Multi-level Governance[1]

Yannis Papadopoulos

Introduction

Several studies focusing on different policy sectors, in diverse national and local environments, find broad convergence toward a policy-making style dominated by cooperation among government levels and between public and non-public actors. 'Governance' as a particular style of governing refers to 'sustaining co-ordination and coherence among a wide variety of actors with different purposes and objectives such as political actors and institutions, corporate interests, civil society, and transnational governments' (Pierre, 2000: 3-4). In its 'multi-level' form, it involves 'a large number of decision-making arenas differentiated along both functional and territorial lines, and interlinked in a non-hierarchical way' (Eberlein and Kerwer, 2004: 128). It implies the formulation or the implementation of public policies by networks involving public actors (politicians and administrators) belonging to different decisional levels, together with various non-public actors (economic agents, interest representatives and stakeholders, experts).[2] Deliberation, bargaining and compromise-seeking are the rule in governance arenas, which are characterised by cooperative relations between governmental units attached to different territorial levels (sub-national, national, European, etc.), and by collaboration of these units with various non-public bodies (associations, third-sector organisations, firms, etc.) instead of topdown policy making. This chapter exposes the reasons why this – at first glance promising and in all likelihood necessary – shift to less 'dirigist' forms of policy making can generate problems with respect to the quality of our democracies. This is a largely neglected issue in a research field which is dominated by managerial concerns about governance performance: based on a survey of about 1,600 projects included in a 'Connex' database on EU governance (GOV-

1 This chapter was originally published in the European Law Journal, Vol. 13, No. 4, July 2007, pp 469-486. It is reproduced here by kind permission of the author and the journal publisher, Blackwell Publishing. Research for this chapter has benefited from generous funding by the Swiss federal government (Secrétariat d'Etat à la recherche).

2 See the definition by Skelcher (2005: 90): 'Networks engage mainstream state, federal, regional, and local governments in interactions with arm's length public bodies including quasi-governmental agencies, single-purpose boards, public-private partnerships, and multi-organizational collaborations'.

DATA), Kohler-Koch (2006: 5) concludes that not more than 17% of them address questions of democracy or legitimacy.

Problems with respect to democracy are caused by a deficit of democratic accountability of governance structures. This deficit mainly stems from four properties of network governance: the weak visibility and uncoupling of networks from the democratic circuit; the weak presence of citizen representatives in networks; the multi-level aspect; and the prevalence of 'peer' forms of accountability. After explaining the accountability problems generated by each of these properties, I conclude with a model for decision making that may alleviate the accountability deficits.

Accountability can be defined as 'a relationship between an actor and a forum, in which the actor has an obligation to explain and to justify his or her conduct, the forum can pose questions and pose judgement, and the actor may face consequences' (Bovens, 2007). Stated somewhat differently, 'A is accountable to B when A is obliged to inform B about A's (past or future) actions and decisions, to justify them, and to suffer punishment in the case of eventual misconduct' (Schedler, 1999: 17). One should note that this definition of accountability combines justification by A to B with the availability to B of sanctions vis-à-vis A. What is more, the constraint for justification depends on the availability of effective sanctions (not necessarily the utilisation of sanctions, but their 'shadow'). Such a resource in the hands of the accountability 'holder' means that the actions of the accountability 'holdee' (Behn, 2001) will not remain without consequences for him or for her, and that the decision about the positive or negative character of these consequences is in the hands of the accountability holder. However, the two dimensions do not need to be simultaneously present: courts, for instance, are compelled to provide reasons for their decisions, but they cannot be sanctioned for them;[3] while MPs can be sanctioned without being (formally) obliged to justify their decisions.

Grant and Keohane (2004: 42) are right in claiming that 'we should resist the temptation to narrow the issue of accountability to that of democratic control'. They mention several other forms of accountability (administrative, fiscal, legal, etc.). In addition, even political accountability is not necessarily democratic. In eighteenth century England for instance, the parliament claimed that the ministers of the Crown should be accountable to it, even though it was not democratically elected. And even the European Parliament was not (directly) democratically elected until as late as 1979 (although it is true that its role as an accountability holder was weak). A thorough survey of accountability issues would require scrutiny of who is accountable to whom, for what, and through which procedures, what kind of arguments and justifications are provided by the accountability holdee, and what kind of sanctions are available to the accountability holder. Being exhaustive in that respect for complex forms of multi-level governance would go beyond the scope of this article. The chapter also disregards the rhetoric justifications used

3 Note, however, that in some systems judges may not be re-elected or are even subject to recall.

in the framework of accountability,[4] and focuses on the (arguably limited) role of public and democratic forms of accountability to citizens and parliaments of actors involved in network governance. In other words, it scrutinises the democratic anchorage (Sørensen, 2005: 348) of network forms of governance, that is, the possibility for those affected by collectively binding decisions formulated or implemented by policy networks, and/or for those representing them, to hold participants of these networks accountable by sanctioning them. It is often argued that horizontal and cooperative decision-making procedures operate in the shadow of the hierarchy, i.e. the options taken by actors who cooperate are subject to state approval, which usually takes the form of parliamentary ratification. To what extent do actors participating in policy networks operate in the shadow of democratic control, and in case of limitations to this control, to what kind of factors are they attributable?

Possible deficits in political accountability are not only the object of normative concerns, but can generate political problems too, leading to governability or legitimacy deficits. Such deficits are not only the objects of critical normative assessments, but also become the targets of anti-establishment political 'entrepreneurs' (Papadopoulos, 2002). Thus, accountability of decision makers is not only a goal to be achieved by political systems claiming to be democratic, but also a means for their legitimation in environments where democratic values prevail. The availability of effective accountability mechanisms forces policy makers to anticipate the ex post control by policy takers, and to act in the shadow of their sanction, which produces a 'deterrent' (or disciplining) effect (Behn, 2001: 14-16).[5]

For accountability to be enforced in contemporary political systems where the institution of binding mandates is no longer *au goût du jour*, both mechanisms are necessary. The 'institutionalisation' (Schmitter, 2004) of retrospective control by the governed requires publicity of the actions of political elites and justification of their actions by them, in other words their 'answerability' (Schedler, 1999), which reduces informational asymmetries between 'agents' and 'principals' due to delegation.[6] Answerability strongly induces rulers to anticipate the retrospective control by the governed (Koenig-Archibugi, 2004: 237-238). The damoclean sword of control fosters responsiveness to the preferences of the accountability holder: the more de-

4 Goodin (2003: 364) distinguishes between different forms of arguments likely to be supplied by actors requested to account on their actions, their intentions, the (sometimes unintended) results of their actions, and so on.

5 As Schmitter (2004: 49) puts it, the most accountable leaders are those who have nothing to fear from accountability. Mansbridge (2003: 526) however correctly maintains that, notwithstanding its current diffusion, 'anticipatory representation' based on 'anticipated reactions' does not involve accountability in its classic form: 'The representative acts only as entrepreneur, preparing to offer and offering a product to a *future* buyer' (emphasis added). Anticipatory representation can fit accountability only in its classic form under the assumptions that voters remain the same and do not modify their preferences from one election to another.

6 'Principal-agent' models are often used to describe accountability problems: for a recent overview, see Bendor *et al* (2001: 191).

cision makers feel that they act in the shadow of possible sanctions, the more it will be rational for them to endogenise the preferences of their 'principal'. The idea that the citizenry should be the ultimate 'principal' is central to democratic accountability, although in reality the mass public is not the only judge of governmental performance (think about the role of constitutional courts, or of external agents such as the International Monetary Fund for some countries). Political actors are accountable to a number of 'forums' which are not their democratic 'principals'. Also, the 'harder' accountability mechanisms are (Bovens, 2005),[7] the more effective we can expect them to be in ensuring responsiveness. In that sense, genuine accountability mechanisms do not rest on a 'logic of appropriateness' – rulers behave in a responsive manner because they feel they have to – but on a logic of 'consequentiality': rulers behave in a responsive manner because they anticipate the costs of unresponsive behaviour. It should finally be added that accountability and responsiveness must be conceptually distinguished (Bartolini, 1999: 435): Benevolent dictators are responsive to the needs of their followers without being accountable, whereas behaving in a responsible manner and displaying 'leadership' qualities in democracies requires politicians to make decisions that may well contradict the preferences of their constituencies.

The Accountability Problem in Network Governance

It is expected that network forms of governance will lead to decisions enjoying strong 'output' legitimacy (Scharpf, 1970), because their content is more appropriate, or because they are better accepted by target groups. In other words, network governance is expected to be conducive to technically more adequate and politically more realistic decisions. However, the consequences of network governance for democracy have long been neglected. The literature originally stressed that more 'horizontal' forms of policy making are more responsive to the concerns of policy takers, because in governance the latter are integrated into the policy-making process, and thus appear as 'co-producers' of the collectively binding decisions that affect them.[8] However, as suggested by Renate Mayntz (1997), and more recently again by Mark Bevir (2006), cooperative governance is not conceived primarily in terms of its potential for democratisation of policy making, but meant as a solution to functional problems, like the management of interdepend-

7 An example of an allegedly powerful accountability forum today is the media, and it is no accident that contemporary democracies have been defined by Manin (1997), a major theorist of representative democracy, as 'audience democracies'. However, if the incumbents fail to follow the recommendations formulated by the media this does not entail any automatic sanction, so that we should speak here of a 'soft' accountability mechanism.

8 See, for instance, the European Commission's plea for 'fostering participatory democracy'. Non-governmental organisations (NGOs) 'are held in high esteem because it is assumed that they contribute to the formation of European public opinion, they provide feedback so the Commission can adjust its policy, they contribute to managing, monitoring and evaluating EU projects, and their involvement helps to win acceptance' (Kohler-Koch, 2000: 525).

ence between various collective actors or concerns with compliance by policy takers.[9] As several recent works point out (Bache and Flinders, 2004; Benz, 1998; Benz and Papadopoulos, 2006; Papadopoulos, 2003; Papadopoulos, 2005), governance by policy networks in fact generates a number of problems with respect to democratic accountability. In this article, I identify and scrutinise four of them.

The Weak Visibility and Uncoupling of Networks

Lack of visibility impedes accountability in primarily two respects. First, decisional procedures in policy networks are often informal and opaque, as this is deemed to facilitate the achievement of compromise. Second, networks dilute responsibility among a large number of actors. This is the 'problem of many hands' or 'paradox of shared responsibility' (Bovens, 1998: 45-52), which can be viewed as the negative side of multi-centric decision making, at least as long as guidelines for 'collaborative' accountability (Behn, 2001: 72-74) remain 'fuzzy' (Flinders, 2005: 230). Even if these problems are attenuated through provisions for access to information and good governance, the latter are no substitute for traditional accountability mechanisms that should give the controllers the opportunity to sanction the controlled (Héritier, 2003). Transparency lacks the element of sanction: it induces the accountability holdee to provide justifications for his or her action, but if these justifications are not considered satisfactory, the accountability holder has no possibility of imposing any sanctions. Publicity is a necessary condition for democratic accountability but not a sufficient one: if exposure to media scrutiny, for instance, induces politicians to behave in a 'responsive' (perhaps also populistic manner), this is only because negative reporting by the media can convince voters to sanction unresponsive politicians in forthcoming elections.

Also, policy networks are often uncoupled from the official representative bodies, whose capacity to exert effective oversight over such parallel decisional circuits is questionable.[10] Analytically, visibility and 'coupling' should be distinguished: visibility has to do with the ability of controllers to watch and monitor behaviour, while coupling has to do with their ability to influence ex ante the behaviour of the controlled, or to sanction it ex post (or both). But, of course, effective control is not possible in the absence of visibility, or if networks operate in remoteness from democratic institutions. In network governance, the initiative and control functions of parliaments are then, in all likelihood, weakened, with parliaments possibly confined to the role of ratifying bodies. True, parliaments have the formal right to overrule decisions made by policy networks (Voelzkow, 2000: 273-276). The question, however, is to what extent this is a credible threat. The capacity of representative bodies to nullify decisions prepared in networks

9 According to Wolf (2002: 40), 'the primary normative guideline for governance is not democracy but legitimacy'.

10 The concept of 'post-parliamentary' governance has been coined to depict that phenomenon (Andersen and Burns, 1996).

can be questioned above all for sheer lack of expert knowledge.[11] One should 'bring the state back in' into the debate on network governance: the state is not 'hollowed out' simply because networks require management and steering, and this is largely done by public actors (Peters, 2006). However, this does not solve the problem of accountability because it can be reasonably hypothesised that 'meta-governance' functions (the governance of governance networks) will rather be devolved to bureaucrats rather than be directly operated by elected bodies. In a sense it is rational for parliamentarians to delegate some of their governance or meta-governance competencies if the information costs for the exertion of these functions are too high for them. But for parliamentarians to be able to subsequently veto proposals made by their 'agents', they again need to have access to information. Thus, the problem remains (except in cases where politicians can credibly argue and decide along strictly ideological lines).

Remoteness from parliaments and voters can be the object of deliberate institutional design (as in the case of autonomous bodies, courts, etc.), in order to make institutions less sensible and less responsive to short-term political concerns. Yet remoteness also produces – most probably unintended – cognitive limits to the capacity to perceive correctly what is happening in policy arenas. MEPs for instance – for their part directly accountable to the electorate – demonstrate a lower accuracy in their perceptions of policy issues than members of national parliaments, including typically European issues, such as the common currency or the abolition of national borders. As regards voters, 40% are not able to identify the policy positions of European transnational parties on unemployment policy, which is closely related to the familiar left-right divide, and the situation is worse for typically European issues (Andeweg, 2005: 13-16), especially as regards 'the everyday policy-making and implementation' (Olsson, 2003: 285). In sum, remoteness aggravates informational asymmetries to the detriment of accountability holders, thus causing prejudice to the exercise of accountability.

There is therefore a risk that decisions will be made by actors other than those regarded as legitimate decision makers by ordinary citizens or by members of the affected communities. Mair (2005), for instance, considers that the EU exemplifies this by assigning a limited role to party democracy, and goes so far as to claim that through a socialisation (or habituation) effect this can result in citizens becoming more generally accustomed to the decline of the role of representative institutions in policy making. It has also been argued that a sphere of (problem-solving oriented) '*politique des problèmes*' – dominated by governance arrangements in 'backstage' policy making – is to a large extent disjointed now from the 'frontstage' sphere of '*politique d'opinion*', which is the traditional realm of party com-

11 This is clearly an empirical issue and of course institutional arrangements are of relevance too. On European matters, the competencies of the European Parliament are not comparable to the competencies of national parliaments on national matters, which depend in turn on the system of government and on parliamentary resources. Also oversight of EU legislation by national parliaments is subject to considerable cross-country variation (Benz, 2004).

petition but seems to play merely a symbolic role (Leca, 1996: 345-246).[12] The relevant actors are not the same in the two spheres, furthermore, the goals and rules of the game tend to differ. This can raise 'coupling' problems between dissimilar logics: for instance, Lehmbruch (1999) when looking at Germany stressed the lack of compatibility between the competitive logic of party politics and the emphasis on negotiation and cooperation within the federal multi-level governance arena. In addition, when the sphere of 'policies' is disjointed from the sphere of 'politics', the effectiveness of accountability procedures is undermined. The retrospective evaluations of office holders on the grounds of their policy achievements, and the prospective evaluation of candidates (incumbents and members of non-governmental parties) on the grounds of their pledges, are hardly possible. The incumbent parties are held responsible for political decisions whose formulation in fact largely escapes their control. Of course; this is not new: ministerial responsibility implies, for instance, that ministers are considered responsible for problems of 'maladministration' even though it is unrealistic to expect them to be aware of all actions undertaken by their subordinates. However, network governance increases the number of actors who are involved in the policy process without being democratically authorised *ex ante*, and without being subject to democratic control *ex post*. It therefore amplifies the fictitious character of political responsibility. In more recent years, governing parties have increasingly been 'punished' for their performance in office: electoral losses of incumbent parties are higher than in the past (Strøm *et al*, 2003). It may therefore be argued that nowadays elections are at the same time a more drastic and a more symbolic accountability mechanism, and that this is a symptom of the disjuncture between the competitive logic of 'politics' and the cooperative logic of 'policy making'.

The Composition of Policy Networks

In response to the criticism that policy networks operate in isolation from democratic institutions (which is, after all, an empirical question), it may be objected that most of their members are authorised by some 'principal' to participate, and are thus subject to control regarding their actions. Also, it appears that the role of politicians within policy networks is not as marginal as might be feared, depending to a large extent on institutional configurations (see the empirical studies by Auel, 2006; Taiclet, 2006). Yet, even when politicians play a significant role in policy networks, this is no guarantee of their responsive behaviour, both because of a tendency to instrumentalise networks for own strategic goals, and because of strong executive dominance over the parliament. For instance, according to a comparative study of three policy sectors in seven European democracies (Kriesi

12 The EU is particularly emblematic in that respect: '*politique d'opinion*' on European matters is virtually absent, with the recent exception of referendums that are increasingly utilised on issues of European integration.

et al, 2006: 354), state actors remain the most powerful group in policy making. If this strongly qualifies the idea that 'governance' means a 'hollowing out' of the state, this is not necessarily good news for accountability. Although it is not clear from the study who these state actors are, their influence in the policy-making process is higher than the influence of political parties, which are the democratically legitimate actors for preference aggregation and policy formation.

Anyway, it should be considered that policy networks are largely composed of top-level bureaucrats, policy experts and interest representatives. Some of these actors are only indirectly accountable to the citizenry due to a lengthy 'chain of delegation' (administrators), or only to their peers (experts) or to limited constituencies (interest group negotiators). Therefore, several actors taking part in policy networks are not necessarily mandate holders, are not constrained by electoral pledges and do not have to anticipate electoral sanctions. With respect to accountability, their presence, however, raises quite different problems: public administrators and leaders of interest groups are present by virtue of their representational properties (albeit remotely connected to the 'demos' in the case of administrators, or connected to a narrow part of it in the case of leaders of interest groups), while the presence of others is justified on quite different grounds (experts on the grounds of knowledge, private firms on the grounds of their blackmailing, i.e. 'exit' power). Apart from experts, the individuals participating in policy networks are collective actors in the sense of representing collective interests, be they those of the state, or of various societal segments and sectors (either those who have a reputation to veto policy, or those 'stakeholders' who manage to argue convincingly that their preferences must be given weight because of their high intensity). They are delegates accountable to principals, but for none of them are citizens the direct principal.

High rank bureaucrats are accountable to their minister, but this is administrative, not political accountability, lacking the public dimension. Democratic control is much attenuated by the long chain of delegation. Bovens (2005) identifies, in that respect, a series of principal-agent relations: from citizens to parliamentarians, then to the cabinet, then to civil servants (and, in addition, increasingly to independent agencies). Further, new *en vogue* public management techniques leave more leverage to administrators, so that the democratic 'answerability' of their decisions and activities is reduced, and democratic control through citizens' 'voice' is increasingly replaced by 'customisation' (i.e. by reliance on feedback by individuals as 'clients' or 'service users'; see also below). True, the problem of administrative discretion is not specific to governance networks. It has been on the research agenda for several decades, since the first influential studies of bureaucracies inspired by organisational sociology. It acquires, however, a new dimension in network governance, where the administration pools considerable external expertise. I do not intend to resuscitate the old and simplistic theories of technocratic power: the influence of experts depends on administrations being receptive (after all science and politics are functionally differentiated spheres), and experts seldom share the same views (even less on highly controversial issues). But an intriguing issue is that in order to claim credibility, experts have to convince others of their independence. They should not appear as the vehicles of the preferences of any 'principal' to which they are accountable.[13] Experts are only credible if they can demonstrate the autonomy of science from politics, and they must demonstrate that their discourse rests on different premises than the discourse of politicians or interest groups.

Experts are of course subject to 'peer review' within the scientific community and risk loss of reputation. Control is here internalised by the profession, but again this soft and 'horizontal' form of accountability is not political or public accountability. And if experts are in a sense also 'authorised' to act (by virtue of their acknowledged intellectual capital), they are not delegated by a 'principal' whom they represent, but are usually selected by the administration. Therefore, there is no guarantee that those who are co-opted (perhaps because they are the least critical) are also the most distinguished according to the self-referential criteria of the scientific system. The requirement of expertise combined with independence is very similar to the requirement that increasingly leads national and European policy makers to insulate some decisional spheres from the arena of partisan politics and electoral competition. The delegation of power to various independent bodies and agencies ('agencification') has indeed been justified by the need to ensure the credibility of those entrusted with decision making, and this credibility is deemed to be primarily safeguarded through independence and expertise according to the 'fiduciary' principle (Majone, 2001; 2002). In the EU system, there are connections between independent regulatory agencies and network governance: regulation by national agencies is influenced by processes of mutual learning and diffusion of policy recipes at European level through informal networks of national regulators (Eberlein and Grande, 2005; Martens, 2005).

Network governance also implies the cooperation of political power holders with non-public actors. One should distinguish between two sorts of the latter: interest groups and non-governmental organisations (NGOs) on the one hand, and private firms on the other. Although it is difficult to distinguish the rationales behind these two forms of cooperation, partnerships with NGOs can mostly be attributed to a 'community' orientation of policy making, while partnerships with (and outsourcing of public tasks to) private actors can be attributed to the influence of neo-liberal thought and new public management doctrines. Accountability problems differ accordingly: interest groups and NGOs are accountable to their members ('internal' accountability; cf. Koenig-Archibugi, 2004: 236-237) and sometimes also to donors. This can be considered partial accountability, neither to the general public nor to the populations affected by their actions

13 This is complicated by the fact that experts' independence is often unrealistic. Empirical studies tend to show that the most competent in a field are also those who are related to the interests in competition in this field. See Barthe *et al* (2005: 53).

('external' accountability).[14] It is also argued that these organisations do not escape problems of elitism (such as in the neo-corporatist model). This is no privilege of NGOs; the same was repeatedly said about parties ('iron law of oligarchy', 'cartelisation'). However, partisan representation is regulated by electoral competition, whereas pressures from public authorities to deal with a small number of interlocutors representing encompassing social segments reinforce monopolistic trends in interest representation (Offe, 1981). Large private corporations for their part are primarily accountable to their shareholders, but even this form of capitalist accountability is not always well developed in corporate governance. More fundamentally, this poses again the problem of partiality and lack of external accountability, as these firms are not accountable to those who may be subject to their externalities (workers, residents in neighbouring areas, etc.), except through the market (NGOs, for instance, threaten to boycott firms that are reluctant to apply social and environmental standards). But, again, this is not political accountability.

The 'Multi-level' Aspect of Governance

In addition, network governance can be 'multi-level', consisting of complex structures cutting across decisional levels. This is exemplified by policy-making in federal states, but more centralised states are affected too: from 'below', social differentiation renders policy implementation contingent on compliance by policy addressees, and from 'above', internationalisation (think about World Trade Organisation regulations) and Europeanisation require multi-level cooperation. Accountability is further inhibited by this multi-level aspect of governance.

Multi-level governance entails cooperative intergovernmental relations between sub-national and national authorities, or between national and supranational organs: multi-level government. The interdependence of decisional levels requires their cooperation, notwithstanding the formal division of competencies between them (that may be accompanied by vertical accountability of lower to upper levels), and this cooperation often takes place in weakly visible policy-making structures. Federal or quasi-federal systems like the EU (for a recent discussion, see Thorlakson, 2006) are characterised by a formal division of decisional competencies across levels, often justified on the grounds of subsidiarity. But problems of scale caused by the need to produce efficient decisions, or the fragmentation of power resources between actors, have led to a 'competence mix' and to cooperation schemes even in pure systems of dual federalism (Thorlakson, 2003). This occurs, for instance, in the phase of policy implementation when the central level is highly dependent on the resources of the constituent units (leading to a dialogue in

14 The distinction between internal and external accountability partly overlaps with the distinction between what Gutmann and Thompson (2004: 39) call respectively 'electoral'and 'moral' constituents.

the EU between the Commission services, national and possibly also regional administrations). Formal verticality becomes thus '*Politikverflechtung*', generating several accountability problems.

First, negotiations across levels are often deemed to be more successful if they take place under conditions of informality which impede accountability. Second, as '*Politikverflechtung*' rests on mechanisms operating along the intergovernmentalist logic and implicating sometimes multiparty executives, it can exacerbate problems of dilution of responsibility ('many hands'). Decisions are taken by representatives of collective bodies in processes involving a multitude of them. The problem of shared responsibility is amplified in cases such as that of EU structural funds policy, where cooperation between public actors across levels is paralleled by cooperation with non-public actors in partnership forms.[15] Besides, even actors that are democratically accountable in principle are only fictitiously accountable because of a lack of information on their positions on the side of principals. The accountability problem has to do with the lengthy 'chain of delegation', making the policy processes visible only to those principals who are closer to network members. In addition, multi-level negotiations tend to involve actors who are subject to administrative rather than democratic accountability, such as national and sub-national bureaucracies who can enjoy considerable discretion.[16] Accountability problems are even more acute in the case of the EU administration: the Commission is itself more weakly accountable than national governments, and individual Commissioners do not have the same hierarchical relation to the administration as national ministers (Verhey, 2006: 19-20). Moreover, even actors who are directly subject to the control of their electorates are faced with the problem of 'two-level' accountability: they are accountable for their actions not only to their constituencies, but also to their negotiation partners. Such 'two-level' games have usually been perceived as opening strategic windows of opportunity for those participating in them. It is instead the constraints posed by such games that need to be emphasised here, because participants have to satisfy, in a sense, multiple 'forums'.[17] The same is true in a context of 'deliberative supranationalism' (Joerges and Neyer, 1997: 274), where network participants are also constrained by 'two-level arguing' (Risse, 2006). 'Comitology' committees in the EU are examples of multi-level governance in its technocratic version, being composed of experts and of administrators attached to

15 Empirical scrutiny tends however to disconfirm the openness of partnerships. Schmidt (2006: 680) maintains that 'EU-mandated pluralist consultation in regional policy – which expected "horizontal co-operation" or "partnership" with civil society in the structural funds process – produced little more than statist forms of consultation in French and in German regions as well as in the UK'.

16 On the influence of European and national bureaucracies upon the Council, see Curtin (2005).

17 For reasons of trust building, accounts must be given to negotiation partners even though the latter have not mandated those who must give account to them (see also above on professional, and below on 'peer' accountability).

different levels and subject to this kind of 'two-level' accountability (Pollack, 2003).

'Peer' Accountability in Networks

Relations between participants in networks pose different problems with respect to public accountability, depending on the status of the actors involved. However, all forms of network governance generate a favourable climate for the development of 'peer' accountability (Benner *et al,* 2004: 199). This is a form of accountability working through embeddedness. According to Goodin, it is typical for third-sector organisations, but may apply more generally to network forms of governance: it is 'based on mutual monitoring of one another's performance within a network of groups, public and private, sharing common concerns' (Goodin, 2003: 378). Participants are then deemed to be also (and perhaps primarily) accountable to their negotiation partners, usually in a 'soft' sense.[18] Durable cooperative interactions between partners are expected to generate self-limitation, empathy and mutual trust. This assumption is made both by rationalist research on cooperation and discourse-oriented research on deliberation. Peer accountability is part of a more general trend where 'principles of informal role/control have risen in importance in comparison to formal accountability (principles)' (Saward, 2005: 13). The open method of coordination in the EU is a good case in point (see Benz, 2007). This form of accountability is sustained by mutual interdependence that, in a sense, derives (even though this may sound too cynical), above all, from mutual blackmailing capabilities. The sheer fear of 'naming and shaming' is deemed to yield disciplining effects because 'free riders' or unreliable actors risk loss of reputation on behalf of their partners, who will consider them as untrustworthy in the future and, in a sense, will no longer agree to 'invest' in them.[19] The standardising effects produced by the threat of losing credit present some similarities with the effects expected from 'horizontal' systems of checks and balances. In parliamentary bicameralism, for instance, institutional actors involved in 'nested games' are induced to anticipate each others' reactions, possibly to deliberate together, and thus to reach agreement more easily. Yet soft accountability mechanisms within networks are distinctive through the lack of

---

18 This also presents similarities with mechanisms of '*légitimation croisée*' (cross-legitimation) between representatives of the central state and local notables at the periphery that have been observed by works of the *Centre de sociologie des organisations* in France. For a theoretical synthesis of this research tradition, see Crozier and Friedberg (1981).

19 Offe (1992) speaks about a 'Gesetz des Wiedersehens'. 'Naming and shaming' is also expected to be an efficient mechanism of mutual adjustment in 'soft' law. However, as in the case of the growth and stability pact, the most powerful countries do not seem to be strongly embarrassed by such naming and shaming, confirming that power is 'the ability to talk instead of listen, the ability to afford not to learn' (Deutsch, 1963: 11).

formal sanctions, the focalisation of accountability on individuals and the frequently missing democratic or even simply 'bottom-up' legitimation of participants.

It can indeed be expected from policy networks that they will produce, through deliberation or bargaining and by virtue of peer accountability, Pareto-optimal outcomes. They can even prove to be more respectful of criteria of social justice than majoritarian decision making (Papadopoulos, 2003: 492-493). For peer accountability to function effectively, however, networks must be sufficiently representative and pluralist, i.e. not exclude weaker interests or actors whose preferences do not coincide with the network's 'mainstream' orientation. Whether this is always the case seems debatable. And even if the network is pluralistic, the diversity of perspectives does not guarantee that these perspectives are representative of society at large. In order to be included in networks, actors must possess resources that are unevenly distributed (expertise, blackmailing capacity, preferences considered as intense, etc.). In addition, interest selectivity is not only caused by inequalities, but also by the imperatives of governability: there can be reluctance to include actors who are themselves not willing to 'play the game'. Not only have deliberative modes of governance been criticised by radical theorists for requiring superior argumentative skills from their participants (Sanders, 1997: 349; Young, 2000: 37-40), but anecdotal evidence suggests that self-governing networks tend, in addition, to reduce associative pluralism and intra-organisational diversity by imposing an official paradigm and by failing to co-opt actors who do not comply with this paradigm (Wälti and Kübler, 2003). This is not only a loss of social pluralism, but can also undermine policy efficiency. The lack of 'requisite variety' in policy networks can lead to the formation of 'group-think' or to what Sunstein (2001) calls 'enclave deliberation'. This impedes critical reflection, which is necessary for accountability. It is also detrimental to problem solving because this kind of deliberation favours conformity with convictions that may rest on erroneous causal hypotheses. For ideological pluralism to be preserved, an exit option must be available to network actors ('opting-out clauses'). On the other hand, it is well known that such clauses favour a bargaining game with threats based on each one's blackmailing power and also inhibit problem-solving deliberation (it is no accident that corporatist devices rely on a design that increases the costs of exit). A lack of pluralism may also limit the optimality of resource allocation. This may be due to deliberate strategic behaviour on the part of 'insiders', but it may also simply result from the necessity for mutual trust building, which may end up in collusion. Lord (2004: 114) stresses the danger 'that instead of balancing and checking one another, networks or their members may collude to suspend competitiveness between themselves, to reduce prospects of challenge from the constituencies to which they are supposedly accountable and to freeze new entrants out of access to the benefits of engagement with the political system'. For instance, rational choice approaches inspired by the Olsonian paradigm, but also critical neo-marxist approaches of corporatism, tend to emphasise the risk of rent seeking within weakly pluralist networks ('iron triangles') at the expense of third parties. 'There is a very real risk that they [mutual accountability networks] will degenerate into a complacent "old boy network", their accountability function blunted by mutual interest', write Harlow and Rawlings (2007).

In addition, the requirements of mutual accountability within peer groups can weaken public accountability. There is a trade-off related to the presence of multiple 'controllers' with different demands:[20] peers on the one hand; reference groups on the other. The necessity to build mutual trust discredits actors who are prone to making strategic use of 'two-level games' and who are likely to 'free ride'. In case of 'group-think', it may however also marginalise those who simply manifest their scepticism about some of the network's common goals. One has to prove one's loyalty to the network by demonstrating that one is a credible and committed interlocutor. This kind of 'peer' accountability can hardly be achieved without some loss of accountability 'at home'. The 'logic of influence' tending to prevail among elites involved in mutual deliberation and negotiation seldom coincides with the 'logic of membership' consisting of mirroring the preferences of their constituencies (Schmitter and Streeck, 1999). The narrowing of the preference gap between collective actors in 'summit' negotiations and deliberations implies (at least if no vertical learning processes occur) the widening of the preference gap between the leadership and the rank-and-file within the represented organisations. In supranational governance, such a loosening of control by 'principals' is amplified by the lengthy chain of delegation. We also noticed that for 'peer' monitoring to work effectively some degree of intra-network variety is necessary. However, it then becomes more difficult for the external public to identify who is at the origin of network outputs, especially when they result from compromise. In addition, compromise seeking and problem solving may require 'legitimate confidentiality' (Schedler, 1999: 21), while democratic accountability may prevent solutions that cannot be 'sold' with populist justifications. Consequently, increased accountability can also lead to 'subterfuge' as blame-avoidance behaviour. Marcinkowski (2001), for instance, maintains that 'informalisation' strategies are employed in policy-making processes in order to avoid media scrutiny; Bovens (2005) stresses risk-avoiding behaviour from actors perceiving to be the objects of 'excess accountability';[21] and Philp (2005: 21) asserts that accountability often generates only an appearance of conformity. Self-presentation strategies of politicians enacted with the help of marketing consultants ('spin doctors') in the context of a political system increasingly developing into an 'audience' democracy point in this direction. Therefore, there are good reasons –

20 This trade-off should be distinguished from 'redundancy accountability' described by Scott (2000: 52). The latter refers to the tendency to supplement traditional mechanisms of accountability by the horizontal mechanisms of the market, in which overlapping (and superfluous) accountability mechanisms reduce the centrality of any one of them (see also Vos, 2005: 14). Instead of a redundant extension we observe here a partial substitution of accountability mechanisms.

21 Not to mention the propensity of 'watchdogs' to focus sometimes on 'scandals' rather than on 'normal' behaviour.

at least in policy makers' minds – not to favour genuine accountability in strongly mediatised public spaces.

Conclusion and Prospects for Accountability

This chapter suggests that network forms of governance entail a number of accountability problems. 'Shared responsibility' and lack of visibility are aggravated by the frequent 'multi-level' aspect of these forms of governance. The relations between actors involved in networks are weakly exposed to public scrutiny, or to the scrutiny of the legitimate, democratic and representative bodies. This is not to say that actors involved in governance networks are not accountable at all. They are subject to 'peer' or professional accountability, to reputational and market accountability, to fiscal/ financial, administrative or legal accountability (Benner *et al,* 2004: 199-200). There is no guarantee, however, that such 'diffuse' or 'composite' control mechanisms (Costa *et al*, 2003; Héritier, 2003: note 29) can be effective, as they operate in a fragmentary and uncoordinated way without forming a coherent system. In addition, the problem of a lack of political and democratic accountability remains: only some network actors are subject to it, and control over them can be merely indirect or partial. In sum, the following points should be stressed:

- In network and multi-level forms of governance the direct democratic accountability of policy makers is weakened.
- On the other hand, there is a 'multiplication of control mechanisms' (Costa *et al,* 2003: 670).
- Actors in such accountability 'forums' may have a distinct agenda from democratic 'principals' with whom policy makers are in a relationship of delegation and representation.
- Those who control *ex post* are thus not necessarily the same as those who formulate mandates *ex ante*.
- The accountability forums are dispersed and do not form a coherent accountability system, so that the picture of a 'patchwork' might be an adequate description here.
- Part of the accountability mechanisms at work are of the 'light' or 'soft' type (indirect, not institutionalised, through moral commitments and social pressure, exposure to the public sphere, etc.), with the risk of being 'toothless' (Schedler, 1999: 16-17).
- As a result, the efficiency of a (syncretic) 'marble cake' of accountability mechanisms including (perhaps too) 'many eyes' that operate in a 'soft' manner is debatable.
- Finally, in network and multi-level forms of governance, there may not only be a trade-off between democratic accountability and policy efficiency (the

'input-output' dilemma), but also a trade-off between democratic accountability and other 'peer' forms of accountability.

Some would argue that, given the increased complexity of contemporary decision-making procedures, democratic accountability has become illusive. Regarding the issue of transparency in transnational private governance, for instance, Scholte (2002: 292) critically concludes that 'most people (including many democratically elected representatives) have not even heard of private sites of global governance'. However, there is no sufficient reason why multi-level governance networks should not be accountable to democratic institutions at different levels, which should be able to exert effective oversight over their operation. It may thus be argued that there is a need for a 'parliamentarisation' of multi-level governance systems.[22] However, such a (in principle welcome) reform strategy also faces limits and should by no means be seen as sufficient to enhance accountability. This is particularly true for the EU multi-level governance system:[23] by contrast to national settings, where governance can be conceived of as 'government plus' (networks of experts, non-governmental groups, civil society actors, etc.), governance in the EU is best described as 'government minus' (Sbragia, 2002: 6). Even if the European Parliament continues, for instance, to gain influence over EU policy making, this will not automatically solve other problems that weaken the influence of party representatives in the exercise of their role as accountability holders (think about the relative weakness of European party federations), or that weaken their legitimacy to act in that respect (think about the 'second-order' character of European elections). Considering these limits, I conclude by suggesting a model to improve democratic accountability in multi-level systems, borrowed from work done together with Arthur Benz (Benz and Papadopoulos, 2006). This should be seen as a complement to better accountability using institutions such as courts or ombudsmen.

We envisage a decisional pattern characterised by a functional separation of power between policy formulation in networks, and by constituent and veto power dedicated to institutions that are authorised and accountable to citizens. Formally authorised institutions should first set the 'meta-governance' procedural rules for fair participation and for accountability in network forms of governance. Although sometimes the formalisation of networks (provisions about selection of participants, mode of operation, etc.) becomes an open political issue, it would be innovative to assign explicitly the design function to the democratically authorised institutions (as we noticed, such a function is often delegated to members of

22 See, for instance, Van Gerwen (2005: 344-368) and the proposals made by Holzinger and Knill (2000) for the EU.

23 Interestingly, Majone (2006: 621) who does not consider the democratic deficit of the EU as really problematic (given the nature of European integration), by contrast finds the 'accountability deficit' to be a 'real problem' for the EU.

the bureaucracy).[24] These institutions should also have the final say on policy outputs, by being an effective locus of critical scrutiny over proposals formulated by governance networks, which have for their part the advantage of pooling expertise and of facilitating acceptance by 'stake-holders'.[25] This is no institutional innovation per se: formally things do work according to this pattern in national settings, and increasingly so at EU level too. Yet, in order to perform their constituent and veto functions effectively, democratically authorised institutions should acquire additional resources in terms of legal instruments, and also in terms of time, information, intelligence, professionalism or organisation. In national, regional, international and multi-level governance, citizens (by referendum), national parliaments or elected governments should fulfil the constituent and veto functions, even though delegation to governments would play a stronger role at the supra- and international levels. Actors in networks should then have to convince, in communicative processes, the legitimised veto players about their policy proposals, while veto players would be forced to supervise participation and policy making in governance effectively. At the same time, learning mechanisms should be developed in order to prevent policy blockages by veto players: to give an example, parliamentary committees should base their proposals more frequently on hearings of experts and interest representatives (that could be public and mediatised).

Such a pattern of decision making can serve as a benchmark to be approximated for all network governance situations, in order to increase the chances for improving their democratic accountability, and thereby their legitimacy. It should replace the current uncoupling of network governance from legitimate representative structures not by a tight coupling, which might lead to vetoing and policy blockages, but by loose coupling, creating interfaces that can be beneficial for mutual learning (Benz, 1998).[26] The creation of such interfaces would require institutional innovation. For instance, particularly in a context where representative politics are also increasingly delegitimised, it does not suffice to redress the imbalance between network and parliamentary governance. A further step is required, which is a closer familiarity on the part of the mass public with the realities of complex decision-making processes, and thereby an increase in its evaluative competence that would permit the reduction of informational asymmetries. 'Deliberative opinion polls' (Fishkin, 1995), for instance, on some major policy choices formulated by networks can be instrumental for such an empowerment, under the condition that they are not confined to the role of mere participatory experiments, as is the case today.[27] They should be combined, for instance, with petition rights such as those

24 Some scholars (Sørensen, 2005; Schmitter, 2006) have reflected on principles for 'chartering' governance arrangements that meet the requirement of 'democratic anchorage'.

25 We leave aside here the issue of the implementation of decisions, which can again be delegated to policy networks, but also requires oversight by formally authorised bodies.

26 Other forms of loose coupling can be found in the linkages between 'governance councils', administrative agencies, parliaments and the judiciary in the framework of 'democratic experimentalism' (Dorf and Sabel, 1998). See also Eberlein and Kerwer (2004: 132-133) for an application to the OMC.

27 See, for instance, an evaluation of the Danish deliberative opinion poll on the Euro (Andersen and Hansen, 2007).

that were foreseen in Article I-47.4 of the Constitutional Treaty. In sum, models of decision making should be proposed and discussed that:

- redress the imbalance between network and parliamentary governance by making the former more accountable to the latter;
- empower not only representatives but also ordinary citizens on complex issues;
- avoid stalemates produced by the lack of mechanisms of mutual learning between network members, political representatives and voters.

As a matter of fact, introducing a higher dose of public, democratic and popular accountability without setting up, at the same time, mechanisms of mutual learning by the involved actors can yield unintended negative outcomes, such as a lack of policy efficiency, and therefore also problems of governability that may ultimately lead to a decrease of (output) legitimacy. Institutional design should be cautiously carried out so as to avoid such 'perverse' or 'boomerang' effects.

References

Andersen, V. N. and Hansen, K. M. (2007). How Deliberation Makes Better Citizens: The Danish Deliberative Poll on the Euro. *European Journal of Political Research, 46 (4),* pp.531-556.

Andersen, S. S. and Burns, T. R. (1996). The European Union and the Erosion of Parliamentary Democracy: A Study of Post-Parliamentary Governance. In S. S. Andersen and K. J. Eliassen (Eds.), *The European Union: How Democratic Is It?* (pp.226-251) London: Sage.

Andeweg, R. (2005, March). De super and ex post? Political Representation and Europeanisation. Paper presented at the workshop of Connex Research Group 2, Leiden.

Auel, K. (2006). Multilevel Governance, Regional Policy and Democratic Legitimacy in Germany. In A. Benz and Y. Papadopoulos (Eds.), *Governance and Democracy. Comparing National, European and International Experiences* (pp.44-62). London: Routledge.

Bache, I. and Flinders, M. (2004). *Multilevel Governance.* Oxford: Oxford University Press.

Barthe, Y. and Gilbert, C. (2005). Impuretés et compromis de l'expertise, une difficile reconnaissance. In L. Dumoulin, S. La Branche, C. Robert and P. Warin (Eds.), *Le recours aux experts* (pp.43-62). Grenoble: Presses Universitaires de Grenoble.

Bartolini, S. (1999). Collusion, Competition and Democracy, Part I. *Journal of Theoretical Politics, 11 (4),* pp.435-470.

Behn, R. D. (2001). *Rethinking Democratic Accountability.* Washington: The Brookings Institute.

Bendor, J., Glazer, A. and Hammond, T. (2001). Theories of Delegation. *Annual Review of Political Science, 4,* pp.235-269.

Benner, T., Reinicke, W. H. and Witte, J. M. (2004). Multisectoral Networks in Global Governance: Towards a Pluralistic System of Accountability. *Government and Opposition, 39 (2),* pp.191-208.

Benz, A. and Papadopoulos, Y. (2006). Actors, Institutions and Democratic Governance: Comparing Across Levels. In A. Benz and Y. Papadopoulos (Eds.), *Governance and*

Democracy. Comparing National, European and International Experiences (pp.273-295). London: Routledge.

Benz, A. (2007). Accountable multilevel governance by the Open Method of Coordination? *European Law Journal, 13 (4)*, pp.505-522.

Benz, A. (2004). Path-dependent Institutions and Strategic Veto-Players—National Parliaments in the European Union. *West European Politics, 29*, pp.875-900.

Benz, A. (1998). Postparlamentarische Demokratie? Demokratische Legitimation im kooperativen Staat. In M. T. Greven (Ed.), *Demokratie – eine Kultur des Westens?* (pp.201-222) Opladen: Leske and Budrich.

Bevir, M. (2006). Democratic Governance: Systems and Radical Perspectives. *Public Administration Review, 66 (3),* pp.426-436.

Bovens, M. (2007). Analysing and Assessing Accountability: a Conceptual Framework. *European Law Journal, 13 (4),* pp.447-468.

Bovens, M. (2005). Public Accountability. In E. Ferlie, E. Lynne and C. Pollitt (Eds.), *The Oxford Handbook of Public Management* (pp.182-208). Oxford: Oxford University Press.

Bovens, M. (1998). *The Quest for Responsibility.* Cambridge: Cambridge Unversity Press.

Costa, O., Jabko, N., Lequesne, C. and Magnette, P. (2003). Introduction: Diffuse Control Mechanisms in the European Union: Towards a New Democracy? *Journal of European Public Policy, 10 (5),* pp.666-676.

Crozier, M. and Friedberg, E. (1981). *L'acteur et le système.* Paris: Editions du Seuil.

Curtin, D. (2005). Delegation to EU Non-Majoritarian Agencies and Emerging Practices of Public Accountability. In D. Gerardinet, R. Munoz and N. Petit (Eds.), *Regulation through Agencies in the EU. A New Paradigm of European Governance* (pp.88-119). Cheltenham: Edward Elgar.

Dorf, M. C and Sabel, C. F. (1998). A Constitution of Democratic Experimentalism. *Columbia Law Review, 98,* pp.267-463.

Deutsch, K. W. D. (1963). The Nerves of Government. Models of Political Communication and Control. New York: The Free Press.

Eberlein, B. and Grande, E. (2005). Beyond Delegation: Transnational Regulatory Regimes and the EU Regulatory Stage. *Journal of European Public Policy, 12 (1),* pp.89-112.

Eberlein, B. and Kerwer, D. (2004). New Governance in the European Union: A Theoretical Perspective. *Journal of Common Market Studies, 42 (1),* pp.121-142.

Fishkin, J. S. (1995). *The Voice of the People.* New Haven: Yale University Press.

Flinders, M. (2005). The Politics of Public-Private Partnerships. *British Journal of Politics and International Relations, 7 (2),* pp.543-567.

Goodin, R. E. (2003). Democratic Accountability: The Distinctiveness of the Third Sector. *European Journal of Sociology, 44 (3),* pp.359-396.

Grant, R. and Keohane, R. O. (2004). Accountability and Abuses of Power in World Politics. *American Political Science Review, 99 (1),* pp.29-44.

Gutman, A. and Thompson, D. (2004). *Why Deliberative Democracy?* Princeton: Princeton University Press.

Harlow, C. and Rawlings, R. (2007). Promoting accountability in multilevel governance: a network approach. *European Law Journal, 13 (4),* pp.542-562.

Héritier, A. (2003). Composite Democracy in Europe: the Role of Transparency and Access to Information. *Journal of European Public Policy, 10 (5),* pp.814-833.

Holzinger, K. and Knill, C. (2000). *Eine Verfassung für die Europäische Federation. Kontinuierliche Weiterentwicklung des Erreichten.* Jean Monnet Working Paper 7/00. Available at http://www.jeanmonnetprogram.org/papers/00/00f1401.html

Joerges, C. and Neyer, J. (1997). From Intergovernmental Bargaining to Deliberative Political Processes: The Constitutionalization of Comitology. *European Law Journal, 3,* pp.273-291.

Koenig-Archibugi, M. (2004). Transnational Corporations and Public Accountability. *Government and Opposition, 39 (2)*, pp.234-259.

Kohler-Koch, B. (2006). Research on EU Governance: Insight from a Stock-Taking Exercise. *Connex Newsletter, 3*, pp.4-6.

Kohler-Koch, B. (2000). Framing: The Bottleneck of Constructing Legitimate Institutions. *Journal of European Public Policy, 7 (4)*, pp.513-531.

Kriesi, H., Silke, A. and Jochum, M. (2006). Comparative Analysis of Policy Networks in Europe. *Journal of European Public Policy, 13 (3),* pp.341-361.

Leca, J. (1996). La "gouvernance" de la France sous la Cinquième République. Une perspective de sociologie comparative. In F. D'Arcy and L. Rouban (Eds.), *De la Ve République à l'Europe* (pp. 329-365). Paris: Presses de Sciences Po.

Lehmbruch, G. (1999). Verhandlungsdemokratie, Entscheidungsblockaden und Arenenverflechtung. In W. Merkel and A. Busch (Eds.), *Demokratie in Ost und West* (pp.402-424). Frankfurt am Main: Suhrkamp.

Lord, C. (2004). A Democratic Audit of the European Union. Basingstoke: Palgrave.

Mair, P. (2005). *Popular Democracy and the European Union Polity*. European Governance Papers (EUROGOV) No. C-05-03. Available at: http://www.connex-network.org/eurogov/pdf/egp-connex-C-05-03.pdf

Majone, G. (2006). The Common Sense of European Integration. *Journal of European Public Policy, 13 (5)*, pp.607-626.

Majone, G. (2002). Delegation of Regulatory Powers in a Mixed Polity. *European Law Journal, 8 (3),* pp.319-339.

Majone, G. (2001). Two Logics of Delegation. Agency and Fiduciary Relations in EU Governance. *European Union Politics, 2 (1),* pp.103-122.

Manin, B. (1997). *The Principles of Representative Government*. Cambridge: Cambridge University Press.

Mansbridge, J. (2003). Rethinking Representation. *American Political Science Review, 97 (4),* pp.515-528.

Marcinkowski, F. (2001). *Die Politik der Massenmedien.* Cologne: Halem.

Martens, M. (2005). Run-Away Bureaucracy? Exploring the Role of National Regulatory Agencies in the EU. *Arena Working Paper No. 30.* Available at: http://www.arena.uio.no/publications/working-papers2005/papers/wp05_30.pdf

Mayntz, R. (1997). Politische Steuerung: Aufstieg, Niedergang und Transformation einer Theorie. In R. Mayntz (Ed.), *Soziale Dynamik und Politische Steuerung. Theoretische und Methodologische Überlegungen* (pp.263-292). Frankfurt am Main: Campus.

Offe, C. (1992). Thesen zur öffentlichen Anhörung der gemeinsamen Verfassungskommission zum Thema Bürgerbeteiligung/Plebiszite. Unpublished manuscript.

Offe, C. (1981). The Attribution of Public Status to Interest Groups. In S. Berger (Ed.), *Organized Interests in Western Europe* (pp.123-158). Cambridge: Cambridge University Press.

Olsson, J. (2003). Democracy Paradoxes in Multilevel Governance: Theorizing on Structural Fund Systems Research. *Journal of European Public Policy, 10 (2),* pp.283-300.

Papadopoulos, Y. (2005). Taking Stock of Multilevel Governance Networks. *European Political Science, 4,* pp.316-326.

Papadopoulos, Y. (2003). Cooperative Forms of Governance: Problems of Democratic Accountability in Complex Environments. *European Journal of Political Research, 42 (4),* pp.473-501.

Papadopoulos, Y. (2002). Populism, the Democratic Question, and Contemporary Governance. In Y. Mény and Y. Surel (Eds.), *Democracies and the Populist Challenge* (pp.45-61). Basingstoke: Palgrave.

Peters, B. G. (2006). The Meta-Governance of Policy Networks: Steering at a Distance, but Still Steering. Paper presented at the Conference on Democratic Network Governance, Roskilde.

Philp, M. (2005). Against Accountability. Paper Presented at the Third ECPR Conference, Budapest.

Pierre, J. (2000). Introduction: Understanding Governance. In J. Pierre (Ed.), *Debating Governance* (pp.1-10). Oxford: Oxford University Press.

Pollack, M. A. (2003). Control Mechanism or Deliberative Democracy? Two Images of Comitology. *Comparative Political Studies, 36 (1-2),* pp.125-155.

Risse, T. (2006). Transnational Governance and Legitimacy. In A. Benz and Y. Papadopoulos (Eds.), *Governance and Democracy. Comparing National, European and International Experiences* (pp.179-199). London: Routledge.

Sanders, L. (1997). Against Deliberation. *Political Theory, 25,* pp.347-376.

Saward, M. (2005). Authorisation and Authenticity: Does Democracy Really Need Political Parties. Paper Presented at the ECPR Joint Sessions Workshop on Democracy and Political Parties, Granada.

Sbragia, A. M. (2002). *The Dilemma of Governance with Government.* Jean Monnet Working Paper 3/02. Available at: http://www.jeanmonnetprogram.org/papers/02/020301.pdf

Scharpf, F. W. (1970). Demokratietheorie zwischen Utopie und Anpassung. Konstanz: Universitätsverlag Konstanz.

Schedler, A. (1999). Conceptualizing Accountability. In A. Schedler, L. Diamond and M. F. Plattner (Eds.), *The Self-Restraining State* (pp.13-28). Boulder: Lynne Rienner.

Schmidt, V. A. (2006). Procedural Democracy in the EU: the Europeanization of National and Sectoral Policy-Making Processes. *Journal of European Public Policy, 13 (5),* pp.670-691.

Schmitter, P. C. and Streeck, W. (1999). The Organization of Business Interests. Studying the Associative Action of Business in Advanced Industrial Societies (Discussion Paper 99/1). Cologne: Max-Planck-Institut für Gesellschaftsforschung.

Schmitter, P. C. (2004). Governance in the European Union: A Viable Mechanism for Future Legitimation? In A. Benz and Y. Papadopoulos (Eds.), *Governance and Democracy. Comparing National, European and International Experiences* (pp.158-175). London: Routledge.

Schmitter, P. C. (2004). The Ambiguous Virtues of Accountability. *Journal of Democracy, 15 (4),* pp.47-60.

Scholte, J. A. (2002). Civil Society and Democracy in Global Governance. *Global Governance, 8 (3),* pp.281-304.

Scott, C. (2000). Accountability in the Regulatory State. *Journal of Law and Society, 27 (1),* pp.38-60.

Skelcher, C. (2005). Jurisdictional Integrity, Polycentrism, and the Design of Democratic Governance. *Governance: An International Journal of Policy, Administration, and Institutions, 18 (1),* pp.89-110.

Sørensen, E. (2005). The Democratic Problems and Potentials of Network Governance. *European Political Science, 4,* pp.348-355.

Strøm, K., Müller, W. C. and Bergman, T. (2003) (Eds.) *Delegation and Accountability in Parliamentary Democracies*. Oxford: Oxford University Press.

Sunstein, C. (2001). *Republic.com*. Princeton: Princeton: University Press.

Taiclet, A. F. (2006). Governance, Expertise and Competitive Politics. The Case of Territorial Development Policies in France. In A. Benz and Y. Papadopoulos (Eds.), *Governance and Democracy. Comparing National, European and International Experiences* (pp.63-80). London: Routledge.

Thorlakson, L. (2006). Building Firewalls or Floodgates? Constitutional Design for the European Union. *Journal of Common Market Studies, 44 (1),* pp.139-159.

Thorlakson, L. (2003). Comparing Federal Institutions: Power and Representation in Six Federations. *West European Politics, 26 (2),* pp.1-22.

Van Gerwen, W. (2005). *The European Union: A Polity of States and Peoples.* Stanford: Stanford University Press.

Verhey, L. (2006, February). Political Accountability in a European Perspective. A Position Paper for Comparative Research. Paper presented at the Workshop Political Accountability from a European and Comparative Perspective, Maastricht.

Voelzkow, H. (2000). Von der funktionalen Differenzierung zur Globalisierung: Neue Herausforderungen für die Demokratietheorie. In R. Werle and U. Schimank (Eds.), *Gesellschaftliche Komplexität und kollektive Handlungsfähigkeit* (pp.270-296). Frankfurt am Main: Campus.

Vos, E. (2005, May). Keeping Independent Agencies under Control. Paper Presented at the Connex Workshop Delegation and Multilevel Governance, Paris.

Wälti, S. and Kübler, D. (2003). "New Governance" and Associative Pluralism: The Case of Drug Policy in Swiss Cities. *The Policy Studies Journal, 31 (4),* pp.499-525.

Wolf, K. D. (2002). Contextualizing Normative Standards for Legitimate Governance Beyond the State. In B. Gbikpi and J. R. Grote (Eds.), *Participatory Governance. Political and Societal Implications* (pp.35-50). Opladen: Leske and Budrich.

Young, I. M. (2000). *Inclusion and Democracy.* Oxford: Oxford University Press.

How to Achieve Governability in Multi-Level Policymaking: Lessons from the EU Structural Funds and EU Environment Policy

Hubert Heinelt

This chapter examines the characteristics of multi-level policymaking in respect of the EU structural funds and EU environment policy in order to draw some general conclusions about opportunities and constraints – or conditions – of achieving governability in a multi-level system. This endeavour is challenging in at least two respects. First, given the restricted scope of a single chapter, it is the case that the characteristics of multi-level policymaking in these two examples cannot be described in detail. However, these characteristics can be found in research findings published elsewhere.[1] Second, the notion of governability used in this endeavour has not only to be clarified but also has to be justified, because governability, as used in this chapter, reflects a particular way of understanding how to govern public affairs effectively as well as legitimately. In addition, because these governing activities are seen as embedded in a multi-level system, the notion of the latter has also to be considered.

The chapter starts with the clarification of the use of the terms 'governability' and 'multi-level system' in Section I. The following section reflects on the characteristics of the two EU policy areas under consideration (Section II). Finally, some general conclusions about the conditions required to achieve governability in the EU multi-level system are highlighted in Section III.

What Does Governability in the EU Multi-Level System Mean?

From the perspective of political science reflections on governability should not be restricted to the question of whether or not certain policy objectives – like 'cohesion' (the decrease of regional and social disparities) or 'sustainability' (reduction in energy consumption, emissions etc) – laid down in programmes or other policy documents are achieved (see Knill and Liefferink 2007: 145-155 for general reflections on the effectiveness of implementation). This may be sufficient for applied policy studies or for an efficiency-oriented analysis of (financial) inputs and outputs (see Beugelsdijk and Eijffinger, 2005; Cappelen *et al.*, 2003; Castells and Espasa Quer-

1 See apart from the contributions in Parts II and III of this volume, Hooghe, 1996; Heinelt and Smith, 1996; Bache, 1998; Bailey and Propris, 2002; Heinelt *et al.*, 2005 on the EU structural funds; and Heinelt *et al.*, 2001; McCormick, 2001; Heinelt and Smith, 1996; Jordan, 2005 on EU environment policy, as well as contributions in Kohler-Koch (2003) and Bache and Flinders (2004).

alt, 2003). As demonstrated in the recent debate on the 'financial perspective 2007-2013' of the EU (see Bachtler and Wishdale, 2005), such studies are strongly linked to policymaking (see Becker, 2005; Heinemann, 2005), which is not bad in itself. However, one has to be aware about the predisposition of such debates to lose the opportunity of reflecting on the basic political logic of governing public affairs in the multi-layered spheres of EU politics. Furthermore, there is the danger that such studies can easily be captured (and some obviously are; see Sapir, 2003) by those actively involved in policymaking, who are part of what is being researched.

Instead, governability should be considered as the ability to steer and to control societal interactions (in this respect, governability refers to what is called 'Steuerungsfähigkeit' in German; with reference to the EU, see Grande and Jachtenfuchs, 2000). Against a background of widely discussed (and accepted) complexity and contingency in modern society, this ability to steer and control has to be conceptualised in a way such that the picture of an all-powerful guiding and controlling entity is *not* the outcome. Instead, emphasis should be placed on context-related choices faced by groups of actors so that they can influence purposefully and act interactively with their current and future situations. From this perspective – which has already been pointed out in contributions to the early debates on policy networks focussed on governance aspects (especially those of German and continental European scholars; see Marsh, 1998) an actor-related capability comes into play indicating on the one hand that actors are not in a position to govern their social environment completely, i.e. there are exogenously given constraints, but on the other hand emphasising that actors can influence their social environment with (potentially) available policy instruments or on the basis of given (or changeable) institutional settings (Scharpf, 1986: 12). From this perspective, governability can be related to (or focussed on) *endogenously, i.e. politically determined* constraints and opportunities for policymaking to realise what is desired and known by actors and perceived as collectively achievable by them (Scharpf, 1988a: 63-64; see also Mayntz, 1997: 192).[2] In this respect governing a modern (functionally differentiated) society is not in principle impossible (as was argued in the 1980s; see the Luhmann-Scharpf controversy; Luhmann, 1989; Scharpf, 1989). Instead, first, the ability to govern, i.e. to influence deliberately societal interactions, has to be clarified depending on the specific issue under consideration. Second, specific actor-related and (endogenously) politically determined opportunities to develop certain strategies and to pursue them have to be identified. Such opportunities are clearly related to institutional and organisational conditions which may or may not allow for or support collective political actions. In certain circumstances political actors may not be able to govern their societal environment completely but may be able to change policy instruments or organisational

2 I am using here and below the terms the 'desired', the 'known' and the 'achievable' as apparently strange translations of parts of the following statement by Scharpf (1988: 63-64; *italics* by H H). "Die Rede [ist bei Steuerungsfähigkeit; added by the author] nicht von exogen bestimmtem Nicht-Können, sondern von endogen – aber nicht unüberwindlichen – Schwierigkeiten der Politik, das *Gewünschte*, *Gewußte* und *objektiv Erreichbare* auch zu tun."

rules with the aim of deliberately influencing their societal environment. In other words, and to define a kind of bottom line, actors can develop a capacity to reform the instruments for changing their social environment in line with their (agreed) policy objectives. Whether or not actors are actually able to achieve what is intended by a particular reform is another question (see Mayntz, 1997: 192), but from an actor-centred understanding of governability they need to demonstrate a capacity to react politically to reform failure by altering the definition of the problem, by questioning the reasons for the failure and by changing the policy instruments, i.e. a new reform.

However, such a view on endogenously defined governability is dependent on how the ability to govern a certain issue is perceived within the relevant 'policy arena', i.e. in our examples the development of regional and social disparities and the protection of the environment. This raises the issue that the societal surroundings/settings, which are to be influenced or altered by particular policy instruments according to the 'desires' of involved actors, can not be intellectually filtered through something 'objectively achievable', but only through what is known within the 'policy arena' or what can be conceptualised as politically hegemonic knowledge or a knowledge base.[3] Although it is clear that political knowledge does not develop independently from discourses in society (and in academia), it is obvious that what is perceived as governable (and how) is dependent on processes taking place within the political system. In the case of cohesion policy, this becomes clear when taking into account the paradigm shift in the 1980s, the intrusion of New Public Management (NPM) ideas in the late 1990s (see Heinelt and Malek, 2002) and the current debate on competitiveness and the strengthening of (urban) growth poles (referred to in the so-called Lisbon process). The same applies to the shift away from the 'command and control' approach and the emphasis placed on sustainability in the environment policy of the EU in the 1990s (see Heinelt *et al*, 2001; Heinelt and Töller, 2003; Knill and Liefferink, 2007). Against this background, a distinction between what is determined politically as possible (and necessary) and what is an exogenously fixed 'mission impossible' may be blurred. Nevertheless, the question has to be raised, what are the endogenous political but not irresolvable constraints on policymaking to achieve what is desired, known and perceived as possible by the actors involved?

To answer this question is not easy in any circumstances, but is even harder in the context of EU multi-level policymaking where not only (exogenously) feasible conditions in the individual member states (and their regions) differ, but what is desired, known and perceived as achievable by the multitude of actors involved at different levels and stages of policymaking is also very varied.

---

3 It is not the point here to reflect the broad debate on knowledge and policy and/or organisational learning. But what should be mentioned is that in this debate the notion of the knowledge base is commonly related to two dimensions: a normative one and a cognitive one where the latter would include some understanding of causality (see Heinelt *et al.*, 2001: 33-40; Heinelt *et al.*, 2005: 33-40). For preliminary results of an ongoing research project on governance and knowledge funded by the Sixth Framework Programme of the EU, in which the author is involved, see Heinelt (2008: 102-109).

Taking into account the debate on the development and the current specificities of the EU polity stimulated by the multi-level governance approach, it is important to emphasise that this approach has to go beyond the 'traditional' international relations theories of (neo-)functionalism and intergovernmentalism (Marks *et al.*, 1996; see for a short overview Bache and Flinders, 2004a: 2-3). Even more important to emphasise – at least for this chapter – is the multi-level governance approach which highlights the implications of a polity characterised by penetrating into the centre of the (nation) state and distributing tasks and competences between different nested territorial levels.

What does this mean for the question of how to achieve governability in multi-level policymaking? Maybe penetration into the centre of the (nation) state and the distribution of tasks and competences over nested territorial levels can fit in with a constellation of differing feasible conditions in the individual member states (and their regions) and varying desires, knowledge and perceptions of the multitude of involved actors. Therefore, it is worth looking at what characterises multi-level policymaking in the areas of the EU structural funds and environment policy in order to identify features and mechanisms in such constellations which might provide conditions to achieve governability in the sense outlined above.

Characteristics of the EU structural funds and the EU Environment Policy

The EU structural funds

The history of the EU structural funds points towards a continuous capacity for reform and does not confirm the 'joint decision trap' hypothesis that has been often associated with policymaking in the EU multi-level system (Scharpf, 1988b).[4] How can this capacity for reform be explained, taking into account the specific conditions of redistributive policies (Scharpf, 2001; Heinelt, 1996: 18-19)? The formation of the structural funds as a redistributive policy has typically been explained by reference to package deals and side-payments in the context of major steps towards European integration. But is this sufficient, and what is the explanation for the further development of the structural funds and their relatively high stability over time? Furthermore, the EU structural funds have demonstrated that they are on the one hand leaving a lot of room for national and regional adaptation and variation but on the other hand are shaping domestic regional (and labour market) policies. How can this kind of 'Europeanising' be explained?

In some of the previous literature (Marks, 1993; Hooghe, 1996; Heinelt and Smith, 1996), the main hypothesis has been that specific policy networks (actor relations) in the EU multi-level system are important. According to this hypothesis, the

4 The following sub-section is based on Heinelt *et al.,* 2003: 135-138.

structural funds and their development as well as their adaptation at the national and regional level can be characterised as follows (Heinelt, 1996: 16-17):

- Key players are not only regularly present at particular points in time at the European level, when decisions have to be made on programme structures and budgeting. Due to the specific requirements of the policy field that funding measures must be dealt with according to programme targets and the flow of EU subsidies must be co-ordinated with national funding programmes, permanent policy networks have had to be created at the implementation level. These implementation networks form a permanent structure, and the key actors involved from the EU, the member states and the sub-national level have built a policy community (Heclo and Wildasky, 1974: 389) which has been held together by common interpretations of issues over the years.
- The decision network through which decisions have to be made about funding objectives and resources after individual programme periods have expired consists of a structure made up of member states and the Commission. However, this network structure does not exist in isolation from the implementation networks which formed while the programme was being implemented, because the latter involves both the Commission and the departments of national governments as well as the sub-national interests directly involved. This is most apparent in the case of the monitoring committees used for evaluation and ensuring regular contact between key local players, national programme agencies and the Commission.
- The stability and continuity of policy networks in relation to the structural funds result in redistribution and funding objectives, funding resources and the implementation strategies remaining constant themes for the actors involved, and thus allow for 'organised feedback loops' in a multilevel policy arena (Marks, 1993: 403). Thus policy reactions can be continually fed into political processes which not only relate to problems of implementation but also to policy issues and may result in changes in policy goals and objectives.

This seems to be a theoretically convincing hypothesis. Empirical research (for instance by Malek, 2002; Heinelt *et al.*, 2005) on the historical development of the structural funds from the 1950s to the end of the 1990s and their implementation in a number of member states does, however, throw some doubt on the validity of this hypothesis. According to these findings there is little evidence for a highly integrated policy network that creates 'organised feedback loops' between policy implementation and policy reform. On the contrary, there is considerable evidence for a high degree of fragmentation within the policy network in the policy field under scrutiny. Fragmentation can be observed along at least four different lines:

- Vertical fragmentation can be identified between implementation and policy reform networks in member states. European decision-making on the revision of structural funds regulations as well as on funding objectives and the allocation of resources at the EU level is undertaken by top-level representatives of the member states (together with the Commission) who lack close contact with those involved in the implementation of structural funds. The key players in the reform processes create a decision arena of their own without close links to the implementation of the funds.

- Horizontal fragmentation of policy specific implementation networks can be found in member states. Within the member states (to varying degrees) administrative structures (as well as their surrounding societal networks) are fragmented between different funds and policy areas. Implementation networks in the field of regional policy (i.e. the ERDF), for example, rarely interact with implementation networks in the field of labour market policy (i.e. the ESF). This fragmentation is made more likely by variation in implementation rules and routines between different policies.
- Horizontal fragmentation of fund specific actor structures can be identified within the European Commission. In much the same way as in the member states, administrative structures within the Commission are fragmented into different Directorates-General (DGs), each of which is responsible for a separate fund.
- Vertical fragmentation between implementation and policy reform networks can be noted in the Commission: Within each DG, the units, which are responsible for implementation in the different member states, are clearly separate from the units, which are responsible for co-ordination and more general 'political' tasks, including policy reform.

These fragmentations are not only formal organisational characteristics. They shape formal and informal interactions and influence communication and, thus, the transfer of experience and knowledge. In the light of these fragmentations, policy reforms in the field of EU structural funds cannot be explained by the existence of a closely knit policy network that encompasses both policy implementation and policy reform and by direct, sustained personal interactions between actors in a single policy community. How can the hypothesis on the crucial importance of policy networks for the development of EU structural funds be modified in the light of these findings? This question will be taken up after a brief look at the key features of EU environment policy.

EU environment policy

'Environmental policy is seen as a case *par excellence* of "the dispersion of authoritative decision-making across multiple territorial levels" (Hooghe and Marks, 2001: xi; cited in Fairbrass and Jordan, 2004: 148) and in this respect as an EU policy characterised by multi-level governance. However, in view of its main regulatory character, it can be argued that it differs significantly from a redistributive policy like the structural funds. With regulatory policy, networks can be found in which the link is considerably looser or more temporary (Hèritier, 1993) between (a) those actors who affect decisions on rules or procedures; (b) those who take these decisions; and (c) those who take into account rules or procedures and check that they are followed. Thus there is only a limited possibility of forming a policy community which has a common view of required actions. This is important not only in relation to the potential for developing a consensus-oriented approach geared towards problem solving based on agreement and a common definition of interests, but is also important in encouraging (or not) transformation of policy by means of interactions in policy networks. For regulatory policy it is plausible to assume considerably more fragile 'issue [specific] networks' (Heinelt, 1996: 17). From this point of view, fragmentation and diversity can be seen as a basic feature of environment policy due to its regulatory character.

Furthermore, environment policy is composed – to an even higher degree than structural funds interventions – of different sub-policies or *sector-specific* measures – like water protection, air pollution control, waste management, chemical control or the protection of endangered species. Each one consists of a number of individual instruments regulating emission, product and process/production standards as well as environmental quality objectives in a 'substantive' way, i.e. by prescribing certain limits/thresholds or concrete goals (see Knill and Liefferink, 2007: 41-43 and 48-51; in the case of air pollution control they identify 18 different regulations). This diversity implies a highly fragmented distribution of responsibilities and tasks particularly in the administrations of member states but also within the Commission, even in DG Environment itself.

But there are also *overarching measures* – like environmental impact assessment (EIA) and strategic environmental assessment (SEA) or the enterprise related eco-management and audit scheme (EMAS). These measures aim at overcoming the compartmentalisation of the policy field resulting from the sector-specific measures in a 'procedural' way, i.e. by prescribing ways in which individual objectives as well as overarching principles of EU environment policy – like prevention, precaution, integration or sustainable development (see Knill and Liefferink, 2007: 27-35) – can be achieved in a given case (e.g. in decisions on planning permission or in an enterprise: see Heinelt *et al.*, 2001b; Knill and Liefferink, 2007: 41-43 and 46-48). These measures leave not only a lot of discretion at the level of implementation in the member states but also at the level of their case-related application (see Heinelt *et al.*, 2001a and Heinelt and Smith, 2003 for EIA and EMAS).

Critical accounts of EU environment policy have to address the consequences of fragmentation and diversity. This applies first of all to interest intermediation between the member states (or their governments) at the EU level. It can not only be characterised as preventing EU legislation which could negatively impact on the competitiveness of their economies. More important, 'regulatory competition' (Héritier *et al.*, 1996) can be seen as a main feature of policymaking. It avoids the costs of adapting domestic organisational arrangements to 'new' regulations. This reflects the European decision-making undertaken by top-level representatives of the member states (together with the Commission) who lack close contact with actors involved in the implementation of EU legislation.

But 'regulatory competition' in this sense not only affects the strategies of member states in decision-making at the EU level but also the implementation of EU legislation. Here, the blocking of organisational change is a main motive of governmental actors, although 'Europeanisation' and especially the spread of particular norms and policy objectives cannot be denied (see below). Against this background the 'implementation deficit' of environment policy (see Jordan *et al.*, 1999) is a consequence of a fragmented multi-level system in this policy field.

More specifically, the 'implementation deficit' has been explained by the fact that objectives defined at the EU level cannot be properly achieved because domestic actors at the national as well as at the 'operational' level are acting independently. It has been argued that the European Commission – neither directly linked to the implementation of EU legislation nor able to control its application– depends heavily on non-governmental organisations (environmental groups) as 'watchdogs' to secure compliance (Heinelt and Meinke-Brandmeier, 2006; Koutalakis, 2004).

In this respect, the 'sub-national mobilisation' of environmental groups as well as their involvement at the EU level by EU institutions (the Commission and the European Parliament) has to be interpreted as a special feature of multi-level governance (see Fairbrass and Jordan, 2004: 162-163). However not only does the 'sub-national mobilisation' of environmental groups differ greatly between member states, but the involvement of environmental groups at the EU level is characterised by differences between these non-governmental organisations in relation to their individual interests or objectives (as well as their organisational capacities). Therefore, fragmentation is a main feature of interest intermediation in respect of these kinds of societal actors.

Against this background, fragmentation can be observed in the field of environment policy in respect of the following:

- Those actors who take decisions on environmental legislation at the EU level or who affect them are clearly not linked to those who implement this legislation or check that it is followed.
- Within member states the key players in decision making at the EU level do not have close links to those implementing environmental legislation.
- Implementation networks in the member states are highly fragmented horizontally in line with different sub-policies. This applies not only for typical sector-specific measures like air pollution control but also for land use planning policy, for which overarching measures have been established. In the latter it is obvious that the 'vested' interests of developers as well as of local authorities quite easily become hegemonic in defining an 'appropriate' land use in line with policies aiming at fostering local and regional (economic) competitiveness.

- Non-governmental actors trying to influence environment policy are horizontally fragmented not only at the EU and national levels but also at the implementation level because of their highly diverse interests and preferences.

Thus, multi-level governance in the field of environment policy can be characterised by "complex, uncertain, and contested decision-making" (Fairbrass and Jordan, 2004: 163) Nevertheless, "learning on the part of member states" (ibid) and "other involved actors" can be observed. How to explain this?

Achieving Governability by Loose Coupling

Do these observations question the relevance of linkages between different actors and layers within multi-level governance – or is it the nature of these linkages which has to be reviewed? Contrary to earlier literature, particularly on the EU structural funds, linkages between the different actors and levels are not tightly horizontal and vertical, but rather loosely coupled. Against this background a hypothesis could be put forward that governability is a result of policy networks characterised by different aspects of loose coupling between relatively autonomous actors.[5]

The expression "loose coupling" has its origin in older approaches developed in connection with organisation studies, which emphases that a "coupled" unit in an organisation as well as an organisation coupled with others can secure "its own identity and some evidence of its physical or logical separateness" (Weick, 1976: 3), although they are dependent on and influence each other. Based on an increasing use of the expression of "loose coupling" – as a result of which its meaning has became more and more blurred – Orton and Weick (1990) helpfully identified different applications of the concept. Orton and Weick (1990: 204 *et seq.*) draw a distinction between a "unidimensional" and a "dialectical interpretation" of loose coupling. The first considers tight and loose coupling as extremes. Therefore, it puts systems characterised by closeness and openness or by "independent" and "responsive components" in opposition to each other. In contrast, the 'dialectical interpretation' of loose coupling (adopted here) emphasises the coexistence of closeness and openness as well as of "distinctiveness" and "responsiveness". This interpretation highlights the fact that units separated by processes of differentiation are able to secure autonomy and to develop specific logics and orientations for their actions even though they still depend on and interact with each other (Orton and Weick, 1990: 205). This increases the opportunity for actors to operate more effectively with respect to specific problems and situations, whilst being at the same time oriented to common objectives and linked by overriding rules. In other words, it is the coexistence of co-ordination and autonomy, the ambiguity of overarching objectives and rules and selectivity on the part of key players that creates the conditions under which developments can come about quite quickly, and adaptability can be secured (Weick, 1985: 164-165).

5 Parts of the following section are based on Heinelt *et al.*, 2003: 138-142.

This applies not least to developments which can be related to the term "organisational learning" (Valve, 2006). This is especially the case for any analysis that adapts the idea of "unconventional forms" of organisational learning (Wiesenthal, 1995)[6] which can be connected to the concept of loose coupling. As the use of the idea of "unconventional forms" of organisational learning questions the ability of organisations to resist the influence of external pressures, so it emphasises the sensitivity of organisations to those external influences and the consequent organisational learning by "intrusion", i.e. by "invasion" of new members with different "ideas" and new knowledge, tolerable dissent of members, and interaction of organisations with different rules and cognitive maps (Wiesenthal, 1995: 145-147). Therefore, they are open to new development and policy options, or organisational changes which flow from the coexistence of closeness and openness as well as co-ordination and autonomy.

This means, on the one hand, that it is necessary to take serious account of the phenomena of differentiation, i.e.

- the *internal organisational fragmentation of collective actors*,[7] particularly in respect of (i) the vertical fragmentation between implementation and policy reform networks in the member states and (ii) the horizontal fragmentation of the different levels of implementation networks in the member states as well as of the European Commission (in DGs and their units) in line with specific responsibilities for individual funds, policies, sub-policies and even programmes;
- the functional differentiation between a decision-making arena on the EU-level and (task specific) implementation arenas in the member states or regions;
- the sequentialisation of decisions at the different levels of vertically fragmented policy sub-systems and between these sub-systems in terms of a break-up of the entire reform and implementation processes into manageable chunks that are repeatedly processed at various levels and between the vertically fragmented parts of the decision system. [8]

6 The expression "unconventional forms" of organisational learning is used in contrast to "conventional forms" of organisational learning developed by Argyris (1976) and Argyris and Schön (1978).

7 See, for such phenomena, the argument put forward by Renate Mayntz. According to her a "strong internal differentiation of the political-administrative system" is related to the "observed change of fulfilling political tasks which can be described by a tendency to govern partial tasks through and in bargaining systems" (Mayntz, 1996: 157; translation by the author). The internal differentiation of the political-administrative system is almost a basic requirement for bargaining by which "the societal problems of interdependencies can get on the agenda of governmental actions" (ibid.), and "intra-governmental bargains" are crucial for avoiding the danger that "the shift of political decisions into sectoral policy networks only leads to fragmentation" (ibid.).

8 It should be noted that these are probably not the only phenomena of differentiation within the two policy areas – and even not for EU policies in general. But they are the most relevant ones for these policy areas.

On the other hand, we have to consider coherence mechanisms which can bring about loose coupling of the phenomena of differentiation. Such mechanisms include:

- accepted rules and norms for the exchange of information and for co-ordinating actions;
- ideas or paradigms (like sustainability or partnership) which suggest specific objectives for actions as well as definitions and measures through which problems can be solved in a way which is commonly perceived as appropriate;
- coupling institutions (like the monitoring committees in the case of the structural funds) where interactions are bound within a specific organisational context, i.e. where actors are forced to meet, to interact and to explain/justify their particular choices of action;
- the anticipation of an authoritative final decision by an indirectly involved authority, for example, the "shadow of hierarchy" within an organisation or the possibility of a political decision (i) at a higher level in the negotiation system (e.g. by the Council) or (ii) from a higher level with a network of organisations (e.g. by the Commission);
- and the existence of a public sphere – whether a sectoral or professional one – which can complement the 'shadow of hierarchy' in so far as the relevance of the afore mentioned rules and norms as well as ideas or paradigms is emphasised and their violation can be criticised in a public setting.

Whilst the phenomena of differentiation reflect the autonomy of the units or parts of a system, the coherence mechanisms provide opportunities for coupling. This addresses the core of the "dialectical interpretation" of loose coupling, i.e. "to combine the contradictory concepts of connection and autonomy" (Orton and Weick, 1990: 216).

Loose coupling can be a result of the coherence mechanisms, but there is no inevitability in the development and the effectiveness of these mechanisms, and without them functional differentiation and organisational fragmentation can result in governance failure. The effectiveness of the coherence mechanisms depends on an alignment of orientations and routines of the – individual as well as collective – actors. This applies to "ideas" or paradigms as well as for the different dimensions of rules and norms for the exchange of information and the co-ordination of actions. Also, the anticipation of a possible final authoritative decision of an indirectly involved authority – especially a hierarchical intervention – could shape the incentive structure of actors, but could also lead to evasive manoeuvres by the (formally) subordinated actors. This is reflected in the "dialectical interpretation" of loose coupling "with its recognition of numerous structural dimensions, its emphasis on simultaneous coupling and decoupling, and its portrayal of structures as malleable through managerial intervention" in that it forces researchers "to move more deeply into the human workings which underlie organizational structure" (Orton and Weick, 1990: 218).

The emphasis on "simultaneous coupling and decoupling" is particularly relevant with respect to hierarchical, one-sided and power-based options and competences for making and enforcing decisions. In a multi-level system of joint decision-making they can lead to vetoes and blockages as well as to a reduction in the openness and the "feasible set" of involved actors (or units). Nonetheless, even in loosely coupled systems the binding nature of interactions has to be enforced in order to avoid individual units becoming (too) independent and a real "decoupling" of collective actors is taking place.

As highlighted above, the internal organisational differentiation of collective actors, the differentiation (sequentialisation) of decisions at different levels, as well as the functional differentiation between a decision-making arena at the EU level and implementation arenas in the member states/regions represent specific intra- and inter-organisational capabilities in a system of EU multi-level governance which have been shown to be conducive to the development of innovative policies, responsive to their environment. They provide the actors involved in a multi-level system with space for taking decisions and they offer area-related opportunities for institutional evolution and organisational learning. However, the various forms of differentiation need to be loosely coupled by specific coherence mechanisms. Otherwise there would be the risk of fragmentation in organisations and isolation of single sub-units within certain policy areas which, in turn, could lead to implementation deficits and to the collapse of newly gained insights and new outlooks.

Possible coherence mechanisms include the acceptance of rules and norms for the exchange of information and the co-ordination of actions (e.g. informal and formal norms for procedures), "ideas" or paradigms suggesting specific objectives for actions, as well as definitions of and solutions to problems. Furthermore, the option of a clear decision imposed on the actors by an indirectly involved authority within an organisation or the possibility of a political decision at a higher level in a bargaining system, as well as the option of being 'named' and 'shamed' in public, are crucial to enforce the coherence mechanisms referred to above. In this respect, the "shadow of hierarchy" can be complemented by the "light of the public".

If coherence is guaranteed by such forms of loose coupling, then inter- and intra-organisational differentiation may prove to be a precondition for adaptation and learning processes by the units involved – especially by those at the 'operational' level – as well as for governability with regard to the achievement of general policy objectives according to differing contextual conditions, whilst specific coherence mechanisms ensure that the actors still relate to each other within the frame of a multi-level system.

The fragmented structure and coherence mechanisms have not been developed and linked in a systematic and consistent way.[9] They have emerged incrementally

9 One can draw lessons from these findings and try to develop design principles for European governance arrangements reflecting these advantages. But this was not the purpose of this chapter. For an attempt to develop "generic design principles for European governance arrangements" focussing on the achievement of effectiveness and legitimacy, see Schmitter (2002).

from pragmatic decisions determined by the specific structures of the EU level governance system, as well as through the various path-dependencies of policymaking in member states. In other words, the array of formal and informal options open to actors in EU decision-making to secure the role of "veto players" as well as the divergence of organisational structures in member states, which shape the development and implementation of the structural funds and environment policy at the EU level, prevent a successful systematic and consistent design.

Nevertheless, there have been successful political attempts to structure the multilevel system of the EU which have had important consequences. This is demonstrated in the case of cohesion policy by the introduction of the principles of programming, implementation and partnership through the 1988 reform as well as by the partial withdrawal of the geographical units of the Commission from the implementation arenas after the reform of 1999, or the move away from the command and control approach in the case of environment policy in the early 1990s. Although there is some evidence that these attempts had been influenced by scholarly debate (see Hooghe, 1996a; Heinelt *et al.*, 2001; Heinelt and Malek, 2002) they are mainly based or derived from the "intelligence of practice". In brief, through their involvement in EU decision-making, actors are able to use favourable (historical and/or organisational) conditions to place their specific definition of the "right" problem and a corresponding "adequate" perspective on the relevant action to take in a hegemonic position. This constitutes policy or organisational learning.

These reflections on loose coupling may provide an answer to the question how governability can be achieved in multi-level policymaking. Differentiation – usually seen as the reason for governance failure – can be used to realise what is desired, known and perceived as achievable by key actors, providing coherence mechanisms are developed and used. This is crucial because what is desired, known and perceived as achievable by key actors differs over time and space, according to historical and territorial contexts. Such a perspective:

- denies the desirability of assimilation and uniformity, linked to a vision of state-based or state-like policymaking, and
- emphasises on the one hand the important influence of diversity but on the other hand and at the same time tries to secure integration through fundamental rules and norms.

In this respect the EU structural funds represent more or less a success story of a European model of policymaking because a high degree of diversity at the regional and national level can be observed when it comes to the implementation of a common funding scheme.[10] This diversity allows not only the adaptability of the scheme to specific spatial institutional as well as social and economic conditions but also to what is desired and known and perceived as commonly achievable by the actors involved in implementation. At the same time the acceptance of overall policy objecti-

10 For the concept of 'democractic experimentalism' (within a 'directly-deliberative polyarchy') see Cohen and Sabel, 1997; Dorf and Sabel, 1998; Sabel and Zeitlin, 2007.

ves and particular rules for adapting the scheme have been secured – which leads to coherence of policymaking and in the political interventions in this policy area. Furthermore, the EU structural funds demonstrated on the one hand the ability to change policy objectives and particular rules for adapting the scheme over time according to (i) changing conditions (particularly further steps towards European integration and enlargement) as well as (ii) political debates about the effectiveness and legitimacy of this (re)distributive policy. On the other hand these changes have been achieved without losing core understanding of what the policy is or should be about. However, it may well be that these characteristics of the EU structural funds are fragile. It is, for example, an open question (which will be answered in the near future) how the recent reform of the structural funds – which put the strengthening of 'competitiveness' (in line with the Lisbon process) alongside the cohesion objective – and Eastern enlargement will affect this policy field.

The example of EU environment policy points to weaknesses in a European model of policymaking represented by the structural funds and in multi-level policymaking in general. If fragmentation is too extensive and far-reaching and not counterbalanced by strong coherence mechanisms integration of political interventions cannot be achieved. The result is just a 'nominal policy' by which not only sub-policies with different objectives and instruments but also diverse practices are subsumed under a common label. More important, a shared understanding of what the problems to be addressed are about, how these problems can be solved, and which policy objectives should be achieved by particular policy instruments gets lost, although general principles, like prevention, precaution, integration or sustainability that address such a basic understanding, may have been established (see Knill and Liefferink, 2007: 27ff). Instead, actors act independently – if not unconnectedly – (according to what they "desire" and "know" and what they perceive as achievable) in specific layers of the EU multi-level system and within different organisational units and sub-policies located at these layers. Under such conditions governability is hardly likely to be achieved. However, 'overarching measures' – like environmental impact assessment and strategic environmental assessment or the enterprise related eco-management and audit scheme – offer opportunities to reach a loose coupling in the afore mentioned way in the field of environment policy, because they prescribe (or least offer opportunities) to clarify in a particular case how individual objectives as well as the overarching principles of the EU environment policy can be achieved.

References

Argyris, C. (1976). Single-Loop and Douple-Loop Models in Research on Decision Making. *Administrative Science Quarterly, 21*, pp.363-375.

Argyris, C. and Schön, D. A. (1978). *Organizational Learning. A Theory of Action Perspective*. Reading/Mass: Addison-Wesley

Bache, I. (1998). *The Politics of European Union Regional Policy. Multi-Level Governance or Flexible Gatekeeping?* Sheffield: Sheffield Academic Press.

Bache, I. and Flinders, M. (Eds.) (2004). *Multi-level Governance.* Oxford: Oxford University Press.

Bachtler, J. and Wishlade, F. (2005). *From Building Blocks to Negotiating Boxes. The Reform of EU Cohesion Policy.* European Policy Research Paper Number 57. Available at: http://www.eprc.strath.ac.uk/eprc/documents/PDF_files/EPRP_57_From_Building_Blocks_to_Negotiating_Boxes.pdf

Bailey, D. and De Propris, L. (2002). EU structural funds, Regional Capabilities and Enlargement: Towards Multi-Level Governance? *Journal of European Integration, 24 (4)*, pp.303-324.

Becker, P. (2005). *Der EU-Finanzrahmen 2007-2013. Auf dem Weg zu einer europäischen Finanzverfassung oder Fortsetzung der nationalen Nettosaldopolitik.* Berlin: Stiftung Wissenschaft und Politik.

Beugelsdijk, M. and Eijffinger, S. C. W. (2005). The effectiveness of structural policy in the European Union : an empirical analysis for the EU-15 during the period 1995-2001. *Journal for Common Market Studies, 43 (1)*, pp.37-51.

Cappelen, A., Castellaci, F., Fagerberg, J. and Verspagen, B. (2003). The Impact of EU Regional Support on Growth and Convergence in the European Union. *Journal of Common Market Studies, 41 (4)*, pp.621-644.

Castells, A. and Espasa Queralt, M. (2003). Do structural actions contribute to reduced regional disparities in the European Union? In B. Funck and L. Pizzati (Eds.), *European integration, regional policy, and growth* (pp.167-176). Washington DC: World Bank.

Cohen, J. and Sabel, C. F. (1997). Directly-deliberative Polyarchy. *European Law Journal, 3 (4),* pp.313-342.

Dorf, M. C. and Sabel, C. F. (1998). A Constitution of Democratic Experimentalism. *Columbia Law Review, 98 (2)*, pp.267-473.

Fairbrass, J. and Jordan, A. (2004). Multi-level governance and environmental policy. In I. Bache, and M. Flinders (Eds.), *Multi-level Governance* (pp.147-164). Oxford: Oxford University Press.

Grande, E. and Jachtenfuchs, M. (Eds.) (2000). *Wie problemlösungsfähig ist die EU?* Baden-Baden: Nomos.

Heclo, H. and Wildavsky, A. (1974). *The Private Government of Public Money.* London/Basingstoke: Macmillan.

Heinelt, H. (2008). Demokratie jenseits des Staates. Partizipatives Regieren und Governance. Baden-Baden: Nomos.

Heinelt, H. (1996). Multilevel Governance in the European Union and the structural funds. In H. Heinelt, and R. Smith (Eds.), *Policy Networks and European structural funds* (pp.9-25). Aldershot: Avebury.

Heinelt, H., Kopp-Malek, T., Lang, J. and Reissert, B. (2005). *Die Entwicklung der EU-Strukturfonds als kumulativer Politikprozess.* Baden-Baden: Nomos.

Heinelt, H., Kopp-Malek, T., Lang, J. and Reissert, B. (2003). Policymaking in Fragmented Systems. How to Explain Success. In B. Kohler-Koch (Ed.), *Linking EU and National Governance* (pp.135-153). Oxford: Oxford University Press.

Heinelt, H. and Malek, T. (2002). Neuere Steuerungsformen im europäischen Mehrebenensystem. In M. Knodt and T. Conzelmann (Eds.), *Regionales Europa, europäische Regionen* (Mannheimer Jahrbuch für Europäische Sozialforschung, Vol. 6) (pp.69-86). Frankfurt am Main: Campus.

Heinelt, H., Malek, T., Smith, R. and Töller, A. E. (2001a). European Union Environment Policy and New Forms of Governance. Aldershot: Ashgate.

Heinelt, H., Malek, T., Staeck, N. and Töller, A. E. (2001b). Environmental Policy. The European Union and a paradigm shift. In H. Heinelt, T. Malek, R. Smith, and A. E. Töller (Eds.), *European Union Environment Policy and New Forms of Governance* (pp.1-32). Aldershot: Ashgate.

Heinelt, H. and Meinke-Brandmeier, B. (2006). Comparing Civil Society Participation in European Environmental Policy and Consumer Protection. In S. Smismans (Ed.), *Civil Society and Legitimate European Governance* (pp.196-218). Cheltenham: Edward Elgar.

Heinelt, H. and Smith, R. (Eds.) (1996). *Policy Networks and European structural funds.* Aldershot: Avebury.

Heinelt, H. and Töller, A. E. (2003). Sustainability, Innovation, Participation and EMAS. In H. Heinelt, and R. Smith (Eds.), *Sustainability, Innovation and Participatory Governance. A Cross-National Study of the EU Eco-Management and Audit Scheme* (pp.11-21). Aldershot: Ashgate.

Heinemann, F. (2005). *EU-Finanzplanung 2007-2013. Haushaltsoptionen, Verteilungswirkungen und europäischer Mehrwert.* Gütersloh: Bertelsmann-Stiftung.

Héritier, A. (1993). Policy-Netzwerkanalyse als Untersuchungsinstrument im europaischen Kontext: Folgereungen aus einer empirishchen Studie regulativer Politik. In A. Héritier (Ed.), *Policy-Analyse, Kritik und Neuorientierung* (pp.432-447). Opladen: Westdeutscher Verlag.

Héritier, A., Knill, C. and Mingers, S. (1996). *Ringing the changes in Europe. Regulatory competition and the transformation of the State.* Berlin: de Gruyter.

Hooghe, L. and Marks, G. (2001). *Multi-level Governance and European Integration.* Oxford: Rowman and Littlefield.

Hooghe, L. (Ed.) (1996). *Cohesion Policy and European Integration. Building Multi-level Governance*. Oxford: Oxford University Press.

Jordan, A., Brouwer, R. and Noble, E. (1999). *Innovate and Responsive? A longitudinal analysis of the speed of European Union environmental policymaking 1967-1997.* CSERGE Working Paper WM 99-02. London: University of East Anglia and University College London.

Knill, C. and Liefferink, D. (2007). *Environment Politics in the European Union*. Manchester: Manchester University Press.

Kohler-Koch, B. (Ed.) (2003). *Linking EU and National Governance.* Oxford: Oxford University Press.

Koutalakis, C. (2004). Environmental compliance in Italy and Greece. The role of non-state actors. *Environmental Policy, 13 (4)*, pp.754-774.

Luhmann, N. (1989). Politische Steuerung. Ein Diskussionsbeitrag. In H. H. Hartwich (Ed.), *Macht und Ohnmacht politischer Institutionen* (pp.12-16). Opladen: Westdeutscher Verlag.

Malek, T. (2002). *Politikgestaltung auf europäischer Ebene*. Baden-Baden: Nomos.

Marks, G. (1993). Structural policy and multilevel governance in the EC. In A. W. Cafruny and G. G. Rosenthal (Eds.), *The State of the European Community. Vol. 2: The Maastricht Debate and Beyond* (pp.391-410). Longman: Lynne Rienner Publishers.

Marks, G., Hooghe, L. and Blank, K. (1996). European integration from the 1980s. State-centric v. multi-level governance. *Journal of Common Market Studies, 34 (3),* pp.341-378.

Marsh, D. (1998). The development of the policy network approach. In D. Marsh (Ed.), *Comparing Policy Networks*. Buckingham: Open University Press.

Mayntz, R. (1996). Politische Steuerung: Aufstieg, Niedergang und Transformation einer Theorie. In K. von Beyme and C. Offe (Eds.), *Politische Theorien in der Ära der Transformation* (pp.148-168). Opladen: Westdeutscher Verlag.

Mayntz, R. (1997). *Soziale Dynamik und politische Steuerung. Theoretische und methodologische Überlegungen*. Frankfurt am Main: Campus.

McCormick, J. (2001). *Environmental Policy in the European Union.* London: Palgrave.

Orton, J. D., and Weick, K. E. (1990). Loosely Coupled Systems. A Reconseptualization. *Academy of Management Review, 15 (2)*, pp.203-223.

Sabel, C. F. and Zeitlin, J. (2007). *Learning from Difference. The New Architecture of Experimentalist Governance in the European Union.* European Governance Papers (EUROGOV) No. C-07-02. Available at: http://www.connex-network.org/eurogov/pdf/egp-connex-C-07-02.pdf

Sapir, A., Aghion, P., Bertola, G., Hellwig, M., Pisani-Ferry, J., Rosati, D., Viñals, J. and Wallace, H. (2003). *An Agenda for a Growing Europe. Making the EU Economic System Deliver*. Report of an Independent High-Level Study Group established on the initiative of the President of the European Commission, Brussels. Available at: http://www.swisscore.org/Policy%20docs/general_research/sapir_report_en.pdf

Scharpf, F. W. (1986). War die Massenarbeitslosigkeit unabwendbar? Von der Schwierigkeit beschäftigungspolitischer Optionen. In H. E. Maier and T. Schmid (Eds.), *Der goldene Topf. Vorschläge zur Auflockerung des Arbeitsmarktes* (pp.9-37). Berlin: Wagenbach.

Scharpf, F. W. (1988a). Verhandlungssysteme, Verteillungskonflikte und Pathologien der politischen Steuerung. In M. G. Schmidt (Ed.), *Staatstatigkeit, International und historisch vergleichende Analysen* (pp.61-87). Opladen: Westdeutscher Verlag.

Scharpf, F. W. (1988b). The Joint-Decision Trap. Lessons from German Federalism and European Integration. *Public Administration, 66,* pp.239-278.

Scharpf, F. W. (1989). Politische Steuerung und politische Institutionen. In H. H. Hartwich (Ed.), *Macht und Ohnmacht politischer Institutionen* (pp.17-29). Westdeutscher Verlag: Opladen.

Scharpf, F. W. (1993). Positive und negative Koordination in Verhandlungssystemen. In A. Héritier (Ed.), *Policy-Analyse. Kritik und Neuorientierung* (pp.57-83). Wiesbaden: Westdeutscher Verlag.

Scharpf, F. W. (2001). *What Have We Learned? Problem-Solving Capacity of the Multilevel European Polity*. MPIfG Working Paper 01/4. Cologne: MPIfG.

Schmitter, P. (2002). Participation in Governance Arrangements: Is there any reason to expect it will achieve "Sustainable and Innovative Policies in a Multi-Level Context"? In J. R. Grote and B. Gbikpi (Eds.), *Participatory Governance. Political and Societal Implications* (pp.51-69). Opladen: Leske & Budrich.

Valve, H. (2006). Evaluating social learning potentials generated by EU structural funding programmes. *Innovation, 19 (2),* pp.171-187.

Weick, K. E. (1976). Educational Organizations as Loosely Coupled Systems. *Administrative Science Quarterly, 21 (1)*, pp.1-19.

Weick, K. E. (1985). *Der Prozeß des Organisierens*. Frankfurt: Suhrkamp.

Wiesenthal, H. (1995). Konventionelles und unkonventionelles Organisationslernen. Literaturreport und Ergänzungsvorschlag. *Zeitschrift für Soziologie, 2*, pp.137-155.

II. Multi-level Governance and the Structural Funds: Still a World of Harmony?

The Development of the Structural Funds: A Success Story?

Simona Piattoni

Introduction

This chapter outlines the evolution of the structural funds in order to tease out the overt and covert goals that have informed this important policy instrument and to try to assess the degree of success with which they have been met. Rather than examining the structural funds' financial endowment and degree of economic success, it analyses both their narrower and broader political goals and their institutional implications. The objectives served by the structural funds, we will see, are far from being purely economic, but also encompass issues such as improvement of administrative performance and support for citizenship building. Based on secondary evidence, this chapter assesses whether the structural funds have indeed fulfilled these objectives or have instead become 'a solution for all problems'. It concludes that, given the multiplicity and multifariousness of the goals served, it is impossible to draw a conclusive balance sheet.

Policies normally serve both substantive and procedural goals. They aim at solving real issues as well as experimenting with new ways of doing things. They also serve a symbolic function. While this is normally understood as a way of dodging thorny issues and skirting difficult responsibilities, in a complex political system like the European Union symbols matter more than ever. Consensus is often built around words which, for their positive connotation, muster wide agreement. Although, and perhaps because, the precise meaning of these concepts is fuzzy, they create a space for convergence towards rather disparate specific objectives. 'Cohesion' appears to be one such term, which has managed to create consensus for multiple and potentially contrasting goals whose precise content and implications were not clear in the beginning and cannot perhaps be fully spelt out even now. It has also created the opportunity for experimenting with a new mode of governance, 'multi-level governance', which can be employed also in other policy realms, for example environmental policy.[1] Apart from cohesion, many other terms of this kind can be found in

1 Multi-level governance is characterised by the active involvement of different levels of territorial government as well as social partners and members of civil society organisations in the definition, implementation and evaluation of structural policy goals and actions. This new mode of governance has been perceived as challenging established hierarchies and as inducing a redefinition of centre-periphery and state-society relations and has given rise to a wave of regional mobilisation throughout Europe (see Hooghe and Marks, 2001 and Bache and Flinders, 2004).

discussions of the evolution of structural policy, such as subsidiarity, partnership, proximity, neighbourhood. It is the open-ended nature of these terms which makes them so precious and durable, as they can be used in different ways at different points in time and can serve as a catalyst for discussion as well as reconciliation.

Structural Policy: An Overview

Structural policy in the EU – the financial support of investment aimed at sustaining economic development or countering economic decline – dates back to the 1950s, at a time when it was usual to speak of the European Economic Communities (EECs). The first fund to be established, in 1960, was the European Social Fund (ESF). Together with the European Investment Bank (EIB) already established in 1957, the ESF was supposed to underpin industrial 'reconversion', particularly from steel and coal industries – which, as a consequence of the war, had hugely overexpanded – to other, more peace-related industries, and to help weather the costs in terms of unemployment and retraining that this implied. In the 1970s such reconversion became necessary on other grounds, as both industries had become economically unsustainable as well as being unhappily associated with war-related production. The ESF was in 1962 joined by the European Agriculture Guarantee and Guidance Fund (EAGGF) which provided money to help stabilise the price of certain agricultural products (the Guarantee section) and to enable farmers to switch from relatively abundant, hence not profit-making, products to relatively scarce ones, from which a greater profit could be secured (the Guidance section).

The economic crisis of the 1970s brought about a general expansion in the scope for structural policy. 1975 was the birth year of the third and probably best known fund, the European Regional Development Fund (ERDF), which was aimed at redressing the economic problems of entire territories within member states and not just of single industrial or agricultural sectors. Despite its name, ERDF was initially neither European nor regional in scope, amounting to little more than a reimbursement, under the heading of 'regional policy', of part of the money that member states contributed to the European Community budget. Between 1975 and 1985, European structural policy slowly evolved. The Commission managed to gain incrementally greater control over the allocation of funds, moving from a system which attributed funds to member states according to fixed quotas to a system which set flexible ranges of variation within which the actual amount of funds allocated to each member state reflected the extent to which the funds' objectives could be seen in the member states' projects. Moreover, the Commission managed to control a small slice of the structural budget for targeted experimental programmes under its direct supervision.

In 1988, this policy was completely overhauled thanks to skilful steering by the then Commission President, Jacques Delors. Preceded, in 1986, by the sunset experiment of the Integrated Mediterranean Programme (IMPs) – aimed at helping the Mediterranean regions of Greece, France and Italy to switch from typically Mediterranean products (olives, citrus, etc.) to greater value-added and prospectively (in view of accession to the EU by Portugal and Spain) less common products – this experiment constituted a major turning point in the life of European regional development policy. This development has been comprehensively studied (see Wishlade, 1996; Bache, 1998) and has served as an empirical testing ground for nascent 'multi-level governance' theorisation (see below). Yet, the history and evolution of European structural policy was not over. Since then, this policy has been enriched by an additional sector-specific fund, the Financial Instrument for Fisheries Guidance (FIFG), in 1994, and a comprehensive new fund directed at countries whose per capita GDP was lower than 90 per cent of the European average at the time, the Cohesion Fund, in 1993. By this time, the name of this structural, mainly regionally-directed policy, had become known as cohesion policy and its declared aim was the promotion of 'social and economic cohesion' among the different regions of the European Union (Hooghe, 1996).

The rationalisation effort and the apparent equilibrium point reached at the end of the 1980s was soon to be undone by new developmental challenges mostly connected with successive rounds of enlargement. Since the late 1980s, the structural funds have been through three new reform rounds. The 1993 reform simplified to some degree the procedures for the submission, implementation and evaluation of the structural funds to be disbursed in the 1994-1999 period and, according to some accounts, allowed member states to regain some of the control over structural policy that they had handed over to the Commission. Even so, some goals could be addressed by simply tinkering with the criteria for the allocation of the existing funds, e.g. the addition in 1995 of Objective 6 (for the support of sparsely populated regions of the European north) to the menu of existing ERDF objectives. Following the recommendations of the Agenda 2000 document approved at the Berlin summit, the 1999 reform put more emphasis on the social and environmental sustainability of development as well as on the concentration of effort and simplification of procedures. These two reform rounds (1993 and 1999) also placed greater emphasis on the participation of lower-level governments and civil society representatives in the monitoring of the structural funds and this was reflected in the creation of the Committee of the Regions (CoR), in 1992, which provided an institutional forum for regional and local concerns and gave their representatives consultative powers over a range of policy issues.

The latest enlargement rounds of 2004 and 2007, though, required the creation of specifically targeted financial instruments. This is the case for the Poland and Hungary Aid for the Reconstruction of the Economy (PHARE), established in 1989, the Instrument for Structural Programmes for Pre-accession (ISPA) and Support for Pre-accession measures for Agricultural and Rural Development (SAPARD) funds created in 1999 to help, first just Poland and Hungary, then all Central and East European Countries (CEECs) retool their agricultural, industrial and administrative capacity and prepare for accession. The latest reform discussions (2004-06), in preparation for the 2007-13 programming period, attempted to further rationalise structural action. Three main lines of action – convergence, competitiveness and co-operation – now subsume the previous objectives (which, in the meantime, had been reduced from six to three) as well as the Community Initiatives which had been kept going through finance from three Funds – ERDF, ESF and the Cohesion Fund (see below).

While the structural funds are available, as of January 2007, to all 27 member states, other instruments have been created to address the more specific problems of additional prospective members, particularly the Western Balkan states. In addition to these programmes and the immediate relief programmes such as ECHO, future accession countries receive regional aid through the Community Assistance for Reconstruction, Development and Stability in the Western Balkans (CARDS) programme which supports investment, institution-building and other stabilisation measures. It should be clear from this overview that the scope of structural policy has expanded over time to accommodate newcomers to the EU and has consequently addressed new problems and taken on new objectives.

It should not be forgotten that, since 1979, several other specially funded programmes have been created to tackle specific goals related to industrial and agricultural transformation (e.g. RECHAR, KONVER, TEXTILE, LEADER), workforce training and retraining (EQUAL, EQUAL NOW), technological upgrading (STAR, STRIDE), tourism promotion and inner city renovation (URBAN), inter-regional and inter-municipal co-operation (INTERREG, EUROCITIES-sponsored programmes), and so on. These and other Community Initiatives began as pilot programmes with which the Commission tried new ways of tackling specific regional development problems. They served as a wedge which the Commission inserted, in the 1970s into the rigid structure of the original funds to create a space for a truly European policy, and represented an important testing ground for innovative ideas and approaches as well as a significant entrepreneurial lever for the reform of the flagship programmes. The number and scope of these Initiatives were later drastically reduced and only a few such programmes (LEADER+, INTERREG, EQUAL, URBAN) were still active in 2006 and have since been subsumed under the heading 'co-operation' in the regulation governing the 2007-2013 period.

Goals and Objectives of Structural Policy

In order to decide whether the structural funds have been 'successful', we need to identify the goals that they were meant to serve. We must also ask success 'for whom' and in terms 'of what'? European structural policy has multiple stakeholders: member states and their regions, European institutions and citizens at large, economic interests and civil society organisations. Different actors assess the same policy from different angles and according to different criteria, so there cannot be one single measure of success. Indeed, the very notion of 'policy' has been questioned by the public policy literature (Sabatier, 2007): policy definition is now considered as much part of the political process as its implementation or evaluation. Structural policy is no exception. It can be argued that next to explicitly stated goals, normally identified by single, evocative words, implicit objectives of an institutional and procedural nature have been pursued, that can be teased out only through more complex forms of words. While the former capture people's attention and serve the Commission's need to communicate effectively the purpose of its policies to its disparate publics, the latter reveal the more concrete interests of the main stakeholders. It could be further argued that the institutional and procedural objectives reveal the ambition to develop a new mode of governance (here to be understood in its polity and politics dimensions), while the broad evocative goals point to the multi-level nature of this policy (see Bache and Conzelmann, this volume).

At least eleven pairings of explicit policy goals and implicit polity and politics objectives can be attributed to the structural funds (see Table 1 below).[2]

Table 1: An Overview of the Goals and Objectives Served by the Structural Funds

Explicit (policy) goals	*Implicit (polity and politics) objectives*
Free trade	Ensure peace
Harmonious growth	Ease the construction of the SEM
Integration	Compensate for economic vulnerability
Cohesion	Sustain creation of EMU
Subsidiarity	Rebalance inter-institutional relations
Additionality	Fix the budget
Partnership	Close the democratic deficit
Ownership	Improve administrative capacities
Active citizenship	Close the democratic deficit
Proximity	Ease EU widening
Competitiveness	Relaunch European integration

Normally, the explicit goals receive wide coverage not only in official documents, but also from press releases and public events, while the implicit objectives need to be extrapolated from detailed regulations and ferreted out through skilful interviews with the actors directly involved. The former are apparent to the wider public; the latter require the work of dedicated scholars. For all of these goals, it is easy to detect that mix of idealism and pragmatism, of compromise and innovation that so often characterises the dynamics of the European Union. We know that in the EU stumbling blocks often become starting blocks for sprinting towards greater integra

2 Clearly this is a personal reading of the history of the structural funds which other scholars may easily challenge. It is equally clear that the same goals and objectives often coexisted and overlapped for long periods of time and that the temporal sequence should be interpreted flexibly.

tion. The contradictions and the ingenuity contained in these developments are aptly captured by simple, but powerful, words which mark the life of EU institutions and policies. Each goal is reviewed in turn and then an interpretation is offered for why first-order goals are couched in such lofty terms and why they get translated into second-order objectives with more practical consequences.

Free trade to ensure peace

At the time the first two structural funds – the EAGGF and the ESF – were created, the most urgent objective Europe-wide was reconstruction. European leaders were acutely aware of the need to avoid any form of intra-European conflict, whatever its nature. It is therefore safe to say that the first substantive goal of the structural funds was to contribute to social and economic reconciliation by helping the reconstruction of European economies. As the second world war can be explained, among other factors, by the interwar escalation of bilateral devaluations in an attempt to maintain the competitiveness of national industries, which in turn led to the elevation of tariff barriers and to a general turn towards autarky, so the reconstruction of national economies was intended to avoid the reproduction of such a hostile situation and should instead ideally give rise to an integrated European economy (Keynes, 1919). This was the dream of the political and administrative elites of the continental states which signed the Treaty of Rome in 1957. In embarking on reconstruction, European elites wanted to avoid repeating the interwar mistakes and strove to create a web of economic interdependencies which would contain any attempts at hostile competition.

The sectors which most logically lent themselves to this experiment in the creation of 'concerted interdependence' were steel, coal and agriculture. Agriculture had been the classical sector in which tariff barriers had been applied in the past and tariff wars had exploded to wreck diplomatic relations between states. Steel and coal were sectors at risk of overproduction – an overproduction which would almost inevitably be absorbed by stocking up war-related products – and divestment should ideally be co-ordinated between states. By helping stabilise incomes in the agricultural sector and absorb the social and economic displacement caused by divestment in steel and coal, the first structural funds were meant to contribute to the attainment of both a substantive and a procedural goal: peace and free trade. Agreement between the first six members of the EEC was relatively easy, as each had either a big agricultural or a big steel and coal problem, or both. The first wave of enlargement brought new problems to the fore and led to the statement of new explicit and implicit goals.

The entry of Denmark, Ireland and the UK into the Community in 1973 posed new redistributive problems. The UK was going through a momentous industrial crisis and scholars worried about Britain's apparently unstoppable industrial decline. Under this considerable pressure, Britain applied again for entry into the EC and was admitted together with long term commercial partners, Ireland and Denmark. Understandably, the issue of helping declining industrial regions was brought up almost immediately. The 1970s were not only putting the mature industries of the European core under stress, but were also exposing the fragility of the least industrialised regions of European, the northern and southern peripheries. A 'marriage of convenience' was thus struck between the UK, Ireland and Italy in pressuring the EC for the creation of a specific fund dedicated to structural action in both declining and developing regions, the ERDF.[3] It was clear that, if the creation of a common market in Europe was to become a reality, too large a discrepancy in per capita GDP, in levels of productive infrastructure, and in quality of training would stand in the way.

Harmonious growth to ease the construction of the Single European Market

For a market to be truly 'common' everyone has to be able to participate in it and take advantage of it. To be excluded by such invisible, yet formidable, barriers such as lack of jobs and minimal standards of living was clearly (politically) unacceptable. Influential in ushering in the structural policy area of the EC, the European regional development policy (ERDP), alongside the common market and the common agricultural policy, was the Thomson report (Commission of the European Communities, 1973) drafted at the request of the Commission in order to study how to achieve "a continuous and balanced expansion" (p. 2). This influential report highlighted how the benefits of the budding common market were accruing mostly to the core regions of the Community, which were becoming increasingly stronger, and were penalising the peripheral regions of Europe, which were becoming increasingly weaker.

Redistributive action which would address structural industrial problems (in addition to those of agriculture which were taken account of by the Guidance section of the EAGGF) would help also fix the European budget, which was felt by the UK government to be unacceptably biased. The UK was contributing substantially to the European budget through its sizeable VAT levies, whilst it was taking too little out because of its minimal participation in agricultural policy (particularly the Guarantee section of EAGGF). The already well-off agricultural areas of continental Europe (particularly in France, but also in the Netherlands and Denmark) were particularly favoured. The stand-off – which featured particularly France and Britain, but also involved other member states – was resolved thanks to the creation of the ERDF in 1975. Although it was not enough to completely offset the imbalance created by the

3 The phrase 'marriage of convenience' is often used to describe the deal struck in Italy after unification between northern industrialists and southern agrarians aimed at allowing the free circulation of agricultural products while keeping nascent industries protected from international competition. It is possible to see the common agricultural policy and the European regional development policy as striking a similar, though reversed, compromise between protected agrarian interests and competitive industrial sectors.

much more sizeable CAP, it was still crucial for securing a working compromise for the entire Community.

For a while, the goal of ERDP was described as that of fostering a 'more harmonious growth', that is, it was justified by referring to the words already contained in the Preamble of the Treaty of Rome. A new round of enlargement brought about a new turn in structural policy and suggested new objectives and new instruments. In 1981, Greece had joined the Community and in 1986 the admission of Spain and Portugal was about to be realised. The Integrated Mediterranean Programmes (IMPs) represented the bargaining chip which was offered to Greece in exchange for its consent to the accession of Spain and Portugal to the Community (Marks, 1993; Pollack, 1995). Greece was officially concerned that Spain and Portugal would flood the common market with typical Mediterranean products, in which all three countries specialised, and drive their prices down. The IMPs were thus conceived as a temporary measure to help Mediterranean regions adapt to this new competitive situation. Funds were made available to economic operators in Mediterranean regions to help them switch from traditional, low-profit crops to new, higher-profit produce or to new activities (such as the industrial transformation of agricultural produce or tourist activities). The beneficiaries, according to the European philosophy of 'leaving no one behind', were the regions of Greece, Italy and France bordering on the Mediterranean Sea.

Integration to compensate for economic vulnerability

The core element of the 1988 reform, from a polity-construction point of view, lies in the innovative ideas it encapsulated, which were the result of many years of reflection and experimentation. First of all, it was decided to abandon the collation of national maps of needy regions and create in its stead a European map of regions in need of financial support. This implied a switch from a nation-wide to a Europe-wide redistributive system that was meant to give increased efficacy to structural action but also to grant greater room for manoeuvre to the Commission and perhaps even facilitate the shifting of primary allegiances among European citizens from the state to the Community level. Second, the reform introduced several novel concepts, first tried out in the IMPs, that were supposed to ensure greater effectiveness to structural policy such as 'integration', 'additionality' and 'programming'. Integration meant that the funds, although managed separately, were supposed to be used jointly to attack specific problem areas. Additionality signalled the tug-of-war between the Commission and the member states over which level should ultimately decide where and how the funds were to be spent. Programming was supposed to lend continuity to the funding effort without disbursing money between too many projects.

The concept of integration, in particular, was central to the administrative architecture of the IMPs. It was becoming clear that one of the most glaring limitations of the structural funds was their rigidly separated administration, which made them easy to monitor but awkward to utilise. It was also becoming increasingly clear that any effective developmental action would need to attack the same problem from many angles, ranging from the creation of infrastructure to workforce retraining, from support of capital investment to marketing skills development. It was also the logical premise for the shift of responsibility to, or at least for the direct involvement of, the lower levels of government in the decision-making process, that is, for the creation of a 'multi-level' mode of governance. The code word for this more self-conscious developmental approach was 'integration', as many instruments were to be integrated towards the one and the same goal.

What mattered even more than the creation of a new Cohesion Fund was, in the mid 1980s, the reform of the structural funds. Both were part and parcel of the agreement among the largest member states to help the newer and poorer member states to move towards European economic averages. The merit for 'the reform' is rightly attributed to the mastery of Jacques Delors, who managed to win one of the largest ever increases in financial endowment from the Community budget for European regional development policy, chipping away at the endowment for the CAP. This reform has given rise to a heated debate about the nature of European decisions, whether they reveal an intergovernmental logic of quid pro quo exchanges (Bache, 1998; Pollack, 1995) or rather the force of an institutionalist logic (Hooghe, 1995, 1996; Keating and Hooghe, 1996) or, again, neither of the two, but rather the need to weave complex multi-level arrangements in order to make things work in the EU (Marks, 1992, 1993, 1996). This debate is still unresolved, because the competing explanations are placed at different explanatory levels, being more concerned with Council decisions (the intergovernmental theory), the complex network of interactions which precede and follow such decisions (the neo-functionalist approach), and the day-to-day implementation of the decisions and their impact on centre-periphery relations both domestically and at the European level (the multi-level governance approach).[4]

Cohesion to sustain the creation of the EMU

By 1988 European member states were clearly gearing up for the creation of an Economic and Monetary Union (EMU) and were discussing the potential repercussions of imposing the same monetary regime on widely different European economies. The danger of 'asymmetric shocks' was haunting the economists, whilst the politicians worried about how to deal with national governments which were relinquishing such a significant (even in symbolic terms) sphere of sovereignty as control of the national currency. It was widely felt that the imposition of the same macro-economic regime on to highly differentiated economies would further exacerbate the

4 The main references are: Hooghe and Marks (1996, 2001), Marks and Hooghe (2003), Bache and Flinders (2004). See also Piattoni (2005).

existing disparities and create unpopularity with the single currency (let alone the symbolic implications of abandoning national currencies). Economic evidence was inconclusive. The Cecchini Report (Commission of the European Communities, 1988), for example, argued that regional disparities across EC states had decreased while those within states had increased. What was certain, however, was that some regions were more vulnerable than others to the challenges from the recently completed Single European Market (SEM) and would have become even more fragile after EMU (Marks, 1996).

Soon after the accession of Portugal and Spain into the Community, however, 'cohesion' became the key word for describing the efforts of European member states and institutions to promote economic growth and social integration. This term, immediately associated with the Cohesion Fund eventually created in 1993 and directed at those member states whose national per capita GDP was less than 90 per cent of the European average (at the time, Greece, Ireland, Portugal and Spain), was meant to cover the entire gamut of policies aimed at reducing regional disparities within the EU. The term cohesion reflected the new concern that, as the European Community was expanding more and more towards the south of Europe, the centre-periphery cleavage was becoming more economically relevant and politically salient than the developing-declining or the agrarian-industrial differences. The internal social and economic cohesion of the Community, and not just the creation of a single European market, was at stake. In its formulation as well as in its implementation, the Cohesion Fund was not a 'regional' fund as it involved only the central administrations of the recipient countries and was directed at upgrading the infrastructural endowment throughout the territory of the member state. However, with its generous financial endowment (15.1 billion ECU during the 1993-1999 period), its concentration on just four countries of the European Community (a novelty in the EC scenario), and with the reform of the structural funds which was undertaken at the same time, 'cohesion policy' effectively replaced 'regional policy' as the official shorthand expression of the multi-faceted effort by the EC to attack the problem of economic and social disparities across the Community. Cohesion, moreover, had the added advantage of avoiding any reference to a specific territorial level, like the region, which was becoming an increasingly contentious issue in the mid 1980s.

Subsidiarity to rebalance inter-institutional relations

The notion of subsidiarity deserves particular attention because, contrary to other EU catchwords, which appear to dull the senses with their positive and gentle ring, it was rather the object of conflict between national and regional authorities which has not yet been fully resolved. Stemming from the social christian tradition to which Delors himself belonged, subsidiarity originally indicated the notion of leaving matters, which are not clearly public, to the private sphere. In the context of the European Community of the mid 1980s, it was interpreted as suggesting that policy decision and implementation should be left to the level of government closest to the problem at hand. According to some, the Commission used it as a wedge to open up a breach in the front of the governments of the member states in order to claim control over regional development policy. Bogged down in intergovernmental strife related to budget contributions and a more general lack of agreement on the ultimate political goals of the Community, in the 1980s the process of integration seemed to slow down.

With hindsight it can be argued that regional development policy was the means by which Delors shook the Community out of its sclerosis and gave new impetus to the integration process. To this end, an instrumental alliance was struck between the Commission and the regions of Europe (Tömmel, 1992). Subsidiarity was therefore used to indicate that developmental issues should be left to that level of government which was closer to the issue, in this case the regional level, but at the same time that supervision over the redistributive logic of the policy should be given to the European Commission. A 'multi-level alliance' had been forged to overcome a political as well as institutional stalemate.

This strategic move from above was met by a corresponding surge from below of regional identities, movements and parties. Regional identities had been reawakening for quite some time. Examples include the 'Celtic renaissance' of the late 1960s in the UK and France, the mobilisation of national regionalism in the historic regions of Spain after the end of dictatorship, the *de facto* federalisation of Belgium along ethnic-linguistic lines and the more recent invention of territorial identities in northern Italy (for a fuller account, see Keating, 1998). Whether these stirrings were expression of a switch from materialist to post-materialist values (Inglehart, 1977), signalled a shift from a demand for 'right to options' to 'right to roots' (Flora et al., 1999), or rather reflected resurgent regional communities and economies (Sabel, 1988), regional movements and parties strongly characterised politics in the late sixties, seventies and eighties.

Subsidiarity thus became the code word which justified the closer involvement of regional authorities in the structural funds. A big debate developed in the discipline about whether such involvement was mere façade or also substantive, whether it covered merely the implementation of the structural funds or also the predisposition of the programme, whether it concerned only the later phases of the policy or also the earlier phases, whether national governments were being deprived of part of their sovereignty from below as well as from above or were using the Commission to better serve their national goals.[5] What is certain is that the financial endowment of the funds was greatly increased, so much so that regional policy appeared to challenge the primacy of the CAP as the redistributive policy of the Community and that regional authorities were more closely involved in the decision-making processes although in different degrees and capacities in the different member states.[6] Moreover, renewed attention was paid to lagging (Objective 1) regions and stronger emphasis

5 Scholars have tried to assess whether European regional policy has indeed empowered the regions. See, for example, Bullman (1996), Bomberg and Peterson (1998), Bache and Jones (2000), Heinelt *et al.* (2003), Bourne (2003).

was put on the need to programme accurately the axes of intervention so as not to diffuse the effort but rather to obtain maximum results. Indeed, from a procedural point of view, the shift from a 'project approach' to a 'programme approach' was the most significant innovation of this period, together with new emphasis on monitoring and on ex-ante and ex-post evaluation.

Additionality to fix the budget

The issue of national contributions to the Community budget once again boiled over in this period and powerfully shaped the implementation of the reformed regulations of the structural funds. The issue of Britain's 'over-contribution' to the EC budget became crucial and got caught in the battle over additionality. The UK government still claimed that it was contributing to the EC budget more than it was taking out and that such an over-contribution was not justifiable on economic grounds. In particular, the issue of additionality became a testing ground in the tug-of-war between the Commission (on the 'supranational side') and the UK and the other member states (on the 'intergovernmental side'). Eventually, it was the British Commissioner, Bruce Millan, who took on the task to impose the 'supranational approach' onto the British government, as probably only a fellow countryman would be a credible spokesman. Summarising a long debate, in practice the British government refused to produce evidence that the financial resources it received from the structural funds were being added to equivalent British funds and were not replacing the British regional development effort. The Commission threatened to use the only weapon it could unilaterally use: to halt the release of funds to declining mining areas under the Community Initiative RECHAR. In the end, the Commission won the battle of principle, but the UK took the opportunity to extract a 'UK rebate' in every budgetary round (the details can be found in McAleavy, 1993, 1995).

The additionality issue exposed what had lurked behind the scenes for a while: the member states were not willing to contribute to the EU budget sums over which they had little or no control and a sense of European solidarity was still missing. In particular, the net contributors to the EU budget (the UK, but also significantly Germany) were beginning to claim 'value for money'. Whilst a too outspoken intergovernmentalist position would have been considered inappropriate for Germany – neither domestic nor international actors would have accepted it – a 'no-nonsense' approach to the funds was defensible. Germany, then, became the promoter of a new turn in structural funds management which put greater emphasis on ex-ante and ex-post evaluation of structural funds implementation, particularly in terms of the congruence of initial objectives with final results (and less in terms of sheer economic impact of the funds, which was very difficult to assess anyway). Efficiency clauses made the release of a certain percentage of the funds dependent on the attainment of certain expenditure targets, under threat of taking away these sums and

6 On the europeanisation of structural policy, see Bache (1999), Börzel (2002), Gualini (2004).

redistributing them between the more efficient regions. Effectiveness and 'value for money' thus allowed Commission and member states to reconcile their (until then) divergent objectives: freedom to pursue a 'supranational' approach to structural action on the part of the Commission, and 'intergovernmental' concern that this space for manoeuvre would not be used to sustain undeserving regions, on the part of the member states.

Partnership to close the democratic deficit

After Maastricht, the main issue concerning the European Union had become its 'democratic temper'. It was widely felt that the increasing powers of EU institutions had to be counterbalanced by greater participation of citizens in the decision-making processes and greater accountability of these institutions to the various societal stakeholders. This general concern with EU democracy also involved the structural funds and, more broadly, the role of regional representatives in EU policymaking. In 1992, the Committee of the Regions (CoR) had been created to give an institutional voice to regional and local authorities over policy issues of direct pertinence. Although the opinions of the CoR were not binding and the matters on which its opinions were sought were limited, still the creation of the CoR was welcomed as a major step forward particularly by those regions or federal states which, being endowed with substantial institutional power at home, had been clamouring for a greater role at the European level as well.[7]

The CoR began its activities with great enthusiasm under the directorship of leading regional governmental figures such as Jacques Blanc and Pasqual Maragall, who became respectively first president and vice-president of the CoR in 1994. While issuing opinions on a number of prescribed matters – such as regional development policy, education, training, youth policy – it also issued its 'own opinions' on a host of different matters as a way of making the 'regional voice' heard. Unfortunately, as the opinions of the CoR were not binding, the initial enthusiasm soon subsided, even though the CoR kept fighting for (and gradually secured) increasing 'institutionalisation'.

The concern for democracy and participation also affected the structural funds regulations. The 1999 regulations toned down to some extent the managerial impetus of the previous set of regulations, responding to the complaints raised by some

7 The 'Europe of the Regions' movement had been launched by German Länder which, reviving the catchphrase of a French scholar (du Granrut, 1994), had meant to protest against their net loss of decision-making powers, particularly in some policy fields such as structural development, which had paradoxically emerged from the 1988 reform. On the uneven impact of the 1988 reform on different types of regions, see Jeffery (1995). On the Committee of the Regions, see Anderson (1991), Jeffery (1995), Christiansen (1996), Warleigh (1999). On regional mobilisation, more generally, see Rhodes (1995), Hooghe (1996), Hooghe and Marks (1996), Keating and Hooghe (1996), Loughlin (1996), Jeffery (2000), Bukowski *et al.* (2003).

regions about the excessive red tape connected with the funds. Greater emphasis was put on the involvement of a larger array of 'social partners' in the monitoring committees which included non-governmental organisations, pressure groups and civil society organisations. Their contribution was considered fundamental for the identification of more appropriate developmental strategies and for achieving the stated goals. Partnership, both 'vertical' across governmental levels, and 'horizontal' between public and private actors, was the word that best captured the idea that shared decisions were better decisions. The entry of Austria, Finland and Sweden in the EU in 1995 infused the structural funds with greater neo-corporatist zeal but also added new objectives to structural policy. In the spirit of 'giving something to everyone', a sixth objective was added onto the existing five to cater for the sparsely populated regions of Nordic Europe. It had become clear at that point that while cohesion remained the ultimate goal of the funds, such a goal would be pursued through different lines of action which responded to the specific needs of the new member states.

Ownership to improve administrative capacities

Clearly, the red tape involved in the utilisation of the structural funds had reached such proportions that the controls which were for a good cause were starting to have serious countereffects. Regions, particularly the more efficient ones, were demanding greater flexibility in the management of the funds and a shorter preliminary procedure: in a word, they claimed ownership of developmental programmes. Inconsistencies also remained at the Community level. Whilst the regions had to adopt an 'integrated' approach by applying different funds to solve complex developmental problems, the Commission still requested separate fund-by-fund accounting, thus imposing double accounting on them. The main innovation of the 1999 regulation was to have simplified the procedure for the Objective 2 regions, allowing them to skip one negotiation step and directly submit a Single Programming Document to the Commission at the beginning of the programming cycle, while the main substantive innovation was a greater emphasis on developmental sustainability, to be understood in both social and environmental terms. This clearly reflected the opening up of structural funds management to social concerns beyond national and subnational governments and, in general, greater concern for popular legitimacy of this policy. The creation of structural funds 'consultative tables' at the national, regional and infra-regional level in several countries clearly shows an attempt to experiment with 'post-parliamentary' democracy. More generally, the multi-level mode of governance, inaugurated amidst contradictions in the realm of cohesion policy, has been extended as an appropriate mode of governance to other policy areas in which different levels of government and civil society actors are relevant stakeholders.

Slowly the idea that more than just money should be circulated through structural action started to gain ground. The reason why, in some countries such as Italy, large sums of structural funds were left unspent had been identified with inefficiency in the regional administration (with reference to Italy, Giuliani and Piattoni, 2001; Brunazzo and Piattoni, 2004). This suggested that one of the goals of the structural funds should also be the upgrading of administrative capacities at the regional level.[8] The Commission imposed stricter procedures for the appropriation, release and spending of funds and requested periodic reporting on the attainment of financial and substantive goals.[9] To avoid shifting the blame across administrative levels, it was requested that managing authorities should be identified at the beginning of each programming cycle and be charged with the supervision of the entire operation. Monitoring committees had been already created in 1988 to promote dialogue between the different administrative and governmental levels as well as with 'social partners' (trade unions, employers' associations, local authorities) and to ensure steady progress towards goal achievement or to allow for a timely retargeting of objectives. Finally, external evaluation was requested at the end of the programming cycle. Best practices were made known throughout the Union to promote emulation.

Active citizenship to close the democratic deficit

The preparation, release and discussion of the White Paper on Governance (Commission of the European Communities, 2001) focused Europe's attention at the turn of the century. By now, the issue of citizen participation, that had been first raised after the surprising results of the Maastricht referendums, had become the most important issue for the European Union. The impending enlargement to Central and Eastern European countries (CEECs) gave rise to general reflection about the notion of European citizenship – whether it could ever exist, how widely should it be granted, which rights exactly it implied – and, even more fundamentally, about the related notion of European identity – whether it could ever develop, what features should characterise it, whether it would supplant or supplement national and regional identities.

If European citizenship had any meaning at all, it had to imply greater participation in important policy decisions, such as those related to the future development of one's region. Regional policy and the structural funds found themselves once more at the core of these debates. The two main channels envisioned by the White Paper on Governance for reducing the gap between European institutions and citizens were civil society organisations and regions. These latter, in particular, were considered to be the institutional level at which active citizen participation was most likely and

8 In Italy, low levels of structural funds utilisation were more the result of the lack of coordination mechanisms between the central and the regional governmental level than sheer lack of administrative capacities in Italian regions, although some were clearly less effective than others. On this issue, see Giuliani and Piattoni (2001, 2006).

9 These were the main features of the 1993 regulations that some authors have interpreted as embodying a sort of 'counter-reform' of the 1988 reform which gave back to member states some of the ground they had temporarily lost (Pollack, 1995).

made more sense. The debate on the forthcoming reform of the funds, which had already begun in 2002, made clear from the beginning that a major redistributive effect from west to east and from older to newer member states would follow the next enlargement round. It soon became clear that this effect could be at most mitigated but not forestalled, without risking the very idea of European citizenship. New modes of governance were therefore devised to encourage greater civil society and regional participation in EU policymaking and to overcome (as smoothly as possible) the increased difficulties involved in opening up decision-making processes to so many new actors.

Proximity to ease EU widening

The imminent enlargement to ten new member states was perceived as being qualitatively (and quantitatively, at least from the point of view of the number of countries involved) different from the others and as requiring reflection on the ultimate goals and direction of the European Union. Union 'widening' could be pitted against 'deepening' with the implicit assumption that the greater the number of member states and of European citizens, the narrower their involvement in EU decision-making processes and the more remote would be the EU institutions. At the same time, 'widening' carries with it the need to better specify Community rules in order to accommodate much larger numbers of state representatives within European institutions, and therefore lead to more 'deepening'.

In particular, during the preparatory phase of accession, the term proximity was coined to convey both the efforts to reach out to the prospective member states (and regions) by creating links and networks of co-operation and to signify the need to make structural policy more visible and comprehensible to the citizens of the regions. Once more, an attempt was made to overcome the legitimate fear that enlargement would harm the poorer regions of the current EU 15, which would have been undercut by eastern competition, without necessarily allowing them to seize this opportunity to redirect investment abroad to exploit cheaper labour costs. Again the idea was that of creating functional interdependencies to make enlargement more profitable for everyone.

Competitiveness and the re-launch of European integration

Lastly, one of the major outcomes of the debate that led to the Lisbon Strategy (2000) was that the objective of the European Union was to make the European economy into the 'most competitive knowledge-based economy in the world'. The structural funds have been reinterpreted in that vein, though emphasis has shifted from structural, fixed investment to human, knowledge-based investment. The Lisbon target seems very far away and very hard to reach. What is more realistic for the structural funds is to keep the process of European integration going, catering particularly to the structural needs of both the past and future enlargement countries. Beyond the CEECs, attention is already turning to the Balkans, the Caucasus and North Africa. For the Balkans in particular, the interest of the EU to pacify the area, encourage development, secure human rights and promote democracy is very real and present. In some ways, it looks as if the EU has come full circle back to its initial goal: 'peace and prosperity' or, rather, 'peace through prosperity' and 'prosperity through peace'. Programmes like CARDS are directly aimed at securing regional peace as a pre-condition for economic take-off. If the experience of the fifteen could be replicated in the twelve new member states and the eight or so prospective candidates, then the structural funds might be considered to be a real success story.

The inter-regional dimension of structural policy – particularly Community Initiatives like INTERREG and URBAN – should not be underestimated. Despite being a less visible feature of intervention, the sustained effort by the Commission to encourage the creation of cross-border links at the regional and municipal, rather than at the national level, deserves attention. These initiatives may in fact be interpreted as a conscious attempt at creating those functional spillovers that some believe drive European integration. This regional 'para-diplomacy' (Keating and Aldecoa, 1999) may quietly resolve questions that, if tackled at the national level, are likely to get mixed up in complicated diplomatic relations and never resolved. The realisation of an 'ever closer union' may indeed be better fostered by working at the periphery rather than at the centre. This, too, is a way of promoting European integration. Indeed, whenever vetoes by member states seem to block the integration process, the Commission seeks strategic alliances with lower level actors, be they regions, interest groups, language minorities or future member states.

Reflections

Are the structural funds a success story? The answer is not easy. They have served many goals, but an overall assessment is difficult. I will try to do so by regrouping the many goals analysed above into three main categories: economic and social cohesion (the explicit policy goals), and administrative and political cohesion (the implicit polity and politics objectives).

Economic and social cohesion (policy). In some countries, structural funds were clearly instrumental in spurring or sustaining a real developmental take-off (Ireland, Spain, Portugal) that would probably have taken much longer without their contribution. In other countries, results were rather disappointing and the funds appeared like a patch on a bad sore for which other cures are necessary (this seems to be the case still for Italy, Greece, and perhaps some of the newer member states).[10] It is in general very difficult to separate the economic impact of a specific measure from all

10 On the impact of regional policy in different member states, see Bache (1998), Börzel (2002), Gualini (2004).

other relevant variables and give it a specific weight. Would Ireland have developed so spectacularly had it not received structural funds and Cohesion Fund monies? It is difficult to say, but certainly the combined effect of the structural funds and the Cohesion Fund has underpinned a growth spurt which was probably founded on domestic factors.

Administrative cohesion (polity). By this term I mean the attempt to bring the administrative (governmental) capacities of all regions to a similar level and the diffusion of a 'European way of doing things' across regions and policies. Here, too, the picture is mixed. Some regions did learn and imported EU standards and procedures into their overall programming. Others clearly dragged their feet, feigned ignorance or simply ignored the possibilities. However, exposure to EU administrative methods has at least alerted all regions to the importance of certain practices, such as programming, partnership and evaluation (Piattoni, 2003, 2006). Multi-level governance has developed into a new mode of governance for all those policies where several territorial jurisdictions are fundamentally involved.

Political cohesion (politics). Has a sense of European citizenship been infused in all EU member states? Did regions succeed in bringing EU institutions closer to the citizenry? Are people aware of the existence of the structural funds and appreciate their redistributive effects? Unfortunately, with the notable exception of some countries and despite the Commission's ability in coining evocative terms, the structural funds are often unknown to the wider population who are simply not aware of the amount of money coming from the EU to certain infrastructural or developmental projects. They are even less aware of being citizens of a larger political entity rather than their nation state or region.

So, are there any criteria according to which the structural funds may be considered as a success? I believe so. The first and most evident is that they have been institutionalised and entrenched as one of the main items on the EU budget. Every member state has taken something from them, probably more so than the common agricultural policy. Many of the terms that have emerged from structural action – subsidiarity, partnership, cohesion, proximity – have become part of our vocabulary and of the cognitive maps with which we analyse and evaluate EU policymaking. The second criterion of success is that the structural funds have helped European integration along by serving, at different points in time, as an insurance against market uncertainties, a device for unblocking decisional traps, a focal point for decision-making, a lever to foster democratic stabilisation, a new mode of governance. In a word, if European integration has come a long way, both in terms of deepening and in terms of widening, it is due to some degree to the structural funds.

References

Anderson, J. (1991). Skeptical reflections on a Europe of the regions: Britain Germany and the ERDF. *Journal of Public Policy, 10 (4),* pp.417-47.

Bache, I. (1998). *The Politics of European Union Regional Policy. Multi-level Governance or Flexible Gatekeeping?* Sheffield, Sheffield Academic Press.

Bache, I. (1999). The Extended Gatekeeper: Central Government and the Implementation of EC Regional Policy in the UK. *Journal of European Public Policy, 6 (1),* pp.28-45.

Bache, I. and Jones, R. (2000). Has EU Regional Policy Empowered the Regions? A Study of Spain and the United Kingdom. *Regional and Federal Studies, 10 (3),* pp.1-20.

Bache, I. and Flinders, M. (Eds.) (2004). *Multi-Level Governance.* Oxford: Oxford University Press.

Bomberg, E. and Peterson, J. (1998). European Union Decision Making: The Role of Sub-national Authorities. *Political Studies, 46,* pp.219-235.

Börzel, T. (2002). *States and Regions in the European Union. Institutional Adaptation in Germany and Spain.* Cambridge: Cambridge University Press.

Bourne, A. (2003). The Impact of European Integration on Regional Power. *Journal of Common Market Studies, 41 (4),* pp.597-620.

Brunazzo, M. and Piattoni, S. (2004). Negotiating the Regulation on the structural funds: Italian Actors in EU Regional Policy-making. *Modern Italy, 9 (2),* pp.159-72.

Bullman, U. (Ed.) (1996). The Politics of the Third Level (special issue). *Regional and Federal Studies, 6 (3),* pp.3-219.

Bukowski, J., Piattoni, S. and Smyrl, M. (Eds.) (2003). *Between Europeanization and Local Societies. The Space for Territorial Governance.* Lanham: Rowman and Littlefield.

Christiansen, T. (1996). Second Thoughts on Europe's 'Third Level': The European Union's Committee of the Regions. *Publius: The Journal of Federalism, 26 (1)*, pp.93-114.

Commission of the European Communities (1973). *Report of the Regional Problems in the Enlarged Community (Thomson Report).* (COM (73) 550 final). Brussels: European Commission.

Commission of the European Communities (1988). *Research on the "Cost of Non-Europe": Basic Findings (Ceccini Report).* Luxembourg: Office for the Official Publications of the European Communities. (see also Cecchini, P. (1988). *The European Challenge: 1992.* Aldershot: Wildwood House).

Commission of the European Communities (2001). *White Paper: European Governance.* (COM (2001) 428). Brussels: European Commission.

Du Granrut, C. (1994). *Europe, le temps des regions.* Paris: LGDJ.

Flora, P., Kuhnle, S. and Urwin, D. (Eds.) (1999). *State Formation, Nation Building and Mass Politics in Western Europe. The Theory of Stein Rokkan Based on His Collected Works.* Oxford: Oxford University Press.

Giuliani, M. and Piattoni, S. (2001). Italy: Both Leader and Laggard. In E. E. Zeff and E. B. Pirro (Eds.), *The European Union and the Member States. Cooperation, Coordination and Compromise* (pp.115-142). Boulder: Lynne Rienner.

Giuliani, M. and Piattoni, S. (2006). Italy: Back to the Future or Steps Towards Normality? In E. B. Pirro and E. E. Zeff (Eds.), *The European Union and the Member States. Cooperation, Coordination and Compromise* (pp.85-106). Boulder: Lynne Rienner.

Gualini, E. (2004). *Multi-Level Governance and Institutional Change. The Europeanization of Regional Policy in Italy.* Aldershot: Ashgate.

Heinelt, H. et al. (2003). Policy-Making in Fragmented Systems: How to Explain Success. In B. Kohler-Koch (Ed.), *Linking EU and National Governance* (pp.135-153). Oxford: Oxford University Press.

Hooghe, L. (Ed.) (1996). *Cohesion Policy and European Integration, Building Multi-Level Governance*. Oxford: Clarendon.

Hooghe, L. (1995). Sub-national Mobilization in the European Union. *West European Politics, 18 (3),* pp.175-198.

Hooghe, L. and Marks, G. (1996). 'Europe with the Regions': Channels of Regional Representation in the European Union. *Publius: The Journal of Federalism, 26 (1),* pp.73-91.

Hooghe, L. and Marks, G. (2001). *Multi-Level Governance and European Integration.* Lanham: Rowman and Littlefield.

Inglehart, R. (1977). *The Silent Revolution. Changing Values and Political Styles among Western Publics.* Princeton: Princeton University Press.

Jeffery, C. (1995). Whither the Committee of the Regions? Reflections on the Committee's 'Opinion of the Revision of the Treaty on European Union'. *Regional and Federal Studies, 5 (2),* pp.247-57.

Jeffery, C. (2000). Sub-National Mobilization and European Integration: Does It Make Any Difference? *Journal of Common Market Studies, 38 (1),* pp.1-23.

Keating, M. and Hooghe, L. (1996). By-passing the Nation State? Regions and the EU Policy Process. In J. Richardson (Ed.), *European Union: Power and Policy-Making* (pp.216-229). London: Routledge.

Keating, M. (1998). *The New Regionalism in Western Europe. Territorial Restructuring and Political Change.* Cheltenham: Edward Elgar.

Keating, M. and Aldecoa, F. (Eds.) (1999). *Paradiplomacy in action: The Foreign Relations of Subnational Governments.* Portland: Frank Cass.

Keynes, J. M. (1919). *The Economic Consequences of the Peace.* London: Macmillan.

Loughlin, J. (1996). 'Europe of the Regions' and the Federalization of Europe. *Publius: The Journal of Federalism, 26 (4),* pp.141-62.

Marks, G. (1992). Structural Policy in the European Community. In A. Sbragia (Ed.), *Euro-politics. Institutions and Policymaking in the 'New European Community'* (pp.191-225). Washington, DC: The Brookings Institution.

Marks, G. (1993). Structural Policy and Multi-Level Governance in the EC. In A. Cafruny and G. Rosenthal (Eds.), *The State of the European Community. Vol. 2, The Maastricht Debates and Beyond* (pp.391-410). Boulder: Lynne Rienner.

Marks, G. (1996). An Actor-Centred Approach to Multi-Level Governance. *Regional and Federal Studies, 6 (2),* pp.20-40.

Marks, G. and Hooghe, L. (2003). Unravelling the Central State, but How? Types of Multi-Level Governance. *American Political Science Review, 97 (2),* pp.233-43.

McAleavy, P. (1993). The Politics of European Regional Development Policy: Additionality in the Scottish Coalfields. *Regional Politics and Policy, 3 (2),* pp.88-107.

McAleavey, P. (1995). European Regional Development Fund Expenditure in the UK: From Additionality to 'Subtractionality'. *European Urban and Regional Studies, 2 (3),* pp.249-53.

Piattoni, S. (2003). Regioni a statuto speciale e politica di coesione. Cambiamenti interistituzionali e risposte regionali. In S. Fabbrini (Ed.), *L'europeizzazione dell'Italia. L'impatto dell'Unione Europea sulle istituzioni e le politiche italiane* (pp.108-138). Roma/Bari: Laterza.

Piattoni, S. (2005). La 'governance multi-livello': sfide analitiche, empiriche, normative. *Rivista Italiana di Scienza Politica, 35 (3),* pp.417-45.

Piattoni, S. (2006). National and Local Governments: Institutional Rebuilding and Politics in the Balkans. In B. Dallago (Ed.), *Transformation and European Integration. The Local Dimension* (pp.45-63). Houndmills: Palgrave.

Pollack, M. (1995). Regional Actors in an Intergovernmental Play: The Making and Implementation of EC Structural Policy. In C. Rhodes and S. Mazey (Eds.), *The State of the European Unon. Vol 3: Building a European Polity.* Boulder: Harlow.

Rhodes, M. (Ed.) (1995). *The Regions and the New Europe. Patterns in Core and Periphery Development.* Manchester: Manchester University Press.

Sabatier, P. A. (2007). *Theories of the Policy Process.* Boulder: Westview Press.

Sabel, C. (1988). The Re-emergence of Regional Economies. Mimeograph.

Tömmel, I. (1992). Decentralization of Regional Development Policies in the Netherlands. A New Type of State Intervention? *West European Politics, 15 (2),* pp.107-125.

Warleigh, A. (1999). *The Committee of the Regions. Institutionalising Multi-Level Governance?* London: Kogan Page.

Wishlade, F. (1996). EU Cohesion Policy: Facts, Figures and Issues. In L. Hooghe (Ed.), *Cohesion Policy and European Integration: Building Multi-Level Governance* (pp.27-58). Oxford: Clarendon.

Structural Funds and Institutional Design: Policy Learning and Adaptation in Cohesion Countries*

Panagiotis Getimis, Leeda Demetropoulou and Christos J. Paraskevopoulos

Introduction: Europeanisation and Domestic Institutional Change

Contemporary studies on EU public policy-making and the associated academic debate about governance in the EU are currently concentrated on the interactions between the Europeanisation of public policy on the one hand and the domestic structures of the member states on the other. Given the Europeanisation of the structures, cultures and processes of public policy-making, accompanied by the emergence of a more pluralistic policy environment at the EU level, it is difficult to identify any field of public policy, which is not subject to some degree of EU influence (Mazey and Richardson, 1993; Scharpf, 1994; Goldsmith, 1993). On the other hand, the size of the Commission's "adolescent bureaucracy" (Mazey and Richardson, 1993: 10) is considered to be relatively small, with regard to EU policy objectives (Goldsmith, 1993). In that respect, the establishment of a distinct regional policy at the EU level in the 1980s has been viewed as an innovative, redistributive instrument with a potential impact on the socio-economic cohesion of the EU (Mitsos, 2001).

Obviously, this trend is linked to the *problematique* of governance in the EU, whereby the member states are facing the challenge to adapt their institutional and policy-making structures to the EU multi-layered policy-making environment. In particular, the notion of 'multi-level governance' (MLG) in the EU (Marks, 1993; Kohler-Koch, 1996; Caporaso, 1996; Marks *et al.,* 1996; Bache and Flinders, 2004) implies that sub-regional, regional, national and supranational authorities interact with each other in two ways: first, over different levels of government (vertical dimension); and, second, with other relevant actors at the same level (horizontal dimension). Although it could be argued that this system of governance might merely reflect the multiplicity of the governance structures in the member states, the multilevel system of governance in the EU is said to be an outcome of the Europeanisation of public policy-making. Given, however, that the notion of Europeanisation can have several meanings and refer to a wide variety of processes, (that is historical, cultural, institutional) (Featherstone, 2003) there is therefore a need for

---

* This paper draws on the research outcomes of ADAPT, an EU 5th Framework Programme-financed comparative study of the impact of Europeanisation on domestic institutional and policy change in cohesion and CEE countries, completed in autumn 2003.

definition/clarification. In the context of public policy-making, Europeanisation is primarily viewed as a process of institutional and policy adaptation as a response to EU policies, but also as the process by which national policies are transferred up to the European level and become the objective of collective decision-making processes (Paraskevopoulos and Leonardi, 2004). Thus, the Europeanisation process refers to the complementary notions of opening up the structures of the traditional nation state to informal and formal rules stemming from the supranational level, and, consequently, to their adaptation to the EU multi-level system of governance. In this respect, the Europeanisation of public policy constitutes an enduring and long-standing challenge to the administrative structures of the member states and hence it is viewed as a positive external shock for promoting institution building, learning and policy-making innovation at the domestic (national and sub-national) levels of government.

In regional policy in particular - and especially in the case of Greece and other cohesion countries - Europeanisation is viewed as an *independent variable* that crucially affects and challenges well established structures within the domestic systems of governance and plays an important role in the administrative restructuring and devolution processes within member states by enhancing institutional capacity at the sub-national level. In particular, its impact on regional and local policy-making is supposed to be twofold: a direct one, by providing increased resources through redistribution and a new set of rules and procedures for the formulation and implementation of development policies; and an indirect one, by shaping intra-regional interactions and thus promoting local institutional capacity through the creation of intra-, inter- and trans-regional networks that support local development initiatives.

Given the complexity of the multi-level governance structures within which the adaptation process takes place and the distinctive character of the policy-making structures at the EU level,[1] however, the degree of '*adaptational pressures*' facing the domestic institutions and policy-making structures in order to comply with European rules and regulations in public policy in general and regional policy in particular, is particularly high in unitary and centralised states like Greece and other cohesion countries. Nevertheless, the presence of a high degree of adaptational pressure constitutes a necessary but not sufficient condition for domestic institutional and policy change. Indeed, there is evidence to suggest that the latter is crucially conditioned by the presence of specific institutional structures at the domestic level of governance that may facilitate or inhibit the adaptation process (Börzel and Risse, 2000; Paraskevopoulos, 1998b, 2001a,b). In other words, although the Europeanisation process plays a key role in the transformation of the domestic systems of governance in general and the public/regional policy-making structures in particular, domestic

1 Although significant variation from one policy area to another is seen as a main feature of the EU policy-making structures and practices, it has been argued that the EU institutional structure is more federal than unitary and its policy-making processes more pluralist than statist (Schmidt, 1997). In that respect, it has been predicted that the more centralised and unitary member states are likely to face stronger adaptational pressures than decentralised and federal ones (ibid.).

institutions and especially specific features of the pre-existing institutional infrastructure at the national and sub-national levels of government do matter for adaptation (Garmise, 1995; Lenschow, 1997; Jeffery, 2000; Paraskevopoulos, 1998b, 2001a,b; Risse *et al.*, 2001; Börzel, 2001; Keating *et al.*, 2003). In that respect, specific features of pre-existing institutional structures at the domestic level of government constitute a crucial *intervening variable* between Europeanisation and domestic policy and institutional change (*dependent variable*) that can account for the pace of the adaptation process.

There are two kinds of mediating mechanisms/logics in the new institutionalist literature that can account for domestic institutional and policy change as a response to Europeanisation: rational choice and the sociological approach (see *inter alia* Börzel and Risse, 2000). The former is based on the *'logic of consequentialism'* and points to the role of redistribution of resources and a consequent differential empowerment of actors at the domestic level. Thus, it conceives of important institutions for the domestic policy-making arena, the presence of *multiple veto points* and existing *formal institutions* as crucial mediating factors that affect domestic actors' capacity for action and hence policy and institutional change. This process has been conceptualized as *'single-loop learning'* (Argyris and Schőn, 1978), whereby actors acquire new information and alter strategies but pursue given, fixed interests. The latter focuses on the process of *social learning* as a fundamental mechanism of domestic change. It identifies *networks* (either epistemic communities, or advocacy and/or issue-specific) and *informal institutions*, namely political and organisational cultures and social norms, as 'thick' mediating mechanisms that affect actors' preferences through the '*logic of appropriateness'*, leading to the re-conceptualisation of their interests and identities, thereby facilitating learning and socialisation processes (Risse *et al.*, 2001; Checkel, 2001). In other words, the process of social learning emphasises the importance of largescale participation in the policy-making process by a wide variety of social actors, i.e. civil society, private sector etc. In this theoretical framework, the role of experts as agents of policy change is crucial through their increased capacity for the diffusion of new information and knowledge (Hall, 1993; Checkel, 1999). On the other hand, informal conventions, namely social norms, play a key role as 'glue providers' for the re-stabilisation of the relations between actors involved in the learning process (see Sabel, 1994; Paraskevopoulos, 1998a,b; 2001a,b). Thus, *'single loop'* learning is significantly affected by the intended and unintended consequences[2] of the redistribution of power and resources between the supranational, national and sub-national levels of government within the EU, and subsequently by the degree of decentralisation and administrative restructuring of

2 The impact of the 1988 reforms of the structural funds on the redistribution of power between the levels of government, by strengthening the role of the sub-national level and establishing direct linkages between supranational, national and sub-national authorities through their role in managing and monitoring Operational Programmes (OPs) of the Community Support Frameworks (CSFs) may be seen as a characteristic case of unintended consequences initiated by institutional or policy reforms at the EU level. Moreover, the core of these reforms remained unchanged even after the 1993 reforms put forward after the negotiations over the 1994-99 structural funds programme (see Pollack, 1995).

the state. *Social learning*, on the other hand, implies a continuous loop of interaction in that compliance with EU policy-making norms and regulations is achieved through the transformation of actors' identities and interests that changes in the broad institutional environment bring about (Checkel 2001). Obviously, this differentiation corresponds to the broader distinction (within the academic debate about how 'paradigm change' occurs in public policy) between *interests*, *ideas/norms* and *institutions* as fundamental conceptual tools/variables affecting change in public policy styles in general (Hood, 1994, 1998; Rose, 1993, 2002). In that respect, the evidence from Greece and other cohesion countries, suggests that, however important the role of formal institutional structures and multiple veto points may be, they do not seem to seriously impede policy change. What, arguably, matters for the learning process in regional policy in these countries is the presence of an administrative capacity at the domestic level of governance and involvement in the policy-making process of networks of non-state actors, such as independent experts and/or the private sector, and informal norms, namely social capital, conducive to the building of co-operative culture (see Paraskevopoulos, 1998a,b; 2001a,b; Paraskevopoulos and Leonardi, 2004).

Overall, the process of Europeanisation of the systems of governance in regional policy plays a crucial role in shaping public/private relations and promoting networking at the regional and local levels. Hence, its impact on endogenous local development capacity is twofold: a direct one, by providing increased resources, and an indirect one, by shaping intra-regional interactions and thus promoting the creation of intra-, inter- and trans regional networks that support local development initiatives. However, it is important to emphasise that the Europeanisation of regional policy itself is not a "homogeneous" and "cohesive" process in which "highly integrated policy networks" create organised feedback loops (Marks, 1993; Heinelt *et al.*, 2003). On the contrary, there is evidence of organisational and functional differentiation at all levels of governance (EU, national, regional, local), which enables actors' participation, institutional innovation and organisational learning and adaptation. It should be stressed, however, that there is a danger of fragmentation of regional policy in specific policy areas, programmes and projects. The forms of this inter- and intra-organisational differentiation, as well as the forms of the cohesion mechanism that try to avoid fragmentation and separation, vary from country to country (Kohler-Koch, 2005). This is consistent with the existing distinction in the literature between two types of MLG, whereby Type I is mostly associated with the traditional 'state-centric' approach to governance and the concept of 'Europe of the Regions' as its institutional blueprint, whereas Type II identifies more closely with the emergence of task-specific, flexible and temporary institutional innovations, focused primarily on the implementation of the structural funds, such as policy networks (Hooghe and Marks, 2001). Thus evaluation of the institution-building process should constitute an integral part of the overall evaluation of the impact of structural funds programmes.

This chapter evaluates the history of the "structural funds-induced" transformation of the institutional infrastructure at both the national and sub-national levels of government and the learning capacity of the pre-existing structures in three cohesion states: Greece, Ireland and Portugal. In particular, it focuses on the capacity for institutional innovation which may be facilitated by the planning, implementation, monitoring and evaluation procedures of the Community Support Frameworks (CSFs), that is by the Europeanisation of structural policy in general. It also discusses the current trends in the reformed EU structural policy, which emphasise the role of institution building as an intrinsic element of the policy-making process in both the cohesion and the new CEE member states.

European Regional Policy and Institutional Change in Greece

Greece's entry into the EC/EU in 1981 coincided with a major change in Greek politics: the coming to power of the first PASOK (Pan Hellenic Socialist Movement) government. Thus, the period of Greece's response to the challenge of adjustment to the new European environment in the 1980s was marked by the presence of a new, socialist government, which came into power with a strong commitment to decentralisation, devolution of power and encouragement of civic participation in the policy-making process. In that respect, the initiation of the EU's Integrated Mediterranean Programmes (IMPs) in the mid 1980s marked a departure from a project-oriented and sectoral towards a programme-oriented and integrated approach to development thereby fuelling the formation of a coherent EU regional policy. This coincided with and gave impetus to the reform of the system of centre-periphery relations, involving - formally at least - decentralisation of power, extensive institution building and experimentation with new (for Greece) forms of civic participation in the policy process[3] (Mitsos, 2001; Paraskevopoulos, 1998b, 2001b). With the introduction of the first CSF in 1989 a coherent regional policy was further strengthened with the adoption of a multi-annual programming approach and the introduction of the concepts of partnership, additionality, proportionality and subsidiarity as dominant policy principles (Paraskevopoulos, 2001b). In Greece, despite the experience of the IMPs, the introduction of the CSFs brought about a completely new policy environment that actors had to cope with, especially in the areas of policy planning and implementation. This new environment was characterised by a system of multi-level planning, involving sectoral programmes at a national scale (the national component) and Regional Operational Programmes (ROPs) for each of the thirteen regions of Greece, as well as, by innovative (for Greece) institutions for actors' participation in policy-making at each level of government, such as the Monitoring Committees of the Operational Programmes (CEC, 1989, 1993). However, although, undoubtedly, both the IMPs and the first CSF functioned as catalysts for the development of a

3 Institution building involved the creation of thirteen administrative regions in 1986 and an elected second tier of sub-national government at the prefectural level in 1994.

plethora of new institutions at the sub-national level, such as development agencies, and/or for the upgrading of existing institutions, the weakness of the overall institutional infrastructure, marked by the role of clientelism in the policy process, led to poor policy outcomes (Paraskevopoulos, 2001b). In the unfavourable political climate of the early 1990s, accompanied by the deterioration of the macro-economic situation and the intense pressure to meet the Maastricht criteria in order to qualify for joining the EMU, an increased concern for accelerating the pace of development as a way of catching up with other member states appeared to be gaining ground in domestic policy discourse. This trend was underpinned by arguments about the generally bad condition of almost any sector of the country's physical infrastructure, as well as, by reference to what other comparable cohesion countries, notably Portugal and Ireland, had already done or were doing. In fact, there was a widespread feeling that the funds of the first CSF, having been dispersed on several small-scale, regional projects across the country, had had much less impact than they would have had if they had concentrated on large-scale infrastructure projects. However, it should be stressed that this was a tacit knowledge-based and not expertise-informed debate. Nonetheless, the issue of transparency and efficiency came to the fore and crucially influenced the planning and implementation processes of both the second and third CSFs. This shift in the policy process from emphasis on participation towards taking economies of scale seriously and therefore towards large-scale infrastructure projects undoubtedly led to a significant improvement of infrastructure in crucial areas where the country was lagging behind. It seems, however, that some kind of recentralisation of policy-making accompanied this shift.

In particular, the emphasis on large-scale projects was accompanied by significant institutional creation, in order to strengthen the capacity of the central state administrative structure, especially of the Ministry of National Economy. Moreover, this trend towards improving central state administrative capacity also reflected increased concern by the EU Commission about the role of the central state bureaucracy in the management of the funds, as became clear with the 1999 regulation of the funds. Thus, the need to allocate responsibilities for planning, management, payment and evaluation led to enhancement of the role of the relevant administrative/political institutions (the central administration of the Ministry of National Economy, the General Secretary, the Minister), as well as to the creation of new institutions, such as the Managing Organisation Unit (MOU), the Managing Authorities for the implementation of the Operational Programmes, the Paying Authority and the Committee of Fiscal Control (Getimis and Demetropoulou, 2004). This trend seems to have led to some sort of reluctant involvement of technocrats (independent consultants, experts) in policy-making and implementation at both the national and sub-national levels of administration (see below). The creation of new municipalities through the compulsory merger of the communes (the so called 'Kapodistrias Plan') in 1997 can be seen as another step in the same direction, namely improving levels of efficiency.

Additionally, emphasis on large-scale infrastructure projects and the subsequent increase of the share of the sectoral/national component of the second and third CSF has also led to an overall increase in the share of private sector involvement in and contribution to the projects, especially at the national level (see Table 1). This involvement, however, although it undoubtedly constitutes a major innovation in terms of public policy-making in Greece, has taken the form of either public-private partnerships (PPPs) and/or concession agreements and is mostly concentrated on large-scale projects and of Europe wide significance.[4]

Table 1: Share of the Private Sector as a Percentage of Total Expenditure (Public and Private) and Community Share as a Percentage of Public Expenditure (Community and National) in the National and Regional Components of CSFs

	Percentage of private sector to total share expenditure		Community share as percentage of public expenditure	
	National component	Regional component	National component	Regional component
CSF I (1989-93)	9.1	7.1	47.1	62.9
CSF II (1994-99)	32.5	19.7	62.9	75.0
CSF III (2000-06)	28.0	13.6	63.5	75.3

Source: Andrikopoulou and Kalkalas, 2003.

The creation of the Managing Organisation Unit and the Joint Steering Committee (JSC) constitute the main institutional innovations involving the use of expertise in the policy process. The MOU is a support mechanism, operating under the guidance and control of the Ministry of National Economy, but external to its civil service structure. The Unit's role is to support public administration by covering specific needs in highly specialised human resources and know-how for the successful implementation of the CSF Operational Programmes that exceed the technical and administrative capacity of the implementing authorities (i.e. organisation of the Man-

4 Such projects include the Athens Airport, the Attiki Odos (*Athens peripheral ring road*), the Attiko Metro (*Athens Underground*), the Rion-Antirion Bridge, and the Egnatia Odos (*Egnatia Motorway*). As for efficiency in policy implementation, however, measured by targets achieved, there is evidence to suggest that with the exception of the projects involving some sort of public-private partnerships (PPPs), Greece lags behind the other cohesion states (CEC, 2001).

aging Authorities, selection and training of personnel, transfer of know-how and provision of organisational tools).

The JSC was established in January 1995 in the Ministry of National Economy, as a sub-committee of the CSF Monitoring Committee, with the aim of improving the system for the development of public works. Both the Greek authorities and the EU Commission saw such an improvement as a prerequisite for efficient realisation of the infrastructure projects of the second CSF and the Cohesion Fund. The Committee focused on three broad areas relating to the development of public works: studies for public projects and planning; the contracting system, including calls for tenders; and the construction of public works. In that respect, a wide range of experts on these issues were directly or indirectly involved in the work of the Committee. There had been two major problems relating to the development of public works in Greece that the Committee tried to deal with: the problem of the so-called 'unusually low/abnormal prices' of public works; and quality control. On the former, a major comparative study, involving France, Germany, Spain, Belgium and the UK, was carried out in an attempt to draw lessons from elsewhere in Europe. Much of this investigation was concentrated on the pros and cons of the famous 'mathematic method' (the so called 'mathimatikos typos'-'μαθηματικός τύπος') for dealing with the issue of abnormal prices. On the problem of quality control, the Committee concentrated on making recommendations for improvement of the function of the External Consultant for Quality Control of Infrastructure Projects (ESPEL), which was established in 1996. On other areas, the Committee was particularly active in relation to concession agreements, the Private Finance Initiative (PFI) and PPP contracts.

In sum, there have been positive developments in respect of the involvement of non-state actors (the private sector and experts) in the policy process and the learning capacity of the domestic policy environment in general, especially since the mid 1990s. However, given that there is no evidence of extensive private sector involvement elsewhere in the policy process, i.e. the ROPs (see Paraskevopoulos and Leonardi, 2004), this may be sporadic and limited only to large-scale infrastructure projects. On the other hand, the involvement of experts, although significant, does not take the form of independent thinktanks, but is based on recruitment to or under the guidance of specific ministries. In addition, Greece's institutional infrastructure is characterised by a low level of social capital and weakness in civil society which is particularly evident in the low level of social trust and trust in public institutions (see Paraskevopoulos, 2005; Paraskevopoulos *et al.*, 2006). This is accompanied by limited and not fully institutionalised fora for dialogue and negotiation, a low presence of PPPs, the dominance of political parties (the so called partitocracy) and clientelism in the policy process and a relatively strong resistance to change closely linked to patterns of interest intermediation. In that respect, statism, namely the centralised, weak administrative structure, has been the main characteristic of the formal institutional infrastructure in public policy in general and in regional policy in particular, with serious implications for the learning capacity of the domestic institutional infrastructure.

Overall, contradictory trends in centre-periphery relations and institutional innovation are the main features of the incremental character of the impact of Europeanisation on domestic policy and institutional change in Greece. On the one hand, structural funds regulations and norms have opened up the process of institutional restructuring at the regional level; on the other hand, the tendency of the pre-existing institutional infrastructure towards centralisation continues to play a key role in the planning and implementation processes of regional policy. Thus, despite the fact that the strengthening of existing institutions and the creation of new ones are widely considered as the main outcomes of the learning process, this strengthening and development of institutions still remains a key challenge for public policy in Greece within the EU MLG structure. Indeed, institution building was significantly absent from the democratisation/Europeanisation agenda during both the first post-authoritarian (1974-81) and, most importantly, the first post-accession (1981-1986) periods. Changes were introduced in 1986 to Greece's statist structure through the introduction of the thirteen administrative regions and in 1994 with the creation of the directly elected prefectural councils. Subsequent changes were also made through the 1997 reorganisation of local government. On the management of the structural funds, Greece has experimented with the introduction of expertise from outside of the administrative structure and has used new approaches for the implementation of cohesion policies (see Paraskevopoulos and Leonardi, 2004).

European Regional Policy and Institutional Change in Ireland

EC membership is seen to have underpinned Ireland's economic success, although a more nuanced account would need to consider a range of other factors, including a succession of corporatist partnership agreements, growth-oriented policies, budgetary austerity in the late 1980s, an inflow of foreign direct investment and the internal market programme. Nonetheless, EC funding, especially from the structural funds, contributed significantly to Ireland's economic growth during the 1990s. Thus, by 2001 GDP per head in Ireland (in terms of Purchasing Power Standards-PPS) was 17 per cent above the EU15 average (CEC, 2004: 2), while simulations indicate that between 1991 and 2002 growth was 2.8 per cent above what it would have been without structural interventions (*op. cit.*, 148). However, regional disparities have not lessened as a result of spending, and recent Central Statistical Office figures suggest that they may even have been growing (see Rees *et al.*, 2004; Rees and Paraskevopoulos, 2006).

Yet EC funding brought not only increased resources but also induced change in Ireland's institutional structures and patterns of governance; in other words, it has significantly influenced the process of the so-called 'Ireland's pragmatic adaptation to Europeanisation' (Rees *et al.*, 2004). Indeed, although the early years of Ireland's membership were marked by low adaptational pressure in regional policy with the state apparatus remaining highly centralised during the 1970s and early 1980s and the Departments of Finance and the Environment acting as the main interlocutors with the Commission and its services, adaptational pressure increased during the late 1980s and throughout the 1990s. Clearly, this trend was brought about by the fundamental shift in EU regional policy from the largely European Regional Development Fund (ERDF)-based funding to national governments on the basis of pre-agreed quotas and indicative ranges, towards the multi-annual programming approach adopted by the structural fund reforms, which led successive Irish governments to work with the EC in formulating national development plans. In this way, the Europeanisation process has impacted in a variety of ways on Ireland's national policy-making processes.[5] There has been an intertwining of domestic and EC policy-making and EC business has been successfully grafted onto the normal business of the various government departments (Laffan, 2000). The type of administrative restructuring that was brought about included adaptation to the role of sectoral departments, increased co-ordination and improvements in policy mechanisms. While institution building has been manifested at the national level through the adaptation of the machinery of central government, and at the sub-national level through the creation of the eight Regional Authorities (1994) and the two Regional Assemblies (1999) following a decision to split Ireland into two regions, the Irish approach to EC policy mirrors the domestic approach to policy-making. It is based on the system of a 'lead department' with each government department managing the area of policy falling within its ambit.[6] The mechanics of policy-making have also been influenced by Europeanisation, particularly the EC's regional policy processes, while a culture of evaluation has been fostered within the administrative system with Ireland being praised for its innovation in methods of analysis. Finally, the move from annual to multi-annual budgeting is another policy-making adaptation initiated by Brussels (see Rees *et al.*, 2004; Rees and Paraskevopoulos, 2006).

With regard to the sub-national level of government, decentralisation of power and resources in Ireland has been limited. In the first two national development plans (NDPs 1989-93, 1994-99), central government departments and their regional bodies were principally responsible for the implementation of the operational programmes. The allocation of management responsibility for the two ROPs in the NDP 2000-06 to the two Regional Assemblies marks the first time that non-central

5 At the national level, a number of new institutions and procedures have been adopted over time to cope with the EU. Various civil service and Oireachtas committees have been put in place. In 2002 both an Interdepartmental Co-ordinating Committee on EU Affairs and a permanent Oireachtas sub-committee for the scrutiny of EU legislation were established. Further institutional innovations have included the establishment of a European structural funds Information Unit (1996) and the creation of a National Development Finance Agency (2003). A National Forum on Europe was established in the wake of the first referendum on the Nice Treaty and has enhanced understanding of EU issues as well as fostering discussion and debate.

6 The role of three government departments, Finance, Foreign Affairs and the Department of the Taoiseach has been enhanced and they play significant co-ordinating roles in European issues while the sectoral / line departments administer specific aspects of European business. Increased co-ordination is evident in policy-making with a consequent diminution in the sectoral approach.

government bodies have been given specific responsibility for such programmes. However, the power that has been given to the Regional Assemblies is restricted and their resource base is quite limited. Additionally, the process of Europeanisation has done little to increase the power of Irish local authorities, although their resources have been enhanced by the financial opportunities inherent in some regional policy interventions. The fact that Ireland was regarded as a single region until 1999 and structural funds money was dispersed via national government indicates the importance of central authority (Keogh, 1994; O'Donnell, 2000).

Moreover, Ireland's adaptation to Europe has led to the emergence and adoption of various mechanisms, including partnerships, increased private participation and changed patterns of interest mediation. Ireland's social partnership model, which emerged in response to the national economic and social problems of the 1980s, has been reinforced by involvement in EC affairs. The strong emphasis on partnership incorporated in EC regional policy since 1988 has reinforced and supported the consensual approach to policy-making in Ireland and has legitimised and entrenched the culture of concertation at both national and local levels. The partnership approach at sub-national level has promoted a territorial rather than a sectoral approach. Furthermore, EC structural funds and interventions such as the LEADER programmes have added financial and authoritative impetus to the local partnerships, which emerged as part of the 'bottom-up' development process. The networks of local partnerships involved in the delivery of EC regional policy programmes are also significant (e.g. Comhar LEADER na hÉireann and Area Development Management Ltd.). These bodies serve to bring the constituent groups together to address shared needs and opportunities and to participate to some extent in agenda-setting and policy-making. Within such a policy environment, involvement in EC programmes since the late 1980s, as well as the practices and procedures required by the Brussels bureaucracy, have combined with the nationally promoted partnership approach to involve a wide range of actors in policy-making. Consultation with the wider public has also become the norm with calls for submissions on policy areas regularly appearing in national newspapers. As part of the preparation for the 1994-99 NDP, an extensive consultation process took place involving social partners, Chambers of Commerce, the Council on the Status of Women, the eight regional authorities, as well as other actors (Fitzpatrick Associates, 2003). For the implementation phase, the range of actors involved in the policy process has widened considerably with local development bodies, private actors and NGOs playing decisive roles. The monitoring phase also involves a significant range of actors. Each Operational Programme (OP) is monitored by a Monitoring Committee comprising government officials, representatives of the European Commission, statutory agencies, the social partners and the Regional Assemblies. Independent private actors such as consultancy firms frequently carry out evaluations of policies and programmes. The widening of the range of actors in the various phases of policy-making has been influenced by but is not totally attributable to Europeanisation.

As for public/private partnerships (PPPs), there is little evidence of their formal presence for the 1994-99 period, although private contributions did form part of the investment in the productive sector and to a lesser extent in the areas of economic infrastructure and local development. In the late 1990s organisations, such as IBEC and the Construction Industry Federation, began to lobby for the introduction of PPPs as essential for the achievement of NDP objectives. It is also notable that the 1994-99 CSF did expect to include private sector expenditure of €2,428 million. However, in common with other member states, the leverage effects of structural fund interventions on private investment are perceived to have reduced for the 2000-2006 period. In 1994-1999 private funds per euro of structural fund expenditure were 0.34 per euro whereas for 2000-2006 the leverage is expected to be only 0.25 per euro (CEC, 2004: 181). In the third NDP (2000-06) it is projected that 134 PPPs will be developed over the 2000-06 period, but this is thought to be optimistic.

In sum, Ireland's formal institutional and public policy-making structure can be characterised by the Westminster model of public administration, namely centralised and relatively efficient public bureaucracy but relatively closed to input from external socio-economic groups during the initial phases of the policy. With regard to the involvement of expertise in the policy process, this takes place primarily at the central state level and takes the form of professional advice and management consultancy rather than independent thinktanks. Additionally, the domestic institutional structure in public policy in general and regional policy in particular is characterised by modest presence on the part of NGOs, albeit fragmented and limited over time, relatively high level of social capital and strong civil society, especially in relation to social trust and trust in public institutions, presence of fora for dialogue and consultation, significant presence of the private sector and PPPs and a relatively high level of resistance to change, especially at the local level.

Overall, Ireland has pragmatically learned to adapt its institutional structures in response to European pressures, albeit in a piecemeal manner, and with some resistance to change both at national and sub-national levels (Rees, 1997). The learning process in Ireland has significantly affected the centralised Westminster-like institutional and policy-making structure. However, its primary impact has been the transformation, rather than the expansion of the existing institutional structure. Thus, institutional innovation has taken place mainly at the central state level and the building of new institutions has been rather limited. Despite its relative efficiency, this institutional structure cannot be considered as favourable for the learning process. Rather, the top-down administrative hierarchy reflects Ireland's pragmatic, ad hoc and cautious stance towards the Europeanisation of policy-making (see Paraskevopoulos and Leonardi, 2004).

When Portugal joined the EC in 1986, there was no national regional policy tradition and macro-economic concerns were considered more important than addressing large regional disparities. Prior to membership, the 1974 revolution had already led to new democratic structures and the growth of elected local bodies, such as municipalities, while the constitution established three tiers of local government: parishes, municipalities and administrative regions. Nonetheless, there was some progress by the early 1980s, with an increasing Europeanisation of public administration, in preparation for membership (Magone, 2001: 121). This included adjustments to national institutional structures, increasing interaction with Brussels, and exposure of public officials to European institutions, policies and practices, all of which challenged Portuguese officials to rethink their approach to public administration and led to the establishment of regional policy as a distinctive policy area for the first time in 1984. As Magone notes 'the administration had to increase its efficiency in view of facilitating the absorption, implementation and monitoring of the structural funds' (*op cit.,* 122). The EC's regional policy, particularly the 1988 reforms and the 1993 Delors II package, increased pressure on Portugal to adapt its approach to regional development and to focus on reducing regional disparities. It also prompted a limited degree of administrative reorganisation at the national level and some deconcentration, utilising the Regional Coordinating Commissions in 1979, but otherwise EC regional policy led to little institutional change at the regional level. But, even if decentralisation did emerge as a key element for political and institutional reorganisation, the deep dualities which divide the country – coastal and inland areas, North and South, urban and rural, as well as an imbalanced distribution of resources and income - continued to favour the concentration of power and administrative bodies in the capital (Rees and Paraskevopoulos, 2006).

Yet, given that Portugal's accession coincided with the first major reform of the structural funds in 1988 and the adoption of a new programming approach to regional development based on National Development Plans and CSFs, this led to the adoption of a complex and wide ranging planning process. In essence, this meant that Portugal had to develop a regional development plan in order to prepare for access to EC structural funds.[7] Thus regional development and the management of the EC structural funds quickly became a priority for the government, reflecting the financial incentives on offer and the need to adapt to meet European policy requirements. In that respect, the RDP for 1989-93 was drawn up after consultation at the regional level, but the decision to prepare and submit a single RDP had been taken by the national government. In a similar vein, for the period 1994-99, the government strategy was to maintain EC funding while simplifying the procedures required under the 1988 reform. Work on the RDP involved participation by the different

7 The government developed an initial plan for regional development for the period 1986-90, but following negotiation with the European Commission, a revised plan, the *National Programme of Community Interest for the Productive Activity*, was agreed (Magone 2001: 126).

ministries, Regional Coordination Commissions, the autonomous regions, local authorities, figures from political, business and financial life and MEPs (Rees and Paraskevopoulos, 2006).

In this way, following EC membership, a number of institutional structures were created at the national level and incrementally adapted in response to EU requirements. The use of CSFs led to the creation of a new structure to manage, monitor, control and assess EC interventions. This was an innovative model for the administrative sector, with the creation of "parallel" bodies specifically designed to manage EC funds. The solution made it possible to decentralise the management of funds within the central administrative authorities and even include the local authorities, and to abide by the principle of partnership established in EC regulations. The institutional structure for implementation of the structural funds during the CSF for 1994-99 broadly adopted the previous model for management, monitoring, assessment and control. Under CSF III (2000-06) a new model for the management of EC funds was developed whereby each regional operational intervention covers and includes the interventions of all ministries in the region, giving the deconcentrated regional departments significantly greater responsibilities (Rees and Paraskevopoulos, 2006).

With regard to non-state actors' involvement in the policy process, there has been an incremental process in Portugal, partly reflecting a slightly stronger civil society than in Greece. At the national level, the public sector, the private sector and NGOs are all represented on the Economic and Social Council, which seeks to promote the participation of economic and social agents in the government's decision-making process. Yet, the most powerful actors remain the Ministry of Planning and the Regional Development Directorate General. Non-state actors have also been involved in the monitoring committees offering a further forum in which to discuss policy. These fora, however, provide limited opportunities for non-state actors to play a role in regional development/policy (Rees and Paraskevopoulos, 2006).

As for the involvement of expertise, experts in Portugal are largely integrated into the existing central government policy-making frameworks. For example, experts are involved on consultative councils and as part of the CSF Observatory. Government departments also use independent experts as part of the evaluation process and external experts are used in the formation of municipal development plans and urban development plans. In relation to the private sector, there is a wide range of profit and non-profit organisations but with relatively little involvement in national or regional fora. There is evidence to suggest, however, that there has been an increase in the number of entrepreneurial associations at local level. The major objective of these associations is to develop lobbying power with regard to national decision makers, namely ministries, in order to obtain financial support. Civil society in Portugal is relatively weak, with NGOs not normally involved in the development of regional policy. The exceptions would appear to be regional business associations (e.g. Leira Regional Business Association), which do play a role in the regional process. Similarly, there is some limited trade union activity, although this tends to be confined to representation on national level bodies. Lastly, agricultural development associations have developed strong links with other NGOs, municipalities and municipal associations. There have been attempts to involve non-state actors in the policy process, arising out of criticism of the first CSF where there was limited civil participation. The second CSF was preceded by a consultative process which involved business associations, trade unions, local civil associations and experts (Rees and Paraskevopoulos, 2006).

Overall, in Portugal there was limited enthusiasm for adaptation to European structures and some resistance by national and local state actors, as well as the public, to the adoption of new institutions. Portugal has met formal EC requirements, if mainly within the context of pre-existing administrative and institutional structures, with limited capacity to change further. However, the increasing role of municipal associations and the mobilisation of civil and entrepreneurial actors, undertaken by the Ministry of Planning and its bodies, has promoted the emergence of a new governance approach to policy-making. This approach emphasises the importance of social networks, civic participation and the creation of mechanisms to obtain consensus. This has been a top-down process, however, and therefore, although civil society and social capital in general are regarded as indispensable for social and economic development and effective policy implementation, in practical terms, levels of civil participation, informal networks and citizen participation and involvement in public matters are still very low. Lacking a strong civil society and facilitative environment Portugal found it difficult to adjust to EC regional policy (see Nanetti *et al.*, 2004).

In sum, EC membership did not lead to a fundamental change in the existing political system, but did lead to significant changes in the relationship between the state and the economy, and led to changes in the role of central and local authorities. New institutional attitudes and forms of behaviour have emerged in response to requirements at various levels: intra- and inter-sectoral adjustments and co-operation, public-private partnerships, public involvement and participation. At the local level, formal and informal means of association and co-operation have been created, alongside the emergence and consolidation of development associations.

Overall, French-style centralisation of policy planning, accompanied by some institutional innovation, especially at the regional and local levels, is the main feature of public policy-making structures in general, and, with some variation, in regional policy in particular. Indeed, the specific features of Portugal's policy-making structure point to: some presence of expertise in the policy process, primarily in the form of experts' associations and from the academic community rather than of independent thinktanks; relatively high level of social capital - well above Greece - especially with regard to trust in public institutions/civil service; significant presence of fora for dialogue at both the central and regional levels of government; significant presence of PPPs, especially at the regional and local levels; and significant resistance to change, primarily at the local level. In a similar vein to Greece, the learning process has resulted in significant and extensive institution building at both central and regional levels since the early 1990s.

Conclusions

The following comparative conclusions and lessons can be drawn with regard to the interaction between Europeanisation of regional policy-making on the one hand and domestic institutional and policy change in the three cohesion countries studied on the other.

First, all the participating countries are facing significant adaptational pressures, albeit to different degrees. One major variable could be the experience of authoritarianism. Although Ireland stands out vis-à-vis the other cohesion countries in terms of effectiveness and efficiency of the domestic institutional structures, it faces, along with Portugal, intense pressures towards decentralisation of policy-making. In Greece, despite the creation of formal institutional structures of territorial governance, the process of substantial institution building did not start until the mid 1990s. In sum, although it is clear that authoritarianism may matter, other crucial variables, such as administrative capacity and the pre-existing institutional infrastructure, may be more important in accounting for variation in the degree of adaptational pressures.

Second, although regionalisation has been - to varying degrees- a dominant feature of intergovernmental relations in all the cohesion countries under consideration, the gate-keeping role of the central state has remained to a great extent unchallenged. One possible explanation may be the underestimation of the crucial role of state-society relations, and particularly of civic culture and identity, as important components of the local institutional infrastructure, in the process of regionalisation and the shaping of the intergovernmental relations and the domestic governance structures at large.

Third, there seems to be a difference between Greece on the one hand, and Ireland and Portugal on the other, with regard to non-state actors' involvement in regional and public policy-making at large. In particular, Greece demonstrates generally low levels of non- state actors' participation in the policy process, which goes hand in hand with the dominant –and hence substitutive- role of political parties. On the other hand, Ireland and Portugal demonstrate a far better policy environment and hence governance structures, characterised by varying but increasing levels of non-state actors' participation in the policy process.

Fourth, there seems to be an east-west pattern in the social capital/civicness divide. In particular, Greece demonstrates a very low level of social capital, accompanied by corruption and clientelism, whilst the situation - though far from ideal - seems to be better in Ireland and Portugal.

Finally, there have been identified varying degrees of resistance to change among the participating countries, closely related to state-society relations. The most crucial is the informal norms and institutions-based resistance, especially in the case of Greece, given that it is possible that this can go hand in hand with formal compliance.

In sum, the evidence from the cohesion countries points overwhelmingly to the presence of Type II multi-level governance structures, involving ad hoc, policy-specific institutional structures in the field, (i.e. policy networks), accompanied by substantial elements of policy conflict. Additionally, with regard to the type of learning identified, it seems that the dominant pattern in the cohesion countries is that of "single-loop" learning, namely as a consequence of the redistribution of resources and hence the differentiated empowerment of actors at the domestic level of governance. In other words, there is not strong evidence of "social" learning taking place. This, however, should not preclude the presence of regional variation within or among the countries concerned.

Bearing all this in mind, the expansion of the list of the conditionality/compliance criteria to include institution building, fighting corruption and so on may be viewed as a major innovation on the part of the EU Commission, with regard to the impact of Europeanisation on domestic institutional structures. Indeed, the focus on such "soft" or "low level", but simultaneously crucial aspects of governance, initiates a break with previous waves of enlargement where negotiations were primarily dominated by key economic and/or policy issues and secondarily by general considerations (qualitative criteria) regarding the domestic socio-political system, namely functioning democracy and human rights.

This, however, should constitute an integral part of everyday public policy-making. Therefore, institution building should be identified as a main priority at both the supranational and domestic levels of governance. Relevant policy tools at the supranational and/or national levels of government could include: conditionality/compliance criteria at all phases of public policy-making (policy design, planning, implementation etc.) linked to institution building; motivation (incentives) related to institution building functions, such as network creation and fighting corruption. Overall, in policy design for regional policy, the processes of institution building, social capital creation, civil society strengthening through enhanced networking, NGO consultation and expertise involvement in the policy process should constitute the EU's key priorities.

References

Andrikopoulou, E. and Grigoris, K. (2003). Greek Regional Policy in the Context of Europeanisation: 1961-2000. In D. Dionysis and P. Argyris (Eds.), *Greece in the European Union* (pp.35-47). London: Routledge.

Argyris, C. and Schőn, D. A. (1978). *Organizational Learning.* Reading: Addison-Wesley.

Bache, I. and Flinders, M. (Eds.) (2004). *Multi-level governance*, Oxford: Oxford University Press.

Börzel, T. and Risse, T. (2000). When Europe Hits Home. Europeanization and Domestic Change. *European Integration Online Papers*, *4 (15).*

Börzel, T. (2001). Europeanisation and Territorial Institutional Change: Toward Cooperative Regionalism? In M. Green Cowles, J. Caporaso, and T. Risse (Eds.), *Transforming Europe: Europeanisation and Domestic Change* (pp.137-158). Ithaca:Cornell University Press.

Caporaso, J. (1996). The European Union and Forms of the State: Westphalian, Regulatory or Post-Modern? *Journal of Common Market Studies, 34 (1),* pp.29-52.

CEC (1989). *First CSF 1989-93, Greece*. Luxembourg: OOPEC.

CEC (1993). *Second CSF 1994-99, Greece.* Luxembourg: OOPEC.

CEC (2001). *Unity, solidarity, diversity for Europe, its people and its territory: Second report on Economic and Social cohesion.* Luxembourg: OOPEC.

CEC (2004). *Third periodic report on economic and social cohesion.* Luxembourg: OOPEC.

Checkel, J. (1999). Social Construction and Integration. *Journal of European Public Policy, 6 (4),* pp.545-60.

Checkel, J. (2001). Why Comply? Social Learning and European Identity Change. *International Organization, 55 (3),* pp.553-588.

Featherstone, K. (2003). Introduction: in the name of 'Europe'. In K. Featherstone and C. Radaelli (Eds.), *The Politics of Europeanisation: Theory and Analysis* (pp.3-26). Oxford: Oxford University Press.

Fitzpatrick Associates (2003). *Ex Post Evaluation of Objective 1, 1994-1999, National Report – Ireland.* Dublin: Department of the Environment and Local Government.

Garmise, S. O. (1995). Economic development strategies in Emilia-Romagna. In M. Rhodes (Ed.), *The regions and the new Europe: Patterns in Core and Periphery Development* (pp.136-164). Manchester: Manchester University Press.

Getimis, P. and Demetropoulou, L. (2004). Towards New Forms of Regional Governance in Greece: the case of Southern Aegean Islands. *Regional and Federal Studies, 14 (3),* pp.355-378.

Goldsmith, M. (1993). The Europeanisation of Local Government. *Urban Studies, 30 (4/5),* pp.683-699.

Hall, P. A. (1993). Policy Paradigms, Social Learning and the State: The Case of Economic policy-making in Britain. *Comparative Politics, 25 (3),* pp.275-96.

Heinelt, H., Kopp-Malek, T., Lang, J. and Bernd, R. (2003). Policy-making in fragmented systems: how to explain success. In B. Kohler-Koch (Ed.), *Linking EU and National Governance* (pp.135-154). Oxford: Oxford University Press.

Hood, C. (1994). *Explaining Economic Policy Reversals.* London: Open University Press.

Hood, C. (1998). *The Art of the State: Culture, Rhetoric, and Public Management.* Oxford: Oxford University Press.

Hooghe, L. and Marks, G. (2001). *Multi-level governance and European integration.* Lanham: Rowman and Littlefield.

Jeffery, C. (2000). Sub-National Mobilization and European Integration: Does it Make Any Difference? *Journal of Common Market Studies, 38 (1),* pp.1-23.

Keating, M., Loughlin, J. and Deschouwer, K. (2003). *Culture, Institutions and Development: A Study of Eight European Regions*. Aldershot: Edward Elgar.

Keogh, D. (1994). *Twentieth Century Ireland: Nation and State*, Dublin: Gill and Macmillan.

Kohler-Koch B. (1996). Catching Up With Change: the Transformation of Governance in the European Union. *Journal of European Public Policy, 3 (3),* pp.359-80.

Kohler-Koch, B. (2005). European governance and system integration. *European Governance Papers (EUROGOV)* No. C-05-01. Available at: http://www.connex-network.org/eurogov/pdf/egp-connex-C-05-01.pdf

Laffan, B. (2000). Rapid adaptation and light co-ordination. In R. O'Donnell (Ed.), *Europe: The Irish Experience.* Dublin: Institute of European Affairs.

Lenschow, A. (1997). Transformation in European Environmental Governance. *EUI Working Papers, RSC No 97/61.* Florence: European University Institute.

Magone, J. (2001). The transformation of the Portuguese political system: European regional policy and democratization in small EU member states. In K. Featherstone and G. Kazamias (Eds.), *Europeanization and Southern Periphery* (pp.119-140). London: Frank Cass.

Marks, G. (1993). Structural Policy and Multilevel Governance in the EC. In A. W. Cafruny and G. Rosenthal (Eds.), *The State of the European Community: The Maastricht debates and Beyond Vol. 2* (pp.391-410). London: Longman.

Marks G., Nielsen F., Ray L. and Salk J. (1996). Competencies, Cracks and Conflicts: Regional Mobilization in the European Union. In G. Marks, F. W. Scharpf, P. Schmitter and W. Streeck (Eds.), *Governance in the European Union* (pp.40-63). London: Sage.

Mazey, S. and Richardson, J. (1993). Introduction: Transference of Power, Decision Rules and Rules of the Game. In S. Mazey and J. Richardson (Eds.), *Lobbying in the European Community* (pp.3-26). Oxford: Oxford University Press.

Mitsos, A. (2001). The Community's Redistributive and Development Role and the Southern European Countries. In H. D. Gibson (Ed.), *Economic Transformation, Democratization and Integration into the European Union: Southern Europe in Comparative Perspective* (pp.306-342). Basingstoke: Palgrave.

Nanetti, R., Rato, H. and Rodrigues, M. (2004). Institutional Capacity and Reluctant Decentralisation in Portugal: Case-study of the Lisbon and Tagus Valley Region. In C. J. Paraskevopoulos and R. Leonardi (Eds.), *Regional and Federal Studies, 14 (3),* pp.403-428.

O'Donnell, R. (2000). *Europe: The Irish Experience.* Dublin: Institute of European Affairs.

Paraskevopoulos, C. J. (1998a). Social Capital and the Public/Private Divide in Greek Regions. *West European Politics, 21 (2),* pp.153-176.

Paraskevopoulos, C. J. (1998b). Social Capital, Institutional Learning and European Regional Policy: evidence from Greece. *Regional and Federal Studies*, *8 (3),* pp.31-64.

Paraskevopoulos, C. J. (2001a). Social Capital, Learning and EU Regional Policy Networks: evidence from Greece. *Government and Opposition, 36 (2),* pp.251-75.

Paraskevopoulos, C. J. (2001b). *Interpreting Convergence in the European Union: Patterns of Collective Action, Social Learning and Europeanisation*. London: Palgrave.

Paraskevopoulos, C. J. (2005). Developing Infrastructure as a Learning Process in Greece. In K. Featherstone (Ed.), *West European Politics, 28 (2),* pp.445-470.

Paraskevopoulos, C. J. and Leonardi, R. (Eds.) (2004). Learning from Abroad (by Comparison): Regionalization and Local Institutional Infrastructure in Cohesion and CEE Countries. *Regional and Federal Studies Special Issue, 14 (3).*

Paraskevopoulos, C. J., and Leonardi, R. (2004). Introduction: Adaptational Pressures and Social Learning in European Regional Policy: cohesion (Greece, Ireland, Portugal) and CEE (Hungary, Poland) Countries in Comparative Perspective. In C. J. Paraskevopoulos and R. Leonardi (Eds.), Learning from Abroad (by Comparison): Regionalization and Local Institutional Infrastructure in Cohesion and CEE Countries (pp.313-352). *Regional and Federal Studies Special Issue, 14 (3).*

Paraskevopoulos, C. J., Getimis, P. and Rees, N. (2006). *Adapting to EU Multi-Level Governance: Regional and Environmental Policies in cohesion and CEE Countries.* Aldershot: Ashgate.

Pollack, M. (1995). Regional Actors in an Intergovernmental Play: The Making and Implementation of EC Structural Policy. In C. Rhodes and S. Mazey (Eds.), *The State of European Union, Vol. 3: Building a European Polity?* (pp.361-390). Boulder: Lynne Rienner.

Rees, N. (1997). Inter-regional co-operation in the European Union and beyond. *European Planning Studies*, *5 (3),* pp.385-407

Rees, N., Quinn, B. and Connaughton, B. (2004). Ireland's Pragmatic Adaptation to Regionalization: The Mid West Region. In C. J. Paraskevopoulos and R. Leonardi (Eds.), Learning from Abroad (by Comparison): Regionalization and Local Institutional Infrastructure in Cohesion and CEE Countries (pp.377-402). *Regional and Federal Studies Special Issue, 14 (3).*

Rees, N. and Paraskevopoulos, C. J. (2006). Europeanisation of Policy-Making and Domestic Governance Structures in Regional Policy: cohesion and CEE Countries. In C. J. Paraskevopoulos, P. Getimis and N. Rees (Eds.), *Adapting to EU Multi-Level Governance: Regional and Environmental Policies in cohesion and CEE Countries* (pp.179-206). Aldershot: Ashgate.

Risse, T., Green Cowles, M. and Caporaso, J. (2001). Europeanisation and Domestic Change: Introduction. In M. Green Cowles, J. Caporaso and T. Risse (Eds.), *Transforming Europe: Europeanisation and Domestic Change* (pp.1-20). Ithaca: Cornell University Press.

Rose, R. (1993). *Lesson-Drawing in Public Policy: A Guide to Learning Across Time and Space.* Chatham: Chatham House Publishers.

Rose, R. (2002). Ten Steps in Learning Lessons from Abroad. *EUI Working Papers, RSC No. 2002/5.* Florence: European University Institute.

Sabel, C. (1994). Learning by Monitoring: The Institutions of Economic Development. In N. J. Smelser and R. Swedberg (Eds.), *The Handbook of Economic Sociology* (pp.137-165). Princeton: Princeton University Press.

Scharpf, F. W. (1994). Community and Autonomy: Multilevel Policy-Making in the European Union. *EUI Working Papers, RSC, No 94/1.* Florence: European University Institute.

Schmidt, V. A. (1997). European integration and democracy: the differences among member states. *Journal of European Public Policy, 4 (1),* pp.128-45.

Preparation for Structural Funds and Europeanisation: The Case of Lithuania

Klaudijus Maniokas

Introduction

The main purpose of this chapter is to outline and explain the development of an institutional infrastructure relating to structural funds in Lithuania in the context of overall institutional changes and from the perspective of Europeanisation. It therefore contributes to understanding of the changes that accession to the EU has brought to the countries of Central and Eastern Europe (CEE).

The accession process and the experience of the first years of EU membership are of particular interest in the context of this book. The Europeanisation process in the former candidate countries of the CEE and the domestic changes associated with it, especially in the field of structural funds, could throw some light on the robustness of the multi-level governance approach. In addition, the accession process can shed some light on the relationship between the so-called new forms of governance in the EU and the multi-level governance concept. Many new forms of governance, such as benchmarking, peer reviews and monitoring were either developed or more widely used in the governance of accession. However, the changes brought about by the accession in the CEE countries do not seem to fit well with the predictions of a classical MLG approach, if it is understood to be a process of deconcentration of central political authority and the emergence of a complex governance network of local, regional and non-state actors. The changes in the CEE countries point instead towards a process of centralisation. This trend suggests a more important role for a range of agencies either created or reformed during the pre-accession period in CEE countries.

The extent of EU influence on the former accession countries has not yet been fully appreciated, though recent academic contributions (Schimmelfennig and Sedelmeier, 2005; Jacoby, 2004; Hughes, Sasse and Gordon, 2004) do throw some light on this issue. The influence of the EU was much broader and intense than was the case for the founder member states and the candidate countries in the course of the previous enlargements. There were four main differences. (i) The influence was broader in scope because of additional membership conditions, such as the Copenhagen criteria and the accession partnerships. (ii) It was more concentrated in time because in just a few years the former candidate countries had to transpose and implement the *acquis*, which had been created and then implemented by member states over many decades. (iii) The receptivity of the candidate states to EU influence made them more sensitive to that influence. This receptivity itself can be attributed to two factors. One was a weak or, in some cases, virtually non-existent institutional structure. This is particularly true for the Baltic States, which were completing a state-building process at that time. Second, the candidate countries had welcomed the *acquis* and other membership conditions as a blueprint for comprehensive transformation and modernisation of the state, the economy and the public sphere. Finally, (iv) the acceding countries were in no position to influence the outcomes of EU policy-making, so could not modify or help to shape decisions.[1]

Given the extent of EU influence on the former candidate countries, and the role of the EU as a model for major reforms in these countries, little is yet known about the purpose, sense and impact of all the reforms associated with the EU. This is particularly clear when comparing the accession process with the transition. The latter had two clearly identified goals: to create a functioning democracy and a market economy. The purpose and content of the accession process had not been questioned by the candidate countries and had not been given any explicit explanation or justification by the EU. This is rather surprising bearing in mind the commonly held view that the EU could not really be regarded as comprising a consistent set of principles and norms governing the functioning of a state. Rather, it is a patchwork of decisions reached as a result of complicated negotiations combined with different sets of side payments (Héritier *et al.*, 1996).

In the context of multi-level governance and structural funds, the governance and impact of accession leads to several interesting hypotheses. For example, the results of Europeanisation suggest that the strategy of the European Commission to enhance the role of regional and non-governmental actors has changed. The explanation for such a change is beyond the scope of this chapter. It could be related to efficiency concerns and the balance of power between different Commission services, as well as to 'old EU' concerns over administrative capacity. However, it seems that Europeanisation of the new member states led to the further centralisation of power in CEE countries. The development of structures for the management of the structural funds reflects this. Moreover, important changes in the balance of power brought about by Europeanisation suggest that the main beneficiaries of this process were not only central authorities. It can be argued that the main institutional winners from the process were the so-called non-majoritarian institutions, which are largely overlooked by scholars using the multi-level governance approach. It is these quasi-independent agencies created and remodelled through the years of accession - and not regional actors - which can be seen as the major winners from accession to the EU and major players in the new multi-level governance networks. The implication is that Europeanisation in the new member states resulted not so much in territorial, but in functional redistribution of power. It is no longer the 'Europe of Regions'. It is about the 'Europe of Agencies'. While these agencies differ in terms of their autonomy and how they work, they are important in almost all Europeanised policy areas in the

1 See Börzel (2002) for the relationship between uploading and downloading.

CEE countries. Structural funds management is no exception. While the implementing agencies created to prepare for the management of structural funds are not as independent as, for example, competition or data protection agencies, they nevertheless fall into the broad pattern of governance promoted by the EU during the long process of pre-accession.

Early indications in the post-accession stage reveal a return to the old principles of governance in the CEE countries, especially in terms of the politicisation of the civil service (World Bank, 2006). However, it cannot be seen as a full return to the early period of transition and EU led reforms. It should be also noted that the CEE countries have been choosing different policies, and the outcomes of Europeanisation differ across countries and in different policy sectors (Schimmelfennig and Sedelmeier, 2005). Regional policies and structures created for the management of the structural funds do differ (Hughes *et al.*, 2004). However, the similar patterns in this as well as in other policy areas, could also indicate convergence, which is much more prominent than in the old EU member states.

Recognition of the role of non-majoritarian institutions might also explain the consequences of the new modes of governance. It seems that these new governance modes bring changes that directly contradict the scenarios based on a classical understanding of multi-level governance. Regional and other units of territorial governance are hardly involved in this complex web of benchmarking, monitoring and evaluating performance. However, different quasi-independent agencies benefit from this approach taking advantage of their expertise and independence.

This chapter first presents the institutional implications of Europeanisation with particular reference to Central and Eastern Europe. It then looks into the preparation for structural funds management. Both the periods of pre-accession and membership are covered. The case study is based on Lithuania's experience evaluated in comparison with other CEE countries. The chapter ends with conclusions and recommendations for further research.

Europeanisation and Enlargement

The still growing literature on Europeanisation could be of help in outlining the direction of change promoted by the EU. However, this literature is rather lacking in providing clear answers. Most of the studies aiming to understand the impact of the EU on public policy and domestic structures in the member states conclude, in the words of Wright and Menon, that the consequences of integration are very patchy, often nebulous and increasingly unpredictable (Wright and Menon, 2001). The studies of Europeanisation largely undermine the initial hypotheses of convergence in public policy styles, solutions and institutional forms and confirm still persisting divergences between the member states. At best, one can refer to clustered convergence and conclude that the Europeanisation of public policy is more robust than the impact on politics and polity (Radaelli, 2004). It could be related to the methods and tools developed for Europeanisation studies. A multi-level governance approach looking into polity implications could therefore be helpful.

Why might it be problematic to apply these theoretical ideas as well as the results of Europeanisation on the former accession countries? One can question whether the idea of adaptational pressure, which, in turn, results from the misfit between European and domestic structures, will in all cases be appropriate for analysis of adaptation in the accession countries. The point is that many EU driven policies and the structures underlying them were new for many accession countries. For example, competition, regional, consumer protection and food safety policies were largely aimed at correcting market failures. Structural and regional policies were also either underdeveloped or developed from scratch. Pre-existing institutional infrastructure was weak. Therefore traditional Europeanisation tools were likely to have limited value in the study of the structural policy of the former accession states. It is more appropriate to see changes in terms of developing new structures as a result of copying either real or the Commission's invented utopian best practices. A multi-level governance approach might better account for the emergence of a new layer of governance in CEE countries as a result of Europeanisation. However, this layer is represented not by regional actors, but by non-majoritarian institutions.

Europeanisation in Central and Eastern Europe: Imitation, Convergence and Regulation

It seems that the dominant logic of Europeanisation in the CEE countries is a mimetic logic based on the search for legitimacy. The functional logic defined by the search for efficiency seemingly played a minor role. This mimetic logic of legitimisation produced very similar institutional solutions, which could be captured by the convergence hypothesis. Preparations for introducing structural policy illustrate the point. Because of the simultaneity and speed of changes in different sectors in the CEE countries, Europeanisation in the accession countries can be seen as a relatively homogeneous process. This is particularly the case in the area of market institutions and structural policy.

The EU had a wide-ranging and deep impact on the institutions of CEE countries. First, the EU accession agenda was very broad and went far beyond the adoption of the *acquis*. It comprised the well known Copenhagen accession criteria such as a functioning democracy, rule of law, market economy and administrative system. Second, due to the asymmetrical nature of the accession process, the EU, especially the European Commission, were able to influence the choice of institutional structures by the candidate states. Technical and financial assistance, including a twinning programme alongside other accession instruments, such as accession partnership, provided the means for having an impact. Third, due to the weakness of the system in CEE countries, institutional models were imported from the EU without much resistance.

The result of this huge EU impact on the institutional system in Lithuania can be summarised by reference to the idea of the regulatory state.[2] It means that the EU has stimulated the development of regulatory policies and the role of non-majoritarian institutions. The latter can be characterised by their relative autonomy from political interference and by their reliance on technical expertise. Using a political criterion, the EU has pushed Lithuania towards consolidation of the autonomy of the judiciary and of public administration. The Public Service Law (1999) and the Law on Courts (2002) can be construed as a concrete result of the impact of the EU. The Public Service Law and other reforms of the public sector resulted in the establishment of a quasi-independent public service. The Law on Courts completed the establishment of the administrative autonomy of the courts.

In the field of economic regulation, the EU has promoted the establishment of a whole set of supervisory institutions. The European Commission pushed hard for isolating those institutions from the political sphere. Therefore, these institutions can be seen as non-majoritarian agencies. Specific laws regulate their competence and the nomination and dismissal of the heads of these institutions is subject to many restrictions. Concrete examples of supervisory institutions reorganised or established under direct EU influence in Lithuania are the Competition Council (under the new Competition Law adopted in 1999), Public Procurement Office (1999), market surveillance institutions such as the National Bureau of Accreditation, State Metrology Service, National Standards Board, Veterinary and Food Supervision Agency, Non-Food Products Supervision Agency (as a result of the reform accomplished in 1999-2000), Lithuanian Bank (made autonomous under a new law on the Lithuanian Bank in 2001), Securities Commission, Insurance Supervision Council, State Energy Pricing Commission, Civil Aviation Administration, Telecommunications Regulations Commission, Consumer Protection Council, Personal Data Protection Council and others. These institutions have been modelled on the experience of different EU member states, but in many cases they are more autonomous than their counterparts in older member states due to the great care taken to ensure autonomy of these establishments by the European Commission.

Regional/Structural Policy in Lithuania in a Comparative Context

Both structural and environment policy have been the subject of similar pressures and tendencies flowing from the non-majoritarian outcomes of europeanisation. However, this has been on a smaller scale than those sectors directly related to the internal market. Environmental policy has expanded in scope and the Environmental Protection Agency was set up and gained important new powers. This agency is not as autonomous as the market surveillance institutions, but it has gained more autonomy as a result of europeanisation (Maniokas, 2002).

2 See Caporaso (1996) for a definition of this idea in relation to other concepts such as the Westhphalian and the postmodern state.

Structural policy development in Lithuania has been marked by an initial confusion about its relationship to regional policy and regionalisation efforts. Preparations for the management of structural funds were initially understood as an essential tool to regionalise the country and to create instruments and institutions for regional policy.

In comparison with old member states, regional policies in CEE countries were less well developed. At the same time, transition reforms led to more accentuated regional disparities within countries. There were also considerable differences between countries. In some countries, like Poland, there was a tradition of regional policy developed by former communist governments. In other countries, such as Lithuania and other Baltic states, regional policy was embryonic. EU influence on the development of these policies was not consistent. It started with an emphasis on regionalisation and regional policy and ended with an emphasis on centrally managed and controlled use of structural funds.

Preparation for the management of structural funds was therefore linked to the development of regional policy in the CEE countries. This, in turn, was marked by confusion over the link between national and EU regional policy. The former candidate countries from CEE countries took the development of a national regional policy as a means to prepare for EU regional policy and in particular the structural funds.

Lithuania had no tradition of strong regional policy. Its regional actors were rather weak. The central authorities realised this during the drafting of answers to the European Commission's questionnaire in 1996 designed to evaluate preparedness for EU membership. No ministry or any other public authority was in charge of regional policy. This realisation prompted the government to place this responsibility on the Ministry of Public Administration and Self Government. This was endorsed by the European Commission. Up to 2000/2001 the Commission encouraged perception of the structural funds to be a matter of regional policy and involvement of regional actors (Maniokas, 2002). Many countries started to devise regional development strategies, laws and programmes, including all these instruments in their broad pre-accession programmes. Lithuania had elaborated a comprehensive normative base, the Law on Regional Development (2002), the regional development programme (2002), and a methodology for the preparation and renewal of regional development plans. Regional development plans were prepared and renewed for all ten of the counties of Lithuania. The European Commission devised a special PHARE 2000 programme, which aimed to build up the capacity of regional actors to manage the structural funds. It tested special grant schemes in three underdeveloped regions of Lithuania. They turned out to be successful.

This process of regionalisation was suddenly halted by a change in the Commission's stance. This was supported by the Lithuanian central authorities (Maniokas, 2002; Nakrosis, 2003). The main responsibility was transferred from the Ministry of the Interior (which had taken over the functions of the Ministry of Public Administration and Self-Government) to the Ministry of Finance. It was a trend that could be observed in many former candidate countries from the CEE. While this initial stage of thinking about structural funds in the context of regionalisation helped to promote regional development throughout the CEE countries and raised awareness of the issue of regional disparities, it also had some negative consequences. Preconditions for a regional policy were created, but the policy remained on paper. The European Commission started to focus on national development strategies and a centralized framework of institutions responsible for the management of structural funds. Most CEE countries were small and almost all had GDP per capita well below the 75 percent threshold. Accordingly, they were considered just one region. The EU made it clear that the need to prepare for structural funds did not require the elaboration and implementation of national regional policies with relevant institutional infrastructure and a full range of appropriate instruments. Instead, what was required was the development of national public investment plans and the strengthening of the central administration (Maniokas, 2002; Nakrosis, 2003). The technical management of different funds and schemes was entrusted to a number of newly created agencies under different ministries. The extent of their autonomy varied and they were not free from political interference, but the participation of regional and local authorities was reduced to a minimum.

The rationale behind the shift of the EU (and the European Commission in particular) from demanding regionalisation to promoting central management structures merits explanation. One study captures the developments in this field and offers a plausible explanation for the changes (Hughes *et al.*, 2004). It is therefore useful to concentrate on the pluses and minuses of the conclusions of this study. The authors argue that the impact of EU conditionality in the area of structural funds was less than clear because the responses from the CEE countries were diverse and depended not so much on EU conditionality as on the tradition of territorial governance. The inconsistency of the EU/Commission's approach, revealing competing views within the European Commission, was also noted. However, there are other ways of interpreting the conclusions. It seems that the governance of the structural funds developed relatively uniformly across the CEE countries. While most of them played with the idea of regionalisation as a way to prepare for the structural funds, the final outcome was highly centralised systems for the management of structural funds. The only major exception is Poland, which managed to create a new level of regional governance based on representative democratic principles. These outcomes correspond closely with the latest Commission view on the conditionalities related to structural funds. This view differentiates between large and small countries recommending regionalisation for the former and centralisation for the latter. The most important point is that there were opportunities to make regional actors more important, but the Commission consciously opted for centralisation.

The change in the Commission's stance is remarkable in the context of multi-level governance. At the beginning of the accession process the Commission was following the line it developed in the late 1980s. It introduced the notion of regional administrative capacities and used instruments like PHARE and evaluation of progress to promote regionalisation (Hughes *et al.*, 2004). The attitude of the Commission changed amid growing concerns over the general administrative capacities of candidate countries in 1999-2001. The Commission was forced by the existing member states to focus on efficient and sound management of future structural funds spending. This imperative became stronger during negotiations, which started in 1998.

The current three-level structural funds implementation system in Lithuania can be seen as a direct result of the change in the EU stance. For the period 2004-2006 Lithuania - as well as many other new member states - decided to manage the structural funds through a centralised system, which was a mix of the characteristics of "differentiated" and "integrated" administrative frameworks.[3] For instance, both EU and national expenditures are managed through a number of budgetary programmes designed specifically for the purpose of financial management. Also new bodies were established to perform specific functions of implementing agencies. Yet the functions of intermediate institutions were embedded in particular ministries.

Although this centralised mixed system has advantages from the efficiency point of view, yet the lack of the regional dimension also means that the system is distant from the applicants and consequently can be less user friendly. Only two implementing agencies[4] – the Business Support Agency and National Paying Agency[5] – have a network of regional units, to which are delegated technical responsibilities for project selection. The remaining implementing agencies have only national offices.

The most important functions such as planning implementation measures and allocating EU structural fund assistance to particular projects are vested in the so-called intermediate bodies. The different sectoral ministries have taken on the functions of intermediate bodies. However, actual project selection is performed by a number of agencies acting as implementing bodies: Human Resources Development Programmes Support Foundation, Central Project Management Agency, Business Support Agency, National Paying Agency, Transport Investment Directorate and Environmental Projects Management Agency.

The level of autonomy of the implementing agencies varies. They cannot be categorised as classic non-majoritarian institutions. However, they have independent legal status and are expected to produce expertise based judgements and decisions. The different and inadequate levels of autonomy of different implementing agencies in their relationship with ministries as intermediate bodies contribute to the risk of capture of these institutions by political groups. However, they continue to operate as new major actors in the management of structural funds. The involvement of regional and other societal actors is very limited. Their inclusion in the project selection process is optional and in most cases superficial. The future of the system is still

3 *Integrated / differentiated* management of the structural funds depends on the extent to which the structural funds are managed through existing national administrative, economic and financial systems or whether administrative, economic and financial systems are set up specifically for the structural funds. *Centralised / decentralised* management of the structural funds depends on the extent to which the management of the structural funds is centralised or decentralised in the territorial-administrative sense (see Taylor *et al.*, 2000).

4 In this programming period, there are six agencies altogether.

5 These two agencies are responsible for structural funds support to agriculture and rural development.

uncertain, but it seems that a large degree of centralisation will be retained. However, it seems that there will be more focus on the reduction of regional disparities in the next financial perspective.

Conclusions

The role of the European Commission partially explains the outcomes of Europeanisation in the former candidate countries and the development of the institutional infrastructure for the structural funds in Lithuania. While these outcomes reflect the nature of the *acquis* and the EU itself, considerable room for interpretation was left to the European Commission on the conditions attached to membership. This was used to push the development of public policy in the former candidate countries towards a utopian model of a regulatory state, characterised by the proliferation of non-majoritarian institutions. This, in turn, forced the candidate countries to focus heavily on policies aimed at dealing with market failures.

Preparation for the management of structural funds is not the most obvious example to use, as it is not related to the regulation of the market, but it indicates a similar trend. The impact of the EU has resulted in the creation of a centralised mechanism of management at central government level, reducing the likelihood of involving regional actors and the creation of a new viable regional layer of government. The initial position of the European Commission was favourable towards regionalisation, but in 1999-2001 this stance radically changed amid growing concerns over the administrative capacities of the former candidate countries and their ability to manage structural funds in particular. This trend therefore is not in line with the predictions of the classical multi-level governance approach. Instead, the influence of the EU resulted in the proliferation of agencies created for the management of structural funds at the central level. The MLG approach, however, is useful in identifying a new layer of governance represented by agencies.

References

Börzel, T. (2002). Pace-Setting, Foot-dragging, and Fence-Sitting: Member States Responses to Europeanisation. *Journal of Common Market Studies, 40 (2),* pp.193-214.

Caporaso, J. A. (1996). The European Union and Forms of State: Westphalian, Regulatory or Post-Modern? *Journal of Common Market Studies, 34 (1),* pp.29-52.

Héritier, A. (2005). Europeanization research east and west: a comparative assessment. In F. Schimmelfennig and U. Sedelmeier (Eds.), *The Europeanization of Central and Eastern Europe* (pp.199-209). Ithaca: Cornell University Press.

Héritier, A., Knill, C., and Mingers, S. (1996). *Ringing the Changes in Europe: Regulatory Competition and the Transformation of the State.* Berlin: De Gruyter.

Hughes, J., Sasse, G. and Gordon, C. (2004). *Europeanisation and Regionalisation in the EU's Enlargement to Central and Eastern Europe: The Myth of Conditionality.* Houndsmills: Palgrave.

Jacoby, W. (2004). *The Enlargement of the European Union and NATO: Ordering from the Menu in Central Europe.* Cambridge: Cambridge University Press.

Maniokas, K. (2002). *EU Enlargement and Europeanisation.* Vilnius: Eugrimas.

Nakrosis, V. (2003). Managing European Union Funds in the Candidate Countries: Administrative Organization and Resource Distribution. In B. Funck and L. Pizzati (Eds.), *European Integration, Regional Policy, and Growth* (pp.201-218). Washington DC: World Bank.

Radaelli, C. M. (2004). Europeanisation: Solution or problem? *European Integration Online Papers, 8 (16).* Available at: http://eiop.or.at/eiop/texte/2004-016a.htm

Schimmelfennig, F. and Sedelmeier, U. (Eds.) (2005). *The Europeanization of Central and Eastern Europe.* Ithaca: Cornell University Press.

Taylor, S., Bachtler, J. and Rooney, M. L. (2000). *Implementing the new Generation of Programmes: Project Development, Appraisal and Selection.* IQ Net. Glasgow: European Policies Research Centre.

World Bank (2006). *EU-8. Administrative Capacity in the New Member States: The Limits of Innovation. Report Number: 36930-GLB.* Washington DC: World Bank.

Wright, W. and Menon, A. (Eds.) (2001). *From the Nation State to Europe?: Essays in Honour of Jack Hayward.* Oxford: Oxford University Press.

EU Structural Funds and Domestic Governance and Policy in Britain

Ian Bache and Thomas Conzelmann

Introduction

This chapter looks at the effects of the EU structural funds on domestic governance and policy in Britain. In doing so, it discusses this as a case of europeanisation, taken here to refer to the 'reorientation or reshaping of politics in the domestic arena in ways that reflect policies, practices and preferences advanced through the EU system of governance' (Bache and Jordan, 2006: 30). This definition delineates the 'subject' of europeanisation (what is europeanised?) and also suggests a causal mechanism: namely, the interactions between domestic and European-level actors in a multi-level system in which a great number of functional policy networks exist. Europeanisation increases the intensity of these interactions and often brings new actors into policy networks. One key question then is whether domestic political processes are merely "reoriented" in the sense that domestic actors respond strategically to the opportunities and/or threats that emerge; or whether a more profound "reshaping" takes place, in which the preferences of domestic actors are changed through engagement with new actors.

One of the prime examples of multi-level governance in the EU is the area of the structural funds. The development, nature and purpose of EU structural funding are set out by Piattoni (this volume). Here we recap briefly that, since 1975, EU regional policy has increasingly become a second layer of regional policy in the member states. In that year, a new European Regional Development Fund (ERDF) was introduced, which paralleled the already existing funds for vocational training and for the restructuring of agricultural economies. The basic objective of the early ERDF was to put additional financial muscle behind the regional policies of member states. In practice, this meant that projects pursued by member states received financial backing from the EU, without, however, the Commission enjoying much influence over the way in which the money was spent. Building on several experiments with giving the supranational layer a greater say, the crucial 1988 reforms installed for the first time autonomous assisted areas of the ERDF (whereas formerly use of the ERDF was delimited to domestic assisted areas), and introduced a new management scheme that loosened the control of national governments over the use of resources. Funds were now disbursed through multi-annual programmes that included monies from the ERDF and other funds and gave the Commission as well as sub-national and societal actors a say through the requirement of partnership.

The implementation of structural funding across different member states and their respective institutional environments have been the subject of much academic interest (see Anderson, 1990; Conzelmann, 1995; Heinelt and Smith, 1996; Heinelt *et al.*, 2005). In addition, there are also a number of studies that look at the effects of structural funding on governance and policy in member states (see Adshead, 2002; Anderson, 1996; Bache and Jones, 2000; Balme and Jouve, 1996; Benz and Eberlein, 1996; Hooghe, 1996; Conzelmann, 2002 and 2006; Gualini, 2003; Smyrl, 1997). This second focus is the one taken here, specifically in relation to Britain. Our basic hypothesis is that Britain is an interesting case for observing europeanisation processes due to the traditionally centralised nature of the British polity and the adverse nature of relationships between Conservative governments and the EU during the 1980s and the first half of the 1990s. From the conceptual perspective of europeanisation, there is a broadly defined 'misfit' between the nature of EU governance and that in Britain; in institutional terms, between the multi-layered and multi-actor EU system and the traditionally strong centralised British state; and, in political terms, between EU political norms of co-operation and consensus seeking and the adversarial style of politics in Britain. In addition, the change of government to Labour in 1997 gives us an important opportunity to observe the importance of domestic party political factors in the europeanisation process.

Governance Effects[1]

In recent years, the British system of governance has experienced significant change, which has accelerated its transformation towards a multi-level polity (Bache and Flinders, 2004a and 2004b; Gamble, 2000; Pierre and Stoker, 2000). Most obviously this is marked by political devolution to Scotland, Wales and Northern Ireland, but there are less obvious changes at other territorial levels (the English regions and municipal and sub-local levels) and in the horizontal dimension to governance, for example in the proliferation of partnership governance (involving various mixes of public, private and voluntary sectors). That much of this transformation has occurred since the election of Labour in 1997 suggests strong domestic explanations for these developments and this paper does not dispute the importance of these – particularly in relation to political devolution. However, over a longer period, the EU has also been significant; particularly in relation to the emergence of English regional governance, the strategies and approaches of local authorities, and the spread of community-led decision-making. These aspects will be dealt with in turn.

1 This section draws on a fuller version published in Bache (2008).

The English Regions

In the 1980s, there was not even an agreed boundary for the English Regions – the most commonly used regional classification was that of the standard region, which originated from the areas covered by the Economic Planning Councils established by the Labour Government in 1965. Different government departments made adjustments to the regional boundaries to fit their needs. The Department of the Environment (DoE) treated London as a separate region, and the DoE, Department for Trade and Industry (DTI) and Department of Transport reallocated counties such as Essex and Hertfordshire out of the South East and into the Eastern region (Church, 1993: 2). Other organisations, such as gas, water, and electricity companies, defined their own regional structures rather than follow the patterns of the standard regions. For its part, the EU used the standard region classification for its purposes, despite the fact that the Economic Planning Councils were abolished in 1979 (Bache, George and Rhodes, 1996: 59)

After the abolition of the Economic Planning Councils by the new Conservative Government, the prospects for the development of English regionalism faded further. The Conservative Government showed no appetite for devolution and rejected interventionist regional policies on principle. The regional dimension of the EU's structural policy entered this vacuum. The government tolerated the EU's regional policy primarily to secure financial reimbursement to the national Treasury, which acted as 'financial gatekeeper' over the distribution of these funds (Bache, 1999). However, this policy became a key part of a renewed push for English regionalism.

Burch and Gomez (2004; 2006) considered the emergence of a 'new English regionalism' in two phases: 1991-1997 and post-1997. In the first phase, they identified the importance of the EU structural funds in shaping administrative processes at regional level (notably partnership) and also in having a 'more modest' regionalising impact. The funds had a 'galvanising effect' and were at the 'very heart' of change, although noting that the degree of change varied significantly across the English Regions according to the degree of EU funding and the response of key domestic players. Burch and Gomez (2006: 95-96) pointed to the effects of the European Regional Development Fund (ERDF) requirements in particular:

> 'The *programming* concept helped to both develop and consolidate the regional tier by creating a clear focus for activities and opportunities for engagement and activism on the part of regional players. Formal requirements to operate on the basis of *partnership* also exerted a powerful regionalising effect by forcing those actors involved in delivering Structural Fund programmes to devise new ways of working with sub-national interests [italics added].

Alongside the impetus provided by the structural funds were domestic factors that gave a push to regionalism, particularly concerns with inter-regional disparities. It is noted that, with the exception of the North East Region, this dissatisfaction did not have popular foundations. The combination of the top-down incentives provided by the structural funds and these bottom-up shifts provided the momentum for strengthened English regional governance from the early 1990s onwards.

Before 1997, the key institutional change at the regional level was the creation of integrated Government Regional Offices (GROs) in 1994. The GROs were designed to strengthen central co-ordination at the regional and local level, particularly in relation to EU and domestic regeneration funds. However, their creation had a number of unintended consequences for the promotion of English regionalism:

- it linked the notions of integrated policy and regional delivery in the minds of Whitehall decision-makers;
- it encouraged the development of regionally focused interest networks;
- it gave a push to regional identities by finally establishing what were to become accepted as the standard boundaries for the English Regions (Bache and Gomez, 2006: 85).

After 1997, the primary force behind English regionalism became constitutional change, with European factors secondary. Labour's devolution programme brought the UK closer to multi-level governance, with devolution to Scotland, Wales and Northern Ireland and the creation of a Greater London Authority. Regional Development Agencies (RDAs) and consultative Regional Chambers were created in the English regions. These institutional developments fell short of the hopes of English regionalists, but this period gave 'critical momentum' to the development of English regional governance and 'provided a platform from which regional players could engage with a far wider range of European issues, such as enlargement, transport and environmental policy' (Burch and Gomez, 2006: 91).

The EU effects in this period are less clear than in the one before: the 'EU-related efforts' (*op. cit.*: 95) affecting the regions were greater, but so were efforts aimed at the regions generally. Again, in this period, the structural funds were the greatest source of EU influence – particularly in shaping the organisational structures in those regions with the largest receipts. For example, the government's decision to give RDAs strategic responsibility for the structural funds prompted several of them to reorganise internally to perform this function. Further, as new regional machinery was developed to co-ordinate both the reception and projection responses to the EU, there was pressure from local authorities and other sub-national actors to be included in these forums, 'an indication of the extent to which partnership working has penetrated the machinery of government' (Burch and Gomez, 2004: 17).

Bachtler and Taylor (2003: 24) provided supporting evidence of the regionalising effect of the structural funds in England. They pointed out that 'elements of structural fund programming are evident in the Regional Economic Strategies drawn up by the English regional development agencies, as well as the integration of government expenditure for regeneration across several policy areas in a "single pot"'. More broadly, research by ECOTEC (2003: 46) recognised the 1989 move towards a regional approach to structural fund programming as 'a factor encouraging a resurgence of regional strategic capacity across the UK' and argued that 'multi-agency approaches to planning stimulated by the structural funds are now increasingly embedded at regional level' (ECOTEC, 2003: 47).

In short, there can be little doubt that the 1989 requirements of reform of the structural funds, particularly in relation to regional programming and regional partnerships, provided the major push for activity at the English regional level in this period. Despite the steering role of central government, EU structural policy reinforced the standard regions as the 'official' boundaries and created embryonic regional networks in England that provided something for the Labour Government to build on from 1997.[2]

The municipal level

Adam Marshall's (2004: 2) study of urban governance suggested a 'distinct, two-way process of Europeanisation … driven primarily by the availability of large quantities of EU Structural Funding'. His contribution took the debate on the effects of EU structural funding away from its usual focus on regions and regionalism, to identify the effects on cities and metropolitan sub-regions. He argued that the EU's principles of partnership and programming have been embraced by domestic actors and spread to other (non-EU) areas of co-operation.

Marshall's case studies, Birmingham and Glasgow, were chosen because of their long histories of interaction with the EU and particularly the structural funds. He acknowledged that the adaptational pressures here would be higher than in cities that have had less consistent interaction with EU programmes. In these cases though, 'downward adaptational pressures have caused urban councils to embrace change and new modes of working'. Specifically, the strategic and holistic approaches to regeneration advanced by EU programming requirements have been adopted by the cities more generally. Bachtler and Taylor (2003: 21-22) also identified the incorporation of EU programming practices in domestic practices in the UK (and other member states).

Another specific EU effect is the increase of participants in local governance through the partnership principle – representatives of business, trade unions, non-governmental organisations and the voluntary and community sector. Marshall (2004: 14) noted that non-governmental actors account for approximately half of the membership of the Strathclyde European Partnership. While the partnership models within each city reflected specific local institutional characteristics, they displayed 'a commitment to joint working, capacity-building and holistic thinking that is less evident in non-beneficiary cities across Britain' (Marshall, 2004: 15).

Marshall's finding that inter-agency working has had effects beyond EU programmes is confirmed by other research. Bachtler and Taylor (2003: 35) illustrated how some partnerships set up for structural funding have formally constituted themselves and taken on a wider role, citing examples in Scotland and Wales. A mid-

2 A study of the Yorkshire and Humber Region (Bache, 2000) illustrates the ongoing importance of sub-regional and metropolitan networks alongside the gradual emergence and identification of a regional elite up to and just after 1997.

term evaluation of the Objective 2 structural fund programmes in the UK found a diminishing effect of the structural funds on partnership working over time. However, this was because partnership working had become embedded in regeneration policymaking to such an extent that it was 'now viewed as being part of the architecture' (Fraser Associates, 2003, cited in ECOTEC, 2003: 45).

Partnership was not a new concept in the UK when the 1989 reform of the structural funds came into effect. However, it was a different beast in UK regeneration policies, used primarily by the Conservative Government to undermine local government and increase the role of the private sector (Bache, 2001). A major contribution of the EU partnership requirement, which sought to empower local and regional authorities, was that over time it broke down barriers to inter-agency working for many in British local government, who came to see it more as an opportunity than a threat. This encouraged new ways of working and the development of new networking skills. In this sense the EU has promoted a more consensual and cross-sectoral approach to politics and policymaking in these areas than was generally the case in the adversarial circumstances of the 1980s.

The sub-municiapl level

Chapman (2006) highlighted an 'increasing emphasis' on the role of the voluntary and community sectors (VCS) in structural fund decision-making. This role is promoted by the partnership principle and given particular encouragement by the European Commission. At the sub-municipal level, the Commission's community economic development (CED) approach to partnership has brought new actors into the policy process. The CED approach funds 'capacity building' measures to facilitate 'bottom-up' approaches to development in the most deprived communities, in which local residents are expected take a lead role.

In her study of the implementation of the EU Objective 1 structural fund programme in the sub-region of South Yorkshire, Chapman portrayed a complex multi-level network of relationships below the level of the region, developed to incorporate community actors in decision-making at various levels. The administration of the programme overall was overseen by the sub-regional programme monitoring committee, chaired by the Director of the Government Regional Office, and including representation from public, private and voluntary sectors, including the Commission, central government departments and local authorities. At the municipal level there were programme links to individual local authorities and colleges, local strategic partnerships and task groups established to assist community partnerships in the development of action plans. Below these were the community partnerships involving residents, which should lead decision-making at this level.

Developing bottom-up approaches to economic and social regeneration is widely acknowledged to be a difficult task. In the South Yorkshire context, support for the VCS was provided by a sub-regional umbrella organisation established by the

Objective 1 programme for that very purpose. Chapman (2006) concluded that the overall effects of the structural funds on the VCS are mixed, although there is evidence of empowerment in some areas. At this level, very specific local factors are often crucial in determining the extent to which community partnerships lead the process of regeneration.

CED is regularly seen as one of the innovative aspects of structural funding (Bachtler and Taylor, 2003: vi) and has been influential over domestic policies for community-based regeneration, such as the New Deal for Communities and the Single Regeneration Budget. Particularly influential was the 'Pathways to Employment' experiment within the Merseyside 1994-99 Objective 1 programme, which was identified by national government as a model of best practice and informed domestic programmes aimed at addressing social exclusion (ECOTEC, 2003: 19).

Reflections on governance effects

The empirical evidence suggests that there has been a distinct EU effect at the regional level and below. This has both a territorial dimension in enhancing the English regional tier, and a governance dimension, through the effects of partnership programming at the regional and local/municipal levels, and through CED below the municipal level. However, while there is a distinct EU contribution to multi-level governance, the overall effects on the British polity of this should not be overstated. Whilst the English regions have undoubtedly been strengthened in the past two decades and there is evidence that the structural funds have played a role, they still remain relatively weak within the UK's constitutional arrangements. The main institutions at regional level are Regional Development Agencies overseen by unelected Regional Assemblies. This weakness was confirmed by the decisive vote (4-1) against elected regional government in the North East Region in November 2004 – the region most likely to vote 'yes'. Other planned referendums in the North West and Yorkshire and Humberside Regions were postponed and the issue dropped down the political agenda. In terms of Type 1 multi-level governance (Marks and Hooghe, 2004; also see Chapter 1 by Conzelmann in this volume), which relates to 'general purpose' jurisdictions, the domestic devolution agenda has been far more significant.

Beyond the regions, there is clear evidence that the EU has promoted Type II multi-level governance, leading to the proliferation of task-specific cross-sectoral bodies at regional, local and sub-local levels. This has intrinsic importance in signalling a shift in the nature of governance and a shifting style of politics towards consensualism. However, just as the English regional tier remains weak within the British system of governance, so does the role of local government and there is no suggestion that this situation has been significantly affected by the EU. Moreover, at this stage at least, no significant claims are made about the political importance of the growing number of bottom-up programmes in Britain.

In summary, Britain is increasingly characterised by multi-level governance and the EU has played a role in promoting this development. Its effects on Type I multi-level governance are less pronounced than on Type II, but nonetheless distinct in both cases.

Policy effects

Against the background of the governance effects of the structural funds, discussed above, this section considers the extent to which EU structural funding has also transformed the instruments of regional policy in Britain, and the ways in which those instruments are used. The EU is relevant for domestic regional policy decisions both through its own regional funding activities and through the control it exerts (via its single market powers) over regional state aids. For reasons of space and consistency with our discussion on governance, we focus here on the effects of structural funding (for a discussion of the domestic effects of state aids, see Conzelmann, 2006).

In order to understand the reorienting effects of the structural funds on domestic policy, it is important to note a number of potential drivers of such effects. First, member states cannot access European funding unless they provide 'matching funds' from domestic sources. Whilst member states are, in principle, free to decide from where to take these funds, an obvious strategy is to 'couple' ERDF funding and domestic regional funds in an attempt to increase the effects of domestic regional policy. Thus, when EU and domestic instruments (assisted areas and eligibility criteria) are incongruent, a certain degree of "adaptational pressure" on domestic policy arises. Second, due to their broad eligibility criteria and their integrated management structures, the EU structural funds are seen by many as relatively innovative means of helping disadvantaged regions and as an instrument for systematically organising the exchange of best practices and policy transfers between individual levels of decision-making. Thus, there is also reason to consider the extent to which the development of policy instruments at domestic level has been influenced by 'learning' from the structural funds model (ECOTEC, 2003: 11; Heinelt, 1996; Tömmel, 2002). Finally, drawing down ERDF funding comes at a price – the Regional Policy Directorate of the Commission and sub-national actors are given a say in how European funds and, by implication, the domestic matching monies, are used by member states. The Commission is in a crucial position here, since it can unilaterally withhold the final approval of the spending plans drawn up by the member states. During the 1990s, it did sometimes use this competence to make strict demands regarding the substance of policy or the process of consulting with sub-national actors (Conzelmann, 2002; ECOTEC, 2003: 12; Hooghe and Keating, 1994; McCarthy and Burch, 1994). We now turn to consider how these factors impacted on British regional policy.

The policy environment

There are two principal branches of regional policy in Britain, namely regional industrial policy, administered by the DTI,[3] and regional regeneration policy, administered by the DoE until 1997, the Department for the Environment, Transport and the Regions (DETR) until May 2001, the Department for Transport, Local Government and the Regions (DTLR) until June 2002, the Office of the Deputy Prime Minister (ODPM) until May 2006 and since then by the Department for Communities and Local Government (DCLG). At the regional level, the RDAs are responsible for the implementation of regional regeneration policy.

Both branches of regional policy are distinct in the kinds of instruments employed and the addressees of the interventions. The main focus of regional industrial policy is on firms that are offered investment support through the instrument of Regional Selective Assistance (RSA). In addition, there are also a number of smaller instruments targeted at small and medium-sized enterprises located in the UK's assisted areas. The main purpose of regional regeneration policy is the renewal of deprived inner city areas through improvements to infrastructure, cleaning up the environment and helping SMEs to thrive. Its most important instrument was the Single Regeneration Budget (SRB) for the period before 2002, and subsequently the "Single Programmes" of the RDAs. Both budget lines address the development needs of sub-national, area-related development partnerships.

The distinction between regional industrial policy and regional regeneration policy is important since the policy effects of EU structural policy play out differently in the two branches. One important factor in this is the increasing differentiation of the ways in which ERDF funding can be used since the 1970s. While the ERDF (like more 'traditional' regional policy schemes; see Bachtler and Yuill, 2001) started as a system of regionally differentiated investment grants, it has expanded its eligibility criteria steadily over the years. Nowadays, it still focuses on productive investment leading to the creation or maintenance of jobs and infrastructure development, but all restrictions on what counts as 'infrastructure' and 'industrial investment' have been removed. As explained on the Commission's regional policy website, 'all development areas are covered: transport, communication technologies, energy, the environment, research and innovation, social infrastructure, training, urban redevelopment and the conversion of industrial sites, rural development, the fishing industry, tourism and culture'.[4] This very broad set of eligible funding areas is supported by the third ERDF priority of developing regional endogenous potentials, which was introduced in 1984 and mainly seeks to create a business environment that is conducive to the success of small and medium-sized enterprises (SMEs).

---

3 Since June 2007 the Department for Business, Enterprise and Regulatory Reform.

4 See *Inforegio Website on the European Regional Development Fund*, http://europa.eu.int/comm/regional_policy/funds/prord/prord_en.htm (as of 27 June 2006).

The 1980s

In this context, it became important that from 1984, the ERDF used percentage ranges instead of fixed quotas in order to determine the distribution of resources among the member states (see Bache, 1998: 58-62). In order to reach the upper limit of funds that could be given to any one member state, it became important for policymakers to avail themselves of a relatively large and differentiated pool of projects that could qualify for co-funding from the ERDF. A set of reforms in 1984 consequently expanded the assisted area coverage of the several instruments of British regional industrial policy (from 27.5 to 36.4 per cent of the UK population) in order to increase the pool of projects that could be used as matching funding for the ERDF. At the same time, aid intensity (i.e. the maximum percentage of public money that could be involved in investment projects) was drastically reduced for many assisted regions while high intensities were still available in the most deprived regions. This move reflected both the scepticism of the Thatcher Government regarding the intrinsic worth of large-scale regional policy as well as the outcome of a consultation exercise, during which 'views on overall coverage tended to favour a tightly drawn inner tier in order to focus resources on the areas of greatest need coupled with the widest possible outer tier to facilitate access to ERDF aid" (DTI, 1984: para. 12). At the same time, the so-called 'Regional Development Grant' (RDG), one of the most important regional policy instruments at the time, was reformed. The changes meant that a higher premium was put on job-related investment and that support for industrial replacement investment was terminated. While the first part of this reform also helped the RDG to qualify for monies from the ERDF, the latter part happened in reaction to a complaint by the European Commission's Competition Directorate about the automatic and not job-related nature of the RDG (see Conzelmann, 2002: 207-10 for an extended discussion). Hence, a first step in the transformation of British regional policy during the 1980s was the larger degree of flexibility that was aimed at increasing its potential to cash in on the ERDF funds.

Post-1988

After 1988, the underlying logic of policy changed for a number of reasons. The most important trigger was the 1988 reform of the EU structural funds mentioned above. The decision to introduce autonomous assisted areas and eligibility criteria for the ERDF (hence, to partly 'decouple' the ERDF from national regional policies) meant that the rationale of designing regional industrial policy in a fashion intended to ease access to ERDF monies vanished. Although matching funds from national coffers were still obligatory, they did not need to stem from regional policy instruments per se, but could instead come from 'horizontal' (i.e. not regionally differentiated) schemes. This changed incentive structure, together with the still unfettered scepticism of the Conservative Government regarding the value of regional industrial policies, led to important reforms to British regional policy. Thus, the year 1988 brought the end for the RDG as the longest standing instrument of regional policy in Britain, while the importance of Regional Selective Assistance (RSA) as the other pillar of regional industrial policy in Britain was greatly enhanced. In practice, RSA (which was eventually terminated in 2004) was henceforth focused mainly on larger-scale investment by internationally mobile capital (see Armstrong, 2001). Since the use of ERDF resources for supporting such forms of regional policy was (and is) viewed critically both by the Commission and Whitehall, the importance of RSA as a source of matching funds for European monies began to decline, while regional regeneration policy became the principal source of matching funds for the ERDF post-1988.

Post-1995: a parallel regional policy

The main instrument of regional regeneration policy in England from the mid 1990s, and one of the most important sources of ERDF matching funds, was the SRB. This instrument was introduced in 1994-5, survived the Labour victory in 1997, and, from 2002 onwards, was merged with the "Single Programme" budgets of the individual RDAs. Both instruments are little more than a budget: while there are rather strict procedural rules, no strings are attached over territorial or substantive eligibility criteria. The basic approach of both instruments is to let sub-national partnerships put projects forward to Whitehall – or, post-2002, the RDAs – and then for government officials to decide whether to make assistance available. The co-ordination between regeneration spending and European funding has been a key concern in both systems. Under the 'old' system, there was an explicit stipulation by the government that bids for SRB assistance should be designed in a way that attracts maximum European funding (ODPM, 2005b: paras. 1.6.7. and 1.6.12). This, together with the relatively loose stipulations concerning eligibility criteria for assisted areas, inevitably led to a strong influence by the ERDF on domestic regional regeneration policy. Second, sub-national partnerships were asked to relate their proposals to strategic development plans for their individual regions, which did not really exist outside the area of EU structural funding during the 1990s. Third, it has been argued that partnerships that have developed within EU-assisted regions are both more experienced in drawing up plans that stand a good chance of receiving SRB funds and are at the same time more capable of managing large-scale regeneration projects in an appropriate manner (House of Commons, 1995, paras 64-5). In sum, there are a number of indications that the implementation of regional regeneration policy both as regards assisted areas and policy priorities was strongly shaped by the European funding regime and also by direct Commission influence during the 1990s. In some cases, there were concerns among regional players that the EU influence resulted in an "insufficient appreciation of national conditions and systems, leading to …

inappropriate approaches or systems". Furthermore, there was domestic criticism of undue influence by EU officials on project selection and "pressure on regions to absorb money into existing aid schemes as a way of spending funds quickly" (Michie and Bachtler, 1996: 43-44).

Post-1997: An integrated policy framework

While the SRB produced a rather haphazard pattern of funding priorities and assisted areas, more consistency has been achieved in recent years through the production of Regional Economic Strategies (RES) under the auspices of the RDAs. One study reported that during the 2000-2006 programming period the conflicts between the European and domestic funding regimes were less intense due to the regionalisation of the UK. "The renewed focus on regional planning in the UK and the development of new regional structures and institutions have secured the integration of Structural Funds with wider regional programmes" (ECOTEC, 2003: 11). The government also acknowledged that, in the course of drawing up the Regional Economic Strategies, "links were made between the emerging RES and the [European] programming documents", so that "the [EU] regional programmes are broadly in line with the economic development priorities set out in the RES" (ODPM, 2005a: 13). Since the process of drawing up the Regional Economic Strategies and the structural funds programming documents for the 2000-2006 period usually ran in parallel in the English regions, it is hard to assess the extent of the 'European' influence on the Regional Economic Strategies. While the greater congruence between domestic and European funding regimes "has partly been achieved through UK policy objectives moving more into line with the approaches promoted through the Structural Funds" (ECOTEC, 2003: 67), it should be noted that it was primarily the domestic reform agenda of the newly elected Labour Government that led to matching policy priorities.

Reflections on policy effects

The net result of the developments discussed above is the emergence of a two-tier regional policy in Britain during the 1990s. On the one side, there are regional regeneration activities that obtain their spatial dimension partly through government decisions, but inevitably also through the designation of eligible areas for ERDF purposes. In this area, domestic and European policies have become entangled to a large degree, so that it becomes difficult to clearly delineate domestic and European policies and to identify causal effects running between the two. The same goes for the policy networks that have formed round these policies. As was outlined also in the governance sections, the implementation networks usually encompass players from both the European and the domestic side, so we can speak of a "reshaping" rather than "reorienting" effect of the EU. On the other side, regional industrial policy continues within domestic assisted areas with little European influence apart from the increasing constraints imposed by EU control of regional state aid (Conzelmann, 2006). The most significant EU effect regarding regional industrial policy is the reorientation of the instruments towards the aim of tapping the ERDF funds during the 1980s. However, with the advent of regional regeneration policy, this motivation vanished. Subsequently, there has been a relatively strong focus of regional industrial policy on attracting inward investment – a priority that as a matter of principle is not co-funded by the EU instruments. Due to the development of this two-tier regional policy, there is in principle no longer strong pressure to make the domestic assisted areas and the ERDF areas congruent.[5]

It is important to note that these effects are caused by the lesser degree of 'coupling' between European and traditional domestic policy instruments that emerged after the crucial 1988 reform of the structural funds. The reforms made it possible to operate a European regional policy in the EU member states with very little direct relation to traditional forms of regional policy (i.e. large scale infrastructure and investment support in peripheral or otherwise disadvantaged regions; see Bachtler and Yuill, 2001). If national governments (as in Germany) insisted on a tight link between European funding and traditional domestic regional policy, conflicts over funding priorities and the congruence between European and domestic assisted areas became much more intense (Conzelmann, 2002: 146-159). This did not happen in Britain due to the more adaptive approach of the Conservative Government, but also due to its lesser belief in the merits of traditional regional policy.

Conclusions

In summing up, we can identify a number of EU-related effects in relation to governance and policy in Britain. With respect to governance, we have observed the enhancement of the regional tier, the emergence of more partnership-oriented, inter-agency work at and between several territorial levels, and the incorporation into domestic governance of practices first developed in EU programmes. In relation to policy, there are clear efforts on the side of the government to design regional policies in a way to make them attractive as co-financing instruments of the structural funds and to facilitate access to the funds. In this way, the EU level increasingly

5 Consequently, more than 40 per cent of the UK population who currently live in an 'Objective 2' area designated for ERDF purposes are not part of an RSA area. This will change in the course of the current reviews of the UK assisted areas map and the drawing up of the National Strategic Reference Framework (NSRF) for the use of structural funds in the 2007-2013 period. Significantly, both review exercises are completely isolated from each other; and the UK government is unlikely to change its position that it "does not accept that the areas eligible for Structural Funds and the Assisted Areas need be identical" (DTI, 1998: para.8).

became an important context within which decisions on the reform and evolution of domestic policies were taken.

While on the surface this seems to be clear evidence of a europeanisation process, its significance should not be overstated. With respect to both the governance and the policy effects, central government has been instrumental in shaping developments rather than simply succumbing to 'adaptational pressure'. In the first phase of the 'new English regionalism', central government sought to steer EU regional policy networks and acted as a financial gatekeeper over the domestic effects of the funds. The creation of GROs by the Conservative Government was partly an attempt to steer the regional networks more effectively, which they proved capable of doing. However, by the late 1990s, GROs were often facilitating rather than steering networks, even where partnership relations had been most problematic. This change was partly through a process of learning induced by EU structural policy. Through experience of partnership working GROs became more comfortable with the practice and less interventionist in detailed processes. If this process of change started in the regional civil service, it became more widespread with the election of a Labour Government in 1997, less opposed in principle to regional policy, less hostile to the EU and enthusiastic about partnership. Yet, while the Labour Government embraced many aspects of the EU's regional policy, becoming a keen advocate of partnership and bottom-up approaches in particular, it also outlined the boundaries of its support and the ongoing centrality of its role. First, by demonstrating that while it has sympathy for regional development and devolved institutions, this does not stretch to conceding control over the financial mechanisms through which EU structural funding is allocated in the UK: the Treasury remains the financial gatekeeper (Bache and Bristow, 2003). Second, the Chancellor of the Exchequer called for a renationalisation of EU regional policy to allow the wealthier member states to reclaim and spend their share of structural funding domestically (Treasury/DTI/ODPM, 2003).

In policy terms, a very similar pattern can be observed. The Conservative as well as the Labour Governments reacted to the changing European context in a flexible manner. Drawing down monies from the ERDF has consistently been a prime motivation in shaping domestic policy instruments, and governments have been ready to change or give up policy instruments that no longer served this purpose. Whitehall has also been content with the relatively strong influence of ERDF funds on regional regeneration policy with respect to the spatial coverage and the kind of activities funded. To the extent that there have been conflicts between Brussels and Whitehall, these tended to focus on the difficult issue of additionality of domestic spending and on certain issues of implementation such as the practices of 'top-slicing' part of the ERDF monies and distributing them outside of the usual programming approaches favoured by the Commission (see Conzelmann, 2002: 231-4). This, as well as the development and retention of a regional industrial policy largely shielded from EU influence and the conflict over the congruence of domestic and ERDF assisted areas demonstrates that the ability of domestic policymakers to control the effects of the funds remains largely untouched.

In this context, the significance of multi-level governance in Britain remains fairly circumscribed. While there is a clear transformative effect in the sense of increased partnership and inter-agency collaboration at the sub-national level, the emerging mode of governance resembles the "Type II" MLG structures identified in the introductory chapter. These governance arrangements are task-specific and, as such, may be disbanded once they have fulfilled their tasks. In addition, it is not yet clear to what extent the differentiated structure of the British polity is important for other policy areas as well. Finally, the central state continues to command greater resources – political, constitutional-legal, financial and organisational – than any other actor within the domestic arena. However, in this changing context, the central state increasingly has to find new and innovative governing tools and instruments to ensure that it remains more than 'first among equals'. In that sense, the emergence of MLG structures in Britain can also be interpreted as one facet of a more far-reaching transformation of statehood in Europe (Schuppert, 2006).

A final observation is that the notion of 'adaptational pressure' emanating from EU requirements infers an unrealistic picture of how europeanisation materialises in regional governance and policy. With respect to policies, it is hard to argue that Brussels prescribes a certain policy model that is then implemented in the EU member states (albeit to varying degrees). The basic outcome of europeanisation is not the change of certain policy instruments, but their different application under the conditions of a changing European context. In this sense, the idea of adaptational pressures implies a degree of coercion that understates the importance of learning in the process of 'europeanisation'. Similarly, with respect to the governance dimension, it is clear that EU policies provided pressures (and incentives) for new structures and processes, but there is also plenty of evidence in the period up to the mid 1990s that most of those introduced were superficial, and that established practices and power relations survived the surface changes. In this period, there was evidence of actors strategically reorientating their practices, but only later was there evidence of reshaping of actors' preferences following a sustained period of interactions within the multi-level networks promoted by structural policy. In the long run, of course, it is this reshaping rather than strategic reorientation that is likely to prove most significant in the changing architecture of governance in Europe.

References

Adshead, M. (2002). *Developing European Regions? Comparative governance, policy networks and European integration*. Aldershot: Ashgate.

Anderson J. (1996). Germany and the Structural Funds: Unification Leads to Bifurcation. In L. Hooghe (Ed.), *Cohesion Policy and European Integration: Building Multi-level Governance* (pp.163-194). Oxford: Oxford University Press.

Anderson, J. (1990). Skeptical Reflections on a Europe of Regions: Britain, Germany, and the ERDF. *Journal of Public Policy, 10(4)*, pp.417–447.

Armstrong, H. (2001). Regional Selective Assistance: Is the Spend Enough and Is It Targeting the Right Places? *Regional Studies, 35 (3)*, pp.247-257.

Bache, I. (1998). *The Politics of European Union Regional Policy. Multi-level Governance or Flexible Gatekeeping?* Sheffield: Sheffield Academic Press.

Bache, I. (1999). The Extended Gatekeeper: Central Government and the Implementation of EC Regional Policy in the UK. *Journal of European Public Policy, 6 (1),* pp.28-45.

Bache, I. (2000). Government Within Governance: Steering Economic Regeneration Policy Networks in Yorkshire and Humberside. *Public Administration, 78 (3),* pp.575-592.

Bache, I. (2001). Different Seeds in the Same Plot? Competing Models of Capitalism and the Incomplete Contracts of Partnership Design. *Public Administration, 79 (2),* pp.337-359.

Bache, I. (2008). *Europeanization and Multi-level Governance: Cohesion Policy in the European Union and Britain.* Lanham: Rowman and Littlefield.

Bache, I. and Bristow, G. (2003). Devolution and the Core Executive: The Struggle for European Funds. *British Journal of Politics and International Relations, 5 (3),* pp.405-427.

Bache I. and Flinders, M. (2004a). Multi-Level Governance and British Politics. In I. Bache and M. Flinders (Eds.), *Multi-Level Governance* (pp.93-106). Oxford: Oxford University Press.

Bache, I. and Flinders, M. (2004b). Multi-Level Governance and the Study of British Politics and Government. *Public Policy and Administration, 19 (1),* pp.31-52.

Bache, I., George, S. and Rhodes, R. (1996). Regionalism in a Unitary State: The Case of the United Kingdom. In Hesse, J. (Ed.), *Regions in Europe II* (pp.57-80). Baden-Baden: Nomos Verlagsgesellschaft.

Bache, I. and Jones, R. (2000). Empowering the Regions? The Political Impact of EC Regional Policy in Britain and Spain. *Regional and Federal Studies, 10 (2)*, pp.1-20.

Bache, I. and Jordan, A. (2006). Europeanization and Domestic Change. In I. Bache (Ed.), *The Europeanization of British Politics* (pp.17-33). Basingstoke: Palgrave Macmillan.

Bachtler, J. and Taylor, S. (2003). *The Added Value of the Structural Funds: A Regional Perspective.* IQ-Net Report on the Reform of the Structural Funds. Glasgow: European Policies Research Centre.

Bachtler, J. and Yuill, D. (2001). *Policies and Strategies for Regional Development: A Shift in Paradigm (Regional and Industrial Policy Research Paper 46)*. Glasgow: European Policy Research Centre.

Balme, R. and Jouve, B. (1996). Building the Regional State: Europe and Territorial Organization in France. In L. Hooghe (Ed.), *Cohesion Policy and European Integration: Building Multi-level Governance* (pp.219-255). Oxford: Oxford University Press.

Benz, A.. and Eberlein, T. (1999). The Europeanization of Regional Policies: Patterns of Multi-level Governance. *Journal of European Public Policy, 6 (2)*, pp.329–348.

Burch, M. and Gomez, R. (2004, July). *Europeanisation and the English Regions*. Paper presented to the ESRC/UACES Conference on Britain in Europe and Europe in Britain: The Europeanisation of British Politics? Sheffield Town Hall.

Burch, M. and Gomez, R. (2006). The English Regions. In I. Bache and A. Jordan (Eds.), *The Europeanization of British Politics?* (pp.82-97) Basingstoke: Palgrave Macmillan.

Chapman, R. (2006). The Third Sector. In I. Bache and A. Jordan (Eds.), *The Europeanization of British Politics?* (pp.168-183) Basingstoke: Palgrave Macmillan.

Church, J. (1993). *The Provision of Regional and Local Statistics: UK Overview*. Paper given to the Statistics' Users Council Annual Conference, 16 November. Esher: IMAC Research.

Conzelmann, T. (1995). Networking and the Politics of EU Regional Policy: Lessons from North Rhine-Westphalia, Nord-Pas de Calais and North West England. *Regional and Federal Studies 5 (2)*, pp.134-172.

Conzelmann, T. (2002). *Große Räume, kleine Räume. Europäisierte Regionalpolitik in Deutschland und Großbritannien*. Baden-Baden: Nomos.

Conzelmann, T. (2006). Regional Policy. In I. Bache (Ed.), *The Europeanization of British Politics* (pp.248-262). Basingstoke: Palgrave Macmillan.

DTI (Department of Trade and Industry) (1984). *Regional Industrial Development*. London: DTI.

DTI (1998). *Review of the Assisted Areas Map. A Consultation Paper*. London: DTI.

ECOTEC (2003). *Evaluation of the Added Value and Costs of the European Structural Funds in the UK. Final Report to the Department of Trade and Industry (DTI) and the Office of the Deputy Prime Minister (ODPM)*. London: ECOTEC Research and Consulting Limited.

Gamble, A. (2000). Policy Agendas in a Multi-Level Polity. In P. Dunleavy, A. Gamble, and I. Holliday (Eds.), *Developments in British Politics 6* (pp.290-307). London : Macmillan.

Gualini, E. (2003). Challenges to multi-level governance: contradictions and conflicts in the Europeanization of Italian regional policy. *Journal of European Public Policy, 10 (4)*, pp.616-636.

Heinelt, H. (1996). Multilevel Governance and the European Structural Funds. In H. Heinelt and R. Smith (Eds.), *Policy Networks and European Structural Funds* (pp.9-25). Aldershot: Avebury.

Heinelt, H. and Smith, R. (Eds.) (1996). *Policy Networks and European Structural Funds*. Aldershot: Avebury .

Heinelt, H., Kopp-Malek, T. and Lang, J. (2005). *Die Entwicklung der EU-Strukturfonds als kumulativer Politikprozess*. Baden-Baden: Nomos.

HM Treasury, DTI and Office of the Deputy Prime Minister (2003). *A modern regional policy for the United Kingdom*. Norwich: HMSO.

HoC (House of Commons) (1995). *Regional Policy. Fourth Report by the Trade and Industry Committee, together with the proceedings of the Committee; Session 1994-95*. London: HMSO.

Hooghe, L. (Ed.) (1996). *Cohesion Policy and European Integration: Building Multi-Level Governance*. Oxford: Oxford University Press.

Hooghe, L. and Keating, M. (1994). The Politics of EC Regional Policy. *Journal of European Public Policy, 3 (3)*, pp. 367-393.

Hooghe, L. and Marks, G. (2003). Unravelling the Central State, But How? *American Political Science Review, 97 (2)*, pp.233-243.

Marks, G. and Hooghe, L. (2004). Contrasting Visions of Multi-level Governance. In I. Bache and M. Flinders (Eds.), *Multi-level Governance* (pp.15-30). Oxford: Oxford University Press.

Marshall, A. (2004, July). *Europeanisation at the urban level: evaluating the impact of the EU on local governance in Britain*. Paper presented to The ESRC/UACES conference on The Europeanisation of British Politics, Sheffield. Available at: www.shef.ac.uk/ebpp

McCarthy, A. and Burch, M. (1994). European Regional Development Strategies: The Response of Two Northern Regions. *Local Government Policy Making, 20 (5)*, pp. 31-38.

Michie R. and Bachtler J. (1996). *Managing the Structural Funds: Institutionalising Good Practice*. IQ-Net Thematic Paper, 1(1). Glasgow: European Policies Research Centre..

Office of the Deputy Prime Minister (2005a). *Realising the Potential of All Our Regions: the story so far*. London: HMSO. Available at http://www.communities.gov.uk/pub/481/ RealisingthePotentialofallourRegions thestorysofar PDF1197Kb_id1139481.pdf

Office of the Deputy Prime Minister (2005b). *Bidding Guidance for the SRB round 6.* Available at: http://www.odpm.gov.uk/index.asp?id=1128130

Pierre, J. and Stoker, G. (2000). Towards Multi-level Governance. In P. Dunleavy, A. Gamble and I. Holliday (Eds.), *Developments in British Politics 6* (pp.29-46). London: MacMillan.

Regional Policy Commission (1996). *Renewing the Regions. Strategies for Regional Economic Development.* Sheffield: Regional Policy Commission.

Schuppert, G. F. (2006). The Europeanisation of National Governance Structures in the Context of the Transformation of Statehood. In G. F. Schuppert (Ed.), *The Europeanisation of Governance* (pp.9-58). Baden-Baden: Nomos.

Smyrl, M. (1997). Does European Community Regional Policy Empower the Regions? *Governance, 10 (3)*, pp. 287-309.

Tömmel, I. (2002). Die Regionalpolitik der EU: Systementwicklung durch Politikgestaltung. In T. Conzelmann and M. Knodt (Eds.), *Regionales Europa - Europäisierte Regionen* (pp.39-68). Frankfurt am Main: Campus.

III. New Fields, New Levels: Bringing Multi-level Governance to New Horizons

Emerging Patterns of Multi-Level Governance in EU Environmental Policy

Christoph Knill and Jale Tosun

Introduction

In the last three decades, the environmental policy of the EU has developed in a remarkable fashion. Starting off as a 'by-product' of economic integration, EU environmental policy developed as a policy field of its own from the early 1970s onwards. Today, it represents a core area of European legislative activities (Jordan, 1999a: 5). This development has been characterised by an ongoing widening and deepening of supranational competences and activities. As the EU dominates the environmental policy agenda of the member states, they are frequently forced to adjust their national regulations, policy instruments and administrative structures to European guidelines (Héritier, Knill and Mingers, 1996; Knill, 2001). It is beyond question that Brussels exerts a considerable influence on the environmental policies of the member states (Sbragia, 2000: 294).

At the same time, however, the member states have managed to preserve a dominant role within this complex multi-level governance structure. On the one hand, this can be explained by the subsidiarity principle for environmental policy which was established by the Treaty of Maastricht in 1992. This principle, which does not apply only to environmental policy but rather constitutes a fundamental principle of European Union law, requires that the EU may act only where member states agree that action by individual countries is insufficient. On the other hand, this dominance is also based on the fact that despite the EU's increasing supranational decision-making competences, implementation has largely remained with member states (Kelemen, 2000: 151).

This multi-layered structure of EU polity with a decision-making authority that spreads across local to supranational levels offers a strong challenge to environmental policy co-ordination in terms of efficiency and legitimacy. In particular, the identification of an 'implementation deficit' has triggered a broad debate about the appropriateness of 'traditional' governance ideas. These discussions culminated in a shift in EU environmental governance at the beginning of the 1990s. This 'new governance' in EU environmental policy abolished interventionist command-and-control regulation in favour of 'context-oriented' governance, characterised by 'new', often procedural policy instruments.

Against the backdrop of these developments, this chapter seeks to answer three main questions. First of all, we are interested in distinguishing the new modes of environmental governance from the 'old' ones. What are the characteristics of the new governance in EU environmental policy? Second, we want to assess the substantive improvement in environmental policymaking due to these instruments. Are the novel environmental policy instruments more effective? And finally, we seek to find out whether the introduction of new governance modes implies a profound change in underlying ideas about governance. Do they entail a genuine transformation of environmental policy governance in the EU?

As we will illustrate in the following sections, the development of preferred governance forms in EU environmental policy is similar to developments that have occurred in other policy fields, e.g. regional policy. And analogous to the experiences in these other policy sectors, the initial enthusiasm about new regulatory approaches has given way to a more realistic assessment of the capability of these instruments.

In order to address our research questions, we proceed as follows. First of all, to reflect the object of this chapter, we outline the development of EU environmental policy as a particular policy field. Second, we point out the most important institutional and legal elements of EU environmental policy in the multi-level governance context. Third, we address the major shortcomings in political steering that emerged from the traditional modes of EU environmental policy governance. This is followed by an overview of the new governance approaches and the corresponding set of instruments, which are discussed in the fifth section. The final section offers some conclusions.

The Evolution of Environmental Policy as a European Policy Domain

Since the beginning of the 1970s we have witnessed a steady expansion of environmental policy activities at the European level. An increasingly dense network of European legislation has emerged, which has now been extended to all areas of environmental protection. This development in EU environmental policy is a little surprising in the light of the legal and institutional conditions which existed in the early days of the European Community (EC). In contrast to other policy fields, EU environmental policy was not explicitly mentioned in the 1957 Treaty of Rome that established the Community. This can be explained by a lack of awareness of the issue at the time, as the European Community was designed primarily to promote economic co-operation (Johnson and Corcelle, 1989: 1).

The Paris Summit meeting of heads of state and government of the European Community's existing and acceding member states in October 1972 can be viewed as the beginning of an independent EU environmental policy. At this conference, a declaration on environmental and consumer policy was adopted, giving the European Commission the task of drawing up an action programme for environmental protection. To this end, an environmental task force was created in the

Commission that was later to develop into the Directorate General for Environmental and Consumer Protection and Nuclear Safety. The Community's first action programme on the environment was adopted in July 1973. By agreeing to this environmental action programme, the members states assigned to the Community an environmental policy mandate (Liefferink, Lowe and Mol, 1993: 2).

The main motive for launching a common environmental policy was driven by the fear that trade barriers and competitive distortions in the common market could emerge due to different environmental standards (Johnson and Corcelle, 1989). EU environmental policy therefore was mainly introduced as a 'flanking policy' to the creation of a common market. A further reason for establishing an EU environmental policy was the growing international perception of environmental problems, as discussed at the United Nations Conference on the Human Environment in Stockholm in 1972. The cross-border nature of certain forms of environmental pollution received particular attention. Alongside these economic and ecological motives, an additional factor can be found in the goal of approximating living conditions in the EU as defined in the preamble and Article 2 of the Treaty on the European Union (TEU). The goals of a 'continual improvement of living and employment conditions' and 'rapid increase in the standard of living' were interpreted by the Community institutions in terms of not only a quantitative, but also a qualitative rise in the standard of living. This interpretation implies that the improvement of the state of the environment is one of the goals of the Community (Holzinger, 1994: 67; Krämer, 2000; Rehbinder and Stewart, 1985: 20).

Despite the fact that environmental policy was built on the legal foundations for trade policy, the output of this first phase can be regarded as a success. Within a decade, a very substantial set of European environmental laws had emerged, with many important areas of environmental policy being regulated at the European level (see Haigh, 2000). By the middle of the 1980s, three additional environmental action programmes had been passed together with about 200 binding legal acts, primarily in the form of directives and regulations (Liefferink, Lowe and Mol, 1993: 2; Weale, 1996: 597; Zito, 1999). This progress can be attributed in part to the pioneering role of individual member states. Germany and The Netherlands in particular lobbied for higher levels of environmental protection (Andersen and Liefferink, 1997; Kelemen, 2000: 150).

With the enactment of the Single European Act (SEA) in 1987, a common environmental policy was explicitly embodied in the EU Treaties. Uncertainty about the legal basis for EU environmental policy was therefore removed. The necessary legal basis for environmental policy activities, which had previously been based on economic integration by the general clauses of Articles 100 and 235 of the Treaty, was replaced by legitimation on the basis of environmental policy goals. This required two substantive changes. First, a new title 'environment' was added to the Treaty, comprising Articles 174-6 (ex-Article 130r-t) of the TEU. These articles included not only provisions on the general significance and goals of EU environmental policy, but also defined the basic principles and decision-making procedures by which these goals were to be achieved. Furthermore, general conditions with regard to the allocation of European and national environmental policy responsibilities and capabilities for action were specified. Second, the introduction of new rules to accelerate economic integration had ramifications for the design of EU environmental policy. These legal changes were based on Articles 18 (ex-Article 8a) and 95 (ex-Article 100a).

The Treaties of Maastricht and Amsterdam have further strengthened the EU's authority and capacity for action. Most importantly, the Maastricht Treaty modified the decision-making procedure. The increased significance of environmental policy becomes apparent in the changes in the decision-making procedure under the Maastricht Treaty. Environmental policy measures on the basis of Article 175 were to be decided by qualified majority voting (QMV), as was already the case for measures relevant to the common market on the basis of Article 95. These changes in the decision-making procedure were followed by a further strengthening of the powers of the European Parliament (EP) in the Amsterdam Treaty. The co-operation procedure introduced with the SEA was replaced by the co-decision procedure, in which the EP and the Council of Ministers have equal power and the Parliament has a right of veto (Judge, Earnshaw and Cowan, 1994). Following the Treaties of Maastricht and Amsterdam, a further Treaty revision was adopted in Nice in 2000. The consequences of this revision for the environmental field were very limited. Since Nice, an attempt has been made to replace the existing Treaties by a new, comprehensive Constitutional Treaty. Due to failed referenda in France and The Netherlands in 2005 and in Ireland in 2008, however, it is unclear whether the changes foreseen in the Constitutional Treaty and the Lisbon Treaty will enter into force. If they do, the most significant change for the environmental policy field would be the revision of the system of QMV.

Another important institutional innovation was the establishment of the European Environmental Agency in Copenhagen in 1994, which hints at a further institutionalisation of EU environmental policy. The most recent undertaking is the Sixth Environment Action Programme of the European Community launched in 2001. It seeks to strengthen European legislation in the priority areas of climate change, nature and biodiversity, environment, health and quality of life, and natural resources and waste.

Although the dynamics of the initial phases have been reduced in recent years, environmental policy reflects an area where supranational policy competences have developed extensively. The next section of the chapter therefore provides an overview of the main actors and institutions active in the formulation of EU environmental policy. By looking closely at how this policy is actually made, we seek to offer a way in to understand environmental policy orientations and governance patterns of EU environmental policy.

Environmental Policymaking in the EU Multi-Level Structure

Environmental policymaking in the EU follows a complex pattern as a result of several factors. It implies the interplay of national and European institutions in a multi-level governance structure. While this does not sound too complicated at first glance, the implications of this complex structure become clearer when attention is paid to the fact that this interaction includes both vertical (EU - member states) and horizontal (among single member states or EU institutions) distribution of decision-making authority. At the supranational level, for instance, there are several institutions that participate in decision-making. The power of these institutions increased significantly from the mid-1980s onwards. By the time of the Treaty of Maastricht the member states were empowered by the introduction of QMV, which intensified the regulatory contest between the member states.

Yet, for illustrating the potential differences for effective governance within this multi-level polity, it is not sufficient to refer to the distribution of decision-making responsibilities. Another important feature of EU environmental policy is that it is more a regulatory patchwork consisting of different instruments, principles and strategies rather than a single coherent body of legislation. To provide a clear picture of environmental policymaking in the EU, we first introduce the main actors. Who are the important actors? What are their responsibilities? Second, we address the policy positions and governance patterns of EU environmental policymaking. What are the most important principles and guidelines?

Central institutions and actors

The most important European institutions in environmental policymaking are the Commission, the Council of Ministers, the EP, the European Court of Justice (ECJ) and the European Environmental Agency (EEA). At the stage of policy formulation, the Commission is the key actor as the regulatory approach that it adopts can be very difficult to change in any major way. Therefore, the Commission's proposals usually define the ground on which governments negotiate (Sbragia, 2000: 298). The Commission, as the 'guardian of the treaties' is, moreover, responsible for controlling the transposition and application of Community law in the member states.

On the decision-making procedure in general, the Council of Ministers is the most important institution since it decides on the adoption of European legislative measures, such as directives and regulations on environmental policy. The co-ordination dilemma that affects multi-level governance in the EU shows up very clearly in the Council. The goal of individual members of the Council is to assert their national interests at the European level to the greatest possible extent, in order to avoid criticism from their own governments, affected societal interest groups and voters. At the same time, it is in the common interest of all members to reach agreement. Nevertheless, the definition of national interests and policy positions in individual cases is often disputed at the member state level. For example, environment ministers from member states, where environmental protection is a comparatively minor priority, have frequently used the negotiations at the European level as a means of strengthening environmental policy concerns at the national level (Collier and Golub, 1997: 237).

Though the powers of the EP can hardly be compared with those of national parliaments, the introduction of the co-operation procedure in the SEA in 1987 led to an extension of the very limited decision-making powers of the EP for all decisions relevant to the common market and thus all environmental policy measures which fell into this category. With the co-decision procedure introduced under the Maastricht Treaty, the EP was empowered to make decisions on an equal footing with the Council; and with the Treaty of Amsterdam, the co-decision procedure was expanded to cover all areas of environmental policy. These developments were important as, from the beginning, the EP played a very active role in strengthening the common environmental policy. However, it is highly questionable whether a parliament with considerably enhanced legislative authority would still be the same parliament from an environmental standpoint.

As the ECJ is responsible for the interpretation of and compliance with primary and secondary Community law, it has made decisive contributions to the formation and development of the EU's environmental policy, particularly during the period when a Treaty basis was lacking. And once environmental protection was incorporated into the Treaty by the SEA, the ECJ played an important role in developing criteria for balancing economic and environmental policy goals. The various decisions of the ECJ on how to interpret the treaties had important ramifications for the development of new legal measures because they changed the potential for action by the actors involved in the decision-making process (Alter and Meunier-Aitsahalia, 1994; McCown, 2006). Moreover, the ECJ also played an important role in the implementation and application of European legislation in the member states – an increasingly explosive political issue.

The EEA does not have any regulatory authority in terms of the development of policy or the implementation of European legislation in the member states. However, it fulfils an essential task through the gathering and processing of information on the state of the environment in the Union. This information is designed to allow for a comparative analysis of the state of the environment in the member states and to provide empirical indicators which can be used as a basis for the design of environmental policy measures at the level of both the member states and the EU (Dilling, 2000).

Besides the institutions at the EU level, there is a growing number of private actors who aim to exert influence on the formation of European environmental policies. In particular since the adoption of the SEA and the realisation of the common market programme, we have seen a dramatic increase in the number of societal actors and organisations at the European level. The primary goals of the European interest groups are gathering information for their members on developments in Brussels and the packaging of their members' interests as well as representing these interests to the Community institutions in the policymaking process (Aspinwall and Greenwood, 1998; Greenwood, 1997; Mazey and Richardson, 2006). As a result, there is an asymmetry with respect to representation by and the assertiveness of different interests at the European level. For environmental policy, this unequal distribution of influence is demonstrated by the overrepresentation of economic interests. Business interest groups clearly outweigh environmental interests not only in terms of numbers, but are also generally better equipped financially and in terms of staff expertise (Hey and Brendle, 1994: 331-387; Mazey and Richardson, 2006).

Finally, the multi-level structure of the EU in the environmental field is complemented by one further element in the role of the EU in international environmental institutions (see Birkel and Liefferink in this volume). In general, the EU has played an influential role in this context. At the same time, EU environmental policy has been driven and influenced by developments at the international level. The UN Conference on the Human Environment in 1972, for instance, became an essential catalyst for the development of EU environmental activities (Jordan, 1999a: 3).

The principles of EU environmental policy

The basic principles of the common environmental policy are codified in Articles 174-176 of the SEA. While Article 174 (1) defines the objectives of EU environmental policy, Article 174 (2) codifies the four central principles on precaution, action at the source, compensation of pollution by the polluter, and integration. The precautionary principle stipulates that environmental policy action should not be taken only when concrete damage has been demonstrated, but instead should be directed at preventing dangers and risks. The principle of action at the source implies that environmental damage should be combated at the source where it originates. The polluter pays principle states that the polluter should bear the costs for the prevention, removal of and compensation for environmental damage. The principle of integration means that the demands of environmental protection should be taken into account during the formulation and implementation of measures in other policy areas of the Union, such as transport, regional or agricultural policy.

Article 174 (3) specifies criteria and restrictions which have to be considered during the development of environmental action programmes and individual measures. Hence the common environmental policy is supposed to consider the current state of science and technology as well as the economic and social development of the Union and the regions. At the same time, the foundations are laid for the introduction of regionally differentiated environmental standards by establishing that the particular environmental conditions in the individual regions of the Union must be taken into account. Previously, the Union was under some pressure to set uniform standards, because environmental protection measures usually had to be based on the harmonisation conditions of Article 94.

Article 176 authorises the member states to maintain or introduce stricter environmental rules than those of the Union. However, the member states are granted this possibility only to the extent that national specifications exceeding those of the EU are in accordance with the goals of the TEU. The result of this is that unilateral national policies are not allowed, for instance, when they stand in the way of the goal of completing the common market. This kind of 'common market relevance' comes into play, in particular, when tradeable products are affected by demands for environmental protection.

On the themes of this chapter, the rules on the allocation of decision-making capacity are of crucial importance. The allocation of environmental policy authority is aligned with functional efficiency criteria. Environmental policy standards, as a rule, should be defined at the level which is most capable of dealing with the problem at hand (see Holzinger, 2000). Addressing environmental problems at an inappropriate level not merely undermines the effectiveness but also the legitimacy of environmental policy. This policy orientation was initially expressed by the principle of the appropriate level of action, which had been laid down in the First Environmental Action Programme of 1973. It stipulated that for each category of environmental problems, in view of their scope and nature, the level of action should be chosen which is most suitable for formulating and implementing the necessary measures. Thus, it is recognised that environmental conditions that vary nationally, regionally or locally, demand different political actions and measures.

The second principle which is related to the allocation of environmental policy authority is the concept of subsidiarity. This principle had already been formulated in the First Environmental Action Programme, then was codified by Article 174 (4) of the SEA and elevated to a general principle of joint action in the Treaty of Maastricht Article 5 (ex-Article 3b). According to this principle, the Community is allowed to become active in the area of the environment only when the 'objectives can be better reached at the Community level than at the level of the individual member states' (Article 174 (4) TEU).

Though both principles are meant to ensure appropriate sovereignty for the member states in terms of environmental policymaking, there is a general tendency to centralise authority at the European level (Holzinger and Knill, 2002; Scharpf, 1994, 137). This transfer of authority to European level institutions reflects general developments in the structure of multi-level governance in Europe (Hooghe and Marks, 2001). It reinforces the conflict between the EU and its member states and their subordinate levels. This holds true in particular for those member states that have federal systems (Garbe, 1996: 37). Federal and strongly decentralised states should experience greater involvement by lower levels of government in environmental policy than unitary states (Liefferink and Jordan, 2004: 41).

In fact, within a palpable multi-level structure such as the EU, the concepts of sovereignty and subsidiarity are closely interlinked. According to Golub (1996), environmental policy represents the clearest example of this connection between sovereignty and subsidiarity. 'The subsidiarity debate forces proponents of integration to address this question of democratic legitimacy when determining the proper allocation of authority for environmental policy' (Golub, 1996: 697).

But the subsidiarity principle can also be used for achieving other goals. For example, some member states have relied on the subsidiarity principle to prevent the EU from becoming active (Holzinger, 1994: 72). Individual member states (the UK in particular) have attempted to promote the re-nationalisation of European environmental policies by referring to the subsidiarity principle (Golub, 1996: 689; Jordan, 1999b). Despite these efforts, though, environmental policy authority between the EU and the member states has not been fundamentally redistributed. Therefore, the de facto centralisation of environmental legislation at the EU level challenges the principles of the appropriate level of action and subsidiarity and represents a genuine co-ordination challenge.

Developing New Patterns of Governance

Concerns about the allocation of authority in terms of the subsidiarity principle as well as the principle of the appropriate level of action stimulated an intense debate about dominant modes of environmental steering (Scott and Trubek, 2002: 8). The subsidiarity principle – which is in the end a reaction to increasing criticism of the bureaucratic culture in Brussels – emphasises forms of governance which to the greatest possible extent 'protect autonomy and are compatible with the Community objectives' (Scharpf, 1993). Thus, interventionist regulations which encroached on member states' room for manoeuvre were no longer as politically legitimate as in the past. According to this line of argument, the subsidiarity principle facilitated the development of new patterns of governance.

The detailed requirements contained in European legislation were not always the most effective means of reaching the targeted policy effects due to varying geographical, political, social and economic conditions at the national, regional or local level (Knill and Lenschow, 2000). With the new governance approach, explicitly aimed at taking different national contexts and conditions into account, the EU attempted to reduce these problems.

But it was not only the subsidiarity principle that triggered discussions about reform of the regulatory approach in EU environmental policy. The discussions were also affected by the identification of an implementation gap in this policy field (Szyszczak, 2006: 492). While the EU's supranational authority expanded in the 1970s and 1980s, implementation of the regulatory output remained with the member states. The latter fulfilled this task unevenly and therefore risked distortions to the internal market (Kelemen, 2000: 151). Over time, the existence of this deficit became well known (Majone, 1995: 8). Even if the problem had been known about for a long time, it did not become politically significant until the beginning of the 1990s. One of the main reasons for this was that some member states started to question the overall legitimacy of EU environmental policy and argued for the 're-nationalisation' of regulatory authority. In doing so, they explicitly referred to the negative results in implementing common policies (Golub, 1997; Jordan, 1999a).

This went along with a shift in research focus. Whilst earlier attempts concentrated on supranational level policymaking (e.g. Héritier, 1999), more recent studies have started asking about the impact of European integration at the domestic level (see Börzel and Risse, 2000; Knill, 2001). Against this backdrop, the effective implementation of European policies gradually moved to the centre of scientific attention, and even became 'politicised' to a considerable extent. As the study by Laffan (this volume) demonstrates, scrutinising the implementation of and compliance with environmental directives is very instructive for assessing the potential of certain forms of political steering. This development paved the way for more detailed studies on the determinants of efficient and effective policy formulation and implementation, for instance, the role of participatory environmental networks (see Koutalakis in this volume).

The debate about new modes of environmental governance also goes along with the broader discussion about the performance of the EU political system. This critical assessment of the EU's problem-solving capacity was triggered by concerns about effectiveness of decision-making and democratic legitimacy (Scharpf, 1999). In addition, concerns about the legitimacy of multi-level governance arrangements emerged (Papadopoulos, 2005; Papadopoulos, this volume).

In summary, the accumulated implementation deficit and concerns about the relationship between the various political arenas made hierarchical co-ordination with its 'old' legal instruments appear highly undesirable. Instead, so-called context-oriented forms of environmental governance gained prominence. They were first introduced by the Fifth Environmental Action Programme, adopted in 1993 (Kronsell, 1997; Lenschow, 1999). Since then, the new approach has received a great deal of attention in the literature (Golub, 1998; Héritier, 2002; Jordan, Wurzel and Zito, 2003; Knill and Lenschow, 1999, 2000; Mol, Lauber and Liefferink, 2000; Sbragia, 2000: 311).

The new governance concept explicitly reflects the diversity of national conditions. Instead of imposing detailed guidelines 'from above', the new approach gives states more flexibility in adapting national arrangements to European requirements. Furthermore, it aims to create positive incentives for voluntary participation and co-operation by various societal actors at different institutional levels during policy formulation and implementation (see Rottmann and Lenschow in this volume).

First, the new approach is reflected in a renewed focus on the definition of policy goals (e.g. with respect to air quality), leaving the decision on the means by which these goals should be reached (e.g. limitation of industrial emissions or automobile exhaust fumes) to the member states. Second, there are more measures which strive for better information and participation by the broadest possible array of state and private actors, such as the Directive on Access to Environmental Information, the Environmental Management and Audit Scheme (EMAS) regulation or the scheme for greenhouse gas emissions trading. Third, hierarchical regulations are being increasingly enhanced by co-operative arrangements and legally non-binding agreements between public and private actors.

This new regulatory approach strongly benefited from the fact that the detailed definition of issue-specific 'command-and-control' requirements often entailed tedious and problematic decision-making processes at the European level. Therefore, interventionist governance proved to be detrimental to the EU's capacity to act. A reduction in the complexity of the European legislative process through using voluntary agreements with industry would result in greater decision-making capacity and adaptive flexibility in European environmental policy (Héritier, 2002; Mol, Lauber and Liefferink, 2000).

The introduction of new modes of EU environmental governance also implied the emergence of a new toolbox of environmental policy instruments. In this context, it is possible to identify a distinction in the literature between substantive and procedural instruments. Substantive instruments are characterised by the fact that they specify concrete demands in terms of policy substance. Procedural instruments, on the other hand, do not lay down concrete policy goals and restrict themselves to the explication of certain rules of procedure, with which member states must comply (Heinelt et al, 2000).

While substantive measures set concrete goals with respect to the improvement of the quality of the environment or the prevention of emissions, procedural instruments are limited to the elaboration of procedural rules. They stipulate certain administrative and legal courses of action, without prescribing the actual result of such courses of action. This reflects the underlying logic of the new approach to environmental regulation.

At the European level, a broad spectrum of procedural rules can be identified (Heinelt et al. 2000). First, substantive measures frequently entail supplementary procedural provisions regarding the course of action to be taken when implementing and monitoring the substantive requirements. Such provisions are typically concerned with authorisation and/or monitoring procedures.

Second, procedural measures have been passed which regulate opportunities to obtain information and to participate in decision-making processes. For example, the 1990 Directive on Access to Environmental Information entails a passive right to information, which means that upon request an individual must be granted free access to all the environmentally relevant information held by national authorities without having to provide evidence of a particular interest in the matter (Kimber, 2000).

A third form of new procedural governance covers the establishment of incentive structures for environmentally friendly behaviour. On the one hand, such measures may be geared towards producers and consumers. An example of this is the EMAS regulation. It defines the procedural rules for the voluntary establishment and certification of environmental management systems in companies. As long as a firm fulfils the conditions of the regulation, it is authorised to use a statement of participation for marketing purposes (Bouma, 2000). The eco-label is based on a similar voluntary incentive structure for the marketing of individual products (Wright, 2000). The recent scheme establishing a market for permits for the emission of greenhouse gases (emissions trading) also fits into this category. Increased scarcity of emission rights will increase their price and thus stimulate technological developments.

On the other hand, there are incentive structures which seek to stimulate environmentally friendly behaviour by member state authorities. These include the strategies of information exchange and publication of the results of the implementation of EU policies, proposed in the Sixth Environmental Action Programme. By these means, member states have an incentive to perform as well as possible, so that their reputation at the European level is not damaged (Héritier, 2002).

Reflections on the New Modes of EU Environmental Governance

At first glance, the overwhelming scientific response to this development gives the impression that EU environmental policy governance has re-entered the 'right' path. However, if one examines more closely the actual contribution of these new instruments to the whole corpus of EU environmental regulation, that first impression is clearly challengeable.

First, we have to address the labelling of this form of governance as 'new'. There was already discussion on environmental governance in the 1980s, stimulated by international organisations. 'This earlier discussion was less concerned with context-oriented forms of governance, but with introducing economic instruments, which were considered substantially more efficient than interventionist measures' (Holzinger, Knill and Schäfer, 2006: 403).

Second, the transformation of EU environmental policy governance should also be viewed as one element of reform discussions at the global level (Lenschow, 1999: 40-41). These shifts in focus were rooted in a global wave of reforms characterised by terms such as privatisation, liberalisation, deregulation, withdrawal of the state, and the emergence of New Public Management (Benz and Goetz, 1996; Kickert, 1997; Wright, 1994). In their comparative analysis of determinants for the uptake of non-traditional environmental policy instruments, Jordan, Wurzel and Zito (2003: 203) stated that the contributors to their edited volume disagreed over the EU's role as the main driving force.

Third, the lack of popularity of these new modes suggests the need for a more realistic perspective. For example, Hey (2000: 85) argued that no general abandonment of typical governance instruments for the sake of purely procedural regulations could be observed in the EU of the 1990s despite such widespread perceptions. Thus, standards and technical norms for products and facilities still played a crucial role in EU environmental policy. Legally non-binding forms of regulation, such as negotiated agreements for private self-regulation, constituted only a very small proportion of the EU's total stock of environmental policy instruments (Héritier, 2002; Jordan, Wurzel and Zito, 2003; Jordan et al,. 2003). In light of this marginal quantitative shift, it is difficult to judge whether the ascribed developments have resulted in a comprehensive re-orientation of environmental governance in the EU. Despite the political rhetoric by the Commission, it remains to be seen whether the current initiatives are symptomatic of a new trend or merely complement the existing spectrum of environmental policy instruments.

Quite apart from the issue of quantitative shift, questions also arise as to the extent to which these new developments have in fact led to improvements in the EU's governance capacity in the environmental field. Comparative research shows that there is no obvious direct causal relationship between the choice of European policy instruments and effective implementation. Instead, successes and failures vary across policies and countries and do not indicate a direct causal linkage between instrument type and implementation performance. The formal, practical transposition of new instruments poses as many problems as is the case for old instruments. These results have been reported in comparative studies (Börzel, 2000; Knill, 1998; Knill and Lenschow, 1998 and 2000) as well as in investigations that focus on individual policies or the implementation of EU environmental policy in individual member states (Bouma, 2000; Kimber, 2000; Wright, 2000).

Recent research has acknowledged that minimising adaptation requirements for national institutions could increase the effectiveness of EU environmental policy. This minimisation combines broad substantive objectives (e.g. quality objectives for air quality) with procedural regulations that require the publication and comparative assessment and monitoring of performance for each member state. In defining policy objectives that are as broad as possible, the institutional adaptation costs can be reduced to a minimum; at the same time, political pressure through transparency and performance comparison can be mobilised to bring about the achievement of policy goals.

These new forms of governance become exposed to view in the 'Open Method of Co-ordination' (OMC) stratagem. This approach was devised during the Lisbon Summit in March 2000 as one of the means for turning the Union into 'the most competitive and dynamic knowledge-based economy in the world, capable of sustainable economic growth with more and better jobs and greater cohesion' (de la Porte, Pochet and Room, 2001: 292). While specific policy benchmarks are set for the Union, national responses are formulated independently and without the threat of formal sanctions. The EU provides a context and enabling structures for co-operation and learning among national policymakers. The regulatory impact of this approach rests on dissemination of best practice and the provision of incentives (peer review) rather than legal obligation and control. Hence, the level of obligation to a regulatory centre is low and a wide range of policy strategies to achieve general EU targets can be chosen (de la Porte and Pochet, 2002; Scott and Trubek, 2002).

At present, this form of 'democratic experimentalism' (Eberlein and Kerwer, 2004: 133) is applied to domains like the information society, research and development, enterprises, economic reforms, education, employment, social inclusion, health care and pensions, i.e. flanking policies for building up the economic union with an emphasis on social cohesion. The concrete design of the OMC varies from policy field to policy field, some emphasising information exchange (e.g. pensions and health), others building up stronger adaptation pressure through cross-national and Commission peer reviews (e.g. employment and to a lesser extent social inclusion). Though the merits of OMC for overcoming regulatory shortcomings have become more visible, it is very underdeveloped in the field of environmental policy (Szyszczak, 2006: 492). Thus, wider use of this promising instrument in EU environmental policy should guide the future political agenda.

Conclusions

In this chapter we have demonstrated how EU environmental policy has matured over the last three decades, culminating in a complex multi-level structure with decision-making competences shared by actors at different levels. Today it is not easy to find elements of environmental policy in member states which have not to some extent been affected by the EU. National governments, however, are still powerful in the multi-level polity system of the EU as they are responsible for implementation. Therefore, it can be stated that a truly multi-level governance scheme has developed in European environmental policy that facilitates co-ordinated actions between supranational, national and subnational actors.

Whilst the institutionalisation of the policy field in terms of substantive matters has largely been a matter of steady evolution, a more dynamic pattern can be observed in respect of governance patterns. A shift seems to have taken place over the past ten to fifteen years from direct intervention to more contextual forms of steering, characterised by new, usually procedural, policy instruments. This development reflects the discussion about new modes of governance in other European policy fields, such as regional policy. In the case of environmental policy, the debate about these new instruments was in the main stimulated by the consequences of the subsidiarity principle as well as by the deficit in implementation. Inadequate implementation flows from the ambiguous and broad formulation of European environmental legislation, which causes difficulties for member states in terms of transposition. Moreover, European regulations burden member states with adaptation costs. In turn, they try to keep these costs low by adopting a 'minimalist' and therefore often ineffective implementation strategy.

The new governance concept is responsive to the diversity of national conditions and gives member states more flexibility in adapting national arrangements to European requirements. Despite these obvious advantages, there is no case for exaggerated enthusiasm about these instruments. Interventionist instruments still dominate the European legislative reality. Research shows that there is no obvious direct causal relationship between the choice of European policy instruments and effective implementation. Therefore, it seems that a genuine transformation in European environmental governance has not yet occurred and a convincing solution to the allocation of authority has not yet been found.

In the debate on the future of Europe, the allocation of competences has become more crucial. Therefore it is necessary to develop more criteria to provide a more precise evaluation of the need to transfer competences to the European level. The impact on some member states, the effects of a national decision on other member states and proof of improved effectiveness can be considered as possible new criteria. This is particularly important against the backdrop of an enlarged Europe, which results in additional regulatory variety and thus an enhanced need for effective and legitimate co-ordination.

References

Alter, K. J. and Meunier-Aitsahalia, S. (1994). Judicial politics in the European Community. European integration and the pathbreaking Cassis de Dijon decision. *Comparative Political Studies, 26 (4)*, pp.535–61.

Andersen, M. S. and Liefferink, D. (1997). *European Environmental Policy: The Pioneers.* Manchester: Manchester University Press.

Aspinwall, M. and Greenwood, J. (1998). Conceptualising collective action in the European Union: an introduction. In J. Greenwood and M. Aspinwall (Eds.), *Collective Action in the European Union* (pp.1-30). London: Routledge.

Benz, A. and Goetz, K. H. (1996). The German public sector. National priorities and the international reform agenda. In A. Benz and K. H. Goetz (Eds.), *A New German Public Sector? Reform, Adaptation and Stability* (pp.1-26). Aldershot: Dartmouth.

Börzel, T. A. (2000). Improving compliance through domestic mobilisation? New instruments and the effectiveness of implementation in Spain. In C. Knill and A. Lenschow (Eds.), *Implementing EU Environmental Policy: New Directions and Old Problems* (pp.222-250). Manchester: Manchester University Press.

Börzel, T. A. and Risse, T. (2000). When Europe Hits Home. Europeanization and Domestic Change. *European Integration Online Papers, 4 (15).*

Bouma, J. J. (2000). Environmental management systems and audits as alternative environmental policy instruments. In C. Knill and A. Lenschow (Eds.), *Implementing EU Environmental Policy: New Directions and Old Problems* (pp.116-133). Manchester: Manchester University Press.

Collier, U. and Golub, J. (1997). Environmental policy and politics. In M. Rhodes, P. Heywood and V. Wright (Eds.), *Developments in West European Politics* (pp.226-242). New York: St. Martin's Press.

De la Porte, C., Pochet, P. and Room, G. (2001). Social benchmarking, policy making and new governance in the EU. *Journal of European Social Policy, 11 (4),* pp.291–307.

De la Porte, C. and Pochet, P. (Eds.) (2002). *A New Approach to Building Social Europe: The Open Method of Co-ordination.* Brussels: PIE Peter Lang.

Dilling, R. (2000). Improving implementation by networking: the role of the European Environment Agency. In C. Knill and A. Lenschow (Eds.), *Implementing EU Environmental Policy: New Directions and Old Problems* (pp.62-86). Manchester: Manchester University Press.

Eberlein, B. and Kerwer, D. (2004). New Governance in the European Union: A Theoretical Perspective. *Journal of Common Market Studies, 42 (1),* pp.121-142.

Garbe, C. (1996). *Subsidiarity and European Environmental Policy: An Economic Perspective.* Basel: Europainstitut der Universität Basel.

Golub, J. (1996). Sovereignty and subsidiarity in EU environmental policy. *Political Studies, 44*, pp.686-703.

Golub, J. (1997). Recasting EU environmental policy: subsidiarity and national sovereignty. In U. Collier, J. Golub and A. Kreher (Eds.), *Subsidiarity and Shared Responsibility: New Challenges for EU Environmental Policy* (pp.35-56). Baden-Baden: Nomos.

Golub, J. (Ed.) 1998. *New Instruments for Environmental Policy in the EU.* London: Routledge.

Greenwood, J. (1997). *Representing Interests in the European Union.* Houndmills: Macmillan.

Haigh, N. (2000). *The Manual of Environmental Policy: The EC and Britain.* London: Catermill Publishing.

Heinelt, H., Athanassopoulou, E., Getimis, P., Haunhorst, K. H., MacIntosh, M., Malek, T., Smith, R., Staeck, N., Taeger, J. and Töller, A. E. (2000). *Prozedurale Umweltpolitik. Umweltverträglichkeitsprüfungen und Öko-Audits im Ländervergleich.* Opladen: Leske und Budrich.

Héritier, A. (1999). *Policymaking and Diversity in Europe. Escape from Deadlock.* Cambridge: Cambridge University Press.

Héritier, A. (2002). New modes of governance in Europe: policy making without legislating? In A. Héritier (Ed.), *The Provision of Common Goods. Governance Across Multiple Arenas* (pp.185-206). Boulder: Rowman and Littlefield.

Héritier, A., Knill, C. and Mingers, S. (1996). *Ringing the Changes in Europe. Regulatory Competition and the Transformation of the State.* Berlin: de Gruyter.

Hey, C. (2000). Zukunftsfähigkeit und Komplexität - Institutionelle Innovation in der Europäischen Union. In V. von Prittwitz (Ed.), *Institutionelle Arrangements in der Umweltpolitik, Zukunftsfähigkeit durch innovative Verfahrenskombination?* (pp.85-101) Opladen: Leske und Budrich.

Hey, C. and Brendle, U. (1994). *Umweltverbände und EG.* Opladen: Westdeutscher Verlag.

Holzinger, K. (1994). *Politik des kleinsten gemeinsamen Nenners? Umweltpolitische Entscheidungsprozesse in der EG am Beispiel des Katalysatorautos.* Berlin: Edition Sigma.

Holzinger, K. (2000). Optimal regulatory units: a concept of regional differentiation of environmental standards in the European Union. In K. Holzinger and P. Knoepfel (Eds.), *Environmental Policy in a European Union of Variable Geometry? The Challenge of the Next Enlargement* (pp.65-107). Basel: Helbing und Lichtenhahn.

Holzinger, K. and Knill, C. (2002). Path dependencies in European integration: a constructive response to German Foreign Minister Joschka Fischer. *Public Administration, 80 (1),* pp.125-152.

Holzinger, K., Knill, C., and Schäfer, A. (2006). Rethoric or Reality? 'New Governance' in EU Environmental Policy. *European Law Journal, 12 (3),* pp.403-420.

Hooghe, L. and Marks, G. (2001). *Multi-level Governance and European Integration.* Oxford: Rowman and Littlefield.

Johnson, S. P. and Corcelle, G. (1989). *The Environmental Policy of the European Communities.* London: Graham and Trotman.

Jordan, A. (1999a). Editorial introduction: the construction of a multilevel environmental governance system. *Environment and Planning C: Government and Policy, 17 (1)*, pp.1-17.

Jordan, A. (1999b). The implementation of EU environmental policy: a problem without a political solution? *Environment and Planning C: Government and Policy, 17 (1)*, pp.69-90.

Jordan, A., Wurzel, R. and Zito, A. R. (Eds.) (2003). *New Instruments of Environmental Governance.* Frank Cass: London.

Jordan, A., Wurzel, R., Zito, A. R. and Breuckner, L. (2003). European Governance and the Transfer of 'New' Environmental Policy Instruments. *Public Administration, 81 (3),* pp.555-574.

Judge, D., Earnshaw, D. and Cowan, N. (1994). Ripples or waves: The European Parliament in the European Community policy process. *Journal of European Public Policy, 1 (1)*, pp.27-52.

Kelemen, D. R. (2000). Regulatory Federalism: EU Environmental Regulation in Comparative Perspective. *Journal of Public Policy, 20 (3)*, pp.133-167.

Kickert, W. J. M. (Ed.) (1997). *Public Managment and Administrative Reform in Western Europe.* Cheltenham: Edward Elgar.

Kimber, C. (2000). Implementing European environmental policy and the directive on access to environmental information. In C. Knill and A. Lenschow (Eds.), *Implementing EU Environmental Policy: New Directions and Old Problems* (p.168-196). Manchester: Manchester University Press.

Knill, C. (1998). European policies: the impact of national administrative traditions on European policymaking. *Journal of Public Policy, 18 (1)*, pp.1-28.

Knill, C. (2001). *The Europanization of National Administrations: Patterns of Institutional Change and Persistence.* Cambridge: Cambridge University Press.

Knill, C. and Lenschow, A. (1998). Coping with Europe: the implementation of EU environmental policy and administrative traditions in Britain and Germany. *Journal of European Public Policy, 5 (4)*, pp.595-614.

Knill, C. and Lenschow, A. (1999). Neue Konzepte – alte Probleme? Die institutionellen Grenzen effektiver Implementation. *Politische Vierteljahresschrift, 40 (4)*, pp.591-617.

Knill, C. and Lenschow, A. (2000). On deficient implementation and deficient theories: the need for an institutional perspective in implementation research. In C. Knill and A. Lenschow (Eds.), *Implementing EU Environmental Policy: New Directions and Old Problems* (pp.9-38). Manchester: Manchester University Press.

Krämer, L. (2000). *EC Environmental Law.* London: Sweet and Maxwell.

Kronsell, A. (1997). Policy innovation in the garbage can: the EU's Fifth Environmental Action Programme. In D. Liefferink and M. S. Andersen (Eds.), *The Innovation of EU Environmental Policy* (pp.111-132). Oslo: Scandinavian University Press.

Lenschow, A. (1999). Transformation in European environmental governance. In B. Kohler-Koch and R. Eising (Eds.), *The Transformation of Governance in the European Union* (pp.39-60).. London: Routledge.

Liefferink, D. and Jordan, A. (2004). Measuring Europeanization and Policy Convergence: National Baseline Conditions. In A. Jordan and D. Liefferink (Eds.) *Environmental Policy in Europe: The Europeanization of National Environmental Policy* (pp.32-46). Routledge: London.

Liefferink, D., Lowe, P. D. and Mol, A. P. J. (1993). The environment and the European Community: the analysis of political integration. In D. Liefferink, P. D. Lowe and A. P. J. Mol (Eds.), *European Integration and Environmental Policy* (pp.1-14). London: Belhaven Press.

Majone, G. (1995). *Mutual Trust, Credible Commitments and the Evolution of Rules for a Single European Market.* Working Paper RSC 95/1. Florence: European University Institute.

Mazey, S. and Richardson, J. (2006). Interest groups and EU policymaking: organisational logic and venue shopping. In J. Richardson (Ed.), *European Union. Power and Policymaking* (pp.247-268). Milton Park: Routledge.

McCown, M. (2006). Judicial law-making and European integration: the European Court of Justice. In J. Richardson (Ed.), *European Union. Power and Policymaking* (pp.171-186). Milton Park: Routledge.

Mol, A. P. J., Lauber, V. and Liefferink, D. (Eds.) (2000). *The Voluntary Approach to Environmental Policy.* Oxford: Oxford University Press.

Papadopoulos, Y. (2005). Taking Stock of Multi-level Governance Networks. *European Political Science, 4 (3)*, pp.316-327.

Rehbinder, E. and Stewart, R. (1985). *Environmental Protection Policy. Integration Through Law.* Berlin: de Gruyter.

Sbragia, A. M. (2000). Environmental policy. In H. Wallace and W. Wallace (Eds.), *Policymaking in the European Union* (pp.293-316). Oxford: Oxford University Press.

Scharpf, F. W. (1993). *Autonomieschonend und gemeinschaftsverträglich. Zur Logik der europäischen Mehrebenenpolitik.* MPIFG Discussion Paper 93/9. Köln: Max-Planck-Institut für Gesellschaftsforschung.

Scharpf, F. W. (1994). *Mehrebenenpolitik im vollendeten Binnenmarkt.* MPIFG Discussion Paper 94/4. Köln: Max-Planck-Institut für Gesellschaftsforschung.

Scharpf, F. W. (1999). *Regieren in Europa. Effektiv und Demokratisch?* Frankfurt am Main: Campus.

Scott, J. and Trubek, D. (2002). Mind the Gap: Law and New Approaches to Governance in the European Union. *European Law Journal, 8 (1)*, pp.1-18.

Szyszczak, E. (2006). Experimental Governance: The Open Method of Co-ordination. *European Law Journal, 12 (4)*, pp.486-502.

Weale, A. (1996). Environmental rules and rule-making in the European Union. *Journal of European Public Policy, 3 (4),* pp.594-611.

Wright, R. (2000). Implementing voluntary policy instruments. The experience of the EU ecolabel award scheme. In C. Knill and A. Lenschow (Eds.), *Implementing EU Environmental Policy. New Directions and Old Problems* (pp.87-115). Manchester: Manchester University Press.

Wright, V. (1994). Reshaping the state. The implications for public administration. *West European Politics, 17 (2)*, pp.102-137.

Zito, A. R. (1999). Task expansion. A theoretical overview. *Environment and Planning C: Government and Policy, 17 (1)*, pp.19-36.

Law into Action: The Struggle to Comply with the Habitats Directive in Ireland, Greece and Finland

Brigid Laffan

Introduction

The Habitats Directive (92/43) is one of the European Union's principal laws for protecting endangered species and habitats in Europe and hence for promoting biodiversity. The Birds Directive (79/409) and the Habitats Directive form the two legal pillars that provide the basis for the Union's ambitious Natura 2000 programme. The main objective of the two directives is to establish a coherent ecological network across Europe of Special Areas of Conservation (SACs) and Special Protection Areas (SPAs) that together will form a European wide ecological network known as Natura 2000. The impetus for the directives came from international conventions, on the one hand, and 'bottom-up' demands from environmental groups, on the other (Fairbrass and Jordan, 2001: 499-518). The transposition and implementation of the two biodiversity directives has been very problematic for the Commission and the member states. There have been numerous delays, political protests, infringement proceedings, court cases and continuing flashpoints throughout the member states (Diaz, 2001).[1] The implementation of the habitats directive was so contentious in France that its implementation was suspended in July 1996 to enable the public authorities to re-launch the process of site designation (Alphandery and Fortier, 2001). As recently as June 2003, the French Government in a submission to the Environment Council highlighted the 'questions and fears of many rural stakeholders' when faced with the directive (European Council of Ministers, 10420/03). The focus of this chapter is on the implementation of and compliance with the habitats directive in three member states, Ireland, Greece and Finland.[2] Prior to outlining the analytical framework of the chapter, we provide a synopsis of the habitats directive to underline the requirements that the member states had to fulfil and on what time scale.

---

1 The member states are obliged to report to the Commission on the implementation of the habitats directive every six years. The national reports are followed by a composite report from the Commission. The first Commission report was issued on 5 January, 2004 as COM (2003) 845 final.

2 This paper is based on the findings of a research project, Organising for Enlargement, that was coordinated by University College Dublin between 2001-2004. The project website is www.oeue.net The papers on Ireland (Laffan and O'Mahony, 2004), Finland (Kinnunen, 2004), and Greece (Andreou, 2004) can be found at www.oeue.net/papers

The Commission, with the support of a number of active conservation groups and MEPs, made a formal proposal for a Habitats Directive in September 1988. Protracted negotiations led to agreement on the text in May 1992 (Fairbrass and Jordan, 2001: 512). The directive, like all EU directives, established both a precise timetable for action by the member states and a detailed specification of what the member states had to do (see Table I). Article three of the directive specified the principal policy instrument, namely, the designation of sites, known as special areas of conservation (SACs) for the protection of endangered habitats of flora and fauna.[3] The designation of sites was to be based on scientific criteria only. Annexes to the directive established a number of habitats and species that were identified as European priorities because of concern for their status. Provision was also made for the subsequent management and conservation of sites, EU co-financing of scientific work leading to the designation of sites, and a reporting requirement for the member states. Each member state had to formally transpose the directive into national law, undertake the scientific work leading to the designation of sites, formally transmit the designated site lists to the Commission, and prepare management plans for the priority habitats and species (see Figure I for an overview of the habitats directive). The timetable for the designation of sites specified three steps. First, the member states had to prepare national lists of sites by June 1995 and transmit these to the Commission. Second, the Commission was to select from these Sites of Community Importance (SCIs) by June 1998 and third, the designation by the member states of Special Areas of Conservation (SACs) by June 2004. The second and third steps were contingent on the first, site designation and transmission of lists to the Commission by the member states. Under Article 5 of the directive, the Commission had the power to request amendments to the proposed national lists from the member states. Hence, the Commission had a formal role in step one of the process. The habitats directive was demanding in terms of its policy instrument (site designation), the privileging of scientific criteria over social and economic ones, its potential impact on different societal actors and its institutional and resource demands for the future management of designated sites.

Figure 1: The Natura 2000 Network

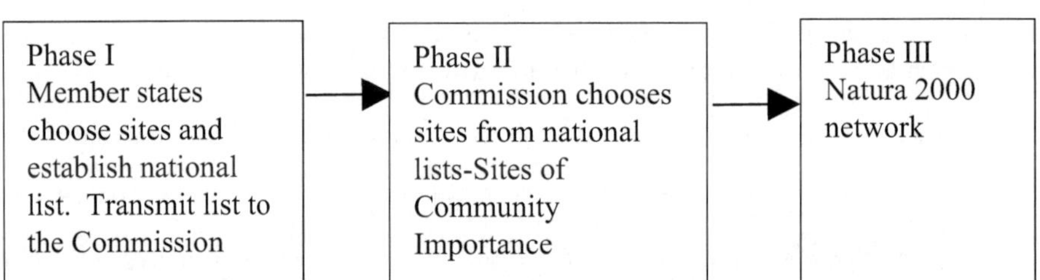

3 The policy instrument for the birds directive was Special Protection Areas (SPAs).

Compliance and Implementation

Compliance and implementation are two interrelated although distinct concepts. Implementation, according to Underdal, refers to the measures that Governments take in order to translate external commitments/laws into domestic laws and policy (Underdal, 1998: 26). In relation to the habitats directive, this included site mapping and designation, consultation with those affected, the preparation and implementation of transposition regulations and the subsequent management of designated sites. Compliance goes further than implementation and relates to 'whether or to what extent countries adhere' to their international commitments (Underdal, 1998: 25). For Haas, compliance 'entails actual change in behaviour' (Haas, 1998: 18). This definition goes beyond formal compliance in terms of the transposition of the directive into domestic law to include the subsequent application of the law. The objective of this chapter is to (a) analyse the struggle to formally transpose the habitats directive into domestic law and (b) to explore the dynamic of site designation in the three member states. The empirical scope of the chapter is limited to phase one of the Natura 2000 process. Two inter-related processes were at work. First, there was the deployment by the Commission of its compliance strategies, a connected national-EU game. Second, there was the generation and mediation of conflict at domestic level, a nested national political game.

The study of the post-decisional phase of EU politics and policy making began in the 1980s (Siedentopf and Ziller, 1988) but only became an important focus of research from the mid 1990s onwards (Collins and Earnshaw, 1992; Mendrinou, 1996; Duina 1997; Haas 1998; Börzel, 2000, 2002, 2003; Dimitrakopolous, 2001; Knill and Lenschow, 1998, 2000; Knill, 1998, 2001; Fairbrass and Jordan, 2001; Mastenbroek, 2003; Falkner, 2003; Falkner et al, 2004; Gange and van Waarden, 2005). Attention to member state compliance and implementation is part of a wider scholarly interest in the impact of the EU on the domestic arena. This branch of enquiry falls under the general rubric of Europeanisation (Goetz and Hix, 2001; Green Cowles et al, 2001; Featherstone and Radaelli, 2003). The literature on compliance and implementation consists of quantitative studies that investigate variation in the levels of transposition across the member states or sectors, studies of delays in transposition and cross-country case studies of the implementation of one or more directives. The literature has identified a variety of different factors that influence national adaptation, notably 'mis-fit' or 'mis-match', domestic administrative traditions and institutional settings, state-society relations, and the number of veto points in domestic political systems (see Haverland, 2003 for an overview).

The literature adopting a case study research design offers a variety of approaches to analysing the implementation of and compliance with European law. Knill and Lenschow, using a neo-institutionalist approach, placed considerable emphasis on national administrative traditions. A key independent variable for these scholars was the degree of embeddedness of administrative traditions (Knill, 1998; Knill and

Lenschow, 1998; Knill, 2001). According to these authors, 'the domestic institutional implications of European policies rather than the choice of policy type are primarily responsible for implementation performance' (Knill and Lenschow, 2000). Haverland focused on the role of institutional veto points and the domestic opportunity structure in his explanation of the impact of domestic opposition to European law (Haverland, 2000). Héritier et al developed an actor centred framework to conceptualise and explain the differential impact of European policies at the domestic level. While acknowledging the importance of institutions, the study paid considerable attention to the 'dynamics of political processes induced by European policy inputs at the national level' (Héritier et al, 2001: 9). The key explanatory variable identified in their study was the reform capacity of the member states. Börzel in her extensive work on implementation and compliance also adopted an actored centred approach with a focus on state-society relations. The key explanatory variables were the 'pull' of domestic mobilisation and the 'push' of supranational actors in pressuring reluctant governments to comply with European directives (Börzel, 2000).

This chapter seeks to add to our understanding of the dynamics of implementation/compliance in the EU by tracing the relationship between domestic mobilisation and the management of domestic conflict, on the one hand, and the compliance strategies of the Commission, on the other. The lack of attention to domestic mobilisation and politics was identified by Mair as one of the shortcomings in scholarship about Europe and Europeanisation (Mair, 2004: 344). The implementation-compliance process is conceptualised as a multi-level process involving EU level actors and domestic actors. A key claim of the multilevel governance approach to EU governance is that ' political arenas are interconnected rather than nested' (Hooghe and Marks, 2001: 4).[4] In order to analyse the dynamics of EU-domestic interactions and intra-state or domestic interactions, the chapter distinguishes between connected games involving national and European actors and nested domestic processes that are endogenous to the three member states. National governments are faced with the dual demands of EU led compliance and domestic politics. The analytical framework used in the chapter is actor centred because the objectives of the chapter are to explore the role of the Commission, a supranational actor, and the way in which domestic actors managed a problematical transposition and compliance process (Héritier et al, 2001; Scharpf, 1997; Richardson, 1996). An actor or agency centred approach does not accord a determining influence to institutions. Rather goal-oriented actors interact within a multilevel institutional setting that exerts influence over them by channelling, facilitating, or constraining their choices and preferences but does not determine them (Héritier et al, 2001). Domestic institutions are seen as intervening rather than independent variables in the implementation of the habitats directive. The two independent variables, identified in the study, are the Commission's compliance powers and domestic conflict concerning the directive. Section three of the chapter identifies the key actors in the

4 It is argued in the multi-level governance literature that the 'Commission has become involved in day-to-day implementation' (Hooghe and Marks, 2001: 24).

implementation process both at EU and domestic level and their respective roles in the process. The institutional setting of the three member states within which these actors interact is outlined. The methodology of empirical process tracing is then used in sections four and five to analyse the interactions among the actors in the period leading up to the formal transposition of the habitats directive into national law, and the process of site designation.[5] Gange and van Waarden (2005) underline the importance of analysing the 'throughput' process in the transposition and implementation of European laws because this process links the same input, the directive, into domestic outputs and outcomes.

Actors and Institutional Settings

The implementation of the habitats directive involved a variety of actors at European and national levels. At the EU level, the two key political actors were the Commission and the European Court of Justice (ECJ). In addition, pan European environmental interest groups had a major influence over the evolution of European environmental policy. The Commission and the Court have distinctive formal roles in promoting compliance with European law. The literature on compliance with international treaties distinguishes between 'top-down' enforcement strategies of monitoring, verification and control and 'bottom-up' management strategies that rely on capacity building, financial assistance and rule interpretation. Tallberg concludes that EU practice challenges this distinction and that the EU is characterised by a 'management-enforcement ladder' that relies on a combination of management and enforcement mechanisms (Tallberg, 2003: 13-14). The management and enforcement mechanisms are formidable resources available to the Commission, in the first instance, and the European Court of Justice (ECJ) once court proceedings are initiated. Notwithstanding reluctance to implement in some cases, the member state governments take into account the enforcement-management ladder available to the EU in their compliance calculus (Underdal, 1998: 7-8). The phased approach to infringement proceedings in the treaties enables the Commission to initiate a process that allows it re-visit the question of transposition and compliance on an iterative basis. In addition to its formal responsibilities as 'guardian of the treaties', the Commission may have responsibilities specified in a directive that enable it to make further demands on governments. For example, in the habitats directive, the Commission had the power to seek amendments to the national lists submitted by the member states.

The key actors at domestic level in the implementation of the habitats directive were the central government ministries, conservation authorities at national and sub-national level, those affected by site designation (mainly landowners) and environmental NGOs. In addition, national parliaments, political parties and courts may have played a significant role depending on the domestic institutional setting.

5 For a discussion of process tracing see King, Keohance and Verba (1994).

National governments occupy a privileged position at the EU-domestic interface as they are the key 'translator devices' of the demands of the EU into the domestic arena and are legally responsible as a 'corporate' actor for compliance with European law. National governments 'Janus like' face the demands of the EU, on the one hand, and demands from their civil societies, on the other. National governments, however, should not be regarded as unitary actors in the implementation process. Inter-ministerial negotiation and rivalry may be a salient feature. Tension between political, official and scientific actors in the state apparatus may also be an important feature of the implementation process. Non-governmental actors are those affected by the directive and environmental pressure groups that would favour the directive and would promote its timely and full implementation. The institutional setting or constellation at the domestic level influences the strategies of the actors and serves to channel opposition.

Four key elements of the domestic institutional setting were identified. First, there was the institutional framework within which nature conservation policy was conducted. Was there an embedded set of institutions at central government level and at sub-national level with capacity to implement and enforce the directive? Second, what was the pattern of state-society relations and the relative power of environmental interests in the society? Third, what were the institutional channels or access points available to those who favoured or rejected the directive? Fourth, what was the domestic legal culture and how available were legal processes to litigants?

The three member states in the study differed on all four dimensions of the domestic institutional setting. The institutional setting in Ireland was unstable during the transposition phase of the habitats directive. The Ministry of the Environment and Local Government negotiated the directive but its transposition was the responsibility of the Ministry of Arts, Culture and the Gaeltacht, because the latter was given responsibility for the National Parks and Wildlife Service (NPWS), the sub-national authority responsible for nature conservation. Prior to this, the NPWS was part of the Office of Public Works based in the Ministry of Finance. In 1994, the NPWS was renamed Dúchas and given responsibility for Ireland's natural and built heritage.[6] The institutional setting in Greece was highly fragmented. Responsibility for nature conservation was the preserve of the Ministry of Agriculture until 1980. In that year, the Ministry of the Environment, Physical Planning and Public Works (YPEHODE) was established with overall responsibility for protected areas. The forestry administration, under the Ministry of Agriculture, retained its responsibility for inland areas. The newly established Environment Ministry assumed responsibility for urban, coastal and marine areas. Hence there was a division between two ministries concerning their spatial responsibilities. A number of other ministries also had responsibility for aspects of conservation. In Finland, the institutional capacity for environmental policy and nature conservation developed early. The Environment Ministry was established in 1972 and

6 The Ministry of Arts, Culture and the Gaeltacht was less important in the governmental hierarchy than the Environment Ministry. The establishment of Dúchas was regarded as an attempt to integrate different facets of conservation in Ireland.

environmental protection had constitutional status. The ministry was responsible for the Finnish Environment Institute and the Regional Environment Centres (RECs), the state's regional offices. The Ministry of Agriculture and Forestry had responsibility for the Forest Park Service and the Natural Heritage Services. The two ministries worked together within a co-operative administrative culture.

The pattern of state-society relations in Ireland was pluralist with neo-corporatist social partnership in the area of economic and social governance. The culture was consultative but societal interests were not highly institutionalised in the system of public policy making apart from the high level process of social partnership. The influence of environmental groups has increased since the 1970s and a small Green Party gained representation in the parliament in 1979.[7] It has not yet however held government office. The balance between farming interests and environmental interests favoured the former. Greek civil society was not characterised by highly organised interests. The system of interest mediation was weak with limited although growing environmental activism. The state has a high degree of autonomy from weakly organised societal interests. In contrast, the Finnish political system was based on high level of access for societal interests, a consultative culture, strong environmental groups and Green Alliance representation in coalition governments.

The third element of the institutional setting was the question of 'veto points' (Haverland, 2000). All three states were unitary states with varying degrees of centralisation. There were no veto points as such. There may however be veto players whose agreement to the terms of implementation may be required.[8] The domestic channels available to those supporting or opposing the directive included governmental channels, parliamentary channels, public protests and the courts. The Irish electoral system, which fosters intense inter and intra party competition, makes individual parliamentarians extremely sensitive to local constituency issues.

The fourth element, the legal culture and accessibility to courts also showed variation across the member states. In Ireland, judicial review through the courts was expensive and protracted. In Finland, there was a highly legalistic culture and a strong system of administrative courts. The Greek system was formally legalistic but characterised by a weakness of compliance. Table 1 provides a summary of the key elements of the institutional setting.

---

7 The Green Party has five deputies in the 2002 Parliament.

8 Both Héritier (2001: 44) and Falkner et al (2004: 466) identified the importance of key actors (veto players) in adjustment to EU policies. Tsebelis defines veto players as individual or collective actors whose agreement is necessary for a change in the status quo. He further distinguished between institutional veto players (generated by the constitution) and partisan veto players (generated by politics) (Tsebelis, 2002: 19).

Table 1: Key Elements of the Institutional Setting

Institutional Setting	Ireland	Greece	Finland
Nature conservation institutions	Unsettled with changes in lead ministry and core conservation services	Highly fragmented with relatively new Environment Ministry trying to establish its presence / credentials	Well established/ institutionalised with shared responsibility between two ministries
State-society relations Influence of environmental interests	Pluralist Medium	Weakly organised civil society Low	Pluralist and highly participatory High
Channels	No veto points but electoral system encourages localism	No veto points	No veto points
Legal culture Access	Common law Costly access to courts	Formally legalistic Weak compliance	Highly legalistic Administrative law courts

Of the three states in the study Finland had the most highly developed capacity for environmental protection, well established institutions, the presence of the Green Party in government, and a pattern of state-society relations characterised by a highly participatory culture. The Irish system for nature conservation was unsettled in the period under review with changes in the lead ministry and the conservation service. That said, the core of the new nature conservation service was based on its predecessor. Environmental groups had grown in influence and a small Green Party had an established parliamentary presence. The institutional setting in Greece was also unstable and the new Environment Ministry was still trying to assert its presence in the governmental system. Environmental parties and groups were politically weaker than in either of the other two member states. Rather than determining the transposition of and compliance with the habitats directive, the institutional setting, it is argued in this chapter, structured interactions between the various actors, affected their choice of arena and influenced their relative weight and influence in the process of negotiation and bargaining. Just how the institutional setting affected the transposition of the directive, the process of site designation and the mediation of conflict is uncovered through process tracing.

The Transposition Phase

All three states were late in the formal process of transposing the directive into domestic law. The transposition phase was essentially a nested domestic game in two of the three states. The Commission formally entered the Greek transposition process when it failed to establish transposition regulations. The transposition phase in Ireland lasted from 1992 when the directive was agreed to 1997 when national implementing measures were put in place. The directive was transposed into Irish law on February 26, 1997 by ministerial regulation (European Communities, Natural Habitats, Regulations). This legal instrument did not require primary national legislation and was thus not the cause of the delay. The period 1992-94 was characterised by inertia in the Irish system as no preparation was made for implementation by the 1994 date. Extensive inter-ministerial consultations began in 1994-95 between the lead department (Arts, Culture and the Gaeltacht) and the Ministries of the Environment and Agriculture on the form of the Regulations (Grist, 1997: 92). During this period, the framing community and their representatives became aware of the significant implications that the directive would have on their land holdings and began their opposition to it (ibid.). According to officials, 'farmers and landowners viewed Habitats as a horrific intrusion' (Interview 02, 22 May, 2003). The then minister came under considerable criticism from the opposition in parliament and from the framing groups. The number of parliamentary questions on habitats rose from 10 in 1992 to 88 in 1997 (Laffan and O'Mahony, 2004). The Irish Farmers' Association (IFA) held a large number of meetings, two per week, around the country on the issue of habitats during this period. The National Chairman of the IFA Sheep Committee criticised the directive as it removed control of land from farmers who would be forced 'to apply to the EU if they wish to engage in any farming activity' (Irish Times, 20 November, 1996). The minister was likened to a hate figure in Irish history, Oliver Cromwell, who had driven the Irish off their land during his Irish campaign in 1649-50. Emotions ran high and those opposing the directive could position their objections in a rhetorical frame that evoked wider societal sympathy. The farmers emerged as important 'veto' players during the transposition phase. Faced with a high level of mobilisation on the ground, the farming groups used all political channels available to them, including the macro process of social partnership to press their concerns on habitats. The key issues for the farming groups were notification to farmers of designation, adequate compensation and an independent appeals board. The conflict about habitats in Ireland raised issues of both distributive and procedural justice (Paavola, 2004: 68). The transposition regulations dealt with some but not all of these issues. The transposition phase of habitats in Ireland was highly politicised and the level of politicisation did not abate in the post-transposition phase.

The directive was transposed into national law in Greece through a Joint Ministerial Decision (JMD) of the Ministries of the Environment (YPEHODE), Agriculture, National Economy, Development, Merchant Marine and Culture. The ministerial decision dated from December 1998, which followed an ECJ ruling against Greece in June 1997 for having failed to adopt the necessary legal measures and to communicate them to the Commission (Case-329/96). As in Ireland, primary legislation was not used as the transposing instrument. The involvement of six ministries in the final implementing instrument underlined the fragmented nature of the institutional setting in Greece. Transposition in Greece was not delayed or hampered by the mobilisation and politicisation of societal groups. Civil society was essentially silent. The key transposition battle took place within central government between ministries. A bureaucratic struggle between the Environment Ministry and the Agriculture Ministry was the primary cause of the delay in transposition. At the heart of the struggle was the question of which ministry would gain competence, status and resources from the transposition and implementation of the directive. The Environment Ministry was the likely winner and the Agriculture Ministry 'was expected to be regulated to a secondary role as opposed to its hitherto dominant position' (Andreou, 2004: 4). The two ministries were unable to overcome their conflict on a bilateral basis. It required the intervention of the Prime Minister's Office to resolve their differences. The transposition instrument largely re-produced the text of the directive, which favoured the Environment Ministry. It was designated the competent authority for Greek participation in the 'Natura 2000' network. Following the formal transposition phase, the Environment Ministry still had the task of building the institutional structures and capacities to actually implement the directive.

Unlike the other two member states treated in this paper, the implementation of the directive in Greece required institution building in the area of nature conservation. The Environment Ministry saw the habitats directive and the wider Natura 2000 process as an opportunity to 'modernize the national system of nature protection' (Andreou, 2004: 6). It used this opportunity to engage in extensive legal change, develop a master plan to amalgamate the sites protected under domestic and European legislation, and create new institutions to oversee nature conservation. The joint ministerial decision of December 1998 made provision for a Natura 2000 Committee that would review scientific data, contribute to the process of designation and propose guidelines for the management of the Sites of Community Interest (SCIs). Proposals for institution building were further augmented by a 2002 law that made provision for 25 Managing Authorities (MAs) to manage 100 Natura 2000 sites. The legality of this development was contested as the original Law 2742/99 stipulated that MAs had to be established on an individual basis by Presidential Decree. In any case, only one MA was actually created in practice. The gap between the formal legal position and the 'living system' of nature conservation remained the central issue in Greece. Legal changes and provisions for new institutional structures and capacities did not translate into practice.

The transposition of the directive in Finland involved amendments to the domestic framework legislation, the Nature Conservation Act (1096/96 and 492/97) and agreement on a specific Decree (169/97). This met the legal requirements of the habitats directive. There was little bureaucratic or political debate on the legislative framework as Finland already had strong nature conservation laws. There was what has been termed a 'silent' phase of preparation for the directive between 1994 and 1997 that coincided with the transposition phase (Kinnunen, 2004: 7). During this period, the nature conservation agencies and nature activists engaged in data collection and mapping potential sites in silence. It has been argued that 'local residents, owners of agricultural land and forests, hunters and other stakeholder groups were excluded from the site designation process' in Finland (Heidanpää, 2002; cited in Paavola, 2004: 71). It was not until a proposed list of sites was published in 1997 and formal hearings began that conflict over the directive emerged.

Different factors influenced the period leading up to formal transposition in the three member states. Opposition emerged most quickly in Ireland and was characterised by a high level of mobilisation among farming interests. The government was left in no doubt that it had a divisive and contentious issue on its hands. The extent of government-landowner negotiation over the transposition regulations underlined the continuing political importance of farming interests in Ireland. The farming groups had high level access to ministers, their advisors, policy specialists, the nature conservation specialists and the wider political system. Their opposition had to be overcome if the directive was to be transposed and applied in Ireland. The situation in Greece was very different. The battle was a bureaucratic one that revolved around competences and resources. The powerful Agriculture Ministry did not want to cede power to the Environment Ministry. The content of the directive was designed to promote environmental protection and thus strengthened the role of the Environment Ministry in Greece. The administrative culture in Greece is characterised by conflict rather than co-operation between different parts of the ministerial apparatus. Civil society, however, was silent. Discussion of the directive did not go beyond the inner circle of government ministries. In Finland, the directive was viewed as a continuation of the domestic nature conservation regime during the transposition phase. There was little evidence of the politicisation that would occur when the list of sites was published. The silent mapping of sites that took place was, however, alien to the Finnish political culture of participation and consultation. Hence issues of procedural and distributive justice would also emerge in Finland.

The Dynamics of Site Designation

Formal transposition of the directive into national law had to be accompanied by a process of surveying sites of community interest, agreement on the national lists of designated sites and their transmission to the Commission. This period proved very problematic for the member states. During this phase, which overlapped with the process of formal transmission, the domestic authorities had to accommodate the demanding process of site mapping and designation, the institutional and political issues that arose from that process and the demand of the Commission for substantial lists so that it could further the process of creating the Natura 2000 network. During this phase, domestic politics met the Commission's role as guardian of the treaties. (See Table 2 for the calendar of transmission from the three member states.) The Commission began to use its enforcement-management ladder during this phase to extract lists from the member states. A change of government in Ireland in June 1997 following the transposition of the directive into national law altered the political dynamics surrounding site designation.[9] The new minister responsible for the directive was from the part of the country that was most affected by designation. So too was the junior minister with responsibility for rural policy. By temperament and political tradition, neither of these two politicians was likely to risk alienating their constituencies in order to comply with a European law. The junior minister argued that the habitats directive was 'a gun to his head' (Interview 03, 25 June, 2003). He and the minister invested considerable political energy in mediating between the farmers and Brussels. By April 1998 only Ireland and Luxemburg had not transmitted any definitive sites to the Commission. The first definitive list of sites was sent to the Commission in August 1998. Prior to that Ireland sent a provisional list of 207 sites in October 1997. The provisional list was in response to a Commission letter of formal notice on April 24, 1996. Unhappy with the provisional list, the Commission sent a second letter of formal notice on 11 July, 1997 in which it once again claimed that Ireland had failed to transmit a full list of sites and adequate site information. In reply, the conservation authorities informed the Commission that the sites would be communicated in three tranches. The Commission regarded the initial list of sites as very inadequate. Faced with a resisting government, the Commission decided to take Ireland to the European Court of Justice. The Court ruled against Ireland in Case C 67/99 on September 11, 2001. In addition to the formal enforcement ladder, the Commission issued very effective threats against the Irish authorities. In a letter dated July 1999, the Commission warned the Government that approval of finances for structural and cohesion funding was a risk because Ireland was 'dragging its feet on designating wildlife sites for protection under the 1992 Habitats Directive' (Irish Times, 17 July, 1999). The ministers concerned perceived this as a real threat. By suggesting that structural funds might be affected, the Commission effectively brought Ireland's core executive on European matters into play. In turn, the Finance Ministry put pressure on the responsible ministry to speed up the process of transmitting lists to the Commission. The relevant politicians were faced with continued opposition from the

9 What was called the Rainbow Coalition (Fine Gael, Labour and Democratic Left) was replaced by a Fianna Fail led coalition. The latter was very critical of the habitats directive while in opposition. Moreover, the minister who was given responsibility for habitats was very sympathetic to the farmers.

farming community and over one hundred parliamentary questions relating to the habitats directive were tabled in Parliament in each year from 1998 to 2001.

Unlike Ireland, the process of site designation in Greece did not lead to the mobilisation of those affected, nor was there a noticeable politicisation of the process. The scientific work began in 1994 when an EU funded project began the process of identifying and mapping habitat and species types in Greece. This produced a scientific list of 296 sites but it was not a national list agreed by the government. It was a 'scientific point of reference' that fed into the process of site designation. A ministerial working group began work in March 1995 on the national list. The process was confined to the ministries and 'local stakeholders were not involved in the consultation process at all' (Andreou, 2004). The working group produced a first list that consisted of 164 sites (SCIs) and 29 (SPAs). The Commission reacted to this list by sending a letter of formal notice to the Greek authorities. Because of the threat of referral, the ministerial working group renewed its work and added 81 SCIs and 23 SPAs to the list. The Greek list was further augmented following recommendations from the first and second Mediterranean bio-geographical seminars. In Greece, the formulation of the list was 'the task of a very limited number of people (essentially officials from YPEHODE and the Ministry of Agriculture, assisted by academics, researchers and occasionally scrutinised by certain influential ecologists)' (Andreou, 2004: 21). This top-down process accelerated the process of site designation but at the cost of 'leaving the national and subnational administration, the most interested actors and the wider public in ignorance' (ibid.).

In Finland the completion of the 'silent' phase was followed by the publication of the proposed Natura 2000 sites in 1997. This formally opened the consultation process in Finland. The publication of the list of sites was greeted by a storm of protests from those affected. The agricultural interest organisation, the MTK, began a regional campaign against the designations. The landowners felt that 'the preparations were made in secret and that they were not heard' (Kinnunen, 2004). The depth of the opposition was symbolised by four farmers from Karvia who went on hunger strike as a protest against the Natura 2000 plan. A total of 14,000 complaints were lodged with the environmental authorities. Of the 14,000 complaints, 9,000 complaints were against newly designated conservation sites in private ownership. The MTK asked for another hearing round given the number of complaints. The Regional Environmental Centres handled the complaints and replied both to the Ministry of the Environment and the landowners. Given the extent of the opposition, the ministry established a ministerial level working group on Natura 2000 to handle the complaints. The purpose of this institutional device was to speed up the process of dealing with complaints as Finland was by this stage coming under pressure from the Commission for non-compliance. The Commission, unhappy with the tardiness of transmitting lists, issued a reasoned opinion against Finland in January 1998 and initiated proceedings before the ECJ in April 1998 in relation to the birds directive. The initiation of infringement proceedings by the

Commission caused a clash with domestic Finnish legal proceedings. If dissatisfied with the non-legal complaints proceedings, the complainants had the right to have their cases reviewed in the administrative law system. Finland's Supreme Administrative Court heard 1,600 cases on Natura 2000. The Finnish authorities refused to transmit a definitive list to the Commission until the administrative court had given judgements on all cases. It was argued that 'being a strongly legalistic country, matters needed to be addressed in a proper legal manner in order to get legitimacy for the decisions taken' (Kinnunen, 2004). During the period April 1997 to August 1998, the environmental authorities were processing complaints and deciding on the list of sites that would be submitted to the government for approval. The total land area in the proposal was 8 per cent less than the area in the original proposal in April 1997. In March 1999 the Council of State decided on the Natura 2000 sites. From then on, the discussion with the Commission revolved around Commission demands for additional sites. The legal battle continued at domestic level. The MKT persisted with its case in the Supreme Administrative Court concerning the basis of Natura area selections but lost it in April 2004.

Table 2: Transmission of National Sites to the Commission

	Ireland No of Proposed Sites	% Total Land Area	Greece No of Sites Proposed	% Total Land Area	Finland No. of Proposed Sites	% Land Area
December 96	0	-	164	-	370	-
October 97	207 Provisional	-	245	-	415	-
February 98	207 Provisional	-	245	-	415	-
February 99	48	-	230	-	1380	-
November 99	138	2.9	230	19.5	1381	13.9
April 2000	259	4.3	234	20.1	1381	13.9
December 2000	317	8.7	234	20.1	1381	13.9
May 2003	364	14.2	236	20.9	1671	17.8
January 2004	381	14.2	239	20.9	1665	14.2

Source: Compiled from successive issues of Nature, DG Environment's Newsletter on Natura 2000 available at **http://europ.eu.int/comm/environment/news/natura/nat16_en**

The dynamic of EU-domestic interaction during the post-decision phase of EU policy making is brought out in the case studies. Claes underlines the 'interactive and dynamic relationship between the EU and the national decision-making level' during the implementation phase (Claes, 2002: 303-304). The exploration of the implementation of the habitats directive in the three member states confirmed the strategic role of the Commission in facilitating domestic implementation and promoting compliance with European law. The Commission engaged in two distinct sets of relationships during this phase. The first was its relationship with the domestic core executives that were ultimately legally responsible for transposition and compliance. Second, it fostered relationships with civil society actors and acted as a support to environmental NGOs at domestic level.

The Commission's enforcement-management ladder proved formidable. The availability and deployment of European sticks had a major impact on the behaviour of national core executives. The requirement to engage with the Commission at each stage in the infringement process meant that those responsible for implementation had to focus their attention on the compliance issue. The legal route of enforcement was used against all three states (see Table 3). It was used against Greece for failure to transpose and was used against Ireland and Finland for failure to transmit adequate lists. Moreover, a case against Greece was the first successful case against a member state for failure to protect an endangered species, the sea turtle, Caretta caretta. Following concerns voiced by non-governmental organisations, the Commission requested the Greek authorities (letter 17 July, 1998) to inform it of the measures it had taken to protect the sea turtles. It also sent a mission to the island of Zakinthos, the breeding ground for the sea turtles on 16-17 July, 1998. The inspection identified a number of issues that were a cause for concern. The Commission was unwilling to accept the assurances of the Greek authorities and issued a letter of formal notice (2 December, 1998). In response, the Greek authorities stated that a draft Presidential Decree had been prepared that would establish a marine park in Zakinthos with an appropriate Management Authority (MA). The Commission argued that this did not amount to 'an appropriate institutional framework' and that measures to protect the species were still inadequate (Court proceedings, C-103/00). The Commission followed this up with a second inspection mission in Zakinthos in August 1999. Although the team found improvements, the protection accorded to the turtles was regarded as still inadequate. Hence, it proceeded with infringement proceedings against the Greek government and the ECJ found against the Greek state in these proceedings. As a consequence of the inspections and infringement proceedings, the Managing Authority for the national marine park at Zakinthos became the first Managing Authority to come into operation. It had a Director, Administrative Board and its own personnel (Andreou, 2004: 15). The Managing Authority had to fight for acceptance in the local community given a perceived clash between nature

Table 3: Infringement Proceedings

Commission Sanctions	Ireland	Greece	Finland
Letters of Formal Notice	(1) Letter of formal notice 24 April, 1996 11 July, 1997 additional letter of formal notice (2) Letter of formal notice 9 October, 1997	(1) Letter of formal notice for non-transposition on 9 August, 1994 No reply from Greek authorities (2) Letter of formal notice re turtles 2 December, 1998	(1) Letter of formal notice re birds directive 10 July, 1998
Reasoned Opinions	19 December, 1998 (2) 8 April, 1998	(1) Reasoned Opinion 21 June, 1995 (2) Reasoned Opinion 15 June, 1999	(1) 17 December, 1998
ECJ Referrals	(1) 25 February, 1999 (2) 27 March, 2000	(1) 8 October, 1996 (2) 17 March, 2000	(1) 17 June, 2000 (2) 29 September, 2002
ECJ Judgements	(1) Case C-67/99 11 September, 2001, the European Court of Justice ruled against Ireland for failure to fulfil its obligations (2) Case C-117/00 judgement against Ireland (13 June, 2002) for failure to fulfil obligations under birds and habitats directives	ECJ judgement against Greece in C-329/96 for non-transposition (2) 30 January, 2002 ECJ judgement Case C-103/00	Judgement against Finland in C-240/00 on 6 March, 2003 Judgement against Finland C-407/03 concerning environmental impact assessments in relation to Article 6(3) of the habitats directive

conservation and economic activity, notably, tourism. It was argued that 'during the early stages of its existence, the new MA faced the opposition of all local stakeholders, who tended to view it as an intruder threatening their economic wellbeing' (op. cit., 19).

The legal route was complemented by bilateral engagement between the Commission and the member states concerning the process of implementation. Commission intervention was triggered by complaints from domestic actors or was driven by internal Commission deliberations. In the case of Ireland, the Commission effectively used the threat of the withdrawal of Cohesion Fund monies as a lever on the domestic core executive to speed up the process of compliance. The December 2002 decision by the Commission to issue a second letter of notice to Greece, concerning the number of SAPs that had been designated, led to a rapid increase in the number from 110 to 154 and the number may be increased again. In the case of Zakinthos, the Commission suspended structural fund payments to the island as a means of exerting pressure on the government and the local authorities.

The relationship between DG Environment and environmental groups at the domestic level was particularly close. The complaints procedure enabled domestic groups to alert the Commission to compliance problems. Such complaints may feed into infringement proceedings. In Ireland, six environmental groups were active in the policy network, An Taisce (Irish Heritage Trust), Friends of the Environment, Birdwatch Ireland, Irish Wildlife Trust, the Irish Peatland Conservation Council and the Irish branch of Coastwatch Europe. Five of these groups received a grant from the Irish Heritage Council in 1999 that enabled them to identify additional sites. This grant allowed them to employ a conservation specialist who in turn identified additional sites. The objective of the group was to increase the number of SACs. They presented a shadow list of 600 sites to the Commission in contrast to 364 sites proposed by the Irish authorities. This information provided the Commission with additional knowledge about habitats in Ireland.

In Greece, eight environmental groups, Arcturos (wild bear protection), WWF Greece, the Hellenic Ornithological Society, MOM (Society for the Study and Protection of the Mediterranean Seal), Archelon (the Sea Turtle Protection Society), the Hellenic Society for the Protection of the Environment and Cultural Heritage, the Hellenic Society for the Protection of the Nature and the Hellenic Centre for the Treatment of Wild Animals were active in promoting the implementation of the Natura 2000 network. In order to increase their leverage, the groups began to act collectively through information and protest campaigns, the organisation of joint conferences and the publication of priorities for action. The groups were active as policy experts and environmental activists. Two environmental groups, WWF-Greece and Archelon, took over the management of the core areas of the marine park at Zakinthos from the state. In addition, the environmental groups had membership of the Natura 2000 Committee and the Management Authorities. The fact that the latter were not yet operational, constrained their ability to further strengthen their presence in the formal institutional system. The majority of complaints to the

Commission concerning the implementation of the habitats directive were submitted by the NGOs.

Environmental groups were strong in Finland and well integrated into the domestic system of public policy making. All major international environmental groups such as Birdwatch, Greenpeace and the WWF had branches in Finland. The most significant domestic group was Finland's Nature Association (SLL). The groups communicated frequently with the Commission and kept it up to date on developments in Finland. They also used their access to the domestic administrative courts system to argue against reductions in the areas under protection. This allowed them to counteract the power of the landowners. It is considered that in Finland, the Ministry of the Environment and the environmental groups won the battle of compliance. Following the judgement against it in the Supreme Administrative Court, the farming organisation MTK wrote to the Commission in May 2004 seeking clarification on a number of issues relating to Natura 2000. Having failed at the domestic level, the farmers group shifted its focus from the domestic to the EU.

Managing and Mediating Conflict

The habitats directive generated considerable political conflict in two of the three member states addressed in this chapter. Conflict in Greece was contained within the bureaucracy because it was characterised by bureaucratic politics between two ministries. That rivalry is likely to continue to influence the application of the directive on the ground as the Agriculture Ministry retains considerable operational capacity. In the two other member states, the habitats directive was characterised by a high level of mobilisation and politicisation. Mobilisation of landowners began earliest in Ireland as farming groups quickly became aware of the potential impact of the directive. This was not a conflict generated by the interest organisations. Rather it represented bottom-up opposition by individual farmers who made their feelings known to their representatives at the numerous public meetings held throughout the country. The continuing influence of the farming community on Irish politics and the nature of the electoral system meant that politicians were extremely sensitive to this conflict (Adshead, 1996). The two ministers with responsibility for the application of the directive after formal transposition were very sympathetic to the landowners. One of these, Minister of State O Cuiv voted against the Nice Treaty in the June 2001 referendum because of an inflexible and unreasonable attitude towards the implementation of certain policies. "This struck me particularly in relation to the habitats directive, where the room for manoeuvre to allow people to continue with traditional activities was very limited and where the EU seems reluctant to facilitate the full compensation of, for example, farmers, who had to de-stock because of the over-grazing of the hills" (Irish Times, June 22, 2001).

Dealing with the objections of farmers was a key priority for the government. It put in place a compensation fund and created an Appeals Board to enable individual landowners to appeal against site designation. Given the cost of judicial review in Ireland, the Appeals Board provided a relatively cost effective channel for landowners. The Appeals Board also created a firewall between the ministers and the landowners and insulated them somewhat from political pressure. The key to unlocking the application of the directive in Ireland was dealing with the opposition from farmers. Effectively, they had to be bought off. Gange and van Waarden suggest that such domestic actors might be called 'frustration players' as in the end the final veto players are the European Commission and the European Court of Justice, which have the formal authority to overrule the vetos of the domestic players in infringement proceedings (Gange and van Waarden, 2005: 16). In the process, the shadow of the Commission acted as a source of necessary pressure on the Irish government. Without it, the government, given its sympathies, would not have developed this model of nature conservation. The conflict did not abate. In December 2002, the main farming organisation organised a 'Keep Out Campaign' to prevent access by the staff of the nature conservation authorities to SAC sites owned by some 15,000 farmers (IFA, Press Release 12 December, 2002). The deterioration in relations between farmers and the nature conservation authority, Dúchas, led to its incorporation as a division in the Environment Ministry. It was renamed the National Parks and Wildlife Service (NPWS). A review of the implementation of the directive that began in September 2003 ended in July 2004 with new levels of compensation for farmers, a code of practice for nature conservation staff in their dealings with farmers, as well as clearer guidelines on the developments that can take place in designated sites.

While the habitats directive gave rise to a very high level of conflict in Finland as well, the mediation of conflict was very different. Environmental groups were much stronger than in Ireland and the Green Alliance was in government. The Minister for Agriculture and Forestry was a non-party minister and the Centre Party, the farmers' party, was in opposition. In addition, Prime Minister Lipponen took the view that the Natura network was a EU matter that 'must be handled according to the nation's "pro Europe" position' (Kinnunen, 2004). The domestic political culture and institutional setting had a major impact on how the conflict was handled. First, prior to the adoption of the national list there was a formal consultation process when the lists were shown in the communities. All complaints were dealt with by the Regional Environmental Centres (RECs) and a special ministerial working group. If this did not lead to agreement, the complainants had access to the system of administrative courts up to and including the Supreme Administrative Court. The Finnish authorities improved the flow of information and offered compensation or the purchase of designated lands. From 2002 onwards, the conflict subsided in Finland.

Conclusions

This chapter has analysed the implementation of and compliance with the habitats directive in three states. The two key independent variables were the role of the Commission in securing transposition and compliance and domestically generated conflict about the directive. The Commission emerged as an important actor in the domestic application of European law. This does not mean that it is involved in the day to day implementation of directives. Rather it had a range of powers and resources that alter the compliance calculus of the member states even when faced with considerable domestic opposition. The phased infringement process allowed it to engage with domestic authorities and extract concessions on a phased basis. Its deployment of other strategies, notably, the suspension or threat of suspension of financial transfers, highlighted the range of instruments that it had available to it. Its links to domestic environmental NGOs were an important part of its strategic arsenal. They provided it with information and formal complaints. The NGOs in turn were strengthened by their access to the EU arena. In countries where environmental concerns were not that embedded or politically strong, it opened up important channels of influence.

The nature and intensity of conflict generated by the directive differed across the three states. The directive marked a major change in nature conservation policy in the three member states. The shift from nature protection predominantly on public lands to protection of specified habitats and species had a major material impact on private landowners, particularly farmers. Landowners mobilised quickly and effectively in Ireland. Individual farmers and their representative organisation were capable of affecting the timing and manner of transposition and compliance. The sympathy of ministers and concerns about the electoral consequences of the directive, meant that the government was willing to continue discussions with them well beyond formal transposition. In Finland, landowners were only let into the process when the list of proposed designated sites was open for inspection and consultation. Thereafter, opposition was channelled through a formal complaints procedure and the system of administrative law courts. The power of environmental groups and their access to the court system meant that the outcome accorded with the policy preferences of the Environment Ministry and the environmental NGOs. In both Ireland and Finland, issues of distributive justice concerning the material impact of designation on landowners and procedural justice concerning their rights to information and consultation about site designation were raised. The time allowed in the directive for transposition and designation was inadequate for the kind of process that would have been required to reduce the fears generated by the directive in farming communities.

The mediation of conflict in Ireland was through political channels, the Parliament and negotiations between the government and the farming representatives. The Nature Conservation Authority found itself in a very difficult position, caught between the demands for designation based on scientific criteria and the sympathy of the politicians for the position of the landowners. Although the appeals procedures was formally based on scientific criteria, efforts were made to get around the science on occasion. Unlike Finland, non statutory processes, the Appeals Board, predominated. In Finland, the mediation of conflict took place within government and through the formal administrative law system. Landowners were less powerful than in Ireland because the pro-farming party was in opposition during this period and environmental groups were manifestly stronger in Finland than in Ireland. By 2002 conflict about habitats had subsided in Finland whereas there were continuing flashpoints in Ireland.

In Greece, there was very limited mobilisation of stakeholders beyond the key ministries. They were effectively kept out of the process. The process in Greece remains at the pre-political stage as effective institutions for the management of the sites have not been established. The new system exists on paper but not on the ground. 'Importing new policy paradigms and creating new institutions that embody them is one thing; taking steps to ensure that the new structures become effective is another' (Andreou, 2004: 22). In Greece, the role of the Commission is not just to push for compliance but also to assist in the building of adequate institutional capacity to foster nature conservation. The situation in Greece 'should be viewed as 'the beginning of a long reform process, whose outcome is still impossible to predict' (ibid.). Based on the experience of the other two states, we can predict politicisation once the directive begins to bite at local level.

References

Adshead, M. (1996). Beyond clientelism: agricultural networks in Ireland and the EU. *West European Politics, 19 (3),* pp.583-608.

Alphandéry P. and Fortier A. (2001). Can a territorial policy be based on science alone? The system of creating the Natura 2000 network in France. *Sociologia Ruralis, 41 (3),* pp.311-328.

Andreou, G. (2004). *Multilevel Governance: Implementing the Habitats Directive in Greece.* OEUE Phase II Occasional Paper 4.3 – 08.04. Dublin: Dublin European Institute.

Börzel, T. (2000). Improving compliance through domestic mobilisation? New instruments and the effectiveness of implementation in Spain. In C. Knill and A. Lenschow (Eds.), *Implementing EU Environmental Policy: New Approaches to an Old Problem* (pp.221-250). Manchester: Manchester University Press.

Börzel, T. (2002). Pace-setting, foot-dragging, and fence-sitting: member state responses to Europeanisation. *Journal of Common Market Studies, 40 (2),* pp.193-214.

Börzel, T. (2003). Guarding the Treaty: The compliance strategies of the European Commission. In T. Börzel and R. Cichowski (Eds.), *The State of the European Union, Vol. 6. Law, Politics and Society.* Oxford: Oxford University Press.

Claes, D. H. (2002). The Process of Europeanization: Norway and the internal energy market. *Journal of Public Policy, 22 (3),* pp.299-323,

Collins, K. and Earnshaw, D. (1992). The implementation and enforcement of European Community legislation. *Environmental Politics, 1 (4),* pp.213-249.

Council of the European Union (2003). *Cover Note 10420/03*. Brussels: Council of the European Union.

Diaz, C. L. (2001). The EC Habitats Directive approaches its tenth anniversary: an overview. *Review of European Community and International Environmental Law, 10 (3),* pp.287-295.

Dimitrakopoulos, D. G. (2001). The transposition of EU law: 'post-decisional politics' and institutional autonomy. *European Law Journal, 7 (4),* pp.442-458.

Duina, F. G. (1997). Explaining legal implementation in the EU. *International Journal of the Sociology of Law, 25 (2),* pp.155-179.

Fairbrass J. and Jordan A. (2001). Protecting biodiversity in the European Union: national barriers and European opportunities? *Journal of European Public Policy*, *8 (4),* pp.499-518.

Falkner, G. (2003). Comparing Europeanisation Effects: From Metaphor to Operationalisation. *European Integration Online Papers, 7 (13)*. Available at: http://ssrn.com/abstract=483482

Falkner, G., Hartlapp, M., Leiber, S. and Treib, O. (2004). Non-compliance with EU directives in the member states: opposition through the backdoor? *West European Politics, 27 (3),* pp.452-473.

Featherstone, K. and Radaelli, C. M. (Eds.) (2003). *The Politics of Europeanisation*. Oxford: Oxford University Press.

Gange, I. and van Waarden F. (2005). *Between Structure and Incident: A Sociological-Institutionalist Appraoch to the Riddle of Transposition Delays of European Food Safety Directives.* Paper presented at the bi-annual conference of the European Union Studies Association in Austin, Texas, March 31-April 3.

Goetz, K. H. and Hix, S. (Eds.) (2001). *Europeanised Politics? European Integration and National Political Systems.* London: Frank Cass.

Green Cowles, M., Caporaso J. and Risse T. (2001). *Transforming Europe: Europeanization and Domestic Political Change.* Ithaca: Cornell University Press.

Grist, B. (1997). Wildlife legislation – the rocky road to Special Areas of Conservation surveyed. *Irish Planning and Environmental Law Journal*, *4 (3),* pp.87-95.

Haas, P. M. (1998). Compliance with EU directives: insights from international relations and comparative politics. *Journal of European Public Policy*, *5 (1),* pp.17-37.

Haverland, M. (2000). National adaptation to European integration: the importance of institutional veto points. *Journal of Public Policy, 20 (1),* pp.83-103.

Haverland, M. (2003). The impact of the European Union on environmental policies. In K. Featherstone and C. M. Radaelli (Eds.), *The Politics of Europeanisation* (pp.203-221). Oxford: Oxford University Press.

Héritier, A., Kerwer, D., Knill, C., Lehmkuhl, D., Teutsch, M., and Douillet, A. C. (2001). *Differential Europe: The European Union Impact on National Policymaking.* New York: Rowman and Littlefield.

Héritier, A. (2001). Differential Europe: national administrative responses to community policy. In M. Green Cowles, J. Caporaso and T. Risse (Eds.), *Transforming Europe: Europeanization and Domestic Political Change* (pp.44-59). Ithaca: Cornell University Press.

Hooghe, L. and Marks, G. (2001). *Multi-Level Governance and European Integration.* Lanham: Rowman and Littlefield.

King, G., Keohane, R. O., Verba, S. (1994). *Designing Social Inquiry.* Princeton: Princeton University Press.

Kinnunen, J. (2004). *Complaints, Farmers on Hunger Strike, Flying Squirrels: The Implementation of the Habitats Directive in Finland.* OEUE Phase II Occasional Paper 3.3 – 08.04. Dublin: Dublin European Institute.

Knill, C. (1998). Implementing European policies: the impact of national administrative traditions. *Journal of Public Policy, 18 (1),* pp.1-28.

Knill, C. (2001). *The Europeanisation of National Administrations*. Cambridge: Cambridge University Press.

Knill, C. and Lenschow, A. (1998). Coping with Europe: the impact of British and German administrations on the implementation of EU environmental policy. *Journal of European Public Policy, 5 (4),* pp.595-614.

Knill, C. and Lenschow, A. (Eds.) (2000). *Implementing EU Environmental Policy: New Approaches to an Old Problem*. Manchester: Manchester University Press.

Laffan, B. and O'Mahony, J. (2004). *Mis-fit, Politicisation and Europeanisation: The Implementation of the Habitats Directive.* OEUE Phase II Occasional Paper 1.3 – 08.04. Dublin: Dublin: Dublin European Institute.

Mastenbroek, E. (2003). The transposition of EU directives in the Netherlands. *European Union Politics, 4 (4),* pp.371-395.

Mair, P. (2004). The Europeanisation dimension. *Journal of European Public Policy, 11 (2),* pp.337-348.

Mendrinou, M. (1996). Non-compliance and the European Commission's role in integration. *Journal of European Public Policy, 3 (1),* pp.1-22.

Paavola, J. (2004). Protected areas governance and justice: theory and the European Union's habitats directive. *Environmental Sciences, 1 (1),* pp.59-77.

Richardson J. (1996). *Policy-making in the European Union.* London: Routledge.

Scharpf, F. (1997). *Games Real Actors Play.* Boulder: Westview Press.

Siedentopf, H. and Ziller, J. (1988). *Making European Politics Work.* London: Sage.

Tallberg, J. (2003). European Governance and Supranational Institutions: Making States Comply. London: Routledge.

Tsebelis, G. (2002). *Veto Players: How Political Institutions Work.* Princeton: Princeton University Press.

Underdal A. (1998). Explaining compliance and defection: three models. *European Journal of International Relations, 4 (1),* pp.5-30.

Multi-Level Environmental Governance and UK Devolution: Weak Administrations Jockeying for Position

Jenny Fairbrass

Introduction

As discussed in greater detail in Chapter 1 of this volume, across the EU a number of parallel processes have been underway for several decades, resulting in novel forms of governance (such as the Open Method of Co-ordination and benchmarking) across a range of policy areas. Many of the changes appear to have been underpinned by principles and practices of voluntarism, subsidiarity and inclusion. As part of this development, the evidence would suggest that the EU level actors (Parliament, Commission and Court) have tried to tap into the resources offered by local and regional authorities and non-state or private actors. As a result, it is argued, EU governance has become increasingly characterised by delegation and dissipation of authority to sub-national and private sector actors, a corresponding decline in hierarchical structures, and the creation of a more network-like pattern in public policy-making. In other words, it has been argued that the label 'multi-level governance' accurately captures the evolving nature of the EU as a polity (Marks and Hooghe, 2004; Hooghe and Marks, 2001; Smith, 2003). Such putative changes require description and explanation.

This chapter contributes to the volume and the debate by exploring developments in EU environmental governance and parallel processes of regionalisation. The chapter focuses on a number of interconnected questions, including *inter alia,* the likely effects of 'new' modes of environmental governance, the consequences of regionalisation for EU environmental governance, and the merits (or otherwise) of the concept of multi-level governance. To explore these issues the chapter presents fresh empirical evidence about regionalisation in the United Kingdom (UK) (labelled devolution) and the development of (EU) environmental governance.

Arguably, environmental policy and the UK provide an excellent 'test case' of the development of EU governance (Fairbrass and Jordan, 2001a; Fairbrass and Jordan, 2002a; Fairbrass and Jordan, 2004; Jordan, 2001) because of the way in which the UK devolution settlement treats the administration of EU relations and environmental policy, and because of the relationship between national and EU policymaking in the area of the environment. Crucially, the Whitehall-Westminster axis (i.e. 'London') retains control over EU matters under the devolution settlement (Cabinet Office, 2001; Bulmer *et al.,* 2002). It is one of the so-called 'reserved powers'. By contrast, environmental policy is one of the devolved policies. However, it is especially important to bear in mind the circumstances surrounding the development of national environmental policy: it is an area that is deeply affected by the EU (Jordan, 2002). Much of what becomes 'national' environmental policy at the member state level is negotiated and determined at the EU level, albeit strongly influenced by member state central government departments. However, crucially, the burden for implementation falls heavily on sub-national government rather than central government.

Moreover, environmental policy is a particularly interesting case because of the difficulty of disentangling the limit and scope of environmental problems. It has not been clear which level of government can or should take responsibility for environmental decisions. In the UK, it could be argued that jurisdictional conflicts are even more likely to arise because of the added complications created by the lack of clarity surrounding the roles and responsibilities of governmental (and non-governmental) actors arising out of the devolution settlement. Accordingly, the chain of events set in motion by the UK government in the late 1990s would seem to afford an excellent opportunity to review and evaluate the evolving nature of EU environmental decision-making and the resulting (if any) systemic change. Devolution in the UK raises questions about emerging patterns of task allocation, roles, responsibilities, actor to actor relationships and the degree of autonomy and influence that can be exercised by actors at the local, regional, national and supranational level of governance.

Furthermore, what makes the UK a particularly revealing case study in relation to regionalisation is that it has traditionally been regarded as a definitive example of a unitary state (John, 1996), an assessment that has been challenged (Rokkan and Urwin, 1983; Mitchell, 2002). Additionally, the form of regionalisation undertaken in the UK is distinctive compared to other EU member states (Hopkins, 2002; Swenden, 2002) in the sense that it has been a top-down process rather than the bottom-up one found elsewhere in Europe (Hopkins, 2002: 18). In other words, the process in the UK rests on the goodwill of the central authority and can, in principle, be rescinded. This contrasts with other European states because regionalisation or federalisation has been enshrined in a national constitution, and, as a result, the regions within many other EU member states are considerably more powerful. As a result, the UK provides a case study in the ways in which ‘weak authorities’ (i.e. the devolved bodies in the UK) grapple with the challenge of attempting to secure political influence (i.e. their efforts to jockey for position) within a wider multi-level governance system.

In order to investigate in detail UK devolution and emerging patterns of EU environmental governance, the research that underpins this chapter has focused primarily on two of the four territories that comprise the UK: namely, Wales and the eight English Regions outside London.[1] The rationale for selecting these two ‘re-

1 The Greater London Authority is distinctive from the other eight English regions and requires separate treatment. This chapter includes data derived from interviews with staff in five of the eight regions outside London.

gions' or 'nations' is based on the assessment that Wales and the English Regions outside London have been granted less extensive powers (Bulmer *et al.*, 2002; Bogdanor, 1999; Norton, 2001; Elcock and Keating, 1998; Jeffery and Mawson, 2002; Swenden, 2002) than either Northern Ireland or Scotland under the devolution settlement. Wales and the English Regions (outside London) might rightly be regarded as the weakest among 'weak authorities'. As a consequence, it is intriguing to observe the strategies and behaviour of the devolved bodies in Wales and the English regions in response to the relatively limited authority that they have been allocated under the UK devolution settlement as they struggle to find creative and resourceful ways of extending their *de facto* policy competence beyond their *de jure* allocation and participate effectively in EU environmental policymaking.

In order to explore the issues introduced above, the remainder of this chapter unfolds as follows. I will first set out a number of claims, conjectures and questions that are used to underpin the subsequent discussion. The next section then focuses on devolution and environmental policy in the UK. Third I will detail the selected case studies (i.e. Wales and the English Regions). The final section provides some concluding remarks.

EU Governance: Claims, Conjectures and Questions

The primary purpose of this section of the chapter is to briefly and selectively highlight some of the key debates arising out of the introductory chapter of this volume and related literature, as a precursor to the more detailed examination of developments in the UK. Here the intention is to reflect on some of the most important claims and conjectures concerning the general character of modern European governance with the aim of identifying significant questions about the development of environmental policy and the parallel process of European regionalisation.

Surveying pertinent literature (Hirst, 2000; Rhodes, 1997; Rhodes, 2000; Richards and Smith, 2002; Pierre, 2000), one of the most prominent contentions to emerge is that many western industrial nations have experienced a shift towards 'governance' away from 'government'. This, it is argued, has increased the number and range of public, private and voluntary sector actors who participate in, and shape, public policy, and this, it is claimed, has caused an increased dispersal of public policy decision-making authority. Such changes are said to obscure the boundaries between government and non-governmental actors in policymaking with the effect that the state becomes a "collection of interorganizational networks" in which no single actor has sufficient power or authority to be able to steer or regulate alone (Rhodes, 1997: 57). If such patterns of policymaking do now prevail, what are the implications for EU governance generally and environmental governance in particular?

Second, scholars concerned with the subject of governance in the EU have grown tired of debating developments in terms of traditional integration theories (e.g.

neo-functionalism and (liberal) intergovernmentalism) and have turned increasingly towards alternative concepts and frameworks. One such approach, which is at heart of this volume, is the idea of *multi-level* governance. (See Bache and Flinders, 2004 and Marks and Hooghe, 2004 for excellent summaries). Whilst, the notion of multi-level governance (MLG) is not without is critics (Jordan, 2001), the approach has been recommended (Fairbrass and Jordan, 2001b; Fairbrass and Jordan, 2004) for highlighting certain critical arguments about the EU as a polity. For example, characteristics such as the mobilisation of sub-national actors, the complex, uncertain and contested nature of EU decision-making, entrepreneurial supranational activity, and unintended policy consequences and learning surfaced in early MLG literature (Marks, 1992 and 1993; Marks *et al.*, 1995 and 1996). In addition, more recently, advocates of the MLG approach (Marks and Hooghe, 2004) have argued that two types of multi-level governance are discernible: Type 1 encompassing general purpose structures; and Type 2 that are thought to be task specific networks. Type 1 governance has been identified in relation to UK structural funding and the English Regions (see Bache and Conzelmann in this volume) but Type 2 networks are also said to have emerged (stimulated by the intervention of the EU in regional policy). The question that arises is what evidence is there for Type 1 and Type 2 MLG in relation to the UK and environmental policy?

Third, moving beyond the more general debate about governance in the EU presented above, it is also important to highlight some of the issues specifically associated with *environmental* governance. Scholars report a shift towards 'new' environmental governance (see for example, Knill and Tosun, Rottman and Lenschow and Koutalakis in this volume). The alleged changes are said to take the form of a shift away from 'command and control' towards new modes such as voluntary agreements, benchmarking and the reliance on private sector actors. Such developments are thought to be part of a search for improved effectiveness and efficiency in regulatory policymaking in the EU, given a history of compliance deficits, slow decision-making, impasses, and an increasing internal diversity within the EU. It is argued that these new forms of environmental governance are likely to lead to consensual decision-making (because the resistance of decision-makers and implementing actors is minimised owing to the low regulatory adjustments required). The key question is whether, in fact, consensual decision-making does result.

If the claims outlined above are correct, there are likely to be a number of potentially very significant implications and consequences. To assess the validity of these conjectures, a number of important questions are posed here about the nature of EU environmental governance and the role of regional actors.

- First, what are the likely effects of 'new' modes of environmental governance? What are the consequences of regionalisation for EU environmental governance? How are the two processes linked? In what ways do they interact? Can they be disentangled?

- Second, do 'new' modes of environmental governance increase or decrease the opportunities for regional actors in the context of devolution? With the introduction of changes to EU environmental governance (e.g. non-binding targets) are there likely to be potentially adverse or beneficial effects on sub-national actors (e.g. marginalisation or increased influence)? What role might business actors play in the context of devolution and environmental policy?
- Third, to what extent have changes to EU environmental governance (as a result of regionalisation and the introduction of new modes of governance) led to the emergence of coalitions among sub-national actors and others (such as other sub-national actors and EU level policymakers)? Under what conditions can one expect coalitions to emerge? What are the objectives of both sides? Are these coalitions more important in the implementation phase in terms of environmental policymaking (as is the case for sub-national partnerships in structural funding policy) or at other stages in the policy cycle? What role do regional actor networks play in environmental policymaking (as compared to structural funding policy)?
- Fourth, given changes in environmental governance, to what extent can they be classified as Type 1 and Type 2 forms of MLG? What do changes in the UK following devolution tell us about EU environmental governance? Does this amount to a transformation of EU governance? Is devolution merely indicative of a more general trend towards decentralisation in the EU rather than a more deep-seated reconstruction?
- Lastly, what mileage is there in the MLG approach with regard to weak administrations and political conflict? Is it necessary to revise MLG to see it less as a consensual mode of governance and more of a conflict driven mode?

Having raised these questions, the chapter now turns to consider the devolution process in the UK.

Background: United Kingdom Developments

This section sets out the background to the empirical case studies that follow in the Section IV of the chapter. In so doing, it focuses on two parallel and interconnected dimensions: first, the process of regionalisation as it relates to the UK; second, the development of environmental governance in the UK set within the broader context of EU environmental policy and policymaking.

Regionalisation in the UK: devolution

In the early part of the twentieth century, Europe was a patchwork of unitary states. Following World War Two, however, in response to a number of crises faced by traditional unitary states, a significant shift occurred. The 'federal principle' appears to have been widely adopted with a resulting trend towards regional government as the norm (Hopkins, 2002: xxi; Bullmann, 1997). Regionalisation, it has been argued (Hopkins, 2002: 24), creates a polity that possesses some but not all of the characteristics typically associated with a federal state (Watts, 1998 and 1999).[2] A regionalised state incorporates an intermediate level of autonomous government between the national and the local level that has final responsibility for policy areas that traditionally have been held by the centre (Hopkins, 2002: 19). Crucially, the regional tier of government may be allocated the ability to create policy that differs from the national norm and regional policy variations may emerge.

Traditionally, the UK has been regarded as a definitive, centralised unitary state (Bogdanor, 1999; John, 1996) because, it was argued, public bodies apart from Parliament do not have an entrenched status and the legal doctrine of *ultra vires* means that local government is dependent on the *largesse* or permission of the national legislature in order to carry out its activities. But, it has also been pointed out (John, 1996) that because the UK lacks a written constitution, the actual or *de facto* distribution of powers is more likely to reflect the resources of the political actors, political tradition and habit. As a result the UK could be regarded (John, 1996: 132) as an administratively decentralised state because of the way in which administrative power has long been divided between Wales, Scotland and Northern Ireland and the decentralisation of extensive financial and decision-making powers to locally elected government. Nevertheless, in the late 1990s, when the UK formally triggered a process of devolution, it began to move beyond 'mere administrative decentralisation' to introduce a distinctive form of regionalisation and pursue a broadly similar pattern to its European neighbours (Figure 1).

In 1998, the recently elected Labour Government passed Acts of Parliament at Westminster that led to the establishment of devolved bodies in Scotland, Wales, Northern Ireland and the English Regions. This development resulted from pressures that had been building up in the UK political system for most of the twentieth century (Bogdanor, 1999; Norton, 2001). When devolution finally came, the powers transferred to the different parts of the UK were unequal, an outcome referred to as 'asymmetrical devolution' (Bogdanor, 1999; Bulmer *et al.*, 2002; Norton, 2001, 261). Scotland was, and remains, the most well endowed having been allocated financial (i.e. limited tax varying powers), legislative and administrative powers to be exercised by the Scottish Executive (SE) and the Scottish Parliament (SP). Northern Ireland's Assembly has more restricted powers than Scotland but less limited than England and Wales, having control over legislative and administrative matters. The powers transferred to Wales and the National Assembly for Wales (NafW) were more confined than those assigned to Scotland and Northern Ireland,

2 It has been suggested (Watts, 1999) that federalisation can arise through one of two processes. It can develop from an aggregation of formerly separate political units, as in the creation of Switzerland or the USA. Or, it may stem from a process that grants constitutional autonomy to political units formerly subordinate within a unitary political system, as in the case of Belgium and Spain. The process of federalisation produces a polity that progressively acquires all of the characteristics of a fully federal state as outlined above.

being restricted to administrative devolution. Arguably, the bodies at the regional level in England outside London (i.e. the Regional Development Agencies (RDAs) and the Regional Assemblies (RAs)) acquired the least powers of all, having been given administrative responsibility only and having no directly elected fora[3] that could 'pass' legislation (either primary or secondary) at the regional level (Bradbury and Mawson, 1997).

Table 1: The UK: A Federal State?

Characteristics of a Federal State	*UK – Post Devolution Features*
Two (or more) orders or government	Central, regional and local government
Directly and democratically elected institutions associated with each order of government	Scottish Parliament, Welsh Assembly and Northern Ireland Assembly directly elected Potential for directly elected regional assemblies in the English Regions
Formal distribution of significant legislative, executive and fiscal powers to each order of government	Only Scotland has significant legislative, executive and fiscal powers
A written constitution that sets out the division of competencies which cannot be amended without the agreement of both orders of government	MoU and associated concordats sets out division of competences but it is not legally binding and the UK Government could rescind powers without the agreement of the regions
A constitutional court that interprets the constitution and tries to ensure that neither order of government illegitimately encroaches on the competences of the other. It also prevents one or several regions from acting against the interests of the other regions	Joint Ministerial Committee has the formal role of acting as the conflict resolution/management body
Mechanisms for safeguarding the interest of the regions at the federal level via either intergovernmental conferences or the presence of a sufficiently powerful second chamber	Absence of formal mechanisms but in practice the central UK Government takes regional interests into account in policy formulation
A symmetrical pattern of shared powers across the nation-state	Asymmetrical pattern

Source: Author

3 The Regional Assemblies do contain elected representatives. However, they have been elected in local elections and form part of local government.

The UK devolution settlement is contained in several Acts of Parliament (i.e. the Government of Wales Act, the Scotland Act and the Regional Development Agencies Act passed in 1998) and related agreements. Aside from the 1998 Acts, the underlying document is the Memorandum of Understanding[4] (MoU) (Office of the Deputy Prime Minister, 2001). This comprises a series of agreements consisting of the main text of the MoU and five supplementary agreements or concordats that apply broadly uniform arrangements throughout the UK covering the following matters: the establishment and operation of a Joint Ministerial Committee (JMC); the co-ordination of European Union policy issues; financial assistance to industry; international relations; and statistics. Finally, there are a number of bilateral concordats drawn up between the devolved authorities and UK central government departments (for example, Department of the Environment, Food and Rural Affairs (DEFRA), 2000). The various documents were designed to 'manage' the devolution process and guide future working relationships between the different tiers of government.

Environmental governance

Even prior to devolution in the UK, an expanding range of government, quasi- and non-governmental actors at all levels had taken an active part in environmental decision-making, contributing to an already rather dispersed pattern of EU environmental governance (Flynn, 2001; McCormick, 1991; Lowe and Ward, 1998) (Figures 2 and 3). For many decades there had been an important wider international dimension to UK environmental policy (Lowe and Ward, 1998: 9-11) and with the UK's membership of EU in 1973, this permitted the involvement of the European Commission, European Parliament and other supranational institutions in national environmental policymaking, resulting in a 'Europeanisation' of policy content, styles and structures in the UK (Jordan, 2002). This accretion of environmental policy competence at the EU level also encouraged the establishment of European or Brussels based non-governmental organisations, thereby adding to the number and range of actors active in UK environmental governance.

Among the governmental actors at the national level were those central government departments charged with environmental responsibilities such as the Department of the Environment, Transport and the Regions (DETR) (although other central government departments also exercised significant powers over matters relating to the environment). Notably, even before the devolution process was triggered, the territorial offices that formed part of the UK government's central machinery, such as the Scottish Office, also played a concrete role in environmental policymaking (Bogdanor, 1999: 111 and 160).

4 The first MoU (Cm 4444) was issued in October 1999 (Lord Chancellor, 1999) agreed between the UK Government and the devolved administrations in Wales and Scotland (not Northern Ireland). This was superseded by MoU (Cm 4806) issued in July 2000 (Lord Chancellor, 2000) to reflect the Northern Ireland Executive Committee's decision to become a party to the agreement, and later replaced by the most recent MoU (Cm 5240), published in December 2001 (Deputy Prime Minister, 2001).

Table 2: Pre-Devolution Environmental Governance in the UK

	Governmental	*Quasi-governmental*	*Non-governmental*
Supra-national	European Union (e.g. European Commission DG Environment and the European Parliament Committee on the Environment, Public Health and Food Safety) Other international organisations		Transnational private business organisations (e.g. TXU Energy and Thames Water plc) Transnational environmental interest groups (e.g. World Wide Fund for Nature, WWF)
National	Parliament Select Committees e.g. House of Commons Select Committees (Environment, Food and Rural Affairs, Environment, Transport and the Regions) and House of Lords Select Committees (EU Environment, Agriculture, Public Health and Consumer Protection) Central Government departments (e.g. DETR, the Treasury, DTI, and Cabinet Office) Cabinet Committees (e.g. Ministerial Committee on the Environment (ENV), and Ministerial Sub-Committee on Green Ministers (ENV(G))	Executive Agencies (e.g. Pesticides Safety Directorate and the Rural Payments Agency) Executive Non-Departmental Public Bodies Joint Nature Conservation Committee Advisory Bodies (e.g. Royal Commission on Environmental Pollution and the Sustainable Development Commission)	Nationally based private business organisations, such as individual firms, national trade associations and professional bodies (e.g. Electricity Producers Association) Nationally based environmental interest groups (e.g. Royal Society for the Protection of Birds and the Campaign to Protect Rural England)
Sub-national	Government Offices in the English regions Local Government: Counties and Unitary Authorities		Locally based private business organisations and environmental interest groups

Source: Author

Table 3: Post-Devolution

Level	*Actors*
Supra-national	European Union institutions e.g. European Commission (DG Environment) European interest environmental and business groups e.g. WWF, Birdlife International, and UNICE
National	Government departments in Whitehall e.g. DEFRA, ODPM, DfT, DTI, and Treasury Parliamentary Committees at Westminster Quasi-government: e.g. the Environment Agency National interest environmental and business groups e.g. RSPB and CBI
Regional	National Assembly for Wales Scottish Parliament and Executive Northern Ireland Assembly Regional Development Agencies and Regional Assemblies in the English Regions Government Offices in the English Regions Regional/national interest groups – e.g. WWF Cymru and CBI Cymru
Local	Government: Local government authorities (e.g. County Councils) NGOs: local interest environmental and business groups e.g. RSPB and CBI Local interest environmental and business groups.

Source: Author

Additionally, prior to 1999, executive agencies and executive non-departmental public bodies, such as English Nature[5] and the Environment Agency[6] (Dixon, 1998: 216-217) that operated beyond (or below) the national government level were already dynamic parties to environmental policymaking. Among the non-governmental actors active at the national level, was an array of private sector, commercial organisations and a growing body of environmental NGOs. At sub-national level (i.e. local or regional) were the long established local authorities, the previously created but intermittently functioning Northern Ireland Assembly and the new Government Offices in the regions (established in 1994) which had played a major role in

5 The 1990 Environmental Protection Act had split the National Conservancy Council's (NCC's) functions into separate country agencies for England, Scotland and Wales. English Nature became responsible for nature conservation matters in England. In Scotland the NCC and the Countryside Commission (CC) were combined to establish Scottish National Heritage (SNH), and in Wales the NCC and the CC were combined to form the Countryside Commission for Wales (CCW)

6 The Environment Agency was formed in the mid 1990s by combining Her Majesty's Inspectorate of Pollution (HMIP), the National Rivers Authority (NRA) and Waste Regulation Authorities (WRAs).

environmental policy (in its implementation if not its formulation) prior to devolution. Along with these organisations there was a plethora of local private sector business organisations and local interest groups (McCormick, 1991: 21-26).

Among the various actors identified above, it was primarily national government departments (such as the DETR) and EU institutions (such as the Commission and the Parliament) that vied for control over environmental policy (Golub, 1995; Fairbrass and Jordan, 2001a and 2001b). Where supranational bodies at the EU level have held sway, it has tended to be as a result of alliances with transnational and national interest groups (e.g. World Wildlife Fund, Birdlife International and the Royal Society for the Protection of Birds) (Fairbrass and Jordan, 2002b). Prior to devolution, sub-national actors such as local authorities had tended to play a limited role in policy-making, though they shouldered much of the burden of implementation.

Prior to 1999, intergovernmental relations between Whitehall and the regions/nations with regard to environmental matters were largely conducted via territorial offices. That is, the Scottish Office, Welsh Office and Government Offices in the English Regions conveyed national policy determined at the centre (in Whitehall or in Brussels) to the regions/nations and would feed back regional concerns to the centre (Government Office for the East of England (GO East), personal communication, April 2, 2004). Even though the 'regions' and 'nations' that comprise the UK had, in many cases, already established offices in Brussels prior to 1999, environmental policy-making with respect to EU level negotiations was highly centralised being largely channelled through the Cabinet Office and UK embassy to the European Union (UKREP). Welsh, Scottish, Northern Irish and English concerns tended to be subsumed within the UK policy line presented in Environment Council of Ministers meetings. As a result, environmental policy tended to be largely "UK" focused, accommodating regional or sub-national concerns and exhibiting little sub-national variation or divergence in terms of the policy positions taken in EU discussions (European Commission – DG Environment, personal communication, March 30, 2004). The one exception to this rule was that there was a perceptible "Scottish position" on a number of issues, fisheries policy being prominent, and on many occasions staff from the Scottish Office would take a leading role during EU negotiations (East of England European Partnership (EEEP), personal communication, March 30, 2004).

Case Studies

The detailed empirical cases presented are Wales and the English Regions[7] outside London. The material[8] is structured around the following issues: task allocation and

7 Interviews were conducted with actors in five of the eight English regions outside London.

8 The discussion presented in this chapter is based on a combination of primary and secondary data. The research commenced with period of documentary analysis in order to establish the *de jure* or formal allocation of powers resulting from devolution. Among the written sources

the *de jure* allocation of environmental policy authority, competition for control of the policy agenda, potential for conflict, information gathering and alliances, policy definition and coherence.

Task allocation and *de jure* powers

Following the 1998 Government of Wales Act and elections in 1999, the NAfW was established in Cardiff. Although it does not have the power to make primary legislation, it does enjoy extensive executive powers and may make secondary legislation (i.e. orders and regulations fixing the detail of implementation). It operates a Cabinet system combined with a strong committee system (Bulmer *et al.*, 2002). Funding for the NAfW is on a block grant basis. It has no powers to vary taxation (Norton, 2001: 269). The powers previously vested in the Secretary of State for Wales were transferred to the NAfW and many of the civil servants that now form part of the Welsh Assembly Government (WAG) previously worked in the Welsh Office (Norton, 2001: 269; Bogdanor, 1999: 159-161). In many ways, the NAfW's powers are restricted but, crucially, it does have power over environmental policy and a number of other policy areas that have direct implications for the environment such as agriculture, highways, housing, town and country planning. These are granted under Schedule 2 of the Government of Wales Act 1998. Very significantly, under Section 121, the NAfW was tasked with particular responsibility for sustainable development, in common with the English Regions. The NAfW has concordats with most functional departments including those with an impact on environmental issues such as the Department for the Environment, Food, and Rural Affairs (DEFRA), the Office of the Deputy Prime Minister (ODPM), and the Department of Transport (DfT).

In England, as part of their modernisation programme (Jeffery and Mawson, 2002; Tomaney, 2002), the Labour Government passed the Regional Development Agencies Act in 1998 which created new actors in the eight English Regions outside London, namely the Regional Development Agencies and the Regional Chambers (now mainly self-styled as Assemblies). The former are business-led bodies with a focus on economic growth, but which also have a duty to contribute to sustainable development under Section 4(1)e of the 1998 Act, and hence environmental policy. The Regional Assemblies (RAs) oversee the work of the Regional Development Agencies (RDAs), with a view to achieving some degree of 'joined-up' government

consulted were Acts of Parliament (i.e. the Government of Wales Act 1998 and the Regional Development Agencies Act 1998), the Memorandum of Understanding (Cabinet Office, 2001), various multilateral and bilateral concordats, government strategy papers and other similar related policy papers. Subsequently, a series of interviews was conducted during a 13-month period from March 2003 to April 2004 encompassing elected members, government officials, national/regional environmental non-governmental organisations (NGOs), and European Commission staff. These interviews elicited data about the *de facto* tasks, roles, responsibilities and interactions of the government actors during the process of environmental policymaking in order to compare those with the *de jure* or formal allocation of powers resulting from devolution.

and accountability at the regional level. They are responsible for devising integrated policies in the spheres of regional planning, transport, housing, economic growth and regeneration, the environment and social inclusion. Although not directly elected, the RAs are stakeholder organisations that comprise elected local authority representatives (about 70 per cent) and social, business and environmental partners (about 30 per cent), which are serviced by paid officials and committees. Given the RAs' relatively limited resources and lack of legislative power, the main mode through which they work to achieve their objectives is one of partnership (East of England Regional Assembly (EERA), personal communication, March 16, 2004; Yorkshire and Humberside Regional Assembly (Y&H RA), personal communication, April 15, 2004; South West of England Regional Development Agency (SWRDA), personal communication, March 23, 2004). These two newly created bodies (i.e. the RDAs and the RAs) work in close co-operation (GO East, personal communication, April 2, 2004; One North East, personal communication, April 6, 2004; South East of England Regional Development Agency (SEEDA), personal communication, March 25, 2004) with the previously established Government Offices in the Regions (GORs). The GORs were initially set up under the Conservative Government in 1994. They were designed to bring central government departments, such as those responsible for environment and education, closer to the regions. As part of the constitutional reform package that was introduced shortly before the 2001 General Election, the GORs were allocated additional resources reflecting the increasing value placed on decentralisation by the UK government.

Competition for control of the policy agenda: increased potential for conflict

Clearly, in a formal sense, devolution has transferred *de jure* policymaking powers to the devolved bodies and altered the formal institutional structures present in the UK (and therefore in the EU). Devolution in the UK, therefore, has created new actors and modified existing ones, thereby altering the institutional configuration in relation to environmental policy within the UK and as part of the broader institutional development of the EU (Figure 4).

However, given the way in which the devolution settlement has been constructed, there remains some uncertainty about the roles and tasks of the various actors (Assembly Member 2, personal communication, March 13, 2003; European Commission – DG Environment, personal communication, March 30, 2004; SEEDA, personal communication, March 25, 2004; WAG – Environmental Protection Division, personal communication, March 12, 2003). However, what is evident is that the new actors in Wales and England have adopted a pro-active (not passive) stance towards EU environmental policy, both in terms of formulation and implementation. They show signs of competing with national level actors (e.g. the DETR) and EU level actors (such as the Commission) for political space. However, despite the alterations to the formal institutional configurations and the informal

Table 4: Pre- and Post-Devolution Compared

	Pre-devolution	*Post-devolution*
De jure distribution of powers and tasks	Among government, quasi, and non-governmental actors at local, national and supranational levels	Among government, quasi, and non-governmental actors at local, regional, national and supranational levels
De facto distribution of powers and tasks	Among government, quasi, and non-governmental actors at local, national and supranational levels	Among government, quasi, and non-governmental actors at local, regional, national and supranational levels
Intergovernmental relations – between Whitehall and regions/ nations	Conducted via territorial offices for Scotland, Wales and Northern Ireland; via Government Offices in the Regions (GORs) in England	Conducted on an intergovernmental basis between London (Whitehall) and Edinburgh (SP), Cardiff (WAG) and Belfast In England: via GORs
Inter-Parliamentary relations – between Westminster and the regions/nations	Not applicable – given that the elected bodies in Scotland, Wales and England had not been created	Dependent on having the same party in government in London, Edinburgh and Cardiff for smooth relations
Governmental relations with EU	UK government (via UKREP) with CoM and CEC Some direct representation from regions and nations of UK to EU institutions via Brussels offices	UK government (via UKREP) with CoM and CEC WAG and SE: via UK Government and increased direct contact with EU institutions via Brussels Offices
Interest groups	Interest representation at local, national and EU level	Interest representation at local, regional, national and EU level
Citizens	Direct elections at local, national and EU level	Direct elections at local, regional (in Wales and Scotland), national and EU level

Source:Author

jockeying for position undertaken by the Welsh and English actors, there appears to have been little or no discernible change to patterns of dominance and subordination. National level central government actors and the European Union institutions remain the chief rivals for control over environmental policy.

Devolution would appear to have increased the potential for conflict (Assembly Member 1, personal communication, March 13, 2003). Nevertheless, to date, little open conflict appears to have arisen. Respondents reported that to date there had been no recourse to the Joint Ministerial Committee (WAG – Sustainable Development Unit, personal communication, March 12, 2003; NafW Brussels Office, personal communication, March 30, 2004).

Information gathering and alliances

One apparent by-product of devolution is the marginalisation of the sub-national or regional government actors (e.g. WAG) from decision-making at the centre in the UK. For example the WAG now finds that it is less likely to be automaticallyincluded in some policy discussions in Whitehall than before devolution. To overcome this problem many of the long standing civil service staff in the WAG rely on their established relationships and networks in Whitehall in order to remain 'in the loop' (WAG – Environmental Protection Division, personal communication, March 12, 2003). Devolution has, therefore, increased the premium on up to date intelligence about forthcoming or developing environmental policy initiatives.

Paradoxically, at the same time, decision-making at the regional level has become more participatory and inclusionary. There is a stronger partnership with civil society in Wales and the English regions (North East Regional Assembly (NERA), personal communication, April 6, 2004; Y&H RA, personal communication, April 15, 2004; GO East, personal communication, April 2, 2004; EERA, peronsal communication, March 16, 2004). This may in part be a compensatory measure on the part of the regional actors, in order to offset the newly emerging problem of being marginalised by the centre at Whitehall.

Crucially, what devolution appears to have transformed, therefore, is the formation of actual and potential political alliances. The regional bodies have sought to establish alliances amongst themselves within the UK. For example, the English Regions Network now provides a forum for discussion and a platform for joint policy development (EERA, personal communication, March 16, 2004). They have also created active networks with other regions across the EU (NAfW Brussels Office (NAfWBO), personal communication, March 30, 2004; WAG-Sustainable Development Unit, personal communication, March 12, 2003). Furthermore, in a way that resembles coalition building among environmental NGOs and the EU institutions, there is evidence that the new actors in Wales and the English regions have identified a potential for influencing environmental policy by joining forces with the European Commission and the Parliament. This behaviour in itself has some precedents. Even prior to devolution Wales and the English regions had established offices in Brussels, mainly focusing on regional funding. However, the formal process of devolution has added weight and purpose to these offices and strengthened relations between the regions/nations and the EU (EEEP, personal communication, March 30,

2004; EERA, personal communication, March 16, 2004; SWRDA - Brussels Office, personal communication, March 23, 2004; Yorkshire and Humberside (Y&H BO) Brussels Office, personal communication, March 23, 2004). As indicated above, the regional governmental agencies now place a higher priority on their contact with the EU and have made organisational modifications to their offices in Brussels in order to reinforce their relationship with EU level policymakers (EEEP, personal communication, March 30, 2004; EERA, personal communication, March 16, 2004; European Commission – DG Regional Policy, personal communication, March 23, 2004; SWRDA - Brussels Office, personal communication, March 23, 2004).

Policy coherence or divergence?

In terms of policy definition, devolution appears to have had at least two main effects. By giving a duty towards sustainable development to both the NAfW and the RDAs, the broader policy agenda has been strengthened. In addition, devolution has already had some impact on the internal coherence of UK environmental policy.

Whilst the English Regions have yet to develop distinctive regional environmental policies, they have begun to identify and act on particular regional priorities. For example, whilst the Regional Sustainable Development Frameworks adopted by many English regions resemble each other and that of the UK central government, they invariably highlight certain aspects that are of special importance to the region. Several have emphasised waste management as a particular priority (SWRDA – Brussels Office, personal communication, March 23, 2004; Y&H BO, personal communication, March 23, 2004). Others regard transport issues as having greater urgency (SWRDA – Brussels Office, personal communication, March 23, 2004).

Similarly, Wales has in some policy areas adopted the same policy line as the UK/England (e.g. with regard to the Water Framework and End of Life Vehicles Directives), in other areas it has taken a different position. For example, Wales took a different line on waste management (WAG - Environmental Protection Division, personal communication, March 12, 2003), genetically modified organisms (GMOs) (WAG - Sustainable Development Unit, personal communication, March 12, 2003), renewable energy (Assembly Member 2, personal communication, March 13, 2003) and land use policy with respect to common land (RSPB Cymru, personal communication, March 11, 2003). More interestingly still, Wales has also begun to formulate policy on issues that, in a strictly technical sense, it has no formal power over (WWF Cymru, personal communication, March 12, 2003). This includes policy on renewable energy and rail transport (Assembly Member 2, personal communication, March 13, 2003; RSPB Cymru, personal communication, March 11, 2003). In summary, devolution has begun to alter the policy agenda in terms of its breadth and degree of divergence.

Conclusions

Having set out the theoretical arguments and having reviewed the empirical data it is now possible to return to the questions raised in above. Taking each in turn the following conclusions may tentatively be drawn.

In attempting to explain developments in EU governance, by evaluating the impact of regionalisation and the introduction of new modes of environmental governance, a significant problem arises. In effect, scholars are trying to locate, fix and 'quantify' what are in effect 'moving goal posts'. Both regionalisation and new environmental governance clearly have had a dynamic effect. However, it is exceedingly difficult to disentangle one from another. Nevertheless, singly they each appear to have further dispersed environmental decision-making authority, although based on the evidence considered here it would seem that devolution has had a more circumscribed impact than the changes introduced via the new forms of environmental governance. Taken in combination they certainly appear to have added to the pressures for the dispersal of decision-making authority and actually resulted in further fragmentation.

The case study evidence about the UK (specifically Wales and the English Regions) would suggest that 'new' modes of environmental governance could increase the opportunities for regional actors in the context of devolution. With the introduction of changes to EU environmental governance (non-binding targets and an increased reliance on private sector actors) there are potentially beneficial effects for sub-national actors leading to increased influence in environmental policymaking. However, the data point to adverse effects with some further marginalisation of sub-national governmental actors.

New governmental (i.e. NAfW and the RDAs) and non-governmental (e.g. RSPB-Cymru and Confederation of British Industry - Cymru) actors have been created at the sub-national or regional level that clearly have the desire and ambition to play a full part in EU policymaking. However, it should be noted that this aspiration is somewhat constrained by a number of factors. First, the NAfW and the English regional bodies lack resources. They are deficient in terms of their financial, informational and legislative resources. These limitations do significantly hinder their attempts to shape environmental policy and implement it. In comparison with business actors in the UK, the regional bodies are at a distinct disadvantage (Fairbrass, 2003). Business organisations clearly command considerable (greater) resources. Second, a factor that contributes to the first, is the necessity for UK environmental policy to be formally channelled through the offices of the UK central government, DEFRA, in order to present a 'UK line'. This restricts the opportunities for the Welsh and English regional bodies to have direct formal relations with EU level policymaking bodies. What emerges from the data is a picture that reveals how actors are included, or rather *excluded* from the policymaking process, not so much on the basis of their formal competences but rather owing to their (limited or inadequate) resource base.

Evidently the Welsh authorities and the English regional bodies are not content to be sidelined because of the formal institutional arrangements. Changes to EU environmental governance (as a result of regionalisation and the introduction of new modes of governance) have driven the creation of coalitions among sub-national actors and others (such as other sub-national actors and EU level policymakers). By way of compensation for their lack of organisational resources (referred to above) the regional governmental actors have sought alternative ways of making direct inputs into EU environmental policy, through, for example, their horizontal networks with other regional authorities within the UK and elsewhere across Europe and via their Brussels based lobbying offices. Moreover, EU level actors such as the Commission and the Parliament very much welcome the input of regional bodies. The former tend to view the latter as a source of political support and information, and will seek them out. In contrast to structural funding policy networks and partnerships, which play a key role during the implementation phase of the policy cycle, the coalitions built by regional actors in relation to environmental policy appear to be more active and critical at the policy formation stage, although even at the later stage of implementation there are efforts to share ideas and other resources with regional governmental actors in other EU member states and other parts of the UK.

In summary, it can be argued that the changes to environmental governance do take the form of both Type 1 and Type 2 MLG. Although in the UK there is little evidence that there has been any genuine decline in formal hierarchical structures, there is evidence of a growing ambition and mobilisation of regional actors in Wales and England, linked to a thickening of horizontal or non-hierarchical networks. The changes to environmental governance in the UK following devolution suggest that environmental governance has become more fragmented and multi-tiered or multi-centred but this does not really amount to a 'transformation' of EU governance. Devolution in the UK appears to be part of a broader more, general trend towards decentralisation in the EU which to date had had a relatively limited impact. However, perhaps the crucial point is that although changes to date have been modest, some seeds have been sown that could result in very different governance patterns in future.

Lastly, in conclusion, it may well be advisable to revise our approach to MLG, seeing it less as a consensual mode of governance and more as conflict driven. Whilst it would seem that on the whole consensus reigns with regard to the relationships between the Welsh and English regional bodies and other actors in the EU's environmental policy area, this partly arises from pragmatic considerations. For example, in a number of areas, it does not make sense for the Welsh and English regions to adopt a different policy line from the UK government (e.g. with regard to the End of Life Vehicles Directive). As a result the conflict resolution mechanism built into UK devolution (i.e. the JMC) has not been called into operation. However, this consensus may be only 'skin deep'. When scratching below the surface, there are signs that there is conflict between the UK government and some of the regional devolved bodies on some issues. For example, the UK government and the NAfW have taken different lines on issues such as GMOs and the Water Framework Directive. The latter is an issue that is deeply political in Wales and a source of conflict with England/the UK. We may, therefore, have to reframe our assumptions about the operation of MLG to see it as a process that encompasses both conflict and consensus, particularly when the actors being evaluated are 'weak administrations' of the type found in the UK in Wales and the English Regions.

In summary, devolution has caused both internal changes to the UK and the EU and to environmental governance. Only time will tell if these changes prove to be enduring and significant in terms of the emergence and empowerment of regional actors. What is clear is that a process of 'jockeying for position' has already begun and is showing some signs of important change.

References

Bache, I. and Flinders, M. (2004). *Multi-level Governance.* Oxford: Oxford University Press.

Bogdanor, V. (1999). *Devolution in the United Kingdom*. Oxford: Oxford University Press.

Bradbury, J. and Mawson, M. (1997) (Eds.) *British Regionalisation and Devolution. The Challenges of State Reform and European Integration.* London: Jessica Kingsley.

Bullmann, U. (1997). The Politics of the Third Level. In C. Jeffery (Ed.), *The Regional Dimension of the European Union. Towards a Third Level in Europe?* (pp.3-19) London: Frank Cass.

Bulmer, S., Burch, M., Carter, C. Hogwood, P. and Scott, A. (2002). *British Devolution and European Policymaking: Transforming Britain into Multi-level Governance.* London: Palgrave.

DEFRA (2000). Concordat between MAFF and the Cabinet of the National Assembly of Wales. Available at: http://www.defra.gov.uk/

Deputy Prime Minister (2001). Devolution: Memorandum of Understanding and Supplementary Agreements between the United Kingdom Government, Scottish Ministers, the Cabinet Office of the National Assembly for Wales and the Northern Ireland Executive Committee. *Cm 5240.* London: The Stationery Office.

Dixon, J. (1998). Nature Conservation. In P. Lowe and S. Ward (Eds.), *British Environmental Policy and Europe* (pp.214-231). London: Routledge.

Elcock, H. and Keating, M. (1998) (Eds.) *Remaking the Union. Devolution and British Politics in the 1990s.* London: Frank Cass.

Fairbrass, J. and Jordan, A. (2001a). Making European Union Biodiversity Policy: National Barriers and European Opportunities. *Journal of European Public Policy, 8 (4),* pp.499-518

Fairbrass, J. and Jordan, A. (2001b). European Union Environmental Policy and the Role of the UK Government: Passive Observer or Strategic Manager. *Environment Politics, 10 (2),* pp.1-21.

Fairbrass, J. and Jordan, A. (2002a). EU Environmental Governance: Uncomplicated and Predictable Policy-making? *CSERGE Working Paper EDM 02-03.* Norwich: CSERGE.

Fairbrass, J. and Jordan, A. (2002b). Interest Representation and Europeanisation: The Case of UK Environment Policy. In A. Warleigh and J. Fairbrass (Eds.), *Integrating Interests in the European Union: The New Politics of Persuasion, Advocacy and Influence* (pp.138-159). London: Europa.

Fairbrass, J. (2003). The Europeanization of business interest representation: UK and French firms compared. *Comparative European Politics, 1 (3),* pp.313-334.

Fairbrass, J. and Jordan, A. (2004). Environmental policy: a case of multi-level governance in the European Union? In M. Flinders and I. Bache (Eds.), *Themes and Issues in Multi-level Governance* (pp.147-164). Oxford: Oxford University Press.

Flynn, A. (2001). Environmental Policy. In B. Jones, D. Kavannah, M. Moran and P. Norton (Eds.), *Politics UK* (pp.611-632). Harlow: Longman.

Golub, J. (1995). The Politics of Judicial Discretion. *West European Politics, 19 (2),* pp.360-385.

Hirst, P. (2000). Democracy and Governance. In J. Pierre (Ed.). *Debating Governance. Authority, Steering and Democracy* (pp.13-35). Oxford: Oxford University Press.

Hooghe L. and Marks G. (2001). *Multi-level Governance and European Integration.* New York: Rowman and Littlefield.

Hopkins, J. (2002). *Devolution in context: regional, federal & devolved government in the Member States of the European Union.* London: Cavendish.

Jeffery, C. and Mawson, J. (2002). Introduction: Beyond the White Paper on the English Regions. *Regional Studies, 36 (7),* pp.715-720.

John, P. (1996). Europeanization in a Centralizing State: Multi-Level Governance in the UK. In C. Jeffery (Ed.), *The Regional Dimension of the European Union. Towards a Third Level in Europe?* (pp.131-219) London: Frank Cass.

Jordan, A. (2002). *The Europeanisation of British Environmental Policy: A Departmental Perspective.* Basingstoke: Palgrave.

Jordan, A. (2001). The European Union: an evolving system of multi-level governance...or government? *Policy and Politics, 29 (2),* pp.193-208

Lord Chancellor (1999). Devolution: Memorandum of Understanding and Supplementary Agreements between the United Kingdom Government, Scottish Ministers and the Cabinet of the National Assembly for Wales. *CM4444.* London: The Stationery Office.

Lord Chancellor (2000). Devolution: Memorandum of Understanding and Supplementary Agreements between the United Kingdom Government, Scottish Ministers, the Cabinet of the National Assembly for Wales and the Northern Ireland Executive Committee. *Cm 4806.* London: The Stationery Office.

Lowe P. and Ward S. (1998) (Eds.) *British Environmental Policy and Europe. Politics and Policy in Transition.* London: Routledge.

Marks, G. (1992). Structural Policy in the European Community. In A. Sbragia (Ed.), *Euro-Politics* (pp.191-224). Washington: Brookings Institute.

Marks, G. (1993). Structural Policy and Multi-level Governance in the EC. In A. Cafruny and G. Rosenthal (Eds.), *The State of the European Community* (pp.391-410). London: Longman.

Marks, G., Hooghe, L. and Blank, K. (1995). European Integration and the State. *EUI Working Paper RSC No. 95/7.* Florence: European University Institute.

Marks, G., Hooghe, L. and Blank, K. (1996). European Integration from the 1980s: State V Multi-level Governance. *Journal of Common Market Studies, 32 (3),* pp.341- 378.

Marks, G. and Hooghe, L. (2004), Contrasting Visions of Multi-level Governance. In I. Bache and M. Flinders (Eds.), *Multi-level Governance* (pp.15-30). Oxford: Oxford University Press.

McCormick, J. (1991). *British Politics and the Environment.* London: Earthscan.

Mitchell, J (2002). Towards a new constitutional settlement? In C. Hay (Ed.), *British Politics Today* (pp.237-258). London: Polity.

Norton P. (2001). *The British Polity.* London: Longman.

Office of the Deputy Prime Minister (2001). *Memorandum of Understanding and Supplementary Agreements.* Available at: http://www.devolution.odpm.gov.uk/memo/pdf/cm5240.pdf

Pierre, J. (2000) (Ed.) *Debating Governance. Authority, Steering and Democracy*. Oxford: Oxford University Press.

Rhodes, R. A. W. (1997). *Understanding Governance.* Buckingham: Open University Press.

Rhodes, R. A. W. (2000). Governance and Public Administration. In J. Pierre (Ed.), *Debating Governance. Authority, Steering and Democracy* (pp.54-90). Oxford: Oxford University Press.

Richards, D. and Smith, M. J. (2002). *Governance and Public Policy in the United Kingdom* Oxford: Oxford University Press.

Rokkan, S. and Urwin D. W. (1983). *Economy, territory, identity: Politics of West European peripheries*. London: Sage.

Smith A (2003). Multi-level Governance: What it is and how it can be studied. In G. Peters and J. Pierre (Eds.), *Handbook of Public Administration* (pp.619-628). London: Sage.

Swenden, W. (2002). Managing Federalism. A comparative overview. In S. Henig (Ed.), *Modernising Britain. Central, devolved federal?* (pp.167-197) London: The Federal Trust.

Tomaney J. (2002). The Evolution of Regionalism in England. *Regional Studies*, *36 (7)*, pp.721-731.

Watts, R (1999). German Federalism in Comparative Perspective. In C. Jeffery (Ed.), *Recasting German Federalism* (pp.265-284). London: Pinter.

Watts, R. (1998). Federalism, Federal Political Systems and Federations. *Annual Review of Political Science, 1,* pp.117-137

Regulatory Effects of Participatory Environmental Networks - The Case of the 'Seville Process'

Charalampos Koutalakis

Introduction

In recent years much of the debate on the future of EU integration has concentrated on enhancing effectiveness and efficiency in regulatory policymaking.[1] Low levels of compliance with EU legislation, slow legislative processes, deadlocked situations and the increasing diversity of the EU are, in brief, the main concerns that justify the growing search for new modes of governance that are different from traditional command-and-control uniformly binding regulatory approaches. New modes of governance cover a wide range of different policy processes such as the open method of coordination, voluntary accords, standard setting, delegation to regulatory networks and agencies, regulation 'through information', benchmarking, peer review, informal agreements, as well as forms of policy experimentation in different economic sectors, where a new mix of public and private goods is sought (Héritier, 2003). They are characterized by the principles of voluntarism (non-binding targets, soft law), subsidiarity (the delegation of decision-making competences to member states or private actors), and inclusion (the participation of all relevant actors in the decision-making process). These "modes of political steering concern both rule-setting and rule-implementation processes including ensuring compliance with international norms" (Börzel, 2002). Since new modes of governance represent an alternative to regulatory requirements (hard law), they are expected to facilitate consensual decision-making by minimizing the resistance of decision makers and implementing actors as regulatory adjustment costs remain low (Héritier, 2001: 9). Consequently, new modes of governance are expected to be politically more efficient and more effective (Héritier, 2003; Jachtenfuchs, 2001; Kohler-Koch and Eising, 1999).

From the end of the 1980s onwards environmental policy has been an area of intense experimentation with such novel regulatory approaches. The literature offers an abundance of explanatory factors that have contributed to the proliferation of new, less coercive, market-based policy instruments at both the EU and individual member state levels (Collier, 1997; Jordan *et al.*, 2003a, 2003b; Lenschow, 2002;

1 This chapter is based on a project *'Smoothing' Eastern Enlargements: Independent Regulatory Agencies and Non-Hierarchical Steering*, which is part of the EU Integrated Project *New Modes of Governance*, financed by the European Commission and coordinated at the European University Institute, Florence. (Contract No. CITI-CT-2004-506392).

Knill and Lenschow, 2000). However, little attention has been paid to regulatory networks, their performance and regulatory effects in terms of policy outcomes. The aim of this chapter is to explore theoretically derived hypotheses from the literature on new modes of governance and delegation to regulatory networks in order to identify the main institutional properties that enhance efficiency and effectiveness in policy formulation and implementation. To explore these issues we proceed as follows. First, we review the theoretical work on delegation to regulatory networks and non-hierarchical steering arrangements as specific features of new modes of governance in environmental policies. Second, we analyse the experience derived from the Integrated Pollution Prevention and Control (IPPC) network(s) organised under the auspices of the IPPC Bureau in Seville in order to assess the scope and effects of delegating regulatory competences to participatory networks. The IPPC Directive (96/61) introduced significant innovations into EU environmental policies. It was the first time that EU environmental policies departed from media-specific regulatory approaches to pollution abatement by introducing an integrated approach that incorporated a single permit system covering all pollutant activities of industry, in water, air and land. These permits are based on 'Best Available Techniques' (BAT).[2] The definition of BAT is delegated to ad hoc co-regulatory sectoral and sub-sectoral networks that comprise the Commission, the member states, business associations, individual firms, environmental organisations, research institutes, universities, plus national and EU regulatory agencies. These networks operate under the auspices of a European IPPC Bureau (EIPPCB) in Seville.

The analysis of the 'Seville process' seeks to assess the regulatory impact of such participatory structures in policymaking. It focuses on two fundamental institutional properties of regulatory networks that the literature suggests are catalysts for the enhancement of effectiveness and efficiency in regulatory policymaking. First, there is the actor dimension, namely the regulatory effects of networks that include all affected interests (firms, private interest groups and non-governmental organizations, national and European agencies and national civil servants). The question is whether a participatory structure is more effective than the traditional legislative process in reducing potential conflicts at the stage of policy implementation. Second, we assess the effects on network participants of non-hierarchical steering arrangements in the decision-making process. Much of our current understanding of the dynamics of transnational regulatory policymaking is based on theories of regulatory competition and notions of a race to the top or bottom in a range of regulatory variation in different policy areas (Radaelli, 2004; Holzinger and Knill, 2004). Regulatory competition between environmentally advanced EU member states that actively seek to enhance their regulatory arrangements at the EU level and laggards that rarely succeed in influencing EU policy developments increase existing differences between member states. To what extent do learning, persuasion and the spread of best regulatory practices facilitated by regulatory networks lead to policy outcomes that differ signi-

2 *Availability* of certain technologies denotes their development on a scale that does not lead to significant negative impacts on economic viability and competitiveness in a given industrial sector or country.

ficantly from those stemming from command-and-control steering modes based on binding legislation? In other words, can new forms of governance reduce the influence of conflicting national interests over the level of environmental regulatory standards, especially in areas that require significant investment in physical and institutional infrastructure? Are they more efficient in facilitating rapid regulatory responses to technological innovations in the area of pollution reduction? What is their degree of effectiveness in achieving the stated objectives of the IPPC Directive (a high level of environmental protection through the diffusion of BAT for pollution reduction) and what forms do regulatory outcomes take in this policy area?

Why Delegate? Dimensions of New Modes of Governance

In its White Paper on Governance, the European Commission attributes an important role to agencies and regulatory networks for the better application of EU rules (European Commission, 2001: 23f). Most of the literature on delegation focuses on the driving forces that condition the incentives of political actors to delegate policy-making competences to independent regulatory agencies and/or regulatory networks operating under their auspices, their institutional design and the consequences of delegation for democratic accountability and control. Rational choice approaches conceptualise delegation to independent regulatory agencies (IRAs) as a response to powerful functional pressures emanating from the expansion of the regulatory role of the state as a distinctive mode of social coordination (Majone, 1994; 1997a). The principal/agent framework that dominates studies of delegation to non-majoritarian institutions, emphasises four explanations as to why delegation to independent regulatory agencies or networks might be beneficial for political efficiency. First, delegation is used to reduce political transaction costs emerging at the stage of negotiations between political actors (Epstein and O'Halloran, 2000; Héritier, 2003: 203). Second, delegation to specialized bodies is seen to facilitate policy continuity given the complexity of socio-economic phenomena, the acceleration of scientific and technological developments and the growth of international interdependence. Everson *et al.* (1999: 21) indicate that "a reason for proposing the creation of European agencies in several areas of economic and social regulation is the perception of EU citizens and economic actors alike, that the present system – with its heavy concentration on rule making and its weak control of the enforcement process – is no longer able to cope with the regulatory challenges of global markets". The high collective stakes attached to these challenges demand continuity in public action, which is not always achieved by political actors because of short-term electoral considerations (Majone, 2001, 1997b). Third, the increasing technical and scientific complexity of many regulatory issues has led to the establishment of agencies and public/private networks which contribute expertise in these substantive matters (Héritier, 2003: 203). Mobilization of all knowledge relevant to public decision-making requires stable relations between peers that minimize bureaucratic or political bias during negotiations (Moe, 1990, 1995). Such a framework is hard to find within public administrations. Finally, agencies and regulatory networks may pave the way for closer incorporation of civil society into governmental institutions. Everson *et al.* (1999: 32) argue that separation from government may make agencies or networks a preferred mechanism for co-opting certain groups into the decision-making process. Thus, agencies and networks function as intermediary institutions between state and civil society. Additionally, agencies and regulatory networks, as depoliticized bodies keen to improve their own public reputation, can contribute credibility and reliability as well as public confidence in regulatory processes and outcomes (Pollack, 1997).

Cross – media pollution prevention policies bring together all the above pressures that encourage political actors to seek alternatives to traditional legislative forms of policy formulation and implementation. Available technology enables or constrains policy options, especially in relation to the stringency of environmental standards and the instruments of monitoring and enforcement. The generation and diffusion of new technologies across a wide spectrum of sectoral economic activities requires rapid regulatory responses that enhance learning capacities and diffusion in those economic sectors and countries with weak economic and knowledge resource bases. Knowledge gaps and uncertainties about the causes of environmental damage, its real dimensions and what constitutes effective remedies require stable continuous interaction between policymakers, economic actors and epistemic communities. Varied ecological conditions within the EU render the adoption of uniform pollution abatement standards ineffective. Variations in the absorption capacities of different geographical areas result in significant regulatory distortions with considerable economic consequences between different polluting activities (Holzinger, 1999). Moreover, in contrast to product standards, economic actors, especially from member states with comparatively weak environmental regulatory regimes may, in the short term, face strong disincentives to comply with environmental process standards that reduce their competitiveness (Scharpf, 1994). As a result, the adoption of environmental standards and the definition of procedural requirements for their implementation have triggered intense competitive pressures between EU member states seeking to avoid high adjustment costs by having to upload their domestic regulatory models and traditions to the EU level. Given the persistent economic disparities between EU member states and the scale of administrative adjustments and financial investments required, regulatory competition has generated a leaders/laggards dynamic in EU environmental policies (Börzel, 2003). The accession of southern European member states (Greece in 1981 and Spain and Portugal in 1986) with weak institutional and administrative capacities and limited or even no prior experience in pro-active environmental policies, coupled with an acceleration of legislative output that followed the launch of the internal market programme, have led to the emergence of a deficit in member state compliance with environmental legislation (Börzel, 2003; Mendrinou, 1996; Tallberg, 1999). The same holds for the recent enlargement to the east. As recent arrivals in the EU, the Central and Eastern European countries (CEECs) faced two serious problems regarding the adoption of EU legislation. First, they did not have the chance to influence European regulations based on their preferences and policy traditions. Second, they often lacked adequate institutional structures and capacities to implement and enforce European regulations effectively. This double disadvantage for the CEECs has led to concern in the new member countries about the full implementation of all EU environmental directives (Baker, 2000; Carius *et al.,* 2000; Homeyer, 2004). Wide differences between domestic economic and administrative capacities highlight limits to the harmonization approach.

Compliance problems point to a fundamental paradox in the current EU regulatory regime. The substantial expansion of the EU's regulatory competences from the 1980s onwards has not been accompanied either by a parallel expansion of the EU's own implementation structures or by powerful enforcement and monitoring capacities. The Commission's DG Environment has comparatively weak monitoring and enforcement capacities compared with other Directorates General, such as DG Competition (Macrory, 1996). The Commission's access to information regarding member states' compliance performance depends on a weak arrangement that involves three main mechanisms: complaints by citizens, business or environmental NGOs; the Commission's own investigations; and petitions and questions in the European Parliament (Koutalakis, 2004). Given the reliance of the Commission on domestic administrations and private actors that are rarely granted institutionalised opportunities to participate in the decision-making process, their systematic inclusion in the policy process seems to provide a viable alternative to the legislative process. The creation of regulatory networks and forums that facilitate exchange of experience, learning and diffusion of best practices between public and private stakeholders reduces the regulatory gap that stems from the unequal distribution of 'say' and 'pay' in EU multi-level governance (Eberlein and Grande, 2005; Dehousse, 1997).

The intensity of the pressures described above determines the Commission's preferences on the institutional design of regulatory networks. Key actors seeking to maximize their influence over policy outcomes attempt to make use of the tension between delegation and control in order to minimize losses from a network's tendency to gain political and bureaucratic autonomy. The higher the pressures experienced by key actors in a given policy area the more competences they will delegate to regulatory networks and the weaker will be their control mechanisms. Institutional design of regulatory networks facilitates or hinders regulatory policy outcomes.

Institutionalist approaches point to two fundamental properties of the institutional design of regulatory networks that enhance effectiveness and efficiency in policy formulation and implementation. First, they include "non-state actors, such as firms, private interest groups, or non-governmental organizations (NGOs) in governance arrangements (actor dimension)"; and second they put "an emphasis on non-hierarchical modes of steering (steering dimension)" (Risse, 2004: 291). In line with theories of deliberative democracy, it is expected that the more inclusive regulatory networks are of diverse interests, the more transparent, effective and efficient their policy outcomes will be (Porte and Nanz, 2004). In multi-level systems that manifest high levels of local and regional diversity such as the EU, participatory network structures that facilitate horizontal coordination and steering between a wide range of public and private actors are expected to strengthen institutional capacity, especially in respect of complex problems with cross-border effects such as environmental pollution (Héritier, 2002). Non-hierarchical, non-manipulative steering forms, for example, 'arguing' and 'persuasion' instead of 'bargaining', are achieved by moving away from majority rules for decision-making (Risse, 2004). These institutional properties are expected to pave the way towards consensual decision-making for policies where consensus between affected interests is difficult to achieve. Non-majoritarian decision-making rules and non-hierarchical policy instruments (learning, arguing, persuasion) have a great potential to alter domestic actors' initial preferences and compliance incentives since those responsible for implementation are participating in both target setting and selection of policy instruments (Héritier, 2001: 9). In effect, they reduce the administrative costs of monitoring and enforcement by public bodies since participants are committed to voluntary self-regulation. These institutional properties facilitate learning and the dissemination of best regulatory practices, especially in conditions of uncertainty regarding both the causes the and optimal solutions to complex problems (Radaelli, 2000).

However, the two institutional properties identified above (the actor and steering dimensions) point to two pertinent problems familiar in the collective network action theories. First, the inclusion of all relevant actors in regulatory network structures increases the problem of coordination. The heterogeneity of decision-making arenas in EU environmental policies that embrace product standards, production processes and sustainability regulations reduces the likelihood of the emergence of a clearly identifiable group of non-state actors (environmental organizations, business groups and citizen associations) capable of generating consensual regulatory outcomes (Prange and Koutalakis, 2005). Moreover, variations in non-state actors' organisational resources (knowledge, expertise and financial resources) to monitor and effectively influence policy developments in the specification of environmental technical standards increases the likelihood of network capture by well resourced actors such as individual businesses and/or industrial associations. The multiplicity and heterogeneity of participants' preferences, coupled with considerable differences in the distribution of their resources, point to the importance of effective steering modes, that is, rules that regulate network interactions and secure stable network functioning. The following sections of the chapter examine systematically the regulatory effects of these two institutional properties in relation to the IPPC network(s) organised under the auspices of the IPPC Bureau in Seville.

The Seville Process: Effective and Efficient?

The IPPC Directive (61/1996) introduced significant innovations in respect of policy content and procedural approaches for the adoption, monitoring and implementation of environmental standards.[3] It was the first time that EU environmental policies moved away from media-specific regulatory approaches to pollution abatement by introducing an integrated approach that incorporated a single permit system covering all pollutant activities of industry (water, air, land) and the efficient use of energy. The IPPC Directive is therefore strong procedurally. Instead of prescribing harmonised emission limit values (ELVs), it provides for co-regulatory processes to identify and disseminate best practices and techniques, taking into account local environmental, technical and economic circumstances. Single permits are based on BAT defined at sectoral and sub-sectoral levels. The permit system applied to new installations since October 1999 and from October 2007 for existing ones. Some new member states have been granted additional periods of grace for their existing installations that in some cases extend until 2012.[4] The definition of BAT is delegated to ad hoc co-regulatory sectoral and sub-sectoral Technical Working Groups (TWGs). The Directive also provides for an Information Exchange Forum (IEF) comprising representatives from member states, large associations and the Commission. The IEF takes an overview of the process, especially in relation to the potential impact of the Directive on industrial competitiveness and employment. It also agrees on the themes to be covered by TWGs. TWGs comprise a large number of actors such as the Commission, representatives from member state governments, industry associations, individual firms, environmental organisations, research institutes, universities, national and EU environmental agencies. These networks operate under the auspices of an EIPPCB in Seville that serves as the network coordinator/facilitator. They facilitate the dissemination of information on BAT based on the benchmarking of best practices described in regularly updated Best Available Technology Reference Documents (BREFs). BREFs have no binding character. Instead, they provide an indicative basis for the adoption of ELVs to be incorporated into single permits issued by the relevant national authorities for each industrial installation covered by the Directive. This decentralised system of permissions allows considerable leverage to domestic authorities to interpret BAT and define ELVs according to local environmental and geographical circumstances, as well as reflecting the technical features of the installation. The technical nature of BREFs and the lack of technical expertise on the part of the Commission to evaluate the compatibility of BAT-based ELVs with broad environmental objectives illuminates the considerable policy relevance of the TWGs. The following sections address the nature of regulatory policymaking within the framework of EIPPCB TWGs by focusing on two funda-

3 OJ L 257 October 10, 1996.

4 These are Latvia and Poland until 2010 and Slovakia and Slovenia until 2011. These installations have to receive a permit by the end of October 2007 but they are obliged to meet emission limit values based on the BAT until the end of the transition periods.

mental institutional properties, namely, the constellation of actors and the steering arrangements governing their interaction.

The actor dimension

Since their establishment in 1996, the EIPPCB TWGs have attracted the attention of a wide range of public and private actors from different countries and industrial sectors. In the first eight years of their operation 33 BREFs were discussed. They cover a wide range of policy sectors and 'horizontal' activities such as energy efficiency, waste treatments (recovery and disposal activities), monitoring systems and economic cross-media issues.[5] Information provided by the EIPPCB on the participants in the TWGs refers to a total of 2,027 public and private actors (Figure 1).[6] Our analysis accounts for both the *territorial* and *functional* dimensions of participation in the TWGs by identifying both national composition and type of actors participating in the process.

On the territorial dimension, we identify two indicators. The first is the number of participants in relation to the total population of each member state. However, this indicator is somewhat misleading, since it does not capture the significance of participation of actors from other member states. In order to provide an account of the incentives for domestic actors to participate in the Seville process, we therefore introduce a second indicator, namely the percentage of industrial facilities in each country that exceed emission thresholds specified in the IPPC Directive. National regulatory authorities are obliged to report these emissions to a European Pollution Emission Register (EPER).[7] The argument is straightforward: the higher the percentage of IPPC industrial plants in a member state that report emissions to the EPER (emissions higher than the IPPC thresholds), the higher the incentives for domestic actors to participate in the process. Participation facilitates not only transfer of experience and expertise on available technological solutions to pollution abatement, but it also safeguards the interests of domestic industry and avoids potential BAT definitions that raise insurmountable adjustment costs. Public and private actors from low polluting member states and/or industrial sectors, especially those involved in the production of niche green technologies, also face strong incentives to participate in the process since the adoption of their technological innovations as

5 A list of BREFs is available at http://eippcb.jrc.es/pages/FActivities.htm

6 The EIPPCB publishes only the contacts of participants in the formulation of each BREF. Based on this information we constructed a database. Each participant is coded by nationality and type of organisation (s)he represents, namely government, EU institution, national ENGO, EU ENGO, research institute, individual firm and national and EU sectoral associations. Research assistance by Gerasimos Kalogiratos on constructing this database is gratefully acknowledged.

7 EPER covers large and medium-sized industrial plants which exceed specified emission thresholds (Annex I of the IPPC Directive). This measure is significant since, according to EPER, 'the threshold values have been fixed at a level that aims to cover about 90 per cent of the emissions from facilities covered by IPPC' (http://www.eper.cec.eu.int/eper/).

BAT would accelerate the distribution of their products in the European market. Figure 1 provides an overview of the national composition of EIPPCB TWGs.

Figure1. National Composition of EIPPCB TWGs

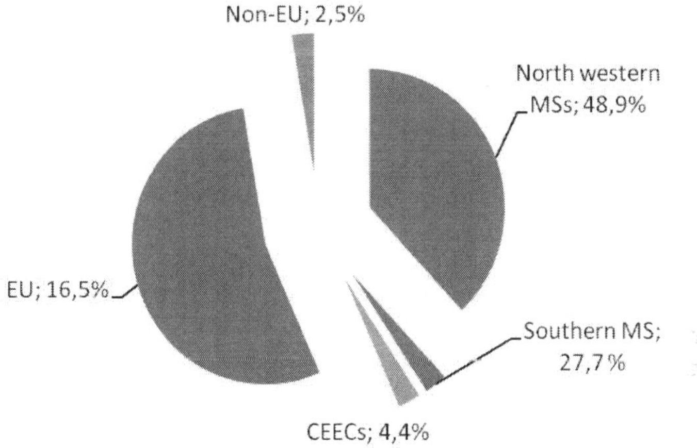

Sources: Author's elaboration based on information provided by the EIPPCB (http://eippcb.jrc.es/pages/FActivities.htm). Data on EPER facilities from European Pollutant Emission Register, 2004 Review, Final Report available at http://eper.cec.eu.int/eper/documents/EPER%20Review%20report,%20final.pdf, p.45. Data on IPPC facilities from European Commission, DG Environment, Analysis of Member States' First Implementation Reports on the IPPC Directive (EU 15), June 2004

The information profile in Figure 1 shows that the overall national participation in TWGs is relatively balanced.[8] Participation rates in member states with a percentage of industrial plants reporting emissions higher than the IPPC thresholds (above the EU average of 20.9 per cent) are considerably higher than a population criterion would suggest (see Appendix I). This is the case for Austria, Portugal, Finland, Greece, Belgium and Germany. The national participation rates for the UK, Ireland and Spain (all with industrial plants reporting emissions well above the EU average) are the only ones that are significantly lower than expected considering their population size. Member states with a low percentage of industrial plants reporting

8 Unfortunately no information on EPER facilities is available yet for the ten new member states.

high emissions had a positive relation of national participation rates to population size. This is the case for Sweden, the Netherlands and Denmark. The national participation rate for Italy and France (both with figures of highly emitting industrial plants lower than the EU average) are the only ones below the expected level taking into account population size. Finally, the 5 per cent participation rate by the CEECs, although not particularly high considering the gravity of pollution problems due to outdated industrial infrastructure, is significant since participation had started long before their accession to the EU. New member states have participated in 16 out of 33 TWGs that were set up after 2001.[9] Their involvement raises important questions about the ability of the Seville process to facilitate smooth adoption and adaptation of new member states to the IPPC requirements.

By way of contrast, analysis of the functional composition of TWGs reveals much higher imbalances than for the territorial dimension (Figure 2). The biggest group of actors participating in the EIPPCB TWGs are national government representatives (44.4 per cent). The latter together with Commission representatives (6.3 per cent) account for approximately half of the participants. Individual firms with 19.7 per cent and industrial associations with 18.4 per cent form the second major category of participants. Research institutes with 8.7 per cent and ENGOs are the actors with the lowest level of participation in TWG. The limited availability of control data allows some comparison between the participation rates of individual firms as a proportion of IPPC and high polluting (EPER) facilities in each member state. According to our estimates, only 0.8 per cent of IPPC facilities and 3.9 per cent of high polluting facilities on the EPER are involved in EIPPCB TWGs. National participating rates by individual firms are evenly distributed across the EU with the exception of Greece that manifests significantly higher levels of participation with 11.4 per cent of IPPC and 45.1 per cent EPER facilities respectively. The Netherlands with 16.3 per cent and Belgium with 11.0 per cent of individual firms also score high rates of participation as a percentage of domestic facilities on the European Pollution Emission Register (see Appendix II).

9 These TWGs are Large Combustion Plant; Large Volume Inorganic Chemicals – Ammonia, Acids and Fertilisers; Large Volume Inorganic Chemicals – Solid and Others; Slaughterhouses and Animal By-products; Food, Drink and Milk Processes; Ceramics, Management of Tailings and Waste – Rock in Mining Activities; Surface treatment of metals; Surface treatments using solvents; Waste incineration, Waste Treatments; Speciality inorganic chemicals; Organic fine chemicals; Polymers; and Energy Efficiency (see http://eippcb.jrc.es/pages/FActivities.htm.

Figure 2. Functional Composition of EIPPCB TWGs

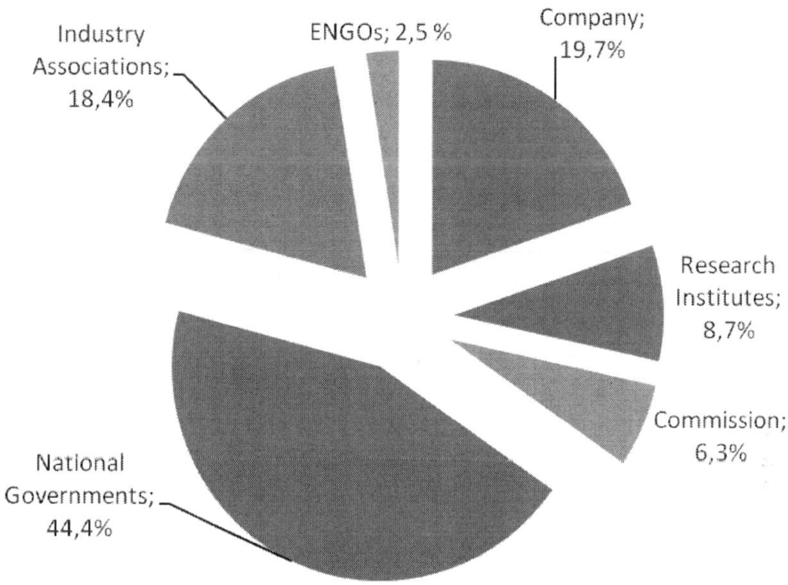

Sources: Author's elaboration based on information provided by the EIPPCB http://eippcb.jrc.es/pages/FActivities.htm).

Industrial associations, however, show a more uneven distribution of participation (Figure 3). The most striking outcome of the analysis regarding national participation rates of industrial associations is that almost half (48.5 per cent) of the participants in that category claim to represent industrial sectors at the EU level. The higher participation rates are attributed to industrial associations from Spain with 10.7 per cent, Germany with 9.7 per cent, Italy with 7.2 per cent, France with 5.4 per cent, and Greece with 3.2 per cent. The rest of the member states score considerably lower rates of participation than these five. Research institutes' national participation rates followed a similar uneven pattern (see Appendix III).

Figure 3. Participation rates of Industrial Associations

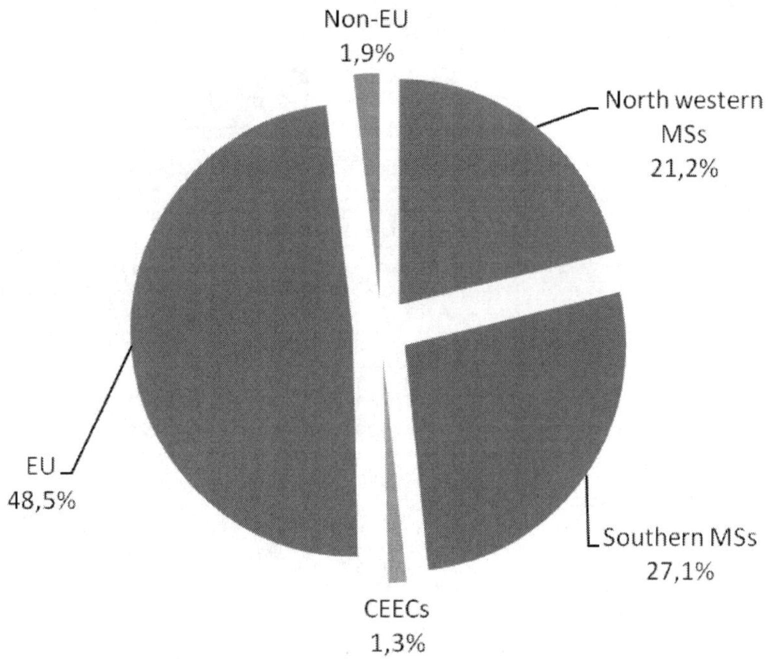

Sources: Author's elaboration based on information provided by the EIPPCB ,http://eippcb.jrc.es/pages/FActivities.htm

Research institutes in three countries (Italy with 29.5 per cent, Spain with 13.1 per cent and Germany with 11.9 per cent) scored relatively high rates of participation in the EIPPCB TWGs. The rest of the member states scored participation rates far below these three countries, with the exception of the CEECs, which with 12.6 per cent scored a higher rate of participation in comparison with all the other categories of actors (Figure 4). Apart from Lithuania, all CEECs participated in TWGs at national rates similar to or even higher than those of the old member states (see Appendix IV). Finally, ENGOs with 2.5 per cent represent the smallest group of participants in the EIPPCB TWGs.

Figure 4. Participation rates of Research Institutes

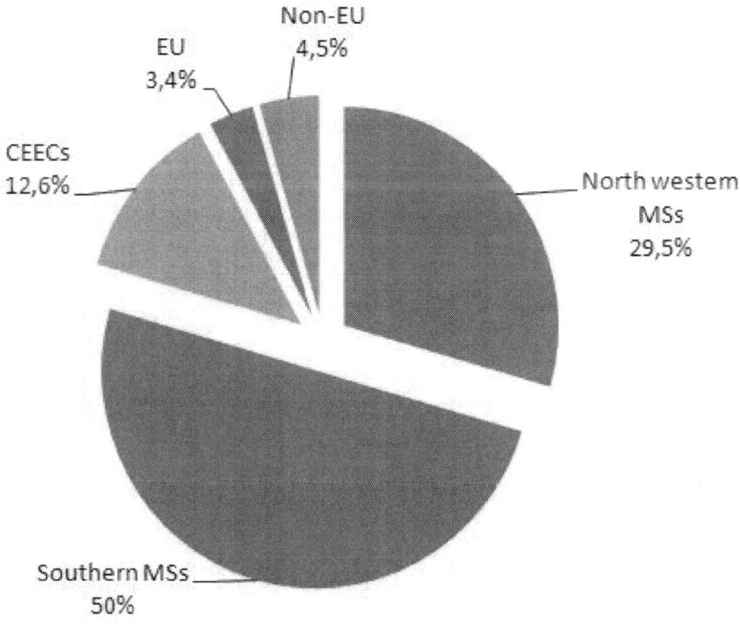

Sources: Author's elaboration based on information provided by the EIPPCB, http://eippcb.jrc.es/pages/FActivities.htm

ENGO participation is dominated by EU umbrella organisations (41 per cent) most notably the European Environmental Bureau that represents 133 ENGOs based in all EU member states (Figure 5). National ENGOs account for the rest, with 57 per cent of ENGO participants from nine member states dominated by German organisations with 29 per cent. The rest of the member states had very modest participation rates. ENGOs from the UK with 8 per cent, France with 6 per cent, Spain with 4 per cent and Poland, Greece, the Netherlands, Denmark and the Czech Republic with 2 per cent are the most visible groups. Finally, another 2 per cent of ENGOs were based in non-EU, mainly EFTA countries.

Figure 5. Participation rates of ENGOs

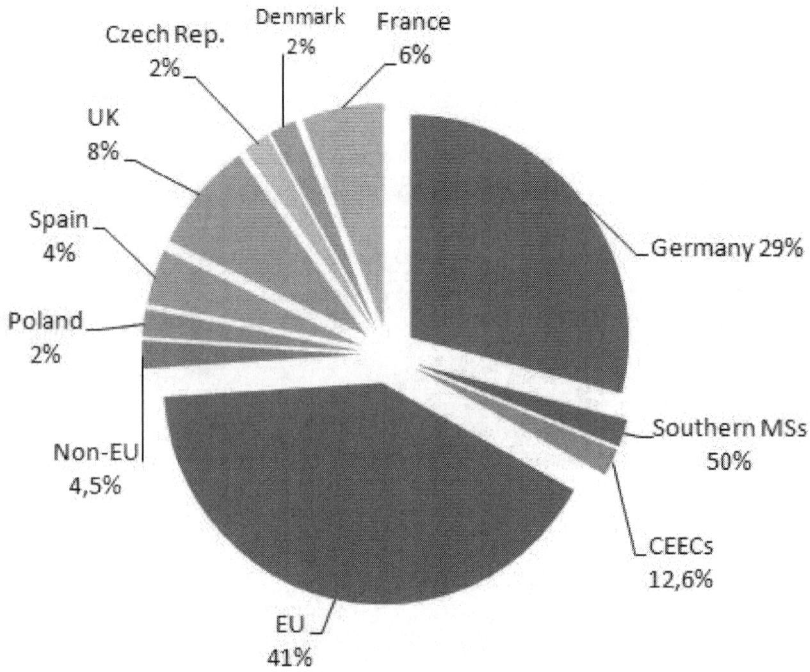

Sources: Author's elaboration based on information provided by the EIPPCB, http://eippcb.jrc.es/pages/FActivities.htm

In summary, analysis of the actor dimension in EIPPCB TWGs reveals considerable imbalances in the functional composition of EIPPCB TWGs. Industrial actors (individual firms and industrial associations) are the most visible group of private actors and the second largest category after governmental representatives. On the other hand, both research institutes and ENGOs are underrepresented in the process. These imbalances can be largely attributed to the framing of the policy problem in the Seville process. BAT identification is a technical issue that requires enormous amount of resources to be devoted by private actors seeking to participate in TWGs.[10] The problem is particularly difficult for ENGOs as they face considerable barriers for participating in the process due to the lack of essential resources (know-

10 A report from an industrial association estimates the requirements for effective participation in TWGs to be approximately €1,000,000.

ledge and expertise) in relation to BAT in different industrial sectors.[11] ENGOs often compensate for their weak resource base through alliances with environmental research institutes. However, participation by the latter is also limited. This considerable functional imbalance raises the issue of winners and losers in the process of regulatory policymaking in the framework of EIPPCB TWGs. Industry are the most influential private actor in the process. However, industrial interests do not represent homogeneous preferences and interests over the type of BAT adopted and the corresponding ELV thresholds. Our analysis does not indicate a systematic over-representation in the process by industrial associations and individual firms in countries reporting either high or low emissions. On the contrary, participation by industrial interests is much more balanced compared with other types of actors. The wide range and heterogeneity of participants coupled with considerable differences in the distribution of resources between them point to the importance of effective steering modes, that is, rules that regulate network interactions and secure stable network functioning. The following section addresses these institutional properties of TWGs, namely the formal and informal modes of interaction between network participants and the institutional mechanisms of network coordination and arbitration in decision-making.

The steering dimension

TWGs facilitate the exchange of information between participants on environmental and economic elements of BAT in each industrial sector. Given the multiplicity of actors with divergent sectoral economic, national and political preferences and interests on the identification of BATs, it is noteworthy that network interactions are governed predominantly by informal rules with no formal conflict resolution mechanisms. The EIPPCB serves as the network moderator. It undertakes all the administrative preparatory work.[12] Decision-making is not based neither on majoritarian nor formal arbitration mechanisms. On the contrary, there is an explicit attempt to seek consensual decision-making through informal practices based on scientific argument and persuasion.

At the informal level, there are three steering mechanisms that arbitrate in cases of profound disagreements and conflicts over the content of BREFs. In the first instance, the EIPPCB plays a central role in reducing potential conflicts, especially during the process of drafting and revising the content of the BREFs. At this stage, the EIPPCB acts as a mediator by contributing to the identification of compromises in difficult issue areas. Through its political independence it manages to 'neutralise' disagreements by distilling the content of the BREFs from political statements and confining the discourse to purely scientific points relating to the validity, accuracy

11 The EEB has campaigned for financial support from the European Commission in order to compensate for imbalanced participation in TWGs (Hey, 2000).

12 The EIPPCB's staff comprises experts temporarily seconded from national ministries and the Commission.

and credibility of data (Sǿrup, 2000). Significant disagreements and political conflicts are also discussed in the IEF that embodies a higher level of representation. Moreover, the Commission retains a discretionary influence over the contents of the BREFs. The Commission's role in the process of applying BAT requirements by the member states is threefold. First, it retains the discretion to intervene and alter the contents of BREFs, especially in cases where the application of agreed BAT based ELVs has a negative impact on the competitiveness of an industrial sector or on employment. Second, the Commission retains the competence to introduce harmonised ELVs when a need for harmonization is identified.[13] Third, the Commission monitors the compatibility of national ELVs with those broadly defined in the BREF documents. It retains its enforcement power (art. 226 TEU) in cases where ELVs significantly depart from lower ceilings outlined in the BREFs. It is still too early to identify whether the Commission's ultimate discretion over the definition of BAT and the application of BAT based ELVs is an element of the 'shadow of hierarchy' in the policy process. However, this element of the 'shadow of hierarchy' is of dubious importance since it would jeopardise and de-legitimize the process.

The weak institutionalisation of network interactions and decision-making rules in the framework of the TWGs has been heavily criticised by environmental organizations. It has been argued that, although it seems to favour consensus, in reality its operation is subject to the unequal distribution of resources in favour of industrial actors (Hey, 2000). It remains to be seen what the effects of the participation and steering modes scrutinised above are in terms of regulatory policy outcomes.

Regulatory Effects: a 'Race to the Mean'?

The procedural nature of the IPPC Directive and the considerable leverage offered to national actors to organise domestic single-permit systems provides a number of ways of accounting for its impact on national institutions and regulatory outcomes in different member states. However, in this chapter we have focussed on the regulatory effects of participatory structures such as the TWGs, in terms of the level of 'indicative' standards adopted by the BREFs.[14] Our analysis draws on information from the first six BREFs (on Cement and Lime, Chlor-Alkali, Iron and Steel, Non-Ferrous Metals, Pulp and Paper and Ferrous Metals). Since many of the BREFs have not yet been completed, our attempt is to identify some tentative trends regarding the regulatory effects of EIPPCB TWGs. The territorial and functional composition of these TWGs does not significantly depart from the aggregate data presented in the previous section of this chapter. In all TWGs around half of the participants represent na-

13 The Commission publishes the results of BREFs in the Official Journal of the EU.

14 BREFs include a wide range of end-of-pipe techniques and processes such as inspection routines, maintenance systems, operating practices and process control methods that are not always quantifiable, but they do prescribe conditions under which certain technologies may lead to optimal outcomes in terms of emission reduction and energy efficiency given the particular characteristics and circumstances of the installation.

tional governments or the Commission.[15] The second largest category is industrial associations and individual firms while ENGOs and research institutes are the categories with the lowest participation rates.[16]

In all the BREFs mentioned above, reports concluded that the adoption of indicative emission range values reflected a compromise between divergent interpretations on what constituted BAT in each of the above sectors. The definition of BAT was less controversial in cases where there were few BAT technologies. In the case of non-ferrous metals and ferro-alloy industries, for example, the main BAT alternatives were the introduction of semi-closed or closed furnaces that have better performance in energy recovery during the smelting process and also reduced dust and fume emissions.[17] Despite the considerable costs involved in the adoption of this technology, it is expected that a BAT will gradually be introduced during the replacement or upgrading of existing open furnaces used by the majority of industrial plants in the sector.

More complicated is the identification of BAT for processes with multiple, tightly integrated production stages that correspond to different operational and technological solutions and varied quality of raw materials. In these cases, multiple indicators have to be balanced and consensus is more difficult to achieve. The predominance of public actors in all the TWGs scrutinised coupled with a relatively balanced participation on the part of high and low polluting industries generates outcomes conducive to bargaining rather than notions of non-hierarchical steering modes such as learning and persuasion through the exchange and dissemination of best available technologies (see Lange, 2002). Information on the regulatory outcomes of the process indicates a tendency to compromise which can be achieved in two ways. First, there is the adoption of a wide range of indicative emission values that correspond to BAT. This leads to the inclusion of the vast majority of IPPC plants in the sector. Such an outcome is not very different from compromises found in the traditional legislative process between EU member states.[18] Second, solutions can be adopted that converge on the 'mean' of the emitting values derived from the data submitted to the

---

15 Public actors' (national government and Commission) participation range from 61.36 per cent in the Pulp and Paper, 59.38 per cent in the Chlor-Alkali, 56.61 per cent in the Cement and Lime, 53.34 per cent in the Ferrous Metals, 53.06 per cent in the Iron and Steel, to 50 per cent in the Non-Ferrous Metals TWG.

16 Industrial associations' and individual firms' participation rates range from 45 per cent in the Non-Ferrous Metals, 41.51 per cent in the Cement and Lime, 39.44 per cent in the Ferrous Metals, 38.78 per cent in the Iron and Steel, 37.51 per cent in the Chlor-Alkali, to 36.37 per cent in the Pulp and Paper TWG. Research institutes' participation ranges from 6.12 per cent in the Iron and Steel, 4.44 per cent in the Ferrous Metals, 3.33 per cent in the Non-Ferrous Metals to zero in the Cement and Lime, Pulp and Paper and Chlor-Alkali TWGs. Finally, ENGOs' participation rates range from 3.13 per cent in the Chlor-Alkali, 2.27 per cent in the Pulp and Paper, 2.22 per cent in the Ferrous Metals, 2.04 per cent in the Iron and Steel, 1.89 per cent in the Cement and Lime, to 1.67 per cent in the Non-Ferrous Metals TWG.

17 For an overview of technical details, see Finkeldei (2000) or the relevant BREF published at http://eippcb.jrc.es/pages/FActivities.htm.

18 Such an approach does not vary a great deal from the experience with other Directives providing for BAT based ELVs such as the Combustion Plant Directive (Börzel, 2003: 89).

TWGs. Both approaches have been applied in a combined way to the BREFs listed above.[19] The convergence to the mean of reported emitting values is justified by references to economic, technological and production parameters that condition the *availability* of best technologies in terms of the percentage of industrial plants falling within indicative emission values.

What is highly contested is the extent to which convergence to the mean of reported environmental performance of plants covered by the Directive denotes a higher level of environmental protection than the one potentially achievable through command-and-control regulatory approaches. To a large extent it reflects different interpretations of BAT by the participants in the policy process. Experts delegated by environmental organisations argue that the current modes of conflict resolution have negative effects on the dissemination of novel environmentally friendly technologies (Lohse and Sander, 2000). Other participants point up the 'pulling effect' of this outcome for these heavily polluting facilities that have to raise their environmental standards to levels that are more realistic considering the amount of investment required for the introduction of novel production processes (Hägstrom, 2000).

Conclusions

Although it remains to be confirmed whether there is a systematic trend for compromise between diverging preferences and interests over the level of indicative regulatory thresholds at the 'mean' of the various national sectoral environmental performances, such a prospect raises a number of key issues regarding the future of the EU environmental regulatory regime. Given the existing division between leaders and laggards in EU member state environmental performance, it would not be too hasty to assume that successive EU enlargements leading to the inclusion of countries with considerably lower production process environmental standards will drive down compromises over the level of environmental standards adopted in participatory networks. In an ever more diverse union, the 'indicative' non-binding character of regulatory standards will potentially reduce compliance deficits, especially in member states that struggle with economic problems and outdated industries. In other words, the tension is between high regulatory standards causing compliance problems in certain member states and/or industrial sectors or lower non-binding standards which are more likely to be applied effectively at the domestic level. In this context, the role of regulatory networks for effective policy implementation through the transfer of experience and the spread of environmentally progressive technologies is crucial. However, the alleged 'political efficiency' and 'policy effectiveness' of co-regulatory networks still remains an empirical question. Experience of the

19 In the Cement and Lime BREF, BAT regarding NO_X abatement corresponds to 200-500 mg NOx/m3. This emission value reflects a compromise between participants' preferences for 100-200 mg NOx/m3 and 500-800 mg NOx/m3 respectively. For a full discussion of technical information regarding the Pulp and Paper, Iron and Steel, Cement and Lime and Chlor-Alkali industries see (Schoenberger, 2000; Suhr, 2000; Hagström, 2000).

Seville process suggests that unless the great imbalance of resources that generates high barriers to entry for potential participants is addressed in a more decisive manner, the constellation of interests will be unlikely to lead to regulatory outcomes that are significantly different from those achieved through conventional legislative processes.

References

Baker, S. (2000). Between Devil and the Deep Blue See: International Obligations, Enlargement and the Promotion of Sustainable Development in the European Union. *Journal of Environment and Planning, 2,* pp.149-166.

Börzel, T. (2003). *Environmental Leaders and Laggards in Europe. Why There is (Not) A Southern Problem.* London: Ashgate.

Börzel, T. and Risse, T. (forthcoming). Public-Private Partnerships. Effective and Legitimate Tools of International Governance?. In E. Grande and L. W. Pauly (Eds.), *Complex Sovereignty: On the Reconstitution of Political Authority in the 21st Century.* Toronto: University of Toronto Press.

Börzel, T. (2002). Non-State Actors and the Provision of Common Goods: Compliance with International Institutions. In A. Héritier (Ed.), *Common Goods. Reinventing European and International Governance* (pp.159-182). Oxford: Rowman and Littlefield.

Carius, A., Homeyer, I. von and Bär, S. (1999). The Eastern Enlargement of the European Union and Environmental Policy: Challenges, Speed and Flexibility. In K. Holzinger and P. Knoepfel (Eds.), *Environmental Policy in a European Union of Variable Geometry? The Challenge of the Next Enlargement* (pp.141-177). Basel: Helbing & Lichtenhahn.

Dehousse, R. (1997). Regulation by networks in the European Community: the role of European Agencies. *Journal of European Public Policy, 4 (2),* pp.246-261.

Eberlein, B. and Grande E. (2005). Beyond delegation: transnational regulatory regimes and the EU regulatory state. *Journal of European Public Policy, 12 (1),* pp.89-112.

Epstein, D. and O'Halloran, S. (2000). *Delegating Powers: A Transaction Cost Politics Approach to Policy Making under Separate Powers.* Cambridge: Cambridge University Press.

European Commission (2001). *European Governance – A White Paper.* (COM (2001) 428). Brussels: European Commission.

Everson, M., Majone, G., Metcalfe, L. and Schout, A. (1999). The Role of Specialised Agencies in Decentralising EU Governance. Report Presented to the European Commission, Florence/Maastricht.

Finkeldei, L. (2000, April). Energy use and process integrated BAT measures. Illustrated by examples from the Non-Ferrous Metals Industries BREF. Paper presented at the European Conference on "The Sevilla Process: A Driver for Environmental Performance in Industry", Stuttgart.

Golub, J. (1998). *New Instruments of Environmental Policy.* London: Routledge.

Hagström, P. (2000, April). BAT process selection and split views. Illustrated by examples from the Cement and Lime and Chlor-Alkali BREFs. Paper presented at the European Conference on "The Sevilla Process: A Driver for Environmental Performance in Industry", Stuttgart.

Héritier, A. (2003). New Modes of Governance in Europe: Increasing political efficiency and policy effectiveness. In T. Börzel and R. Cichowski (Eds.), *The State of the European Union, 6 – Law, Politics, and Society* (pp.199-243). Oxford: Oxford University Press.

Héritier, A. (2002). New Modes of Governance in Europe: Policy Making Without Legislating? In A. Héritier (Ed.), *Common Goods: Reinventing European and International Governance* (pp.185-206). Boulder, Rowman and Littlefield.

Héritier, A. (2001). *New Modes of Governance in Europe. Policy making without legislating.* Project Group Reprint 2001/14. Bonn: Max Planck.

Holzinger K. and Knill C. (2004). Competition and Cooperation in Environmental Policy: Individual and Interaction Effects. *Journal of Public Policy*, *24 (1),* pp.25-47.

Holzinger, K. (1999). Optimal Regulatory Units: A Concept of Regional Differentiation of Environmental Standards in the European Union. In K. Holzinger and P. Knoepfel (Eds.), *Environmental Policy in a European Union of variable geometry? The Challenge of the Next Enlargement* (pp.65-107). Basel: Helbig & Lichtenhahn.

Homeyer, I. von (2004) Differential Effects of Enlargement on EU Environmental Governance. *Environmental Politics, 13 (1),* pp.52-76.

Jachtenfuchs, M. (2001). The Governance Approach to European Integration. *Journal of Common Market Studies, 39 (2),* pp.245-264.

Jordan A., Wurzel R. and Zito A. (2003a). European Governance and the Transfer of 'New' Environmental Policy Instruments. *Public Administration*, *81 (3),* pp.555-574.

Jordan, A., Wurzel, R. and Zito, A. (2003b). *New Instruments of Environmental Goverance.* London: Frank Cass.

Knill, C. and Lenschow, A. (2000). *Implementing EU Environmental Policy.* Manchester: Manchester University Press.

Kohler-Koch, B. and Eising, R. (Eds.) (1999). *The Transformation of Governance in the European Union.* London: Routledge.

Koutalakis, C. (2004). Environmental Compliance in Italy and Greece. The Role of Non-State Actors. *Environmental Politics, 13 (4),* pp.754-774.

Lange, B. (2002). From Boundary Drawing to Transitions: The creation of Normativity under the EU Directive on Integrated Pollution Prevention and Control. *European Law Journal, 8 (2),* pp.246-268.

Lenschow, A. (2002). *Environmental Policy Integration.* London: Earthscan.

Lohse, J. and Sander, K. (2000, April). Is the BREF process a success or a failure? – an NGO perspective. Paper presented at the European Conference on "The Sevilla Process: A Driver for Environmental Performance in Industry", Stuttgart.

Majone, G. (1994). The Rise of the Regulatory State in Europe. *West European Politics, 17 (3),* pp.77-101.

Majone, G. (1997a). From the Positive to the Regulatory State. *Journal of Public Policy, 17 (2),* pp.139-167.

Majone, G. (1997b). Independent Agencies and the Delegation Problem: Theoretical and Normative Dimensions. In B. Steuenberg and F. van Vught (Eds.), *Political Institutions and Public Policy* (pp.139-156). Dordreht: Kluwer Academic Publishers.

Majone, G. (2001). Nonmajoritarian Institutions and the Limits of Democratic Governance: A Political Transaction-Cost Approach. *Journal of Institutional and Theoretical Economics, 157,* pp.57-78.

Majone, G. and Everson, M. (2001). Institutional reform: independent agencies, oversight, coordination and procedural control. In O. De Schutter, N. Lebessis, and J. Paterson (Eds.), *Governance in the European Union* (pp.139-183). Luxemburg: European Commission.

Macrory, R. (1996). Community Supervision in the Field of the Environment. In H. Somsen (Ed.), *Protecting the European Environment: Enforcing EC Environmental Law* (pp.9-21). London: Blackstone Press.

Mendrinou, M. (1996). Non-Compliance and the European Commission's Role in Integration. *Journal of European Public Policy, 3 (1),* pp.1-22.

Moe, T. (1990). Political Institutions: The Neglected Side of the Story. *Journal of Law, Economics and Organization, 6,* pp.213-253.

Moe, T. (1995). The Politics of Structural Choice: Toward a Theory of Public Bureaucracy. In O. Williamson (Ed.), *Organization Theory: From Chester Bernard to the Present and Beyond* (pp.116-153). Oxford: Oxford University Press.

Pollack, M. (1997). Delegation, Agency, and Agenda Setting in the European Community. *International Organization, 51 (1),* pp.99-134.

Porte de la, C. and Nanz, P. (2004). The OMC - a deliberative-democratic mode of governance? The cases of employment and pensions. *Journal of European Public Policy, 11 (2),* pp.267-288.

Prange, H. and Koutalakis, C. (2005). Smoothing Eastern Enlargement through New Modes of Governance? In G. F. Schuppert (Ed.), *Europeanization of Governance – The Challenge of Accession.* Baden-Baden: Nomos.

Radaelli, C. (2004). The Puzzle of Regulatory Competition. *Journal of Public Policy, 24 (1),* pp.1-23.

Radaelli, C. (2000). Policy Transfer in the European Union. *Governance, 13 (1),* pp.25-43.

Risse, T. (2004). Global Governance and Communicative Action. *Government and Opposition, 39 (2),* pp.288-313.

Scharpf, F. W. (1994). Community and Autonomy: Multi-Level Policy-Making in the European Union. *Journal of European Public Policy, 1 (2),* pp.219-42.

Schoenberger, H. (2000, April). BREF on the Production of Iron and Steel - conclusion on BAT. Paper presented at the European Conference on "The Sevilla Process: A Driver for Environmental Performance in Industry", Stuttgart.

Suhr, M. (2000, April). The BREF in the pulp and paper industry BAT for an industry with a large variety of raw materials and products. Paper presented at the European Conference on "The Sevilla Process: A Driver for Environmental Performance in Industry", Stuttgart.

Tallberg, J. (1999). *Making States Comply. The European Commission, the European Court of Justice and the Enforcement of the Internal Market.* Lund: Studentlitteratur.

Appendix I: Data on national Composition of EIPPCB TWGs

MS	National particpation rate (%)	Population %	EPER facilities
A	2.3	1.9	32.5
B	4.2	2.3	23
CY	0.1	0.2	
CZ	1.2	2.3	
DK	2.1	1.2	13.8
ES	0.3	0.3	
FI	2.2	1.2	29.3
F	6.6	12.9	19.9
D	11.6	8.2	23.8
EL	4.3	2.3	25.3
HU	0.8	2.3	
IRL	2.0	0.8	34
I	7.8	12.8	7.6
LV	0.4	0.5	
LT	0.0	0.8	
L	0.4	0.1	
MT	0.1	0.1	
NL	6.5	3.4	3.8
PL	0.8	8.7	
P	8.2	2.2	28.1
SK	0.2	1.2	
SV	0.7	0.5	
E	7.2	8.8	27.1
S	2.0	2.0	17.7
UK	9.0	13.1	38.4
EU	16.5		20.9
Non-EU	2.5		

Appendix II: Data on National Participation Rates of Individual Firms

MS	Individual firms' Participation rates as a proportion to number of IPPC plants (%)	Individual Firms' Participation rates as proportion of firms registered with EPER (%)
A	1.0	3.0
B	2.5	11.0
DK	0.5	3.8
FI	1.1	3.7
F	0.7	3.4
D	0.9	3.8
EL	11.4	45.1
IRL	0.2	0.6
I	0.4	5.7
L		
NL	0.6	16.3
P	1.6	5.7
E	0.5	1.9
S	0.5	2.7
UK	0.8	2.2
EU	0.8	3.9

Appendix III: Data on National Participation Rates of Industrial Associations

MS	Participation Rate %	MS	Participation Rate %
A	0.3	LV	0.0
B	0.8	LT	0.0
CY	0.0	L	0.0
CZ	0.5	MT	0.0
DK	0.5	NL	1.1
ES	0.0	PL	0.0
FIN	0.3	P	5.9
F	5.4	SL	0.0
D	9.7	SV	0.0
EL	3.2	E	10.7
HU	0.8	S	0.8
IRL	0.3	UK	2.1
I	7.2	EU	48.5
		Non-EU	1.9

Appendix IV: Data on National Participation Rates of Research Institutes

MS	Participation Rate %	MS	Participation Rate %
A	1.1	LV	2.3
B	1.7	LT	0.0
CY	0.0	L	0.0
CZ	3.4	MT	0.0
DK	1.7	NL	1.7
ES	0.6	PL	1.1
FIN	0.6	P	6.3
F	5.1	SL	0.6
D	11.9	SV	0.6
EL	1.1	E	13.1
HU	4.0	S	0.6
IRL	1.1	UK	4.0
I	29.5	EU	3.4
		Non-EU	4.5

Source for all appendices: Own elaboration based on information provided by the EIPPCB (http://eippcb.jrc.es/pages/FActivities.htm). Data on EPER facilities from European Pollutant Emission Register, 2004 Review, Final Report available at http://eper.cec.eu.int/eper/documents/EPER%20Review%20report,%20final.pdf, p.45. Data on IPPC facilities from European Commission, DG Environment, Analysis of Member States' first implementation reports on the IPPC Directive (EU 15), June 2004.

"Privatising" EU Governance: Emergence and Performance of Voluntary Agreements in European Environmental Policy

Katja Rottmann and Andrea Lenschow

Introduction

> Up to the present, environmental protection in the Community has mainly been based on a legislative approach ('top-down'). The new strategy ... implies the involvement of all economic and societal partners ('bottom-up') (Official Journal 1993: 17)

The publication of the Fifth Environmental Action Programme in 1993 pointed to a new trend in EU environmental policymaking. This trend had its roots in two parallel debates (Lenschow, 1999). First, it followed a global debate on governance which responded to a loss of problem-solving capacities by central governments and argued both for the unburdening of state administrations and for less hierarchical styles in "steering" the economy and society. Second, the international discourse on sustainable development established a more systemic understanding of the linkages between environmental protection and economic and social development, suggesting the need for more co-operative and inclusive policymaking involving business interests and ordinary citizens as partners in changing behavioural and production patterns.

Inside the EU the "crisis of the state" (or more accurately "crisis of the EU") had become visible through an unsatisfactory record of the "state of the environment" in Europe (EEA, 1998) and some evidence of malcompliance with the – by that time impressive – body of regulations and directives aimed at protecting the natural environment, putting the economy on a more environmentally sustainable basis and ensuring that peoples' health and well-being would not be threatened by environmental pollution (see annual reports on monitoring the application of Community law by the Commission). Hence, there was – in rhetoric at least – a call for new policy instruments, presenting alternatives to the traditionally hierarchical, top-down mechanisms of policymaking and shifting (some) responsibility to private actors. Institutionally, this shift would represent a departure from the principles of co-operative federalism that guided old-style regulatory environmental policy in the EU, with the lower national and regional administrative levels implementing the decisions taken at the centre of the political system in Brussels. "Governance in networks", which of course has always characterised the policy formulation phase, when the

Commission relies heavily on consultations with public and private actors, would now extend further to decision-making and implementation.

This chapter focuses on the emergence and the characteristics of voluntary agreements (VAs) as a particularly interesting new instrument in this context. VAs follow the trend towards less hierarchical steering in the sense that they are not legally binding on the contractual partners. Also, they typically do not define precise and uniformly applicable mechanisms, technologies or institutional arrangements for reaching the agreed target, but allow for considerable flexibility in achieving the common goal. In terms of "privatising" governance and forming networks between public and private actors we can distinguish two forms of VAs: private self-regulation, where private actors voluntarily agree on common standards outside the legal and institutional framework of the EU (i.e. outside a formal multi-level governance context); and co-regulation, where regulatory competences may be formally delegated from EU institutions to private actors (for the EU framework see Section 2). Differences in the formal nature of public-private co-operation in VAs typically correspond to varying intensities of co-operation, although – as we will see below – public-private interaction in self-regulatory formats should not be underestimated. The following table places VAs in a simple typology of regulatory modes.

Table 1: Typology of Public-Private Cooperative Forms in Governing Instruments

		Degree of Public-Private Co-operation	
		Low/Moderate	Moderate/High
Degree of Obligation	High (obligatory commitments)	Regulation (command-and-control)	Regulation with formal involvement of private actors
	Low (voluntary commitments)	VA: Self-regulation	VA: Co-regulation

Source: Rottmann (2005, 19); adapted from Mol *et al.* (2000: 4) and Knill (2003: 65)

While the increase in the number of VAs at the national level is undisputed – in 1997 the Commission counted over 300 in the EU member states, with an upward trend – voluntary agreements at the EU level are less well known and hardly researched. Holzinger *et al.* (2003) argue that the actual profile of new instruments in EU environmental policy and of VAs in particular, hardly corresponds to the rhetoric attributed to them in EU and OECD documentation. There might be a great deal of noise about nothing.

This chapter therefore seeks out actual evidence of VAs in EU environmental policy.[1] In a second step we look for the characteristics of "privatisation" – viewed through the lenses of European debates on 'good' and 'multi-level' governance. In analysing the formulation, design and implementation of two specific EU VAs aiming at the reduction of CO_2 emission in cars (ACEA) and greater energy efficiency in consumer electronics (EICTA), we will investigate the format that public-private co-operation takes and identify some framework conditions for their effectiveness. We will argue that the ongoing EU-level discourse on good governance forms a favourable context for VAs to emerge, but that the EU institutional context – given its multi-level characteristics – poses limits to VA effectiveness. Neither the internal organisation of European industry not the external conditions for inducing private actor commitments (e.g. a shadow of hierarchy) tend to be sufficiently powerful.

Rhetoric and Evidence of Public-Private Governance in the EU

Following the problems in ratifying the Maastricht Treaty in the early 1990s, discussions about appropriate forms of governing 'Europe' spread quickly – both in the EU member states, reflecting primarily the division of competences between the European and national or regional levels (the subsidiarity debate), and inside the European Commission, debating new forms of public involvement as one means of increasing both acceptance and effectiveness of EU policy without fuelling calls for de-regulation and re-nationalising. Inside the Commission this debate culminated in the publication of the (in)famous White Paper on European Governance in 2001 (CEC, 2001). Besides emphasising the need to improve the quality of (traditional) regulatory policy, the Commission called for stronger involvement of civil society not only in the form of old style consultations but increasingly also in the form of self- and co-regulation.

As long ago as 1996 the Commission had published a Communication on VAs (CEC, 1996) which laid down a range of criteria to ensure credibility and transparency in using this instrument. Although the Communication was primarily directed at member states choosing VAs as an alternative to classical regulatory tools, it also established a framework for EU level VAs. These were always to take the form of non-obligatory agreements. However, they could be recognised (informally) by the Commission (in the form of a recommendation or an exchange of letters establishing certain framework conditions).

In 2002 the Commission formulated a Communication specifically on environmental agreements at the EU level (CEC, 2002). Responding to announcements

1 It should be noted that VAs on environmental matters need not be negotiated (or controlled) by authorities responsible for environmental policy. One of the case studies analysed in this paper, for instance, involves industry and the Directorate-General for Energy & Transport; the other does include DG Environment but also DG Enterprise. This, of course, complicates the detection of environmental VAs.

about improving relations with industry and supporting voluntary agreements with clearly defined goals that had been made in the Sixth European Environmental Programme (CEC, 2001: 19) as well as demands from the European Parliament for a legal framework for VAs, this Communication distinguishes between two forms of VAs (see above). Self-regulation implies voluntary agreements which are reached by industry outside any legal framework at the EU level. While the Commission may recognise such VAs, it does not forego the right to initiate formal regulation. Co-regulations, in turn, are agreed within a legal framework. For example, there could be a framework directive delegating responsibility for achieving legally determined environmental targets to private actors.

This chapter focuses on the former variant of VAs, the "privatisation" of both target-setting and implementation. Increasing numbers of VAs offer support to claims of a trend towards new policy instruments which are based on a non-hierarchical rule-making structure and a new balance in state-society relations with more autonomy for private actors. Although small compared to the total number of active directives and regulations, VAs agreed at EU level exceed the number reported in studies sceptical of the spread of new instruments (Holzinger *et al.*, 2003: 118) as well as the number of VAs in most EU member states (except Germany, the Netherlands and Austria) (Bongardt *et al.*, 2005: 13). The first VAs at EU level had already been agreed in the late 1980s. They aimed at the reduction of chlorofluorocarbons (CFCs) in various products. During the three years following the 1996 Communication eight new VAs were brought in, most of them focusing on energy efficiency and CO_2 emissions reduction. By 2006, a total of 23 VAs had been agreed (three representing follow-ups and extensions of prior agreements).[2] Our overview also reveals that several VAs have been terminated or have become obsolete by regulation, hinting at interesting dynamics and tensions both with EU policy makers as well as inside industry. These dynamics and the conditions for reaching effective VAs can be investigated only in detailed case study analysis. The analytical framework for such case studies will be outlined below.

Analytical Framework: Multi-Level and Good Governance in Self-Regulation

Following the approach taken in this book, the analysis of self-regulation allows us to trace 'multi-level governance' in an area where multi-level structures lack formal institutionalisation. From this point of view self-regulation can play three different roles. First, self-regulation may become an *alternative* to policy decisions taken in the multi-level framework of the 'Community method'. Second, suggesting a *complementary* role, self-regulation may operate in the shadow of EU institutions that monitor and control private regulatory activity. Third, VAs may serve as a

2 There is no official register of VAs in the EU. The figure given here is based on research in various DGs in the Commission and large industry associations. As there is no formal obligation that all VAs should be published in an EU document (or in the Official Journal), the number may underestimate the true spread of VAs.

bridge "to initiate European policymaking in areas previously entirely reserved to member states" (Héritier, 2002: 195).

From a more general 'good governance' perspective, VAs are chosen for their potentially superior problem solving capacity compared to traditional regulatory instruments in the EU (Liefferink *et al.*, 2000: 14). They can bypass long-winded decision-making procedures between the Commission, Council and the European Parliament, reduce the administrative burden on the EU and at the national level through building higher levels of acceptance by those affected by environmental policy, and allow for flexible and innovative implementation on the part of the private actors involved (Héritier, 2002; ten Brink, 2002). By contrast, it can be argued VAs raise the possibility that industry merely follows 'business as usual' rather than actively pursuing environmental protection goals. In addition, the selective involvement of private actors and lack of transparency may reduce the legitimacy of the regulatory process (Volpi and Singer, 2002). Hence, a framework for ensuring the effectiveness and legitimacy of VAs needs to be put in place. This chapter focuses mostly on the issue of effectiveness in its analysis, but suggests links to the issue of legitimacy were appropriate.

Table 2 combines features identified in the literature that are likely to contribute to the effectiveness of private self-regulation. We distinguish two dimensions – the internal and external dimensions of self-regulation and the top-down versus bottom-up process of controlling performance. The literature investigating the political (and regulatory) role of corporate associations tends to "bring the state back in". The state (or the EU) provides incentives for private self-regulation by accepting private norms or standards as valid alternatives to legal instruments while at the same time holding the "stick" of regulatory intervention in case industry fails to comply with the agreement (Voelzkow *et al.*, 1987; Mayntz and Scharpf, 1995). In other words, this literature suggests that VAs ought to be placed in the shadow of the hierarchy; hence that state authority and private responsibility must be *complementary* (see above). Most of the "good governance" rhetoric, in turn, tends to perceive VAs at least partly as *alternatives* to the state and focuses on bottom-up dynamics and the general public's involvement to secure both adequate solutions for specific situations and the legitimacy of regulations. Furthermore, the general public may pressure private actors from the outside, for instance through consumption behaviour or public protest.

Turning to the internal dynamics of private self-regulation, effectiveness has been linked to leadership as well as membership structures (Mol *et al.*, 2000; de Clerq, 2002). At the EU level, corporate leadership lies with European peak associations. Compared to national VAs – especially in states with corporatist industrial relations – these associations cannot be expected to be strong in exerting authority over their members. They may nevertheless succeed in building trust among them by providing information, mediating conflicts as well as shielding them from external state/EU or societal pressure. Membership constellations with homogeneous interest structures tend to be the most appropriate for effective VAs, as members are likely to agree on the objectives laid out in the agreement. Otherwise, in heterogeneous constellations, the VA needs to facilitate win-win solutions, trading off the interests of members with very difficult outlooks in order to be effective. Generally, the literature on interest intermediation suggests that small groups are more likely to control the free-rider problem, which may otherwise destabilise co-operation (Olson, 1965).

Table 2: Framework for Assessing Self-Regulation in the EU

	External dimension of self-regulation	Internal dynamics of self-regulation
Top-down	Shadow of EU hierarchy; Legal equivalence of private norms	Leadership of EU association
Bottom-up	Society's involvement and control; Public pressure	Homogeneous membership; Small membership

The following case studies investigate the structure of EU self-regulation in the light of their multi-level governance features and good governance potential. The case studies were chosen in 2005 when their final performance was still uncertain. Roughly speaking, the ACEA case seemed to reveal rather favourable internal conditions and at least moderately positive external conditions suggesting a high potential for effective performance. The EICTA case, by contrast, appeared to suffer from a more problematic internal and external framework suggesting a high probability of failure.

ACEA (Association des Constructeurs d'Automobiles Européens)

The voluntary agreement of ACEA was part of the Commission's strategy to reduce CO_2-emissions from passenger cars. In light of a high level of disagreement among the member states, EU policy makers had stopped regulatory initiatives and aimed at achieving a reduction in CO_2 emissions without defining binding targets in the form of a directive, but by pursuing a voluntary agreement between the association of European car manufacturers, ACEA,[3] and the European Commission.[4] Two Directorates General (DGs) were involved in the agreement: DG Environment and DG En-

3 All European car manufacturers are represented by ACEA. At the time of writing, ACEA had 14 members: BMW, DAF Trucks, Daimler, Fiat, Ford of Europe, General Motors Europe, MAN Nutzfahrzeuge, Porsche, Peugeot Citroen, Renault, Scania, Toyota Europe, Volkswagen and Volvo.

terprise and Industry. The ACEA agreement was signed in 1998 and aimed at reducing CO_2 emissions from passenger cars by 25 per cent to a value of 140g CO_2/km by 2008 compared to 1995 levels.[5]

CO_2 emissions from the transport sector and particularly from cars are an important issue in European climate policy as they contribute significantly to climate change. CO_2 emissions by road traffic increased by 22 per cent between 1990 and 2001 and accounted for 24 per cent of the total man-made CO_2 emissions in the EU 15 in 2001 (Kageson, 2005: 5). Furthermore, these emissions are likely to increase further due to a constantly rising traffic volume. This development stands in sharp contrast to the EU's commitments in the Kyoto Protocol where it agreed to reduce its CO_2 emissions to about 8 per cent below 1990 levels by 2008.

Emergence of the agreement

The European Commission realised quite early on that CO_2 emissions by cars would become an important issue of climate policy. A Directive as early as 1991 stated that the Commission should decide on measures limiting the CO_2 emissions of motor vehicles (OJ, 1991). The Motor Vehicle Expert Group (MVEG) of the Commission was charged with developing appropriate measures. It put forward different proposals such as emission standards and fiscal measures. The discussions in the expert group revealed that the problem of CO_2 emissions from cars would not be easily solved. At that time, member states could not reach a consensus about any legally binding measure (e.g. fiscal measures or efficiency standards). In particular, those member states with a significant automobile industry did not want to agree on measures that would be costly for their manufacturers.

Quite typically for the emergence of VAs (c.f. Héritier and Eckert 2008), once it had become clear that the Commission was working on the topic of CO_2 emissions from cars, ACEA proposed to the Commission the idea of a voluntary agreement in order to provide an alternative to EU regulation. The automobile industry was familiar with this instrument since the German sector association, VDA, had set up a voluntary agreement in 1995. To introduce such an instrument at the European level, the members of ACEA first had to agree on this approach amongst themselves. The main advantage for the automobile industry is that such a VA sets only average targets but leaves it to industry to decide how to achieve them. This means that no technical requirements are made and intervention in the market is avoided. A standard, by contrast, could limit the industry's flexibility to build a wide range of cars from small cars to Sports Utility Vehicles (SUVs) and could eliminate some car models with very high CO_2 emissions. Hence, the manufacturers of big cars such as

4 The title of the agreement is: ACEA commitment on CO_2 emission reductions from new passenger cars in the framework of an environmental agreement between the European Commission and ACEA (ACEA, 2002).

5 In 1995, the average CO_2 emission of the total number of cars manufactured was 186g CO_2/km.

BMW or Volvo clearly favoured VAs whereas the manufacturers of smaller cars may have been willing to agree to an obligatory minimum CO_2 emission standard for all cars. The then President of ACEA, Pieschetsrieder, at that time chief executive officer (CEO) of BMW, was, however, able to convince all manufacturers of the superiority of the voluntary approach. Furthermore, he persuaded some governments in member states with a strong automobile industry to support the project (Rottmann, 2005: 55).

At the same time, internal discussions were taking place in the EU institutions about a possible voluntary agreement. DG Enterprise and Industry as well as the majority in the Council of Ministers favoured a voluntary approach, as they did not want to endanger the competitiveness of European automobile manufacturers by emission standards. DG Environment was more sceptical as the instrument of a voluntary agreement had no legal treaty basis. In the end, the Commission agreed on a voluntary approach taking into account that other measures would probably not be accepted by the Council (Keay-Bright, 2000: 19). As a consequence, it published a Community strategy to reduce CO_2 emissions from cars which consisted of three elements: a voluntary agreement with the automobile industry, a framework for fiscal measures and a fuel economy consumer information scheme (CEC, 1995). This strategy was subsequently approved by the Council. The European Parliament (EP) took a more critical stance. It had not been involved in the development of the Community strategy and made clear that it could not accept a voluntary agreement, which as an informal instrument contained no legal provisions ensuring the institutional involvement of the EP.

After the publication of the Commission strategy on CO_2 and cars, the Commission started to work on the concrete text and targets with ACEA. During discussions between the EP, the Council and the Commission, the European institutions had agreed on an average value of 120g CO_2 /km for new cars by 2005, or at the latest by 2008. ACEA was not willing to accept this target for the voluntary agreement and proposed 167g CO_2 /km by 2005 which in turn was not accepted by the Commission. The negotiations were delayed until 1998 when the Commission and ACEA finally agreed on a 25 per cent reduction target for the year 2008 which meant a value of 140g CO_2 /km. These negotiations took place at different levels of authority between the Commission and ACEA. In the beginning, they started at the working level between two desk officers from DG Environment and DG Enterprise and Industry as well as two engineers from Ford representing ACEA (Keay-Bright, 2000: 21). Later, they were conducted at the highest level between the two relevant Commissioners on the one hand and the president of ACEA on the other. The Council was regularly informed and consulted by the Commission, whilst the EP remained on the sidelines during the negotiation process. "Public participation has been almost non existent, with NGOs only having been consulted once" (Volpi and Singer, 2002: 150). Consequently, the EP and NGOs were very critical of the negotiation process as well as of the outcome of the agreement.

Nature of the agreement

The ACEA agreement consisted of a commitment by all manufacturers belonging to ACEA in 1998, on the one hand, and a Commission recommendation which officially recognised the commitment in February 1999 (OJ, 1999), on the other. The text of the ACEA agreement set concrete targets for the commitment:

- A reduction in the average CO_2 emissions of new cars of 25 per cent by 2008 compared to 1995 to a value of 140g CO_2 /km;
- An interim target of 165-170g CO_2 /km by 2003 which corresponds to a CO_2 emissions reduction of 9-11 per cent compared to 1995;
- The introduction of car models emitting 120g CO_2 /km or less in the EU market by 2000 by some manufacturers (ACEA, 2002: 11).

Furthermore, ACEA agreed to assess compliance with these commitments by a joint monitoring procedure with the Commission as well as by conducting a joint "major review" of the agreement in 2003.

The emission data provided in the monitoring reports were aggregated data and indicated the average for all companies. They did not refer to the achievements of individual companies in order to guarantee data protection (ACEA, 2002: 12). This triggered a lot of criticism by NGOs who complained about a lack of transparency (World Resources Institute and SAM Group, 2005).

It seems that the Commission paid particular attention to include in the text of the agreement some of the criteria laid down in its communication of 1996, such as quantified and staged targets and monitoring of the agreement. This might have helped to convince the EP of the quality and legitimacy of the agreement, although not all the criteria were fulfilled; most notable was the absence of civil society involvement.

During the negotiations on the agreement, the Commission had promised to undertake discussions with the Japanese (Japan Automobile Manufacturers' Association – JAMA) and Korean (Korea Automobile Manufacturers' Association – KAMA) automobile industries for an equivalent agreement. ACEA had feared a competitive disadvantage if other non-European automobile manufacturers were not obliged to reduce CO_2 emissions of their cars. Indeed, the Commission was able to reach a similar agreement with JAMA and KAMA, which for 2009 set the same CO_2 target for new cars sold in the European market.

Furthermore a monitoring decision of the EP and the Council in 2000 (OJ, 2000) obliged each EU member state to provide data on CO_2 emissions from newly registered cars from 2003 on, so that independent verification of the results of the agreement became possible. Until 2003, data on CO_2 emissions had to be provided by the automobile industry. Moreover, the Commission was now required to inform the EP and the Council each year about the progress of the agreement through a Commission Communication.

In sum, within the category of self-regulation and compared to other VAs at the European level, the ACEA agreement was a relatively formal instrument, as it has been recognised by a Commission recommendation. In addition, it was accompanied by the decision of the EP and Council to introduce independent monitoring and the obligation of the Commission to publish the results of the agreement in an annual communication.

Implementation of the agreement

Aside from substantive progress by car manufacturers, the ACEA agreement required mainly monitoring and reporting activities. In particular, this involved two main fields of work: the joint monitoring reports by ACEA and the Commission, and – following the monitoring decision in 2000 – independent monitoring by the Commission and the member states.

At first, the ACEA and the Commission did not agree on the exact form of common monitoring as this had not been specified in the text of the agreement. ACEA preferred a simple monitoring system, e.g. an exchange of letters stating the progress of implementation. The Commission – faced with criticism from the EP and NGOs – insisted on a more detailed monitoring procedure with joint monitoring reports (Rottmann, 2005: 63).

During the early meetings of the implementation phase of the agreement, a common reporting format was developed by the Commission and ACEA. During regular meetings a monitoring report was drafted with both partners agreeing on the text. This text was then adopted by the two relevant Directors-General of the Commission and the President of ACEA. Afterwards, a Commission official prepared the Commission Communication for the EP and the Council on the basis of the joint monitoring report. Both documents were published on the website of DG Environment.[6]

In addition, more detailed meetings at the working level were taking place between the responsible officials of the Commission and ACEA in order to solve technical questions. These meetings established close contact between the Commission and ACEA. The member states were required to allocate resources for the creation of the independent monitoring system, and ACEA paid an independent research institute to obtain the CO_2 emission data.

During the early years of the agreement, the Commission had to rely on ACEA's data. However, after the monitoring decision by the EP and the Council in 2000 independent monitoring became possible. The member state authorities responsible for the registration of new cars now had to include information on CO_2 emissions in the registration procedure and to transmit this information to the Commission. The first monitoring report relying on these independent data was published in 2002.

During the first years of the agreement, ACEA members were able to reduce CO_2 emissions from new cars so that the interim target for 2003 of 165-170g CO_2 /km had already been reached in 2000. However, in the following years, the reduction rate slowed down. By 2004 ACEA members had reduced CO_2 emissions from new

6 See http://europa.eu.int/comm/environment/co2/co2_monitoring.htm.

cars from an average of 185g CO_2/km in 1995 to 161g CO_2/km, which represents a reduction of 13% (CEC, 2006: 3, 9). In its 2006 Communication, the Commission stated that in order to reach the target of 140g CO_2/km in 2008 reduction measures would have to be accelerated between 2004 and 2008. Both responsible Commissioners underlined that the Commission would pursue other measures to ensure that the CO_2 reductions were achieved if the industry did not live up to its commitment.[7]

Potentially undermining the credibility of the Commission's threat of hierarchical intervention, however, were the activities of the high level expert group CARS 21 (Competitive Automotive Regulatory System for the 21st Century).[8] This group was set up by the Commission (DG Enterprise and Industry) and ACEA in 2005 to make recommendations for increasing the competitiveness of the European automotive industry. It was very much focused on competitiveness issues and some conflict over possible future measures to reduce CO_2 emissions emerged. While the Commission wanted to set a target of 120g CO_2/km by 2012, ACEA pointed out that such a target would be too expensive.

As it became more and more obvious that the car industry would not be able to reach their target for 2008, the Commission returned to its earlier legislative approach for reducing CO_2 emissions from cars. In February 2007, it published a communication outlining its future strategy (CEC, 2007), announcing a legislative framework for new cars and vans which the Commission planned to publish by the end of 2007.[9] The reduction was set at 130g CO_2/km by 2012 by improvements in vehicle technology and a further 10g CO_2/km by additional measures such as efficiency improvements for tyres or air conditioning or the use of biofuels, adding up to a reduction total of 120g CO_2 by 2012. Hence, while car industry may not be able to avoid regulatory action, it had succeeded in convincing the Commission that a 120g target for motor technologies alone would endanger its world wide competitiveness.

The Commission tabled a legislative proposal in December 2007 under the co-decision procedure. Immediately, this proposal was heavily contested by car manufacturers as well as some car producing countries, especially those countries that produce cars with high CO_2 emissions, such as Germany. At the time of writing, the proposal is being discussed by the European Parliament and the Council, where it is expected to finish the legislative procedure before the parliamentary elections in June 2009.

---

7 Press release IP/06/1134, "CO_2 emissions from new cars down by more than 12% since 1995", Brussels, 29 August 2006.

8 See http://ec.europa.eu/enterprise/automotive/pagesbackground/competitiveness/cars21.htm for further information.

9 Other pillars of the strategy were measures to promote the purchase of efficient cars such as improved labelling and an EU code of good practice on car marketing and advertising to promote more sustainable consumption patterns.

Evaluation

Two 'top-down' dynamics fostered the emergence of the ACEA agreement. First, there was the threat that regulatory measures would be imposed on industry. The emerging salience of the EU climate policy added some (bottom-up) pressure on all actors to present a solution to this environmental problem and overcome controversies. Second, the ability of the ACEA leadership in bringing about agreement among its members and negotiating bilaterally with the Commission contributed to the decision.

With regards to the performance of VAs, the ACEA case seems to feature a number of quite promising elements, suggesting potential success, but also some hindering factors. Looking at internal industry dynamics, we note that ACEA's role in guaranteeing the implementation process vis-à-vis its members is quite restricted. The Automobile Association mainly provided information and was responsible for negotiating with the Commission. However, the fact that ACEA consists of only 14 members, who form a fairly homogeneous group sharing the common interest to avoid regulation, facilitated effectiveness from the bottom up. The VA represented a win-win situation for the ACEA members, even though some companies won more than others. Consequently, all companies could be convinced to participate in the agreement. However, an uneven commitment and even free-riding was possible because emission data were presented for ACEA as a whole and so avoiding transparency on which company had reduced CO_2 emissions to what extent. The fact that some manufacturers actually performed much better in reducing emissions than others, the former therefore perceiving less of threat when it comes to regulatory measures and indeed speculating on competitive advantages in such cases, carried the risk of destabilizing the agreement.

Also, with regard to the external dynamics, support for a strong environmental agreement was and still is at best mixed. The demand for efficient cars has increased due to rising gasoline prices and is thus an incentive for the car manufacturers to comply with the agreement. Furthermore, the special agreements with the Korean and Japanese car manufacturers levelled the playing field on an otherwise highly competitive market. But still, consumers also ask for faster, bigger and safer cars which are very inefficient.

A special feature of the ACEA agreement was its formal design. In addition to joint monitoring by ACEA and the Commission, the "monitoring decision" by the EP and the Council implied independent monitoring and annual communications on the state of implementation. This means that different European institutions were much more involved in the agreement compared to other self-regulatory arrangements. Based on this monitoring, the Commission was able to control industry's performance. The ACEA agreement thus operated in the shadow of hierarchy which clearly represents an important factor in achieving compliance.[10]

10 This is the core argument of Héritier and Eckert (2008) in their recent study of European VAs in the PVC and paper industry sectors.

Yet, it turned out that the ACEA agreement did not live up to its expectations and that compliance by ACEA was not achieved. From the industry's perspective the VA had succeeded in the sense of postponing any legally binding rules by about 10 years. Furthermore, the VA targets have now been diluted in the 2007 Commission proposal (130g CO_2/km by 2012 by motor technologies instead of 120g) and industry is strongly lobbying for also postponing the deadline from 2012 to 2015. Within the Council, the proposal is still heavily contested as it was already during the mid-1990s. In light of such a powerful lobby against environmental regulation it appears that the eventual success of limiting CO_2 emissions of automobiles is highly dependent on favourable dynamics in the ongoing climate change debate. In the aftermath of the European Council in March 2007 climate change has become one of the most important issues on the European agenda. This situation is putting member states and European institutions under enormous pressure to find a compromise and to establish legally binding rules for the CO_2 reduction of cars.

EICTA (European Information, Communications and Consumer Electronics Technology Industry Associations)

The voluntary agreement[11] by EICTA was established in 2003 and aimed at improving the energy performance of consumer electronics such as television sets or DVD players in standby mode as well as in on-mode. EICTA is a mixed association consisting of national associations as well as big companies in the sector.

This VA was part of the European energy efficiency policy, motivated by both energy security and climate change concerns. In 2000, the Commission published an action plan to improve energy efficiency. In the field of household appliances and consumer electronics it proposed three possible policy instruments: labelling systems and minimum standards for energy efficiency as well as voluntary agreements.

In the early 1990s, Directive 1992/75 (OJ, 1992) introduced energy labelling for household appliances (e.g. freezers, washing machines and dishwashers). Depending on their energy use household appliances are given a label from "A" (very efficient) to "G" (very inefficient). Such a label is intended to foster consumer awareness and to induce the purchase of efficient equipment. Minimum efficiency standards have also been applied in the field of household appliances, for instance, for refrigerators and freezers (OJ, 1996). Minimum standards aim at removing appliances with low energy efficiency from the market.

However in the field of consumer electronics it is difficult to apply these two policy instruments. As consumer electronics are subject to very fast technological development and minimum standards are likely to be outdated soon after they have

11 This VA corresponds clearly to the regulatory mode of self-regulation due to its informal nature. In order to emphasise the voluntary nature, it is called self-commitment. Its title is "Industry self-commitment to improve the energy performance of household consumer electronic products sold in the European Union".

been agreed. The same holds true for a labelling system given that the development of energy efficiency categories takes time.

In contrast, voluntary agreements seemed to provide enough flexibility to adjust to technological development. That is why the Commission – in the case of energy efficiency it is DG TREN (Transport and Energy) – has favoured the voluntary approach in some specific areas. Furthermore, it assumed that voluntary agreements would use fewer internal resources than other instruments because formal institutional routines are reduced to a minimum. Member states supported VAs in the area of energy efficiency as long as they established targets going beyond business-as-usual. They also recognised that VAs could provide fast and efficient implementation. EICTA appreciated the opportunity to reduce the regulatory burden on its members and to keep as much flexibility as possible for developing and selling products in the European market. The EP and NGOs, in turn, took a more critical stance because they feared that targets were not set at ambitious levels and that industry-independent monitoring might be absent (Rottmann, 2005: 76). They should be proven right.

Despite initially rather widespread internal support, EICTA terminated its voluntary agreement in 2007. The dynamics of this story will be traced on the following pages.

Emergence of the agreement

Several studies on possible measures to improve energy efficiency were conducted within the programme SAVE (Specific Action for Vigorous Energy Efficiency) during the 1990s. It turned out that many appliances had a high energy use in standby mode and that there was a high potential to improve energy efficiency in this area. Already in 1996, VAs had been recommended as an instrument to improve the energy efficiency of television sets and video recorders. The Commission organised several meetings with representatives of the consumer electronics industry to discuss the possibility of a VA. After two years of negotiations in 1998, a voluntary agreement to reduce energy consumption by new television sets and video recorders in standby mode was concluded with the industry association EACEM, which later merged with EICTA. The VA was recognised in a Commission notice (OJ, 1998) and set targets for 2000. The targets of the agreement were reached already in 1998 (Bertoldi, 1999: 7).

In 2000, the Commission discussed developing the VA with more demanding targets and an extension of the agreement to the on-mode of television sets. It also discussed an extension of the existing labelling system in order to draw consumers' attention to the energy use of their TV sets or video recorders. This proposal was submitted to the relevant business interests, but the industry was very much opposed. In such a labelling system, top technology television sets would be labelled with an "F" or "G" as they typically use a lot of energy, whereas products that are technologically less advanced could obtain an "A". The industry felt that consumers could be misled by the label with regard to the performance of the product.

In order to prevent the introduction of labelling, EICTA offered a new agreement containing more ambitious targets for energy use in standby mode for TV sets and DVD players as well as initial efforts to reduce the energy consumption of TV sets in on-mode. The proposal was discussed in the Commission and by national experts within the Labelling Committee. This committee had been set up under Directive 1992/75 on the energy labelling of household appliances and was responsible for implementing measures under this Directive. The negotiations between the Commission and member states on the one hand and EICTA on the other took about two years. A conclusion was reached only after EICTA agreed to include in the VA a special voluntary label for TV sets as well. As a result, the Commission and member states agreed to recognise this VA and not to pursue legislation.

Nature of the agreement

The legal status of the VA by EICTA differed from the ACEA agreement. It was not recognised in a Commission recommendation or notice and was thus more informal. Furthermore, there was no provision that the Commission should monitor the agreement or publish annual reports on the state of implementation. Such informality allowed for greater flexibility not only on the part of industry, but also for the Commission which was in no way formally constrained from pursuing other measures to improve energy efficiency.

As proposed by EICTA, the VA covered TV sets and DVD players in standby mode as well in on-mode for some TV models (EICTA, 2003). It consisted of three annexes which related to different product categories: CRT-TV (cathode-ray tube television), non-CRT-TV (TVs with new technologies) and DVD players. Each annex set specified targets for the relevant product group. The targets for CRT-TV were the most far-reaching. They included targets for power consumption in standby mode (not exceeding one watt by 2007), power consumption in on-mode (energy efficiency improvement of 5-10 per cent by 2007) and a label stating the power consumption in on and standby mode as well as the estimated annual energy consumption. The commitments for non-CRT-TV were similar, but did not include an energy efficiency improvement in on-mode as the measurement method still had to be developed. The commitments for DVD players included a target only for the standby mode.

Patterns of industry commitment differed significantly from the ACEA agreement. EICTA *invited* its members to take part in the VA. It was important for the Commission that the participating companies represented a broad market share of about 70-80 per cent so that the VA would have an identifiable impact on the energy efficiency of consumer electronics. Depending on the product category between six and twelve companies entered into a commitment. In 2003, when the agreement was concluded, participating companies represented a market share of nearly 70 per cent for CRT-TV.

These companies had to report annually on the energy performance of their products sold in the EU. The results were put into an aggregated report which was submitted to the Commission. Another item laid down in the EICTA commitment was the establishment of a steering committee which had to verify the results of the commitment. The steering committee consisted of representatives of EICTA, the Commission, some member states and other experts such as the representative of a consumer organisation. Transparency of the VA for the general public was limited; however, as the text of the VA has been taken off the EICTA website and annual reports were not published in a prominent place on the website.

Implementation of the agreement

Similar to the ACEA case, the EICTA VA lay down certain implementation procedures to facilitate and ensure achievement of the substantive targets of the agreements. The most important element of these implementation measures was the reporting procedure. Once the member companies had reported the data concerning the energy use of their products to EICTA, the latter prepared an annual report. This report contained information on the development of the average energy use in standby and in on-mode for each company. As confidentiality was a very important issue, the data were blinded in the sense that the performance of single companies was not revealed.

The annual report was discussed in detail in the steering committee which met two or three times a year. If the report did not satisfy all members of the committee, it had to be changed by EICTA. It should be noted, however, that no independent data collection or monitoring was foreseen in the VA; hence the steering committee fully depended on the industry for information.[12] The consumer organisation, which in contrast to many other VAs was involved in the committee, could not guarantee the accountability of the agreement either as it did not possess the technical knowledge necessary to participate actively in the monitoring process. In order to monitor a voluntary agreement effectively, NGOs would need further resources to fund an expert.

Once the EICTA annual report had been approved by the committee, it was forwarded to the Commission which distributed it to the national experts on the Labelling Committee[13] in order to involve all member states in the monitoring process

12 The text of the agreement refers to a "third party" writing the report for the steering committee and effectively assuming the role of an auditor. In reality, both parties to the regulation were satisfied with EICTA collecting and collating the data itself.

13 This is the "comitology" regulatory committee established through Council Directive 92/75/EEC of 22 September 1992 on the indication by labelling and standard product information of the consumption of energy and other resources by household appliances (OJ L 297 of 13.10.1992, pp. 16-19).

and enhance the legitimacy of the procedure. Member states could always start thinking about legal measures if the targets specified in the agreement were not reached by EICTA. The discussions in the Labelling Committee represented the "shadow of the hierarchy" in this case. In addition, the Commission and member states undertook random checks on the voluntary label. It is indicative of the weak control mechanisms built into the VA that from time to time, Commission officials and member state experts went to big shops selling consumer electronics (e.g. Saturn or Media Market) to see whether they could find the voluntary label on TV sets.

EICTA's influence over its members was rather limited during the implementation process. It could not persuade more EICTA members to join the VA and the market share of participating members was steadily decreasing (in the field of CRT-TV the share declined to about 50 per cent). In particular, the manufacturers of low-price products tended not to participate in the VA as they faced increasing competition from Asian companies which are not members of EICTA and were not committed to similar energy efficiency targets. The risk that the market share of consumer electronics covered by the VA could decrease to such an extent that it would become ineffective was very high.

From 2003 to 2005, two annual reports were published. They showed that the energy consumption of TV sets and DVD players had decreased. However, there were big differences between the participating companies. While some had performed very well, others had not made much effort to increase the energy efficiency of their products.[14] The second annual report shows that some companies performed worse than in 2003,[15] although they still met the interim target concerning standby use (three watts by 2005) (EICTA, 2005).

In 2007, EICTA terminated the voluntary agreement arguing that European producers of consumer electronics faced strong international competition from other producers. Participating in the VA had meant investing resources for the development of more efficient products and for reporting activities. Meanwhile, international (and European) competitors not participating in the VA could put cheap and inefficient products on the market increasing their market share. Eventually, European producers participating in the VA even called for strict EU-wide regulation on energy efficiency as this would impose the same rules on all competitors on the European market.

Such regulatory measures have been on the horizon since 2005, with the adoption of the Eco-Design-Directive (Directive 2005/32/EC on the Eco-Design of Energy-Using Products – EuP). This directive, which adopts a life-cycle perspective, does not introduce directly binding efficiency standards, but foresees the development of legally binding implementing measures for different product groups. In principle, the directive applies to all energy-consuming products (except vehicles for transportation). This means that sooner or later an appropriate implementing measure will

14 While companies are treated anonymously in the report, it nevertheless distinguished between individual companies (1, 2, 3,…).

15 From 2003 to 2004 the sales weighted average standby power consumption increased from 1.75 to 1.87 watt (EICTA 2005: 13).

also be developed for consumer electronics. One option the Commission is considering is a revised labelling scheme that would also work in the area of consumer electronics. While in 2005 industry was still hoping to avoid regulatory action through the VA, the failure to commit a sufficiently large group of producers to the VA targets and hence, the emergence of competitive disadvantages for VA participants have altered the prevalent negative stance on regulatory action and the prospect of the EuP directive has contributed to the termination of the VA.

Evaluation

The EICTA-VA emerged out of a relatively long tradition of policymaking in energy efficiency policy. Next to several funding measures, VAs had been agreed to reduce energy consumption of electrical appliances, including TV sets, in the past. Nevertheless, the discussions about a regulatory framework on labels for TV sets provided the main impulse for a new VA in the consumer electronics industry.

In contrast to the ACEA agreement, there was no formal agreement on either substantive or procedural standards in the EICTA case. Somewhat paradoxically, this made the role of the Commission much more important than in the ACEA agreement, as the Commission negotiated bilaterally and multilaterally with EICTA and the member states and managed the informal interaction of all participants. As the only EU body involved in the VA, the Commission took great responsibility for the implementation process and has been much more actively involved than would be the case in any "normal" Directive. However, there were no formal requirements making the Commission accountable to the EP and the Council, such as a monitoring decision forcing the Commission to communicate with and report to other actors.

The internal factors that might foster compliance were less favourable than in the ACEA case. Although EICTA exercised a similar role in the VA – the provision of information to companies participating in the VA, the preparation of monitoring reports and negotiations with the Commission – its influence in the process of implementation was weaker. The association could not convince all companies in the sector to join the VA. Moreover, the membership structure in the sector was and still is much more diversified compared with the ACEA agreement which makes agreement on a common position more difficult. Voluntary participation in the VA made free-riding an attractive option for companies in the sector. The global nature of the electronics market and the fact that competitors from other continents were not bound to the voluntary agreement either (in contrast to the KAMA and JAMA agreements in the automobile sector) finally led to the failure of this self-regulatory arrangement.

In addition to these unfavourable internal dynamics of the consumer electronics industry, the external dimension was not very conducive to effective implementation of the agreement either. Consumers interested in buying high-tech products generally did not pay much attention to energy efficiency. Moreover, in many cases, the consumers were not informed about the energy use of electronic equipment as a labelling system had only partially been realised. Also, due to the technical nature of the issue, public pressure through the participation of a consumer NGO has not lived up to expectations. Only the Labelling Committee, which was informed by the Commission on the progress made by the consumer electronics industry, imposes some top-down pressure on companies to comply with the VA.

Given these factors it is not surprising that expectations about the performance of the VA have not been met. Neither the achievement of targets nor the efficiency of the agreement was satisfactory. The negotiations took about two years, which is not much faster than an implementation measure. The extension of the 2003 commitment to new aspects of energy efficiency (most notably on-mode of non-CRT-TV) took much longer than expected. Due to international competition which had not been taken into account in the design of the VA, EICTA logically terminated the agreement and supports the adoption of binding rules for all companies in the European market.

Conclusions

We started this chapter by asking whether it is possible to observe a real trend to new modes of governance in EU environmental policy, and a trend towards shifting responsibility to private actors in particular. Noting that the adoption of voluntary agreements is clearly only possible in a limited range of circumstances, namely where the polluters are identifiable, fairly homogenous and sufficiently organised, this study has detected significantly rising numbers of VAs. The total number exceeds data reported elsewhere (Holzinger *et al.*, 2003) and this instrument is used in most member states. In particular, the EICTA example hints at a snowball effect because one VA may trigger other VAs concerned with related issues.

Referring to the factors that might foster the effectiveness of self-regulatory arrangements, which we developed at the beginning of this chapter, it turned out that hierarchical pressure is a crucial factor for implementation and hence the effectiveness of voluntary agreements, given that bottom-up dynamics are highly contingent and the industrial organisation of self-regulatory agreements at the EU level – compared to national patterns – are weak.[16] In the two case studies, the industry associations – ACEA and EICTA – have limited capacities and information to control their members and ensure their compliance with the agreement. Their function is limited to facilitation and co-ordination. The more homogeneous membership constellation in ACEA played a role in formulating moderately advanced standards and in securing an initially decent aggregate performance. Nevertheless in both cases the participating companies are competing market actors joined only by the promise of a mutual 'winning' situation in the form of preventing legislation which would have

16 For a similar conclusion compare Héritier and Eckert (2008).

imposed additional costs for all companies in the sector. Bottom-up pressure from the consumer side played no decisive role, but rather added ambiguity, in our case studies. In short, our findings confirm the well known lessons from the "steering" debate, which highlight the shadow of the hierarchy as a crucial factor in ensuring the effectiveness of industrial self-regulation (Mayntz and Scharpf, 1995). This finding also puts the bottom-up focus in the good governance debate into critical perspective.

Moreover, despite the rhetoric on new governance in which VAs are embedded, public accountability and democratic legitimacy have long been recognised as problems – rather than merits – of VAs (Baldwin and Cave, 1999). The ACEA case showed some awareness of this issue and adopted measures to create accountability through monitoring processes that were independent of industry and regular reporting to the EP and the Council. The EICTA commitment, by contrast, retained its informal status and approached the issue of accountability and input legitimacy by having a consumer protection group participate on the steering committee. However, in terms of numbers as well as capacity this group was outweighed by industry representatives. Therefore, similar to regulatory policies of the EU, voluntary agreements gain public legitimacy not through the democratic and transparent organisation of 'input' but rather through policy output and problem solving capacity.

As for our two case studies, environmental performance (i.e. output) cannot impress. In both cases it took considerable time to reach agreement in the first place (although prior legislative attempts had not looked promising either). Targets have not been met on time, although neither target was considered particularly ambitious. And, most importantly, in the light of poor performance both VAs were terminated eventually. In the ACEA case the Commission has proposed binding legal regulation in 2007; EICTA has terminated the VA calling itself for regulatory action as an alternative to the failing voluntary agreement.

The question of the primary function of VAs at EU-level – building a *bridge* to 'normal' EU regulation or representing an *alternative* to classical regulation – cannot be answered conclusively on the basis of only two case studies. But the ACEA and EICTA case offer some interesting insights. First, both cases suggest that VAs may have become an *unintended* bridge towards EU regulatory action in fields that initially seemed either too controversial or too technical to allow for the adoption of binding legislation. Our cases provide no evidence that the Commission agreed to VAs expecting failure which would enhance its chances of eventually pushing binding rules. But the weak performance of the VAs did let the option of adopting classical regulation shine in a much brighter light than this had been the case before. Second, even when failure was not yet imminent, our case studies suggested that VAs are closely *connected* to, *complementary* or even *dependent* on other policy instruments and the working of the Community method. Besides the badly needed shadow of hierarchy, we note that this is also the case institutionally where self-regulations are neither as exclusively private nor as informal as might be expected. In both case studies, EU institutions and especially the Commission played a crucial role in the formulation and monitoring of the agreement, and informal commitments and criteria link VAs to all parts of the multi-headed apparatus of EU policymaking. Both the EU institutions and the EU interest federations, however, tend to be overstrained in pressuring, controlling or inducing industrial actors to voluntarily conform to certain environmental standards.

Despite these capacity gaps, our analysis reveals that 'failure' may not be the last word. Besides an evident return to classical top-down regulation, VAs appear to trigger rather paradoxical reactions in the EU governance system. Voluntary agreements – heralded as instruments to involve private actors and to reduce the regulatory burden of Community actors – appear to place the Commission centre stage which begins to develop the required capacities. The Commission is the primary partner of industry in the initiation and formulation of VAs. More importantly, it plays a very active role in ensuring policy compliance. The informality of the instrument and the absence of an intermediate level of governance push the Commission to become involved with actual compliance "on the ground". This requires administrative resources and capacities few had anticipated but that seem to develop "on demand".

References

ACEA (2002). *ACEA's CO_2 Commitment.* Brussels: ACEA. Available at: http://www.acea.be/ACEA/brochure_co2.pdf.

Baldwin, R. and Cave, M. (1999). *Understanding Regulation: Theory, Strategy, and Practice.* Oxford: Oxford University Press.

Bertoldi, P. (1999). *Energy efficient equipment within SAVE: Activities, strategies, success and barriers.* Paper presented at the SAVE conference – For an Energy Efficient Millennium, Graz.

Bongardt, D., Dalkmann, H., Hutfilter, S. and Rottmann, K. (2005). *Review of Voluntary Approaches in the European Union. Feasibility Study on Demonstration of Voluntary Approaches for Industrial Environmental Management in China.* Wuppertal: Wuppertal Institut.

Commission of the European Communities (CEC) (2007). *Communication from the Commission to the Council and the European Parliament. Results of the review of the Community Strategy to reduce CO_2 emissions from passenger cars and light-commercial vehicles.* (COM (2007) 19). Brussels: European Commission.

CEC (2006). *Communication from the Commission to the Council and the European Parliament. Implementing the Community Strategy to Reduce CO_2 Emissions from Cars: Sixth Annual Communication on the Effectiveness of the Strategy.* (COM (2006) 463). Brussels European Commission.

CEC (2002). *Communication from the Commission to the European Parliament, the Council, the Economic and Social Committee and the Committee of the Regions -Environmental Agreements at Community Level: Within the Framework of the Action Plan on the Simplification and Improvement of the Regulatory Environment.* (COM (2002) 412). Brussels: European Commission.

CEC (2001). *European Governance. A White Paper.* (COM (2001) 428). Brussels: European Commission.

CEC (1996). *Communication from the Commission to the Council and the European Parliament on environmental agreements.* (COM (1996) 561). Brussels: European Commission.

CEC (1995). *Communication from the Commission to the Council and the European Parliament. A Community strategy to reduce CO_2 emissions from passenger cars and improve fuel economy.* (COM (1996) 689). Brussels: European Commission.

De Clercq, M. (2002). *Negotiating Environmental Agreements in Europe: Critical Factors for Success.* Cheltenham: Edward Elgar.

European Environment Agency (EEA) (1998). *Europe's Environment: The Second Assessment.* Copenhagen: EEA.

EICTA (2003). *Industry self-commitment to improve the energy performance of household consumer electronic products sold in the European Union.* Brussels: EICTA.

EICTA (2005). Industry self-commitment to improve the energy performance of household consumer electronic products sold in the European Union. Final Report based on calendar year 2004 data. Brussels: EICTA.

Héritier, A. (2002). New modes of Governance in Europe: Policy-Making without Legislating? In A. Héritier (Ed.), *Common Goods. Reinventing European and International Governance* (pp.185-206). Lanham: Rowman and Littlefield.

Héritier, A. and Eckert, S. (2008). New Modes of Governance in the Shadow of Hierarchy: Self-regulation by Industry in Europe. *Journal of Public Policy, 28 (1),* pp.113-138.

Holzinger, K., Knill, C. and Schäfer A. (2003). Steuerungswandel in der europäischen Umweltpolitik? In K. Holzinger, C. Knill, and D. Lehmkuhl (Eds.), *Politische Steuerung im Wandel: Der Einfluss von Ideen und Problemstrukturen* (pp.103-129). Opladen: Leske und Budrich.

Kågeson, P. (2005). *Reducing CO_2 emissions from new cars. A progress report on the car industry's voluntary agreement and an assessment of the need for policy instruments.* Brussels: European Federation for Transport and Environment.

Keay-Bright, S. (2000). *A critical analysis of the voluntary fuel economy agreement, established between the European automobile manufacturers and the European Commission, with regard for its capacity to protect the environment.* Brussels: European Environmental Bureau.

Knill, C. (2003). *Europäische Umweltpolitik. Steuerungsprobleme und Regulierungsmuster im Mehrebenensystem.* Opladen: Leske und Budrich.

Lenschow, A. (1999). Transformation in European Environmental Governance. In B. Kohler-Koch (Ed.), *The Transformation of Governance in the European Union* (pp.39-60). London: Routledge.

Liefferink, D., Andersen, M. S. and Enevoldsen, M. (2000). Interpreting Joint Environmental Policy-making: Between Deregulation and Political Modernization. In A. Mol, V. Lauber and D. Liefferink (Eds.), *The Voluntary Approach to Environmental Policy. Joint Environmental Policy-making in Europe* (pp.10-31). Oxford: Oxford University Press.

Mayntz, R. (2004). Governance im modernen Staat. In A. Benz (Ed.), *Governance – Regieren in komplexen Regelsystemen* (pp.65-76). Wiesbaden: Verlag für Sozialwissenschaften.

Mayntz, R. and Scharpf, F. (Eds.) (1995). *Gesellschaftliche Selbstregelung und politische Steuerung.* Frankfurt am Main: Campus.

Mol, A., Lauber, V. and Liefferink, D. (Eds.) (2000). *The Voluntary Approach to Environmental Policy. Joint Environmental Policy-making in Europe.* Oxford: Oxford University Press.

Official Journal of the European Communities (OJ) (2000). *Decision No 1753/2000/EC of the European Parliament and the Council of 22 June 2000 establishing a scheme to monitor the* *average specific emissions of CO_2 from new passenger cars.* OJ L 202 of 10th August 2000, pp.1-13.

OJ (1999). *Commission recommendation of 5th February 1999 on the reduction of CO_2 emissions from passenger cars.* OJ L 40 of 13th February 1999, pp.49-50.

OJ (1998). *Notice pursuant to Article 19 (3) of Council Regulation No 17/62 concerning Case No. IV/C-3/36.494 _ EACEM energy saving commitment.* OJ C 12 of 16th January 1998, p.2.

OJ (1996). *Directive 96/57/EC of the European Parliament and of the Council of 3 September 1996 on energy efficiency requirements for household electric refrigerators, freezers and combinations thereof.* OJ L 236 of 18th September 1996, pp.36-43.

OJ (1993). *Towards Sustainability. A European Community programme of policy and action in relation to the environment and sustainable development.* OJ C 138 5 of 17th May 1993, pp.5-98.

OJ (1992). *Council Directive 92/75/EEC of 22 September 1992 on the indication by labelling and standard product information of the consumption of energy and other resources by household appliances.* OJ L 297 of 13th October 1992, pp.16-19.

OJ (1991). *Council Directive 91/441/EEC of 26 June 1991 amending Directive 70/220/EEC on the approximation of the laws of the Member States relating to measures to be taken against air pollution by emissions from motor vehicles.* OJ L 242 of 30th August 1991, pp.1–106.

Olson, M. (1965). *The Logic of Collective Action.* Cambridge: Cambridge University Press.

Rottmann, K. (2005). *Neue Formen der Governance in der EU: Die Bedeutung freiwilliger Vereinbarungen in der europäischen Umweltpolitik.* Osnabrück University, Master's Thesis.

Ten Brink, P. (Ed.) (2002). *Voluntary Environmental Agreements: Process, Practice and Future Use.* Sheffield: Greenleaf.

Voelzkow, H., Hilbert, J. and Heinze, R. G. (1987). ‚Regierung durch Verbände' – am Beispiel der umweltschutzbezogenen Techniksteuerung. *Politische Vierteljahresschrift, 28 (1),* pp.80-100.

Volpi, G. and Singer, S. (2002). EU-level agreements: a successful tool? Lessons from the agreement with the automotive industry. In P. ten Brink (Ed.), *Voluntary Environmental Agreements: Process, Practice and Future Use* (pp.142-154). Sheffield: Greenleaf.

World Resources Institute and Sam Group (2005). *Transparency issues with the ACEA agreement: Are investors driving blindly?* Available at: www.sam-group.com/downloads/studies/ACEA_Driving_Blindly.pdf.

Living Happily Ever After? How "Going International" Changes the Relationship between EU Member States and EU Institutions in Environmental Policy

Kathrin Birkel and Duncan Liefferink

Introduction

In recent decades, the EU has done its utmost to position itself as a unified and coherent actor on the international scene. In the light of this development, it is striking that this is hardly reflected in contemporary approaches to EU studies; and it is even more astounding that it cannot be found in one of the most popular of the latter, multi-level governance (MLG). After all, MLG has opened up new territories for research in this field, and its foremost thinkers assert that "the separation between domestic and international politics ... is rejected by the multi-level governance model" (Hooghe and Marks, 2001: 4). So far, however, international politics as depicted by MLG has stopped at the borders of the EU.

Nevertheless, the international level is increasingly important. This is shown in the field of environmental politics, where the EU has gone global very actively, claiming international leadership since the run-up to the United Nations Conference on Environment and Development (UNCED), held in Rio de Janeiro in 1992 (Jachtenfuchs and Huber, 1993). In addition, the two aspects of environmental policy which have attracted the most attention in the last decade – climate change policy and the policy concerning genetically modified organisms (GMOs) – have been framed as "international" issues. In both of these cases, the EU has played a crucial role in the development of an international regime.

Given the strong involvement of the EU (institutions as well as member states) on the international scene, it is highly probable that this is not without influence on what is happening inside the EU. It can therefore be argued that attempting to draw a full picture of what is happening inside the EU, e.g. in fields such as environmental politics, is no longer feasible without integrating the international dimension.

But how can this be done? This chapter argues that even in the case of an open approach such as MLG, a simple extension to yet another level runs the risk of dragging hidden theoretical baggage along with it; theoretical baggage that, in the end, could hamper a meaningful extension of MLG. In particular, we deem it relevant in order to be able to "go international" in a sensible way, to highlight MLG's conflictual basis which is inherent in its key concepts. Moving away from the view that it is the materialist-positivist conceptualisation of these concepts that poses a problem in this respect, it is argued that a social constructivist alternative both offers new perspectives on EU matters and provides access points to the international level. Such a conceptualisation no longer precludes the possibility of co-operation between member states and EU institutions and therefore is much more suited to embrace the reality of the international level. Empirical findings – taken from the case of climate change – suggest that, with the EU "going international", co-operation has become a likely path for the future.

The Evolution of MLG

The conspicuous neglect of the international level which has characterised MLG so far comes as a bit of a paradox given the fact that one of the big achievements of this approach was to transpose the governance approach originating from the field of international relations, and to make it suitable for EU studies. It was by adopting the pluri-dimensional model central to governance thought that MLG gave a whole new spatial character to the EU. Before, the EU as seen by both neofunctionalists and intergovernmentalists had principally consisted of two competing blocs ("Brussels" on the one side, the member states on the other), both sharing a formal, governmental character. The "new" vision of the EU, inspired by governance thought, was far more complex:

> "one finds an emerging political disorder; instead of a neat, two-sided process involving member states and Community institutions, one finds a complex, multilayered, decisionmaking process stretching beneath the state as well as above it (…). In short, the European Community seems to be part of a new political (dis)order that is multilayered, constitutionally open-ended, and programmatically diverse" (Marks, 1992: 221).

Gary Marks, the "father" of MLG, thus conceived of a formation that was composed of more than two levels and did not exclusively involve governmental actors.

It was not only in the spatial set-up that MLG differed from traditional EU theories. It also formed a part of the "comparative turn", a new wave of thinking in EU studies which took the European political system as given and did not reflect on where its current shape had come from, thus abandoning the old battle ground between intergovernmentalists and neofunctionalists.

As part of this development, new questions arose that were, at the same time, the old "Lasswellian" ones (who gets what, when, how?) (Rosamond, 2003: 7). In order to be able to address them, it was deemed necessary to adopt new approaches, with a preference for those with a comparative politics background (Hix, 1994:1). The former reliance in EU studies on international relations approaches was seen to have had its day.

Although MLG tried to distance itself from the first generation of EU studies thought (Marks, 1993: 392), it was quite close to neofunctionalism. After all, with an increasing number of actors and levels forming a web of relations, contacts that bypassed the member states became conceivable (Marks, 1993: 402). In addition, it was claimed that both the "decentralization of decision-making to subnational levels of government as well as centralization of new powers at the supranational level" (Marks, 1993:401) created a "centrifugal process in which decisionmaking is spun away from member states in two directions" (Marks, 1993: 402). This raised the key question of whether the role of the state had been weakened, and in this respect suggested a rapprochement of MLG and neofunctionalism.

This issue became more pertinent during the evolution of MLG thinking, not least since, with the Treaty on European Union (1992) and the Treaty of Amsterdam (1997), the 1990s saw more competences redistributed in favour of supranational institutions.

MLG kept track with these developments, and, indeed, a decisive shift is discernible between early MLG accounts and later ones. Whereas, at first, considerable emphasis was put on the relevance of the "added" sub-national level, MLG later seems to have adopted neofunctionalism's former role of emphasising the increasing importance and autonomy of supranational institutions, though no longer in the larger context of European integration but rather in EU internal everyday decision-making. Due to this and MLG's sustained challenge to "state-centric approaches", MLG was more and more seen to fill the gap left by the "abdication" of the neofunctionalist position, viz. its legitimate successor. Again, the focus was on the allegedly conflictual relationship between EU institutions and member states, and member states were deemed to be, at least in the long run, losing out.

Inserting the International Dimension

During this process, the "ML" part of MLG virtually disappeared. First of all, MLG had never taken the international level into consideration; now, the dominance of the sub-national level also lessened. This led George to make the slightly sarcastic statement that "SNAs are still in there, but have become just one part of an argument that reads as a more modern and sophisticated version of Neofunctionalism, although minus functional spillover, which of course is why it needs a new name" (George, 2004: 112).

Instead of reinforcing the sub-national level, the aim here is to introduce the international sphere. It is true that MLG is not unique in ignoring the international level; "navel-gazing" has been a common problem of most EU approaches, and, in particular, "theorizing the EU to date has been characterized by a paucity of attempts to link the process of European integration and the nature of EU governance with developments in the wider world" (George and Bache, 2001: 33). Nevertheless, this is especially striking in the case of MLG, an approach whose very name claims to reflect more than just two levels. It can indeed be argued that, in its early years, MLG has been an approach based on structural policy, which indeed is an "EU only" issue and as such unconnected to the international sphere. However, MLG has largely abandoned this path. Its claims and aspirations now reach far beyond structural policy and are made in policy fields where the international entanglement of both EU member states and EU institutions is rising and becoming more significant.

It is also true that "there is nothing inevitable about multi-level governance ignoring the international level" (George, 2004: 29). Still, given the lack of precedents for such integration, a key question remains: how can it be done?

A straightforward attempt to take MLG one level higher would consist in simply extrapolating MLG's basic assumptions and argumentation. Has EU integration consolidated national states or weakened them? In the latter case, the kind of political order that would emerge (Hooghe and Marks, 2001: 1) would be nearly the same. Taking stock of the distribution of international competences within the EU, one could argue that, in a struggle for power and authority, EU institutions (Commission, Parliament etc.) have been able to appropriate competences that formerly had been in the hands of member states. For example, from the 1970s, the EU has signed international environment agreements alongside member states. This practice was formalised in the Single European Act 1985, which not only provided a legal basis for EU environmental policy, but also, in its Article 130R(5), explicitly acknowledged the EU's competence to enter into international commitment in this field. Since then, the dominant legal form has remained that of the so-called 'mixed agreement', signed and ratified by both the EU and the individual member states. As Sbragia (Sbragia, 1998: 285) remarks, 'the Member States have never recognized international environmental relations as belonging to the exclusive competence of the Community and have gone to some length to ensure that their role is safe-guarded'. Nevertheless, over the past 30 years, the EU has increasingly managed to act on behalf of the member states (Sbragia, 1998). One could argue that this represented a dilution of individual state sovereignty and a loss of member state authority. In this sense, the research agenda would consist in trying to test MLG statements by confronting them with empirical cases of conflict between EU institutions and member states that are related to the international sphere. Jordan, in this context, points out that "some of the most interesting multi-level conflicts within the EU centre on the question of which actor(s) (...) should represent the EU in international fora" (Jordan, 2001: 201). The final aim, then, would be to find out which side had won, and which had lost in this struggle, with MLG "being right" if EU institutions had got the upper hand. There are, however, good reasons for discarding such an approach.

To start with, we can pose the question whether the current constitution of the international level can actually be addressed within the discourse of MLG. After all, it is the declared goal of the EU (both member states and EU institutions) to improve their performance at the international level by acting in a unified manner; in the case of environmental politics, this has been underlined by the creation of a common identity ("international environmental leader"). How does this fit in with the conflictual nature implied by MLG?

Along the same lines can MLG, as it is, still hold on to the predominant features of its original "field of application": EU politics? It can be asked from an empirical point of view whether we are witnessing an increasing number of instances where a coarse member states vs. EU institutions division no longer applies. In environmental politics, for instance, only a few cases fit into this pattern. Insofar as they do, moreover, they tend to be linked to specific issues involving only one or a few member states, rather than a conflict between one full 'camp' against the other. A case in point is the Danish attempt to go further than the common EU standpoint in the revision of the Basel Convention on the shipment of hazardous waste in 1995 (Liefferink and Andersen, 1998: 263). Because of existing internal EU competence in this area and taking into account that a common standpoint had already been officially reached by the Council, the EU's leading role on behalf of the member states was uncontested. Not surprisingly, therefore, the Danish campaign, somewhat half-heartedly supported by the other Nordic countries, led to considerable controversy.[1] Recently, however, cases like this appear to be the exception rather than the rule. Even in major issues like climate change, the EU proves to be in large part able to speak with one voice in the international arena (see below).

In examining these objections to simply extrapolating MLG, we see that, although their nature is fundamentally different, there is a common element. Both objections empirically take issue with the basic MLG assumption that the relationship between the "core players" in the EU is principally conflictual.

The Key Issue of Conceptualisation

The conflictual nature of the relationship is not a mere assumption that MLG makes. It is embedded in MLG's conceptualisation of its key terms. This will become clearer by examining these concepts more closely.

Basically, the central concepts that MLG employs in describing the changing "order" in the EU (and thus the altering relationship between member states and supranational institutions) are "classical" political ones: sovereignty, authority and power. Despite the central role accorded to these terms, however, they are hardly ever explicitly defined or conceptualised – an omission that also holds for MLG's seminal theoretical texts.[2] Possible meanings and interrelations therefore have to be reconstructed from their contextual usage.

Addressing the three concepts in turn, MLG is no stranger in EU studies claiming that state sovereignty is diluted. The observation that "European institutions have obtained… attributions which, in the rest of the world, are in the domain of national

1 On the substance of the matter, though, the success of Denmark's hardline strategy has to be acknowledged, as both the Commission and the Council eventually took on the Danish position.

2 The main source outlining MLG's core business consists of just one text focusing on theoretical building blocks. Although this piece has been published under various titles at different occasions , the variation in content is negligible.

governments" (Alesina and Wacziarg, 1999: 1) or "that something that the EU does was the domain of the states at another time" (Waever, 1995: 417) has been a common impetus for "re-examining" the current status of sovereignty in member states of the EU, and has also inspired MLG. Sovereignty, then, seems to be something that has to do with possessing key competences and controlling the associated processes, notably in the field of decision-making. In fact, it is usually in combination with decision-making that sovereignty is mentioned in seminal texts on MLG (Hooghe and Marks, 2001: 2, 4, 12, 17) in combination with an alleged "loss of control" that the member states have suffered in this area (Hooghe and Marks, 2001: 2, 4, 6, 10, 17). This loss basically refers to the fact that decision-making in the Council is now dominated by the majority voting mode, and that EU institutions have competences of their own.

By depicting sovereignty as a commodity that one possesses in higher or lower quantities, several issues are not raised. First of all, with sovereignty solely depending on the distribution of formal, legal competences, and, at best, the resources to fulfil them, legitimacy moves out of focus. The question is not raised whether the population is in support of a sovereign status, nor whether this status is accorded by the other states in the international system.[3] In this conception, a threat to member states' sovereignty is primarily emanating from their involvement in the EU; the national and, above all, the international level[4] are in this respect far less important.

What exactly distinguishes MLG's notion of sovereignty from its notion of authority remains unclear. First, there is no clear indication in seminal texts with regard to definition or conceptualisation, and, second, there are numerous overlaps between the two notions. Like sovereignty, authority is predominantly coupled to the notion of (formal legal) competences (Hooghe and Marks, 2001: 9, 24). Basically, MLG applies a concept in which "authority is... considered in terms of 'competence', namely the relationship between the tasks an institution must perform and the legislative powers and resources awarded to it that will enable these tasks to be carried out" (Germain, 2000: 209). In addition, and following common usage, the authors use "authority" as a label for the very institution that is in possession of these competences, e.g. when they point out that the Council once was "the sole legislative authority" (Hooghe and Marks, 2001: 17). In general, then, "authority" connotes something that decides, that binds, that is obeyed.

Used in a similar fashion to sovereignty, it shares its blind spots. With authority, just as sovereignty, being depicted as a commodity, the role of the "addressee" is not considered, and neither is the issue of legitimacy.

---

3 Wouter Werner and Jaap de Wilde point out that there are "at least two important audiences for a sovereignty claim to be distinguished – the domestic audience (to whom a claim to sovereignty is a claim to supreme or ultimate authority) and an external audience (to whom a claim to sovereignty is a claim to independence)" .

4 It is true that MLG takes the national level into account by considering the work of non-governmental organisations (NGOs). The way it does so, however, raises two objections. First of all, it may be criticised that MLG focuses on NGOs only insofar as they work together with EU institutions (notably the Commission) and thus boost the latter's position. Secondly, it can be argued that NGOs are not representative of whole populations.

There is, however, one exception to the close relationship between the two concepts. Although sovereignty, in MLG thought, is said to be diluted in the case of the member states, this does not mean that it has automatically "switched" to the EU institutions – quite the contrary. It is striking that MLG authors have preserved "sovereignty" uniquely for "classic" states, as if it is something that is intrinsically linked to the issue of statehood itself.

Authority, on the other hand, is markedly transferable; after all, it is one of the central arguments of MLG that authority is devolved from A (the state) to B (mostly an EU institution) and is thus now shared by those parties. Authority therefore is a classical zero-sum concept.

This makes the connection between authority and power very close. Interestingly, although Marks and Hooghe use the term "power" far less than "sovereignty" or "authority", the theoretical attention they pay to this concept is much higher. To start with, by adopting Dahl's definition of power – that "A has power over B to the extent that she can get B to do something he would not otherwise do" (Hooghe and Marks, 2001: 5) – they establish a clear baseline for their further deliberations. Clearly, this is another zero-sum concept. The "portion" of power that one actor wins, the other forcibly loses (Hooghe and Marks, 2001: 5). Power in this sense, moreover, boils down to "control over persons", the question being "who controls whom" (Hooghe and Marks, 2001: 5).

The link to authority now seems to be that "more" of authority, and thus more of formal legal competences, automatically entails "more" of power. The competences, then, work as a "power resource"; the more competences A possesses, the more power he has. The reliance on institutional competences as "food for power" becomes obvious when, for instance, Marks and Hooghe point out that "the Parliament was almost powerless under the Treaty of Rome" (i.e. it lacked certain competences) or, even more, that the Parliament now has been given "significant agenda-setting powers", powers being used here as a synonym for competences (Hooghe and Marks, 2001: 20).

How MLG conceptualises its key concepts, therefore, has major consequences for the overall picture that is conveyed about the EU. To start with, MLG has a largely positivist-materialist outlook on sovereignty, authority and power, depicting them as (finite) commodities. Sovereignty, authority and power are empirically derived from looking at the distribution of formal competences between actors and an indirect comparison of this distribution to that of former times. By ascribing to the power and authority concepts an intrinsic zero-sum logic, a tendency to presume conflictual behaviour between EU member states and institutions becomes central to this theoretical approach.

Moreover, by treating these concepts as commodities which are distributed independently from their social constitution, MLG ignores numerous questions such as the circumstances in which the redistribution of competences came about or what consequences this brought about from the wider environment. Principally, then, the issue of legitimacy as well as the relevance of the EU's population, and, to a larger extent, that of the international society of states are overlooked.

A Social Constructivist Alternative

In the light of this, a reconceptualisation that has the overall aim of setting a new course for an extended MLG has to fulfil two tasks. To start with, it should provide a link to the international level. Moreover, it should be open enough to allow for consensual behaviour, while not precluding conflicts. In the light of the conceptual analysis outlined above, a first attempt at reconceptualisation primarily consists in challenging the idea that sovereignty, authority and power are depicted as finite commodities that both EU institutions and member states strive for but that only one of them can have. As a second step, one should take account of the potential dependent relationships between these concepts and the international level. It can be argued that an alternative approach of this kind would both enhance the theoretical set-up of MLG and integrate the international level instead of simply treating it as an "add-on".

A social constructivist approach to such reconceptualisation is very promising in this respect. Concepts which are elaborated in this way are more inclusive. None of the terms in question is solely depicted in terms of formal institutional competences and their distribution. Rather, what is crucial is the process of social construction.

The key differences between a social constructivist and a positivist conceptualisation become clear when applied to power, taken as the most basic "unit". What is noteworthy is that MLG has solely focused on the subject of a power relation ("*A*") and turned a blind eye on "*B*", i.e. the object of power. Moreover, by adopting a materialist stance that holding competences equals having power, MLG saw the possession of "power resources" as determining in the sense that they would automatically ensure *B*'s obedience.

From a social constructivist view, however, this is not the case. In respect of "power resources", no automatic link between their existence and successful power exercise can be presumed. Only if *B* ascribes to them some importance or meaning can they reduce the possibility that *B*'s reaction is "negative".

Power resources, then, can at best have a catalytic, but never a mechanistic, influence on the exercise of power. They have to fit the context and must be regarded as meaningful by the object of power. There is always the chance that *B* will resist *A*'s actions.

Given this, the role of authority from a social constructivist perspective is crucial. Since *A*, wanting to exercise power, can never be certain to be successful, he has to think of strategies which are likely to enhance the chances of success. Authority is regarded by many to be the "optimal" and "most sustainable" strategy in this respect. Given that *B* regards *A*'s claim for authority as valid, *A* has to overcome only a minimum, if any, resistance. A relationship between *A* and *B* in which *B* grants *A* authority may therefore be seen as a perfect foundation for an enduring power relation, even if *A*'s authority can never ensure that *B* will "comply" at all times (Barnett and Finnemore, 2005: 170). Authority is, as such, of major political relevance.

In a relationship marked by authority, however, *B*'s stance is even more decisive; it is from him that authority "emanates". Unlike power, authority is not exercised, but enjoyed; it is something that is attributed by others. For whatever reasons, these "others" decide to regard *A*'s demand(s) to be legitimate, and are thus willing to meet them.

This is not to say that *A* has to be satisfied with playing a passive part; he can make an effort to provide reasons why others should deem his intentions to be legitimate. In trying to do so, *A* will most probably draw upon what Badie calls shared myths – i.e. socially constituted knowledge – on which legitimacy is based (Badie, 2001).

This, however, cannot circumvent the possibility that the basis for an authority claim made by *A* changes over time or ultimately disappears. It may be challenged by new "myths" or new "knowledge" that "are cutting across traditional ones and are directly staking out the consensual basis of modern societies in which different collective imaginations of what power should be and how it can be accepted are competing" (Badie, 2001). *A*, then, has to continue to maintain his authority basis either by abiding by his original reasons for legitimation or by thinking of new ones.

Sovereignty, finally, resembles authority insofar as it is conferred to *A* (typically a state) by others. Again, this does not preclude the possibility or even the need for *A* to claim sovereignty and to substantiate this claim by drawing upon "myths" or elements of shared knowledge. But in the end, no claim can hold if it is not regarded as valid by relevant others.

Sovereignty builds on the high political relevance of authority (see above). *Within* a society, people can confer authority on more than one person or unit; according sovereignty to someone or something, however, means that, in case of doubt, this is who or what the highest authority is attributed to (and thus whose demands would probably be followed). Externally, the fact that *A* has sovereignty conferred on it means that it is recognised that *A* enjoys the highest authority internally. Accordingly, in case of doubt, *A* would be the one to be seen to represent the community in question. At least two important audiences for a sovereignty claim can be distinguished – the domestic audience (to whom a claim to sovereignty is a claim to supreme or ultimate authority) and an external audience (to whom a claim to sovereignty is a claim to independence)" (Werner and De Wilde, 2001: 290). In principle, then, there is always the possibility that, despite international acknowledgement of sovereignty, *A*'s sovereignty could be heavily disputed internally – or vice versa.

In a nutshell, for *A* to maintain its sovereignty, it is not essential that it meets any formal requirements such as possessing certain competences. Moreover, the mere fact that a unit has transferred rights or tasks that have so far usually been considered to be "typically sovereign", does not necessarily mean that the unit has lost its sovereignty as such[5] or that, with these tasks or rights, sovereignty has been

5 This would only be the case if the transferral would have destroyed the basis for *B*'s decision to accord *A* this status.

transferred.[6] Sovereignty, as such, as a status, "is something that cannot be partly handed over or pooled; it is an indivisible quality. The rights and powers linked to that status, however, can be handed over to other states or international organizations" (Werner and De Wilde, 2001: 297).

It is, therefore, conceivable that, even if a unit does not fulfil one of the formal criteria, it may have sovereignty attributed to it – and with it, the possibility to act accordingly.

The consequences of such a reconceptualisation for the overall theoretical framework are significant. To start with, it takes away the conflictual "bias" inherent in traditional ideas about MLG. It allows a theoretical picture to emerge which is better suited to grasp the "reality" of international environmental politics. At this level, both EU institutions and member states need to secure authority in order to be allowed to join the international club and make an impact. In the light of this, conventional MLG would have to depart from the assumption that, whatever one actor gains authority-wise, the other has to lose because the relationship between EU institutions and member states are seen as necessarily conflictual. A reconceptualised MLG does not imply this. In examining how both EU institutions and Member States try to secure authority and how they try to achieve legitimacy, something new becomes apparent. This is the fact that it is increasingly difficult for either of them to do this alone. Rather, each side can offer something the other one lacks. EU institutions can argue that they are more effective in representing 25 individual states, but lack the essential criterion of statehood; the individual member states, on the other hand, may lack the impact a grouping of 25 has, but can claim to have the "ticket to the ball" that the EU institutions need.

Thus the point of departure for a "reconceptualised" MLG in the international sphere is quite different from previous thinking about MLG. As it becomes clear that EU institutions on the one hand and member states on the other draw on different legitimation bases, a struggle between them would only occur if the very foundations of one of them was being undermined by the other. Moreover, it is even conceivable that the different authorities become interdependent, i.e. that one actor draws (part of) its legitimation from the other's mere existence or function.[7] If so, it would be fatal for *both* if one actor attacked the legitimation base of the other. Consensual, cooperative behaviour in this case is therefore far more likely.

What is more, by reconceptualising MLG's key concepts along social constructivist lines, an attempt is made to integrate the international level instead of treating it as a further add-on, just another level for the EU institutions and member states to continue their skirmishes (with the focus being based solely on the EU itself). In this revised approach, key concepts are reinterpreted in a way that puts a strong empha-

6 In principle, a simple transfer of sovereignty is not possible, since *B*'s stance on this issue is crucial. What is possible, then, is the transfer of tasks that are deemed to be linked to sovereignty.

7 A simple example would be the establishment of a worker's council in a company. The mere existence of such an institution can boost the legitimacy of the company's management.

sis on the addressee, which, in this case, are other actors at the international level. Thus, the processes at the international level become a substantive part of the story.

MLG in a Global Perspective: The Case of Climate Change

As outlined above, the basic argument flowing from a "reconceptualised" MLG is that, looking at the EU from the international level, it is not the case that both EU institutions and member states seek to enhance their authority independently from each other. "Brussels" cannot do without the member states, since it lacks their "stateness", which, internationally, is the "ticket to the ball" (Waever, 1995: 420).

The EU institutions, in turn, are regarded by the vast majority of member states as a necessity in contemporary times. By this institutional set-up member states want to ensure that they are in a better position to cope with "globalisation" and to be heard and compete on the international scene,

From this perspective, co-operating with and respecting each other enhances the probability that the EU institutions and member states can profit from the authority held by each other, and therefore also increases their agency role.

This is particularly the case when looking at the EU in relation to international environmental politics. Not only did both EU institutions and member states see this arena as a possible arena for establishing the EU as a legitimate and effective actor, "to stand forth as a strong and unified block on the world scene" (Andresen and Agrawala, 2002: 46) but, in this case, the ambitions of the EU were even higher. In the light of the gradual withdrawal of the United States (US) from this field, it can be argued that international environmental politics was seen as an opportunity to boost the international authority of the EU by presenting it as a new, fresh and modern alternative. The EU's leadership aspirations become more understandable if seen from this angle:

"Environmental leadership conveys the image of the EC as a new type of power, dealing with contemporary problems in appropriate terms and contrasts this image with the one of the United States as a traditional military power neglecting problems that cannot be solved by traditional means of foreign policy. 'Leadership' underlines the EC's aspiration to become a super-power, but a modern one" (Jachtenfuchs, 1996: 188).

The EU's external leadership aspirations, moreover, may help to reach internal agreement. This again suggests that if the international level is involved, relations between the EU institutions and member states are not necessarily characterised by a struggle for authority. The history of the EU's climate policy illustrates that the pathway to co-operation can be steep and difficult, but may lead to a situation where neither the EU institutions nor the member states perceive themselves as 'weakened'.

In fact, climate change was the area where the EU's leadership ambitions in the environmental field first surfaced. The Dublin Declaration of 1990, for instance, referred to 'establishing a strong Community position in preparation for the Second World Climate Conference' of October 1990 (cited in Huber, 1997: 149). The ambition was strongly supported not only by the Environment Commissioner at the time, Carlo Ripa di Meana, but also by the influential Forward Studies Unit, functioning directly under Commission President Jacques Delors. Even more important, the need to form a single front in order to push the other major international partners, notably the US and Japan, was basically endorsed by the member states in the Council of Ministers (Jachtenfuchs and Huber, 1993).

During the negotiations on the UN Framework Convention on Climate Change (UNFCCC) at the Rio Conference in 1992, the EU managed to act in a united way (Sbragia, 1998: 299). However, the consensus withered away in subsequent years, due to disagreements about the implementation of EU climate policy, notably the establishment of a CO2/energy tax, and the problem of dividing the costs in a way considered fair by all the member states involved (Huber, 1997).

The negotiations on the Kyoto Protocol in 1997 provided a second opportunity. While the US argued for the use of flexible, market-based instruments without fixed reduction targets for the emission of greenhouse gases, the EU strongly preferred quantified emission limitations and reduction objectives (also referred to as 'QELROS') for all "Annex I" countries, i.e. the developed, industrialised world. In order to promote its position as forcefully and credibly as possible, the EU arrived in Kyoto with a proposal for a 15 per cent emission reduction for the EU as a whole by 2010, relative to 1990. More significantly, in the present context, the proposal included a means for sharing the burden between the member states. When it became apparent during the Conference that the other "Annex I" countries could not be pushed towards similar reductions, the EU moderated its position, unwillingly, but as a unit. Eventually, reductions of 8 per cent for the EU, 7 per cent for the US and 6 per cent for Japan were accepted in exchange for a commitment to a set of flexible instruments, including emissions trading and the possibility to 'buy' emission reduction in developing countries. Soon after the Kyoto meeting, in June 1998, the EU adapted its burden sharing agreement to the new overall target of 8 per cent. Targets for the individual member states ranged from -28 per cent for Luxembourg and –21 per cent for Germany and Denmark to +25 per cent for Greece and +27 per cent for Portugal (Damro and Luaces Méndez, 2003).

With hindsight, the EU's leadership on the climate issue was successful to only a limited extent. Internationally, the issue has stopped short at the US refusal to ratify the Kyoto Protocol. In this sense, one might argue, the EU's leadership had completely failed. Internally, each member state continues to have its own, often serious problems in realising the targets of the burden sharing agreement. But the point to make here is different. At first sight, strong EU co-ordination in the Rio and Kyoto negotiations and the concomitant prominent role of the Commission may appear as a loss of authority on the part of the member states. However, the member states have never seriously contested the EU's international role on the climate issue. It was widely acknowledged that the only possible way to carry any weight against the US and other large countries in the negotiations was to have a joint strategy coordinated by the Commission in collaboration with the Council Presidency of the time. Similar leverage could not have been achieved by the member states individually. Thus, the EU and the member states, rather than playing a zero-sum game for authority between themselves, effectively worked together and jointly increased their authority in the global arena as a result. As a side effect, the pressure created by the Kyoto negotiations eventually facilitated an agreement about the internal distribution of the burden associated with emission reductions.

Conclusions

Inserting the international level into MLG, is after all a necessary yet by no means straightforward task. Instead of simply extending the existing MLG building by adding an additional international floor, this chapter has opted to solidify the groundwork first and to alter or remove components that could hinder its extension.

Consequently, it addressed what it saw as the biggest obstacle: the original conceptualisation of key features of MLG. It was argued that depicting sovereignty, authority and power as (finite) commodities which are closely linked to the distribution of formal competences and follow a zero-sum logic, demonstrates that conflict is a theoretical necessity – a necessity which is inappropriate when attempting to comprehend processes which include the EU in the international sphere.

Reconceptualising these features along social constructivist lines, in contrast, allows other aspects to come to the fore. Authority does take a central role, but not as a hard fought prize in a battle; rather, it opens up the possibility for EU institutions and member states to complement each other, to profit from each other's legitimacy.

This, in turn, is essential for the EU as an actor on the international scene. In order to make an impact, it needs the member states' "stateness" as well as for the EU institutions to act as organisational anchor and motor. This becomes particularly clear in the field of environmental politics, where the leadership claim is an outward sign of the common efforts of both EU member states and institutions – not only to promote the environmental cause, but also to establish the EU as one of the main actors internationally.

Several caveats should be made at this point. The aim here has been to argue for a reconceptualisation of key features terms of MLG in order to be able to extend it to the international sphere. Although we assume that such a revised MLG is also more appropriate for "EU-only" circumstances, the final verdict on whether this truly is the case is a task for further research. By putting forward a reconceptualisation distinct from the materialist-positivist mainstream, it was not our intention to make a plea for a general social constructivist overhaul of MLG. We also do not deny that the extension of MLG could be made on a functionalist argument. We would simply point out that such an argument should be based on a revised view of MLG that offers more room conceptually, for co-operative behaviour between the main actors.

In the light of what has been argued, it could be asked whether, in the course of "internationalisation", EU institutions and member states will finally come to "live happily ever after"? This is neither claimed nor promoted. Looking at the current state of European affairs, there is enough to quarrel about, whether it concerns Treaty revisions, the future of the constitution, or the distribution of competences in new fields like taxation or spatial planning. It is, however, argued that these struggles are hardly ever clear cut and that speaking of them as "struggles for authority" is in the main an exercise in rhetoric.

It is therefore very likely that co-operation is not the only path the EU will travel on in the future. But neither can it be dismissed as just a utopian notion. As we have explored in this chapter, co-operation is both theoretically feasible and empirically plausible, especially with an EU that is increasingly "going international".

References

Alesina, A. and Wacziarg, R. (1999). *Is Europe Going Too Far?* NBER Working Paper No. 6883. Available at: http://www.nber.org/papers/w6883.pdf.

Andresen, S. and Agrawala, S. (2002). Leaders, Pushers and Laggards in the Making of the Climate Regime. *Global Environmental Change, 12, (1)*, pp.41-52.

Badie, B. (2001). Sociology of Legitimacy. In N. J. Smelser and P. B. Baltes (Eds.), *International Encyclopedia of the Social and Behavioral Sciences.* Oxford: Elsevier.

Barnett, M. and Finnemore, M. (2005). The Power of Liberal International Organizations. In M. Barnett and R. Duvall (Eds.), *Power in Global Governance* (pp.161-184). Cambridge: Cambridge University Press.

Damro, C. and Luaces Méndez, P. (2003). Emissions Trading at Kyoto: From EU Resistance to Union Innovation. *Environmental Politics, 12 (2)*, pp.71-94.

George, S. (2004). Multi-Level Governance and the European Union. In I. Bache and M. Flinders (Eds.), *Multi-Level Governance* (pp.107-126). Oxford: Oxford University Press.

George, S. and Bache, I. (2001). *Politics in the European Union.* Oxford: Oxford University Press.

Germain, R. D. (2000). The Central European Bank and the Problem of Authority. In M. Kelstrup and M. C. Williams (Eds.), *International Relations Theory and the Politics of European Integration. Power, Security and Community* (pp.205-225). London: Routledge.

Hix, S. (1994). Approaches to the Study of the European Community: The Challenge to Comparative Politics. *West European Politics, 17 (1),* pp.1-30.

Hooghe, L. and Marks, G. (1997). Contending Models of Governance in the European Union. In A. W. Cafruny and C. Lankowski (Eds.), *Europe's Ambiguous Unity. Conflict and Consensus in the Post-Maastricht Era* (pp.21-44). Boulder: Lynne Rienner.

Hooge, L. and Marks, G. (2001). *Multi-Level Governance and European Integration.* Lanham: Rowman and Littlefield.

Huber, M. (1997). Leadership in European Climate Policy: Innovative Policy Making in Policy Networks. In D. Liefferink and M. S Andersen (Eds.), *The Innovation of EU Environmental Policy* (pp.133-155). Copenhagen: Scandinavian University Press.

Jachtenfuchs, M. (1996). *International Policy-Making as a Learning Process? The European Union and the Greenhouse Effect.* Aldershot: Avebury.

Jachtenfuchs, M. and Huber, M. (1993). Institutional Learning in the European Community: The Response to the Greenhouse Effect. In D. Liefferink, P. D. Lowe and A. P. J. Mol (Eds.), *European Integration and Environmental Policy* (pp.36-58). London: Belhaven.

Jordan, A. (2001). The European Union: An Evolving System of Multi-Level Governance ... Or Government? *Policy and Politics, 29 (2)*, pp.193-208.

Liefferink, D. and Andersen, M. S. (1998). Strategies of "Green" member states in EU Environmental Policy-Making. *Journal of European Public Policy, 5 (2)*, pp.254-70.

Marks, G. (1992). Structural Policy in the European Community. In A. M. Sbragia (Ed.), *Euro Politics. Institutions and Policy-Making in the "New" European Community* (pp.191-224). Washington: The Brookings Institution.

Marks, G. (1993). Structural Policy and Multilevel Governance in the EC. In A. W. Cafruny and G. Rosenthal (Eds.), *The Maastricht Debates and Beyond* (pp.391-410). Boulder: Lynne Rienner.

Marks, G., Hooghe, L. and Blank, K. (1996). European Integration from the 1980s: State-Centric Versus Multi-Level Governance. *Journal of Common Market Studies, 34 (3),* pp.341-78.

Rosamond, B. (2003, March). *(European) Integration Theory, EU Studies and the Sociology of Knowledge.* Paper presented at the 8th biennial conference of the European Studies Association, Nashville.

Sbragia, A. (1998). Institution-Building from Below and Above: The European Community in Global Environmental Politics. In A. Stone Sweet and W. Sandholtz (Eds.), *European Integration and Supranational Governance* (pp.283-303). Oxford: Oxford University Press).

Waever, O. (1995). Identity, Integration and Security. Solving the Sovereignty Puzzle in E.U. Studies. *Journal of International Affairs, 48 (2),* pp.389-431.

Werner, W. G. and De Wilde, J. H. (2001). The Endurance of Sovereignty. *European Journal of International Relations, 7 (3),* pp.283-313.